1990

W9-AED-573

Critiquing Radio and Television Content

Critiquing Radio and Television Content

Peter B. Orlik

Central Michigan University

Allyn and Bacon, Inc.

Boston   London   Sydney   Toronto

To Chris

Always Supportive
Always a Comfort
Always a Franklin

Copyright © 1988 by Allyn and Bacon, Inc.
A Division of Simon & Schuster
160 Gould Street
Needham, Massachusetts 02194–2310

Library of Congress Cataloging-in-Publication Data

Orlik, Peter B.
  Critiquing radio and television content.

  Bibliography: p.
  Includes index.
  1. Broadcasting—Evaluation.   2. Radio criticism.
3. Television criticism.   I. Title.
PN1990.9.C73075   1988   791.44'01'5   88–3462
ISBN 0–205–11643–4

Editorial-Production Services: Wordsworth Associates/Grace Sheldrick
Cover Administrator: Linda K. Dickinson
Cover Designer: Susan Slovinsky
Designer: Pat Torelli

Printed in the United States of America

10 9 8 7 6 5 4 3 2 1   93 92 91 90 89 88

Brief Contents

1   The Essence of Criticism   1
2   The Critic and the Communications Process   19
3   The Species of Criticism   35
4   Knowledge Processing   49
5   Productional Ingredients   73
6   Business Gratifications   99
7   Audience Gratifications   113
8   Probing Ethics and Values   131
9   Aesthetics and Art   155
10 The Logic of Aesthetic Form   177
11 Depiction Analysis   201
12 Symbols, Myths, and Structures   221
13 Composite Criticism   247
    Appendixes   267
    Index   335

Contents

List of Illustrations   *xiii*

Preface   *xv*

1   The Essence of Criticism   1

What Is Criticism?   1
Why Is Radio/Television Criticism Needed?   5
Brief History of Radio/Television Criticism   8
The Critic's Role   11
Notes   17

2   The Critic and the Communications Process   19

Critic Preparation   19
Originator Criticism   21
Message Criticism   26
Medium Criticism   27
Receiver Criticism   30
Notes   33

3   *The Species of Criticism*   35

The Personality/Gossip Feature   36
The Audience Reaction Column   39
The Preview   41
The Program Review   43
The Opinion Essay   44
Conclusion   47
Notes   48

4   *Knowledge Processing*   49

Empirical and Normative Perspectives   49
   Empiricism   49
   The Normative View   52
The Four Ways of Knowing   54
   The Scientist   54
   The Mystic   56
   The Rhetorician   58
   The Critic   60
The Perceptual Triad   64
   The Sensuous Plane   64
   The Expressive Plane   65
   The Productional/Technical Plane   68
   The Planes Combined   68
Notes   72

5   *Productional Ingredients*   73

The Musical Ingredient   73
   Clarity   74
   Execution   75
   Continuity   78
   Aptness of Task   79
   A Musical Summary   82
The On-Stage Skill Ingredient   82
   Radio People   82
   Electronic Newspersons   84
   Other Television Personalities   85
The Stage-Molding Ingredient   87
   Light and Shadow   88
   Horizontal and Vertical Camera Planes   90
   Camera/Character Arrangement   92

Camera in Motion   93
Reaction Shots and Reverse Angles   93
Shot Transition and Duration   94
Aural Transitions and Volume   95
Stage-Molding Summation   96
Notes   97

6   Business Gratifications   99

Bottom-Line Preeminence   100
Ratings, Shares, and Tonnage   102
Scheduling and Flow Analysis   107
Notes   112

7   Audience Gratifications   113

An Audience Uses Overview   113
Entertainment/Time Punctuation   116
Information/Surveillance   117
Escapism/Nostalgia   118
Companionship/Conversation Building   120
Problem Solving   122
Personal Enrichment and Development   125
Catharsis/Tension Release   127
Notes   129

8   Probing Ethics and Values   131

Ethics and Values Defined   131
What Critics Value   135
Freedom of Expression and Media Access   142
The Protestant Ethic and Social Darwinism   145
The Protestant Ethic   146
Social Darwinism   147
Notes   153

9   Aesthetics and Art   155

Interpreting Aesthetics   155
Absolutism   156
Individualism   157

Objectivism   157
Cultural Relativism   158
Biopsychological Relativism   160
A Schools-of-Thought Conclusion   162
Art Defined   163
Outer-Directed Tasks of Art   163
Inner-Directed Tasks of Art   165
The Three Sources of Art   171
Fine Art   171
Folk Art   171
Pop Art   172
Notes   174

10   *The Logic of Aesthetic Form*   177

Organic Unity   178
Theme   179
Thematic Variation   180
Recurrence   183
Transposition   183
Alternation   184
Inversion   184
Balance   186
Evolution   190
Hierarchy   191
The Complete Logic Applied   194
Notes   199

11   *Depiction Analysis*   201

How Is Our Physical Environment Constituted?   202
What Is Society Like?   205
What Consequences Flow from Our Actions?   207
What Are Our Responsibilities?   210
What Are the Standards by Which We Should Evaluate
    Ourselves?   213
Depiction Critiquing in Action   215
Notes   219

12   *Symbols, Myths, and Structures*   221

Symbols and Archetypes   221
Ritual, Mystique, and Myth   227

Thesis, Antithesis, and Synthesis   233
Semiotics   238
Notes   244

13 *Composite Criticism*   **247**

Intrinsic Appreciation   248
Extrinsic Appreciation   250
Intrinsic Evaluation   252
Extrinsic Evaluation   255
Composing the Composite Critique   258
A Final Annotation   264
Notes   264

Appendixes   **267**

A *The Cosby Show:* "Theo's Holiday"   267
B *Ethel and Albert:* "The Income Tax"   297
C Suggested Exercises   315

Index   335

List of
Illustrations

2–1   Criticism and the Communications Process   20

4–1   Michelob Classic Dark "Soy Sauce" Photoboard   61

4–2   Celentano "New Italians" Photoboard   66

5–1   Philips Lighting "Cabin" Photoboard   89

5–2   TV Shot Continuum   90

9–1   Sealtest Dairies "All Natural" Photoboard   166

10–1 Kemps Ice Cream "Peppermint Bon Bon Cow" Photoboard   181

10–2 John Smith's Yorkshire Bitter "Anniversary" Photoboard   182

10–3 True Hierarchy   192

10–4 The Absence of Hierarchy   193

10–5 False Hierarchy   193

11–1 "I Am Michigan" Photoboard   204

11–2 Oldsmobile "Who You Are" Photoboard   214

12–1 Tide "Socks" Photoboard   230–231

12–2 Exxon "Ink Jet" Photoboard   236

12–3 U.S. Navy "Flight Operations" Photoboard   240

12–4 Cadillac "The Dream Realized" Photoboard   243

13–1 Composite Criticism and the Communications Process   263

Preface

Critiquing Radio and Television Content unequivocally contends that radio and television content has the capacity to constitute art. An inherently associated contention is that the material heard and seen over the electronic media is worthy of serious consideration by both critics and literate consumers. If you number yourself among either group, this book should help you make reasoned and relevant judgments as to what to recommend to other people and what to select for your own listening and viewing. If, in addition, you are a broadcast/cable professional or professional-to-be, this book strives to suggest consistent measures by which you can evaluate your own output and that of your competitors as one means of coping with the charges and challenges hurled by intra- and interindustry debunkers and pressure groups.

Make no mistake, our objective need not be to stimulate criticism; radio/television is already more often critiqued than almost any other area of human endeavor. Because virtually everyone in the country owns several receivers, and because the electronic media are delivered to these receivers via the publicly owned spectrum or municipally granted right-of-way, every member of society takes a proprietary interest in broadcasting and cablecasting. Due to the fact that most people have listened and watched since birth, the citizenry also feels itself to be expert judges of media content.

No, the need is not for criticism stimulation but for criticism refinement. Refinement is needed because the fishbowl environment in which the electronic media must function has engendered almost as many yardsticks for evaluation as there are programmatic fishes to be scrutinized. And unfortunately, some of these yardsticks are so specialized or (what is worse) so biased as to be applicable only to a single program type and/or a single special-interest perspective. Largely unserved by the more focused and universal evaluative procedures common to literary, dramatic, music, and visual arts criticism, the critiquing of radio/television content often has become a fragmented exercise at best and one that lacks both the salience of other forms of criticism and the pervasiveness of the medium it seeks to explain.

Also, because the electronic media are comparatively young, there has been little time to develop standards appropriate to their assessment. This view, however, assumes that broadcast and cable are so divorced from other generative enterprises that nothing common to more historic creative activities can be enlisted for the purpose of media evaluation. *Critiquing Radio and Television Content* adopts a much different orientation; we take the position that mature principles of criticism developed for older art forms are equally adaptable to and beneficial for the judgment of radio and television. We also borrow from modern sociology, psychology, and business economics in suggesting a variety of critical perspectives that, despite their divergency, can still be mutually supportive in coming to grips with the multifacetedness that is radio/television product.

Unlike many other writings on broadcast criticism, this volume sees the field as much wider than the world of prime-time television alone. Thus, our purview includes the aural as well as the visual medium, nonprime as well as prime time, and commercials as well as full-length programs. Similarly, cable matter is referenced along with that of open-circuit broadcasting because it is not the delivery system but the content that presents the critical challenge. Consumers listen to and watch output, and the particular technology that happens to deliver this output is quite unimportant—at least, until it technically malfunctions.

The contribution that *Critiquing Radio and Television Content* hopes to make does not entail pushing back the boundaries of graduate school research in semiotics or quantitative research. Instead, this book strives to serve as sensitizer and synthesizer in how to dissect and cope with broadcast/cable material on a day-to-day basis. Rather than presenting one way to evaluate one genre of electronic media content, we here explore several operations that might be used to understand and legitimately evaluate a wide spectrum of radio and television products. In lieu of advocating a single critical approach or methodology, therefore, this book illuminates several such systems, each of which can be independently pursued or abandoned as the reader's interest and philosophy determine.

Through such an orientation, it is hoped that your own critical faculty will be stimulated or, in the words of eminent broadcast observer Robert Lewis Shayon, "revved up" to the enormously important task of electronic media analysis. As Shayon once put it:

The critical faculty, though apparently inactive in many individuals, is actually quietly idling, like a motor. It needs to be revved up, to accelerate critically, and to fire other idling motors. There are motors idling, within critics-in-potential, at just the right rate of revolutions, give or take a tolerable variance. Once revved up, they can hopefully take off to make their own critical contacts.[1]

To lead you to this point of combustion, *Critiquing Radio and Television Content* begins with four chapters that define the critical arena. Chapter 1 delineates the role of criticism and that of the critics who practice it. This is followed, in Chapter 2, by an examination of how such criticism impacts the entire communications process. Chapter 3 then studies the five major species of today's radio/television critique, and Chapter 4 explores how we acquire and manipulate the knowledge that is the wellspring both of message content and the assessment of it.

The next three chapters probe the instruments out of which electronic media product is fashioned (Chapter 5), the business objectives that motivate this fashioning (Chapter 6), and the uses to which audiences are accustomed to put the result (Chapter 7).

With this groundwork laid, the book's last six chapters introduce specific critical orientations that can be used: an ethics and values approach (Chapter 8); a primarily aesthetic vantagepoint (Chapters 9 and 10); a sociological effects schema (Chapter 11); a literary/structural point of view (Chapter 12); and finally, a composite inspection (Chapter 13) that can incorporate and accommodate many aspects of the other perspectives.

Two complete situation comedy scripts comprise Appendixes A and B and are referred to frequently as the subjects of sample analyses. By design, these two episodes (from *The Cosby Show* and *Ethel and Albert* series, respectively) are separated by a distance of thirty years as a means of testing whether certain critical procedures enjoy a timeless utility or endure time-bound limitations to their applicability. Finally, Appendix C provides a list of suggested exercises generated from individual chapter discussions and these same two episode scripts.

If we are to explore broadcast/cable criticism, it is time to end these preliminaries and get on with it in the assurance that what we discover will help us feel more rather than less comfortable with radio/television content and more rather than less self-assured in making judgments about it. Literate persons, from concerned consumers to electronic media employees to paid professional reviewers, can engage in the legitimate and fruitful practice of criticism and should engage in it as a means of improving their own listening/viewing, their own industry, or the guidance service they provide for others. The key is not to be intimidated from this task by the seeming complexity and vastness of the broadcast/cable enterprise, not to be like the title character from *Leave It to Beaver* who fatalistically told his big brother:

Ya know, Wally, I'm glad I don't know as much about life as you do, otherwise I'd be the biggest chicken in the whole world.[2]

Competent people can fearlessly appraise radio and television if they acquire a basic understanding of both the workings of the communications industry and the essential components of human perception and human nature. *Critiquing Radio and Television Content* is dedicated to the furtherance of this cognizance.

Acknowledgments

Thanks are extended to Central Michigan University for granting a University Research Professorship that made the actual writing of this book possible and to Dr. B. R. Smith for making the resources of the University's Broadcast and Cinematic Arts Department available to assist in manuscript preparation. Special recognition goes to Patti Hohlbein for converting a primitively typed draft into final and beautifully word-processed form. Appreciation is also extended to Allyn and Bacon's Bill Barke, who offered immediate and unswerving support to this project, and to Karen Hanson for her editorial shepherding of it toward completion. My gratitude also goes to Grace Sheldrick, Wordsworth Associates Editorial Services, for her expert editorial/production assistance.

Further thanks are due the following respected colleagues who reviewed the manuscript for this book: James A. Brown, The University of Alabama; Edwin L. Glick, North Texas State University; and Robert H. McGaughey III, Murray State University.

I am likewise indebted to *The Cosby Show*'s Director of Public Affairs, Kim Tinsley, and to *Ethel and Albert*'s writer and co-star Peg Lynch for their kindness in providing masterpiece scripts for our analysis and enjoyment.

Special mention also must be made of Dr. Thomas O. Olson, whose brilliant teaching at Wayne State University introduced me to broadcast criticism and imparted a respect for the subject and for aesthetics that has found an outlet in this edition.

Finally, boundless gratitude is extended to my wife, Chris, and our two children, Darcy and Blaine, who put up with a great deal of preoccupied grumpiness while the struggle with this manuscript was under way. Their encouragement and love were and are irreplaceable to this project and this existence.

Notes

1. Robert Lewis Shayon, *Open to Criticism* (Boston: Beacon Press, 1971), 6. Used by permission.
2. Irwyn Applebaum, *The World According to Beaver* (New York: Bantam Books, 1984), 48.

*Critiquing Radio
and Television Content*

The Essence
of Criticism

As used in contemporary conversation, the term *criticism* is afflicted with a multitude of often contradictory meanings. Therefore, before we can begin to comprehend the variety of criticism within the complex context of radio and television, it is essential to determine criticism's essential ingredients.

What Is Criticism?

In everyday speech, when people mention *criticism,* or the act of being *criticized,* they are usually referring to an unpleasant, negative event. Criticism is cast as an evaluative weapon; its sole purpose is the disparagement of the referent at which this weapon is hurled. Taken in this context, criticism must always be viewed as a destructive rather than constructive force that can triumph only at the expense of the object being criticized. If this were criticism's main goal, there would be little point in embracing the subject as a means toward understanding radio and television, since we would only be concerned with how deftly the products of these media could be annihilated. Pushed to the extreme, this is the unproductive pursuit of boycott and bookburning, in which something is removed but nothing is replaced.

Fortunately for criticism and its subjects, there is much more to it than that. Certainly, the procedure can include commentary that points out defects. This, however, is little more than name-calling unless an explanation is given as to *why* these elements are defective and proposals made as to what can be done to rectify such flaws. This rectification, this suggestion for improvement, is essential if criticism is to be useful. In this sense, the exercise of criticism is like the remodeling of a building. In the remodeling process some outmoded or extraneous features must be dissassembled—even destroyed—before the improved edifice emerges. This tearing down is never devastation for its own sake, however, but a necessary prelude to the structure's refinement.

The original Greek work for criticism, *krinein,* means to comprehend or to judge. Clearly, both comprehension and judgment are essential tasks in the critical exercise. The critic who lacks an understanding of the subject matter and material cannot be relied on as a source of trust. An umpire who has never played baseball still may make astute judgments if he has watched many games and mastered the league's rule book. One who has neither seen the game nor read the rules is another matter, however, and probably would cause the contest to descend into chaos. Similarly, a broadcast/cable critic need not have worked in the radio/television industry as long as he or she has extensively studied its workings and products, including, of course, the specific programmatic product under discussion.

Criticism, then, is both a comprehension and a judgment that has the responsibility to formulate positive as well as negative commentary. As Jerry McNeeley discovered in his doctoral dissertation, "Criticism is a carefully considered judgment of the merits and faults of a work of art with the purpose of improving and stimulating interest."[1] That radio and television can be considered art is discussed at length in Chapter 9. The point here is that the hallmark of legitimate criticism is this "carefully considered judgment" of both the work's effective and defective properties. Further, genuine criticism has a goal of expanding and upgrading perceiver attentiveness to the medium under discussion. This characteristic gives criticism a relevance and utility that transcend the single painting or program, composition or commercial, that we are analyzing.

Jerome Stolnitz has pointed out that "we analyze works of art not only in order to understand them better, but also to pass judgment on their *value.*"[2] This concept of valuation is especially important since one cannot appraise something that has no worth. By its nature, criticism that is only negative cannot be criticism at all since it refuses to acknowledge any value in what it demeans. Many alleged broadcast/cable critics fail this crucial test because they disdain the medium they claim to be analyzing. Thus, their writings are not balanced assessments but one-sided diatribes that contribute to neither our understanding of the medium nor the comparative value of the particular media product that is the latest object of their scorn. When seen in this light, the pronouncements of these prejudiced critics stand out as patently unreasonable. In contrast, "the processes of criticism," states Monroe Beardsley, "when they are performed well, have much reasonableness in them."[3]

Just as it is reasonable to assume that nothing created by imperfect human beings can be all good, it is also reasonable to conclude that no human product can be all bad—even if, at first blush, its sole virtue seems to be that a program conformed to its allotted time and did not impinge on the next scheduled show. The legitimate radio and television critic will keep this criteria of reasonableness in mind in compiling the credit/debit balance sheet for a particular programmatic event. Still, the term *balance sheet* must not be taken too literally because seldom, if ever, are the strengths and weaknesses of

a particular show exactly equal. Inevitably, the balance will be tilted to one side or the other, but this inventorying process will have helped media consumers not only to understand the properties of this program, but also, in Stolnitz's words, "to understand them *better*" in future listening and viewing experiences.

Reputable criticism, then, is knowledgeable comprehension, positive/negative ascertainment, and resulting "carefully considered judgment" as a means of "reasonably" estimating the value of the particular work under scrutiny. Through this process, listeners and viewers should become more interested in, and understanding of, similar values, or their absence, in other radio and television content.

The critique is the precisely engineered vehicle that transports this criticism from the mind of the critic to the mind of the consumer. Its precision stems from what Beardsley identifies as "the availability of a kind of method or principled procedure, by which proposed interpretations can be tested."[4] A wide variety of such methods is available in radio/television criticism; some of the major ones will be sampled in subsequent chapters. Whatever the procedure used, however, it should encompass each of the five basic steps that constitute what S. Stephenson Smith calls the critical process:[5]

1. Apprehension of the work by means of sense impressions.
2. Analysis of the work which puts it in perspective and corrects unbridled impressionism.
3. Interpretation of the work to the reader of the criticism.
4. Orientation of the work to its place in the history of similar works.
5. Valuation or the determination of the peculiar as well as the general essence of the work.

Our previous discussion has touched on several of these aspects. We know that the critic must have actually comprehended (apprehended) the program or piece of broadcast/cable continuity through eye and/or ear. He or she cannot simply have heard about its content from someone else (or only read about it in a studio press release). Next, by using what Beardsley refers to as "a kind of method or principled procedure," the critic should inventory the components of the work to get beyond a superficial, initial reaction in order to decipher the media product for the consumer. Since no piece of broadcast/cable content exists in isolation, part of this deciphering will involve the comparison of this creation with current or past program ventures of a similar type. One can, for example, look at Situation Comedy *A* either in terms of contemporary situation comedies with which it must compete for attention, or in terms of past such shows that have helped define the genre. Finally, the particular worth of the program must be determined by weighing its individual merits and flaws so that the creation's individual significance and its significance for its medium both become clear.

To see how Smith's five-step critical process is made manifest, let us first read the following review of the series *L.A. Law* penned by *TV Guide*'s Don Merrill.

L.A. LAW
by Don Merrill

Why are we so enthusiastic about *L.A. Law*? Because it assumes the audience has a modicum of intelligence. Because the characters are interesting and sympathetic. Because the plots make sense and are believable, even though a few picky legal experts might find them a bit simplistic at times. Because in or out of the courtroom, the dialogue is often witty and always true to character, and the acting doesn't look like acting.

This is not, by a long shot, the first television show about lawyers. It is, however, the first one since *The Defenders* (1961–1965) that captures the flavor of the profession, and even *The Defenders* was chiefly concerned with the melodrama of sensational criminal cases. *L.A. Law* is about the attorneys in a successful law firm that handles the entire range of legal matters.

The way producers Steven Bochco and Terry Louise Fisher and their writers approach them, a tax or divorce or child-abuse case can be just as fascinating as a juicy murder. Bochco produced *Hill Street Blues* during its first five years, and Fisher, who created *L.A. Law* with him, is a former deputy district attorney for Los Angeles County. This NBC show, like *Hill Street,* uses an ensemble acting company and basic storylines that carry over from week to week.

Harry Hamlin plays one of the central characters, a hard-working attorney in love (as who isn't?) with Susan Dey, in the role of a deputy district attorney who ran for a judgeship. She was engaged to be married to someone else when they met, and his determined pursuit of her, which went on over several episodes, was funny, moving and absolutely delightful.

The firm's top tax lawyer (Michael Tucker) and a female attorney (Jill Eikenberry) are involved in a middle-aged romance that is also fascinating. But enough about romance—this show is about the law, and a conniving divorce lawyer(Corbin Bernasen) gets some of the more titillating cases. Then there's the Chicano (Jimmy Smits) more interested in his *pro bono* clients than anything else, which infuriates the pragmatic partner (Alan Rachins) who wants only clients who produce income for the firm. Which prompts this outburst from the senior partner (Richard Dysart): "I'm sick and tired of this obsession with fees. If Mr. Sifuentes or any other attorney in this firm sees fit to offer his or her services and time for the public good—that's good enough for me."

Heaven knows it isn't often we get a stimulating new dramatic program these days. Most producers seem wedded to the half-hour format, and those who risk the longer route are afraid they'll lose audience if they don't fill their shows with violent action. Bochco and Fisher assume their viewers have attention spans exceeding that of a Chihuahua, and entertainment interests that might occasionally go beyond chuckling at sitcoms, wondering at the sexual proclivities of the rich folks in nighttime soap operas and wincing at the mayhem in police shows.

Please tune it in. You'll not only enjoy an entertaining show, you may help persuade other producers—and networks—that this is the right direction for television.

This review clearly demonstrates that the critic has apprehended not one, but several episodes of this program and has garnered a number of sense impressions from it (witty, character-consistent dialogue; acting that doesn't look like acting; fascinating, titillating cases; lovable Susan Dey).

Second, Mr. Merrill puts the work in perspective by indicating that this is a show for viewers who possess at least "a modicum of intelligence" and have reasonably mature attention spans and breadth of entertainment interest. He then proceeds to interpret the work; initially by citing its plots, which "make sense and are believable" (a merit), despite the fact that "a few picky legal experts might find them a bit simplistic at times" (a fault). This point is followed by a discussion of some specific examples from the program to illustrate this interpretation and to prove the accompanying assertion about the astuteness of *L.A. Law's* producers.

Fourth, the *TV Guide* writer orients the reader to the fact that "this is not, by a long short, the first television show about lawyers. It *is,* however, the first one since *The Defenders* (1961–1965) that captures the flavor of the profession, and even *The Defenders* was chiefly concerned with the melodrama of sensational criminal cases." He also relates its similarities to a sister NBC show, *Hill Street Blues.* Finally, Mr. Merrill conducts his valuation, which culminates with the observation that by tuning in to *L.A. Law,* "you'll not only enjoy an entertaining show, you may help persuade other producers—and networks—that this is the right direction for television." This statement isolates the general essence of the program but would lack credibility were it not backed up by previous enumerations of the peculiar elements that justify this general statement: the Hamlin/Dey "funny, moving and absolutely delightful" courtship; the "fascinating" middle-aged romance of Tucker and Eikenberry; the clash of values between partners Rachins and Dysart.

Thus, though this *TV Guide* critique is relatively brief, its skilled author has been able to combine, through use of the criticial process, all of the essential ingredients required for reputable criticism:

> knowledgeable comprehension, positive/negative ascertainment, and resulting carefully considered judgment as a means of reasonably estimating the value of the particular work under scrutiny.

Why Is Radio/Television Criticism Needed?

Some people would claim that the very pervasiveness of radio and television makes systematic criticism of them unnecessary. The broadcast/cable media come directly into one's home, after all, so there is no need to propel people to this or that concert hall, theatre, gallery, movie house, or bookstore. Further, since this content is so readily, even automatically, available everyone can make personal choices in the privacy and convenience of home. All that is needed is some sort of program schedule to serve as a menu from which to choose, and for radio, just a simple list of stations and their formats will suffice.

There is no arguing that radio and television are popular, or that they are readily available to virtually every inhabitant of the United States. There is also no debating that listeners and viewers each make thousands of programming choices every year and that many of these people and most of these choices are not motivated by a trained critic's counsel. Yet, it is this availability and popularity that require the attention of astute critics. Former Federal Communications Commissioner Lee Loevinger has written that, "Broadcasting is popular and universal because it is elemental, responsive to popular taste, and gives the audience a sense of contact with the world around it which is greater that that provided by any other medium."[6] This sense of contact, however, can be severely warped if listeners and viewers lack the perceptual training and guidance necessary to (1) make their media choices wisely and then (2) evaluate the success of those choices in terms of the programmatic content to which they were, as a result, exposed.

Advocating that the public needs some sort of advice in media selection and interpretation may seem elitist if not downright dictatorial until one stops to realize how ill-prepared most individuals are to be self-sufficient radio/television consumers as opposed to consumers of other goods, services, and even literary products. Our educational system prides itself on its ability to turn out productive citizens who have learned how to earn a wage, evaluate a purchase, balance a checkbook, and make some sense out of the printed word. Yet, the purchase of electronic media content through the prioritized expenditure of one's time, and the decoding and evaluation of that content via one's own intellect, are subjects seldom, if ever, found in the standard school curriculum.

How many book reports, for example, has the average student had to complete before leaving school? On the other hand, how many media listening or viewing reports have been assigned? That there are probably many times more of the former than the latter is in direct contradiction to the media use patterns those students will exhibit throughout the rest of their lives. Some will seldom, if ever, read a book again, but all will absorb the disjointed equivalent of thousands of book-length narratives through continuous consumption of radio and television content. This immense dissonance between classroom training and real-world behavior exists in the college as well as the grammar school. "To say that the communications media are central to the functioning of our society is to state the obvious," states Everette Dennis. "However, American undergraduate education almost completely ignores the study of mass communication. Unless students major in communications, journalism, or media studies, they can go through college without acquiring more than fragmentary knowledge about mass communication."[7] Recently, print literacy has grudgingly had to share the spotlight with computer literacy, but media literacy remains an unrecognized and unmet need despite the fact that the graduates of our school systems collectively will spend much more time with the software of radio/television than with that of computers.

Because broadcasting and cable are so central to our lives, and because we lack the schooling to understand and evaluate them, the radio/television critique takes on fundamental importance as a vital form of continuing education. In addition, the primacy of the electronic media makes them prime targets for criticism by anyone and everyone regardless of training or expertise. People who would never dare to assess a sonnet or dissect a medical the-ory feel entirely comfortable making the widest and most unequivocal pro-nouncements about radio transmissions and telecasts. Gene Jankowski, president of the CBS Broadcast Group, once observed that we are "living in a country where it is popular to criticize television. Indeed, I often think that some of the more active critics of our medium don't even own sets, because their letters and oral diatribes are occasionally difficult to match with pro-grams. We very often receive mail before the program appears on the air."[8]

This compulsion to criticize is due to more than the pervasiveness of ra-dio/television. It also stems from the fact that, to some legally arguable extent, broadcasting and cablecasting use a public resource and are therefore subject to an especially intense scrutiny by individual citizens and their governmental representatives. Though the public right of way on which cable depends differs in kind and legal precedent from the spectrum space to which a broadcaster is licensed, the popular belief in broadcasters and cablecasters as public trustees (if not as servants) remains undifferentiated and is the breeding ground for even the most self-serving or misinformed commentary.

Because a print publisher owns or leases its presses and delivery mecha-nisms, and because a film studio exhibits its products via the private property of movie houses (and video marts), these two media enterprises escape much of the constant buffeting that is the broadcaster's and, to a lesser extent, the cablecaster's lot. Besides, the First Amendment to the U.S. Constitution for-bids only "abridging the freedom of speech, or of the press." It says nothing about broadcasting or cablecasting; as historically ludicrous as that strict inter-pretation seems, it has served as the conclusion for several judicial decisions and as the belief structure for many pressure groups.

The presence of these three factors—(1) radio/television pervasiveness and popularity, (2) interpretative absence from the school curriculum, and (3) public resource status—mandates a knowledgeable and independent criticism on which people can rely. This body of criticism need not be a buffer for the media; stations, networks, and cable systems generally have shown the financial incentive and legal capacity to take care of themselves. Nor should it constitute a supercensor to which all must adhere. Instead, radio/television criticism can serve what Carl Grabo has dubbed the "creative function": "to point out ways wherein the arts . . . may do their part, aid them to maturity, shape them to their task of awakening sympathy and understanding."[9]

Effective radio/television criticism, then, is not a *protector of* its media but the *builder for* the media of what former *New York Times* critic Jack Gould once identified as "an alert, critical, articulate audience."[10] Like any art form, radio/television can only be expected to advance with, not in opposition to, its audiences. "What does improve in the arts," maintains Northrop Frye, "is the comprehension of them, and the refining of society which results from it. It is the consumer, not the producer, who benefits by culture, the consumer who becomes humanized and liberally educated."[11]

The fact that comprehension-building critical opinion could be advantageous to the broadcaster as well was recognized even in the comparatively early history of the enterprise. In 1930, Leslie Allen of *The Christian Science Monitor* told his readers: "The leaven of intelligent criticism can eventually leaven the whole radiocasting lump."[12] Sixteen years later, the founder and board chairman of CBS, William Paley, stated the matter much less antagonistically when he observed that, as far as professional criticism was concerned, "I believe all broadcasters should welcome it. It is desirable that radio should receive the same sort of intelligent reviewing which books, play, movies, concerts and so on receive. Formal published criticism of individual radio programs promotes better artistic standards all around."[13]

In the final analysis, the question is not should there be radio/television criticism, for this endeavor, especially in its negative, untutored form, is inevitable and unavoidable. Rather, the issue revolves around the need for literate, reasonable analysis by both enlightened consumers outside, and astute professionals inside, the electronic media. The negative, special-interest diatribe will always be with us. However, because it merely signals problems rather than offers solutions, such censure can cause only media retrenchment instead of refinement. Knowledgeable comprehension, ascertainment, and judgment of value, on the other hand, can serve the needs of public and programmer alike. As Arnold Hauser observes, "The problem is not to confine art to the present-day horizon of the broad masses, but to extend the horizon of the masses as much as possible. The way to genuine appreciation of art is through education."[14]

Brief History of Radio/Television Criticism

When compared to the other communicative arts, formal educative critiquing of the electronic media is a fledgling activity. Its history seems even shorter when we discover that its early years were expended in a technical study of delivery systems rather than in looking at transmitted content. Typical of this worldwide popular mechanics approach to the broadcast medium was this 1923 newspaper critique of a radio address by a nation's prime minister:

> The voice of General Smuts . . . was loud and clear in tone but unintelligible in speech as a thunderstorm affected the transmission.[15]

At about the same time in the United States, writer Perce Collison was making a similar thrust. His orientation is typical of that of virtually all radio critiques penned during this century's first three decades. Program content, it seemed, existed to serve the purpose of signal clarity rather than the other way around:

> As a general rule a single voice gives much better results than a chorus. Likewise a few stringed instruments sound better than an entire symphony orchestra. Jazz bands are an abomination and should be absolutely eliminated not because the

public does not like jazz but because the scrambled mess of disjointed harmony that is jazz just cannot crowd into a telephone transmitter.[16]

As Ralph Smith recounts in his landmark study of U.S. broadcast criticism's first thirty-five years, "It was unfortunate for the development of criticism that the scientific journalist seemed interested only in opinions about the electronic functioning of a program and was unable to cope with non-technical criticism."[17] This mechanical orientation undoubtedly contributed to the feeling of many of the intelligentsia that broadcasting was at best applied science and at worst, gritty hobbycraft that lacked any vestige of artistic legitimacy. (One wonders how many eighteenth-century European music critics took a similar approach in evaluating Mozart's pioneering use of the mechanically imperfect clarinet.) At the least, the crystal and wire preoccupations of those early broadcast reviewers set a pattern that later had to be reversed rather than built on.

The nuts-and-bolts view of the medium began to subside only after ready-built radio sets substantially replaced hobbyist-assembled kits. At about this same time, the gravitation of famous (or fame-seeking) personalities to radio, a phenomenon brought about by the medium's newly discovered commercial possibilities, helped replace circuit talk with publicist gossip. The burgeoning popularity of the new medium, combined with the advertising revenues it was now beginning to generate, made radio a prime exposure builder for rising (and falling) stars whose press agents were happy to provide copy to the print journalists who now found themselves covering broadcasting.

These gossipy bits of filler usually were printed beside the newspaper's radio schedule for the listeners' ready reference and at a discrete distance from legitimate literary, drama, and music criticism. Thus, the trend away from science and toward personalities did little to improve the stature of the print media's broadcast coverage. As Smith indicates, "the dealer in chit-chat emphasized only the 'personalities' appearing in a show and was inept at any more profound analysis of it."[18] Because the so-called radio columnists knew nothing about the medium and had been assigned the beat in addition to more conventional chores, this sorry state of affairs was to be expected. The journalist happily printed what the publicist was happy to give him to the virtual exclusion of any substantive broadcast analysis. As late as 1946 (just before the mushrooming of commercial television) a *Variety* study of these broadcast "critics" found that almost 85 percent of them were, in the words of Llewellyn White, "'mostly office boys or old men' who simply print the radio logs, now and then 'highlighting' a few programs in boxes, and for the rest, relying on broadcasters 'handouts' for filler."[19]

Two of the few keen exceptions to the otherwise blunted state of broadcast criticism during this period were the writings of Volney Hurd and his subordinate, Leslie Allen, in their early 1930s columns for *The Christian Science Monitor*. Even though Hurd was primarily a scientific journalist, he was astute enough to branch out from a purely technical analysis of radio; and he paid freelancer Allen to do likewise. In commentary such as the following, which appeared in 1931, Hurd helped put radio's practices and potentials into a larger perspective for his readers:

> As an advertising medium, it is less than half a dozen years old. Another year or two may bring about needful changes in present practices, voluntarily. If it doesn't, an uprising is inevitable among radio listeners. With the dial tuned elsewhere, the offending broadcaster loses his audience to the unoffending. With the switch turned off, a radio receiver is useful to nobody.[20]

Such a thoughtful orientation toward broadcasting was exceedingly rare in the years before World War II. But the onset of that conflict, and the accompanying European prominence of radio as a news and propaganda vehicle, motivated the radio editor of the trade publication *Variety,* Robert Landry, to make this appeal:

> I urge the point that radio channels are so important to democracy that as a nation we would be much better off to have, rather than not have, a widespread corps of professional radio watchmen."[21]

There was little time for, or interest in, radio introspection from 1941 to 1945 as the industry honed its considerable talents toward war bond selling, news coverage, and general morale building. However, a new and much more substantive attention to broadcast criticism emerged in 1946—not from scholars or from the press, but from the federal government. In that year the Federal Communications Commission (FCC) released its "Blue Book," officially known as *The Report on Public Service Responsiblity of Broadcast Licensees.*

This report examined the discrepancy between what broadcasters had promised the FCC they would do to serve the public interest and their actual programming performance. The "Blue Book" documented instances of over-commercialization and a lack of both local and public affairs programming. Its effect probably would have been profound were it not for the fact that one of its principal authors was Charles Siepmann, a former employee of the British Broadcasting Corporation. Siepmann's alien noncommercial background was exploited by industry apologists in an effort to demonstrate that the "Blue Book" was contaminated by foreign ideas (and ideals) that had little relevance to the American radio scene. However, if it did nothing else, the "Blue Book" raised a storm of public controversy about U.S. broadcasting. This storm germinated widespread interest in more, and in more serious, professional critiquing of radio and the just-emerging television.

Scarcely two months later, John Crosby wrote his first daily radio column for the New York *Herald Tribune,* an event Ralph Smith lauds as "the beginning of a new era of criticism."[22] As *Newsweek* magazine later affirmed:

> Previous radio editors were inclined to use their columns for a display of corny and irrelevant wit. But Crosby's followers were learning fast that radio deserved the same adult criticism as music or theatre.[23]

The issuance of the "Blue Book," the advent of the substantive Crosby column, and the simultaneous burgeoning of television all combined to pave the way for the much more robust broadcast criticism of the 1950s and beyond. It must be noted, nonetheless, that this new criticism was unable to replace the old "gossip column" approach but instead had to share the public spotlight with it.

From the 1950s to the present, critics within both academia and the media have contributed immensely to the storehouse of radio/television criticism, even though the aural medium is addressed in only a small percentage of today's output. From the academic community, such scholars as Harry Skornia, Wilbur Schramm, Paul Lazarsfeld, Charles Siepmann, and Llewellyn White paved the way for subsequent studies by scores of experts in communications, psychology, sociology, literature, and linguistics. Some of their works have become popular in their own right or have shared in the popularity of industry critics who have borrowed from them.

Meanwhile, journalist critics including the aforementioned John Crosby, Gilbert Seldes (who is equally accepted as an academic), Jack Gould, Lawrence Laurent, Bernie Harrison, Hal Humphrey, Les Brown, and Robert Lewis Shayon were serving a similar function in the press by producing thoughtful columns that redefined and enlarged the boundaries of radio/television criticism for the benefit of their readers and the industry writers who followed in their footsteps. Recently, observers like Robert Stengel have remarked on what they perceive to be "the evolution of television criticism into something approaching social and cultural commentary. . . . More critics, particularly the newer ones, say they are less interested in simply previewing a single program. Often a program preview is only a vehicle for a broader commentary on the state of television or more."[24] If this trend is significant, and if it continues, there will be more mutual borrowing of insights between academic and industry writers with an even more eclectic style of criticism emerging. Some mechanisms ripe for such sharing are explored later in this book.

The Critic's Role

So far, we have probed the components of legitimate criticism, why it is needed for radio/television, and its uneven progress toward meeting that need. At this juncture, then, it becomes important to clarify the critic's function in a more definitive way than asserting that he or she "engages in" criticism. And because radio/television critics should not allow their task to be dismissed as inferior to tasks of people who scrutinize the older communicative arts, it is vital that the catalog of the electronic media writer's responsibilities begins with expectations established by and for the critics who evaluate these other human endeavors.

A common thread found in much of the writing about the older forms of criticism is the concept of the critic as a guide. Thus, aesthetics scholar

Stephen Pepper maintained that, "The critic is like the helpful guide who shows you just where you can get the best view of the object. . . . You would, in fact, find it for yourself if your interest persisted, but if you follow the directions of the experienced guide it will save you some trouble and pains."[25] Certainly, this is an apt description for an electronic media critic, particularly in terms of the trouble and pain that can result from sitting through an unsatisfying program that could have been avoided if the consumer had been forewarned. Similarly, in speaking of literary reviewers, Monroe Beardsley affirms that, "A critic who offers to improve our acquaintance with literary works by giving interpretations of them takes on the character of a guide. And if he is a discriminating guide, capable of helping us choose best where to spend our limited time, he cannot avoid evaluations."[26] Here, again, the ramifications of this statement for the radio/television critic are profound. The multitude of listening and viewing paths make it impossible for any of us to explore even a fraction of these paths in the time at our disposal. And the less time we have, the more essential a good guide becomes in providing us with evaluative guidance.

To formulate this guidance, F. V. N. Painter observed eighty years ago that "the critic ought to be a person of sound judgment. . . . The critic should have the power to divest himself of prejudice; and, like a judge upon the bench, should decide every question by law and evidence."[27] Though the courtroom analogy may be a bit somber when referring, for example, to a critique of a situation comedy, Painter's stressing of the need for factual impartiality has great relevance. A reviewer who, for example, believes that all situation comedies are inherently frivolous and time-wasting has no right to attempt to evaluate one for us. In fact, as Theodore Meyer Greene stresses, the true critic "must be able to apprehend with sympathetic insight both the trivial and the profound."[28]

The critic's role, therefore requires the surveillance of the total landscape—in our case, the total electronic programming landscape in which everything (from ten-second commercial to multihour documentary) is considered to be worthy of initial attention as a prelude to the adjudication process.

Eminent poet and critic T. S. Eliot was acutely aware of this point when he reflected that, "the critic to whom I am most grateful is the one who can make me look at something I have never looked at before, or looked at only with eyes clouded by prejudice, set me face to face with it and then leave me alone with it."[29] Eliot keenly recognized that the critic's guide function embraced a concern for the unknown as well as the known. Such a responsibility does not permit a writer to discuss with the audience only radio/television content considered unique. Thus, even though it is much easier to explore the event program than the five-days-a-week game show, the conscientious critic will ignore neither in order to orient readers properly to their full range of options.

This is not to say that the resulting critique must conclude that all broadcast/cable content is of equal worth. As Beardsley mentioned earlier, the process of criticism "cannot avoid evaluations," for appraisal is a central component of criticism as we have defined it. The carrying out of this appraisal, however, requires the critic to, in Jerome Stolnitz's words, "make explicit the criteria or yardsticks of value in the light of which he arrived at his judgment. If he fails to do so, his criticism is hopelessly vague and we literally do not know what he is talking about."[30] Whether this yardstick is aesthetic (How beautiful is it?), sociological (What social lessons does it teach?), utilitarian (Is this the most gratifying way to spend my time at the time?), or a combination of these vantage points, it must be revealed to consumers so that each can determine the yardstick's relevance to personal priorities.

In his *L.A. Law* piece quoted earlier in this chapter, for example, Don Merrill gave several reasons many viewers *should* like the show; he also isolated certain elements that would displease others: the complexity of the legal process is not truly portrayed; the program requires an hour rather than a half-hour of one's time; it is short on violent action and requires the investment of significant attention. Although Merrill's context strongly suggests that these deficiencies are really advantages, the viewer with opposite priorities has been given the information necessary to formulate a divergent conclusion. Aesthetics expert Clive Bell addresses the necessity for this approach by insisting that, "it is useless for a critic to tell me that something is a work of art; he must make me feel it for myself. This he can do only by making me see; he must get at my emotions through my eyes. Unless he can make me see something that moves me, he cannot force my emotions."[31]

Up to now, we have looked at the critic's role primarily from the standpoint of how the resulting critique serves the consumer. Also of substantial importance, however, is how the critic assists the creator or (particularly in radio/television) the multiple creators of the work in question. Richard Blackmur refers to this function as "the critic's burden," which he insists is the responsibility "to make bridges between the society and the arts."[32] By opening up lines of communication and understanding between creator and consumer, the critic makes it easier for each to comprehend the needs of the other. In the short term, creators thereby learn what their audience desires now while, for the long term, the audience can be coaxed into a positive anticipation of the more profound expressions of which the creator may be capable.

The recognition of this duty is what causes Carl Grabo to argue that, "The justification of criticism must largely be the stimulus which it provides for original works."[33] Grabo adds that "creative criticism can aid in the dissemination of knowledge, in pointing out to the novelist or dramatist new subjects for his consideration and even, possibly, new techniques with which to experiment."[34] How seldom we think of this function as important to critique construction. Yet, how important it can be to a television script author or a radio copywriter in providing encouragement and stimulation. This is the same reason such professional media writers seek Clios for their commercials and Emmys for their programs. And it is in service to this part of the critic's task that Merrill concludes his *L.A. Law* piece with this request: "Please tune in . . . you may help persuade other producers—and networks—that this is the right direction for television."

Thoroughgoing criticism yields another benefit for creators by leading the audience, in the words of Jerome Stolnitz, "to master the work's complexity. Critical analysis can show us formal inter-relationships which bind the work together, meanings which make up its truth, expressive significance which gives it resonance and depth."[35] This is exactly the service that key critics performed in their assessment of breakthrough television series such as *All in the Family* and *Hill Street Blues*—teaching their readers the "expressive significance" of Archie Bunker's bigotry and the "formal inter-relationships" that cross-stitch *Hill Street's* seeming chaos. Even the allegedly crass and cursory commercial can, if well-executed, possess a complexity and a "resonance" that, when isolated by a perceptive critic, may be a source of admiration.

In seeking to define the components that comprise the critic's role, we have so far relied on the testimony of experts in literary and aesthetic criticism since it is their perspectives that have shaped the world into which the fledgling radio/television criticism was born. Still, the electronic media are now mature enough to have acquired reputable judges of their own, some of the most seminal of whom were mentioned in the previous section. Though largely faithful to the central traditions of literary and aesthetic critique, radio/television critics have formulated specialized additional concerns in order to come to grips with the extra problems and conditions inherent in mass communications. These concerns thus have further enlarged the critic's role that we have been attempting to delineate.

Gilbert Seldes, for instance, believes it is the duty of radio/television critics to propose change. He also adds the further stipulation that "the changes they suggest should all be workable within that [the capitalist] system. This would be more intellectually honest and would also save a lot of time."[36]* A former executive in the system (the capitalist system in general and the broadcasting system in particular), Seldes realized that the immense cost of the medium requires its allegiance to the power structure that funded it. The critic who ignores this allegiance when formulating recommendations is thus embarked on a futile, and probably hostility-producing, course of action. The same could be said of a media critic who refuses to take into account the tenets of the Marxist-Leninist government that is financing the Soviet networks. Inherent parts of the radio/television critic's task, then, are to understand and explain the environmental constraints within which any electronic media organization must operate. (Chapter 6 is devoted substantially to this subject.)

Film critic John Simon supports as well as expands Seldes's viewpoint when he talks about the critic as one who is:

using more and truer touchstones. Good criticism of any kind—of movies, ballet, architecture or whatever—makes us think, feel, respond; if we then agree or disagree is less important than the fact that our faculties have been engaged or stretched. Good criticism informs, interprets, and raises the ultimate questions, the unanswerable ones that everyone must try to answer nonetheless.[37]

Simon's "truer touchstones" encompass both Seldes's concern with systemic workability and the need to use standards that make sense in terms of the category of object being critiqued. Thus, certain rhetorical principles may apply equally to the platform speech and to the radio commercial, but the critic must determine this relevance in advance before using these standards in explaining the commercial to the public. This explanatory process would then help "stretch" that public's perception of the radio advertisement and how it really functions. It would also help laypeople interpret the effectiveness, the validity, and, perhaps, even the morality of this rhetorical functioning as it is manifested in other commercials listeners will hear in the future.

For radio/television, however, this interpretative task must go beyond the critic's comprehension of rhetorical, aesthetic, or ethical principles. As former *Washington Post* critic Lawrence Laurent observed, "This complete critic must be something of an electronics engineer, an expert on our governmental processes, and an electrician. He must have a grasp of advertising and marketing principles. He must be able to evaluate all of the art forms; to comprehend each of the messages conveyed, on every subject under the sun, through television."[38] Laurent's view thus encapsulates Seldes's requirement that the critic take the system (the "governmental processes") into account as well as Simon's demand for "stretching" (for comprehending "messages conveyed, on every subject under the sun").

The critic must take responsibility for this broad comprehension of systems and subjects because the listening and viewing audience members seldom have the contacts and never have the time continuously to acquire and update such a comprehension for themselves. According to former *New York Times* writer Jack Gould, "Critics in a sense are the proxies of the viewers. This does not mean that viewers necessarily will agree with the reviewers. But it does mean that there is the common bond of an independent opinion."[39] Gould's counterpart at the *Chicago Tribune,* Larry Wolters, stated at about the same time that, "The critic alone can serve as a watchdog for the viewer who cannot always speak effectively by himself."[40] Apparently, then, for key radio/television practitioners, a critic's task goes beyond that of interpreter/guide to embrace a willingness to serve as protector of the audience when that course of action becomes necessary.

Finally, we cannot ignore the fact that broadcast/cable reviewers, in surveying an overwhelmingly entertainment-oriented enterprise, must be entertainers themselves if they are to maximize their exposure. The breadth and diversity of their public (as compared, say, to that of the ballet critic) requires that their output be expressed in a manner that is interesting, concise, and even fun to listen to or read. The *Minneapolis Tribune*'s Will Jones candidly admitted to this aspect of his work when he wrote that his columns were supposed "to serve as an entertainment feature for the paper."[41] More than twenty years ago, the trade publication *Television Age* editorialized that "the critic's function today seems to be to amuse and entertain viewers prospective and actual with wit, if not malice."[42] P. J. Bednarski of the *Chicago Sun-Times* showed that this requisite was still relevant well into the 1980s when he confessed to a National Association of Television Program Executives gathering, "If I wrote about issues all week, I would have no readers."[43]

Having readers is of obvious importance to Bednarski and to his newspaper, which has a substantive financial stake in keeping those readers satisfied. It is difficult to imagine, therefore, that the entertainment aspect of a critique will ever cease to be an important component of the radio/television critic's role—at least as far as nonacademic criticism is concerned. The electronic media critique is not just a review of the entertainment programming that has been transmitted over an entertainment-oriented medium. It also itself constitutes one ingredient of a product (newspaper, magazine, or aired broadcast segment) that is being commercially marketed.

This chapter has examined the critic's role first from the perspective of traditional, or nonmass communications criticism, and then from the vantage point of people concerned with critiquing the output of the electronic mass media. By distilling all of these insights, we arrive at a list of a dozen characteristics that, collectively, can be said to constitute the radio/television critic's overall role:

1. To serve as guide/interpreter/proxy for the listener or viewer.
2. To judge/evaluate the worth, and perhaps the effect, of electronic media content.
3. Sympathetically to apprehend the entire range of transmitted content, the trivial as well as the profound.
4. To use and reveal the suitable yardsticks by which content value and/ or effect have been determined.
5. To engage the audience members' emotions in helping them experience the program content for themselves.
6. To construct bridges between the broadcast/cable industry and its audiences.
7. To stimulate new works and techniques on the part of media creators.
8. To educate the audience to appreciate the complexity of radio/television content.
9. To propose feasible change on the part of the media industry.
10. To respect and reveal the systemic limitations within which the electronic media must operate.

11. To extend the horizons and stretch the perceptions of the audience to encompass a greater variety of listening/viewing experiences.
12. To entertain the consumer of the critique.

It is doubtful that any single critique can accomplish all twelve of these functions. It also is problematic that the purview of any one critic is wide enough to embrace them all. The media vehicle that publishes the piece, the type of piece that vehicle mandates, and the training and inclination of the individual critic are all factors that tend to narrow the initial focus. Still, this twelve-point inventory does serve to stake out the parameters and the possibilities inherent in radio/television criticism. At the least, this list should serve to disabuse you of the notion that critics are merely, as Neil Hickey jested, "like people who come down from the hills after the battle and shoot the wounded."[44]

Notes

1. Jerry C. McNeely, "The Criticism and Reviewing of Brooks Atkinson," Ph. D. diss., University of Wisconsin, 1956, p. 2.
2. Jerome Stolnitz, *Aesthetics and Philosophy of Art Criticism* (Boston: Houghton Mifflin, 1960), 188.
3. Monroe C. Beardsley, *The Possibility of Criticism* (Detroit: Wayne State University Press, 1970), 39.
4. Ibid., 57.
5. S. Stephenson Smith, *The Craft of the Critic,* quoted in Ralph L. Smith, *A Study of the Professional Criticism of Broadcasting in the United States 1920–1955* (New York: Arno Press, 1979), 113.
6. Lee Loevinger, "The Ambiguous Mirror: The Reflective-Projective Theory of Broadcasting and Mass Communications," *Journal of Broadcasting* (Spring 1968): 110–11.
7. Everette E. Dennis, "Undergraduate Education Should Stop Ignoring the Importance of the Media," *The Chronicle of Higher Education* (February 4, 1987): 36.
8. Gene F. Jankowski, "The Golden Age Revisited." Speech presented at the International Radio and Television Society, 19 March 1979, in New York.
9. Carl Grabo, *The Creative Critic* (Chicago: University of Chicago Press, 1948), 116.
10. Jack Gould, "Television: Boon or Bane?," *Public Opinion Quarterly* (Fall 1946): 320.
11. Northrop Frye, *Anatomy of Criticism* (Princeton: Princeton University Press, 1957), 344.
12. Leslie Allen, *The Christian Science Monitor,* 31 May 1930.
13. William Paley, quoted in Ned Midgley, *The Advertising and Business Side of Radio* (New York: Prentice-Hall, 1948), 318–19.
14. Arnold Hauser, *The Social History of Art,* vol. IV, *Naturalism, Impressionism, The Film Age* (New York: Vintage Books, 1958), 259.
15. Gideon Roos, "Broadcasting in South Africa," *Finance and Trade Review* (July 1954): 38.

16. Perce Collison, "Shall We Have Music or Noise?" *Radio Broadcast* (September 1922): 434–35.
17. R. Smith, *Professional Criticism,* 9.
18. Ibid.
19. Llewellyn White, *The American Radio* (Chicago: University of Chicago Press, 1947), 123.
20. Volney D. Hurd, "Too Brief to Tune Off," *The Christian Science Monitor,* 28 March 1931.
21. Robert J. Landry, "Wanted: Radio Critics," *Public Opinion Quarterly,* (December 1940): 621.
22. R. Smith, *Professional Criticism,* 45.
23. "Crosby's First Birthday," *Newsweek* (May 19, 1947): 66.
24. Robert Stengel, "Television in Print: The Critic's Choice," *WATCH Magazine* (December 1979): 121.
25. Stephen C. Pepper, *The Work of Art* (Bloomington: Indiana University Press, 1955), 58–59.
26. Beardsley, *Possibility,* 62.
27. F. V. N. Painter, *Elementary Guide to Literary Criticism* (Boston: Ginn and Company, 1903), 4–5.
28. Theodore Meyer Greene, *The Arts and the Art of Criticism* (Princeton: Princeton University Press, 1952), 468.
29. T. S. Eliot, "The Frontiers of Criticism," in *On Poetry and Poets* (London: Faber and Faber, 1957), 117.
30. Stolnitz, *Aesthetics,* 11.
31. Clive Bell, "Significant Form," in Melvin Raeder, *A Modern Book of Esthetics,* 5th ed. (New York: Holt, Rinehart and Winston, 1979), 288.
32. Richard P. Blackmur, "A Burden for Critics," in *The Lion and the Honeycomb* (New York: Harcourt, Brace, 1955), 206.
33. Grabo, *Creative Critic,* 22.
34. Ibid, 39.
35. Stolnitz, Aesthetics, 375.
36. Gilbert Seldes, *The Public Arts* (New York: Simon and Schuster, 1964), 211.
37. John Simon, *Private Screenings* (New York: Macmillan, 1967), 4.
38. Lawrence Laurent, "Wanted: The Complete Television Critic," in *The Eighth Art* (New York: Holt, Rinehart and Winston, 1962), 156.
39. Jack Gould, "A Critical Reply," *New York Times,* 26 May 1957.
40. Larry Wolters, quoted in George Brandenburg, "TV Critic's Role Is Middleman—Wolters," *Editor and Publisher* (December 23, 1961): 39.
41. Will Jones, quoted in George Condon, "Critic's Choice," *Television Quarterly* (November 1962): 27.
42. "But Who Listens?" *Television Age* (September 27, 1965): 19.
43. "TV Critics Take the Stand," *Broadcasting* (January 21, 1985): 72.
44. Ibid.

The Critic and the Communications Process

Having established a definitional framework for what criticism is, why it is needed, its comparatively brief evolution in the radio/television field, and the twelve key tasks of its practitioners, we are now ready to look in more detail at the various forms and focuses this criticism assumes. Even though the range of this activity is wide, it can be initially comprehended by ascertaining how the various analyses of broadcasting and cable center on the components of the communications process.

Consisting, in its most elemental state, of (1) originator, (2) message, (3) medium, and (4) receiver, the communications process is the carrier of all human interaction. Thus, it is both a framework and vehicle for the practice of radio/television criticism, which is itself communication that seeks to decipher previous or previewed communication carried on via the electronic media. As Figure 2–1 shows, criticism can center on any or all of the four communications process components. A writer may choose to concentrate a single critique on one of these elements and therefore subordinate discussion of the other three. But the consequent impact of this decision on the utility of that critique is significant. As we shall see, it is often difficult to comprehend the effectiveness of a message, for example, without at least a cursory knowledge of who produced it, how it was transmitted, and the identity of its intended target audience.

Critic Preparation

Keep in mind what was said in this book's Preface. Anyone, from concerned consumer to broadcast/cable employee to paid professional critic, can engage in the practice of criticism and can determine how that criticism will be fo-

19

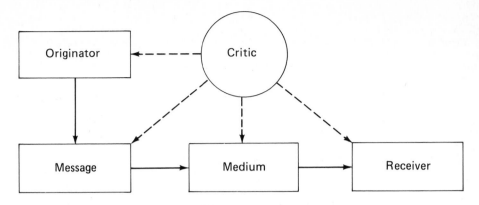

Figure 2-1   Criticism and the Communications Process

cused. As Robert Lewis Shayon, a founder of comprehensive radio/television criticism, recognized, "All people are critical, at different levels of intensity, insight, and awareness. All of us are truly critics-in-being, some more awakened than others. Some don't even know that they are critics; some critics who consider themselves critics of a higher order would benefit from a reevaluation of their competency."[1] The correctness of each individual's analytical performance ultimately must be judged not on his or her official title, but as to whether the evolved critique exhibits the requisites for reputable criticism as defined in Chapter 1:

> Knowledgeable comprehension, positive/negative ascertainment, and resulting carefully considered judgment as a means of reasonably estimating the value of the particular work under scrutiny.

Certainly, the critic's own background will play a significant role in influencing the direction taken in a particular critique. Les Brown, the *New York Times* critic who subsequently became editor-in-chief of *Channels of Communication,* feels that the job of the radio/television critic "if it were done seriously, would seem to call for a renaissance man—or woman—rather than some reject of the newsroom. The qualifications are awesome. Ideally, you have to be equally at home with light entertainment, serious drama, variety, pop music, dance, opera, soap opera, documentaries, politics, sports, news, and game shows."[2] Note, however, Brown's use of the word "ideally." His long experience in the field brought home the reality that, unlike their colleagues covering the other arts, radio/television "reporters and reviewers, for all their skills at writing and gathering information, bring very little background knowledge to the assignment—something that would be unthinkable if the assignment were dance, theater, or music."[3]

Pulitzer Prize winning critic William Henry believes that a less formidable list of qualifications will suffice as preparation for the broadcast/cable critic since that critic's "beat," unlike dance or theater, is familiar to virtually every reader. As Henry sees it, "almost anyone who has gone to college and made something of the experience is capable of becoming an effective television critic. The prime requirements, I think, are curiosity, diversity of interest, and awareness of what's going on in the rest of society."[4] In communications process terms, Henry apparently feels that sensitivity to the receivers and their world is more crucial than a vast storehouse of knowledge on every conceivable message category.

Whether slightly more message or receiver oriented, a critic's background probably is above reproach as long as it avoids special interest attachments to the originator and channel functions. Stating this another way, it is essential that the critic's experience includes a studied detachment from the people and organizations being analyzed. Veteran reviewer Samuel Singer, for instance, maintains that the critic must "avoid personal friendships with anyone about whom you may have to write. . . . To be emotionally involved with any arts professional that you must review is to tie your hands. Anything you write is suspect. . . . You may give as dispassionate a review as is humanly possible, but you will be accused of either praising the performer because he is your friend, or 'leaning over backward' and finding some fault for the same reason."[5] Maintaining such an emotional distance might not seem too great a task, but it becomes a perilous high-wire act when the critic's employer forces him or her to function as a reporter as well. The *Detroit News*'s George Bullard testified about this quandary when he told a University of Michigan audience:

> I don't think they [newspaper editors] realize the problem it creates if you're a critic and a reporter. You might trash Channel 4's local programming on Monday and then on Tuesday go in and say, "Now I'm a reporter. I'm not here to cheap shot you. I'm here to get the facts." Well, they're going to tell you to stick it. If you've ever worked a news beat you know you have to create a relationship with your sources. And being a critic and a reporter puts a strain on you and your sources because they are never quite sure what hat you're wearing when you walk in the door.[6]

A critic's background, then, is a mixture of acquaintance with and avoidance of the creators, content, channels, and consumers it is his or her lot to scrutinize. Let us now examine in more detail the types of subjects likely to be encountered within each communications process category.

Originator Criticism

In examining the sender of the electronic media message, one is seldom looking at a single individual but instead is assessing a group of individuals amalgamated by or into a station, news department, production studio, advertising agency, or network. It must be recognized that in dealing with the originator function, our focus is on message *creators* rather than on message *transmit-*

ters. A broadcast or cable network, for example, constitutes an *originator* when it produces a program itself, but it is solely a *medium* when it transmits content prepared by someone else. In practice, it is often difficult to separate these two enterprises. However, this lack of separation itself can come to constitute a potent topic for critical analysis. Did a new action/adventure show fail because it was poorly produced by a California studio or because the network interfered in decisions about the casting and storyline development? If the latter scenario was the case, it was the fault of the network's serving in an *originator* role. If, on the other hand, the program died because the network was unable to convince enough of its affiliated stations to "clear" (air) it, or because the network scheduled it agaist a competitor's #1 rated show, the blame must be attributed to the network's role as a medium. In order not to seem unduly antagonist towards networks, it is important to mention that a studio also could blunder in the capacity of medium by failing to garner the support of enough large market stations to make possible the first-run (direct to station) distribution of that studio's new miniseries.

Let us return to the topic at hand, to *originator* as differentiated from *medium* critiquing, by citing British sociologist Jeremy Tunstall's definition of *communicators,* his term for people we would label *originators:*

> non-clerical workers within communications organizations—people who work on selecting, shaping and packaging of programmes, "stories" and other messages for transmissions to the ultimate audience.[7]

Notice that Tunstall's communicators are the people responsible for preparing content for transmission; they do not carry out the transmission themselves. Note also that their tasks are not mere transcribing (clerical) functions but involve the actual gleaning and honing of the creative message product. Known by job titles such as scriptwriter, copywriter, director, performing talent, journalist, editor, art director, producer, and (when in decision-making capacities) cinematographer or videographer, these people are the professionals who collectively construct the electronic media's content and form. By virtue of this status, they are also the people whose performance is monitored through criticism of the originator function.

Contributions these originators make are usually assessed as a group product (the MTM organization; J. Walter Thompson Advertising; The CBS News Division) rather than evaluated as individually attributed labors. This is to be expected because, in the words of Charles Wright, "the production of mass communications is an organized social activity, rarely the direct handiwork of a single creative artist."[8] That originator criticism of the electronic media focuses on ensembles more than on soloists does not diminish its legitimacy and should not diminish its utility. The critic, says Eliseo Vivas, should "enlighten the artist on the true nature and meaning of his created object, since the artist may do better or worse or quite differently than he intends."[9] As this variance between artistic intent and artistic result is probably greater for group than individual efforts (given the fact that it *is* a group doing the creating), the exercise of originator criticism in the realm of radio/television would seem to be of conspicuous importance in fulfilling the creator-enlightening task Vivas has identified.

Aesthetics authority Theodore Meyer Greene considers this exploration of artistic intent to be a key element of what he calls historical criticism. "The special task of historical criticism," states Greene, "is that of determining the nature and intent of works of art in their historical context . . . we can hope to understand, so far as lies in our power, what it was that authors or makers of works of art intended to express, and to interpret this intention in the light of *their* interests and cultural background."[10] Obviously, the history of a situation comedy series or a syndicated radio feature will be considerably shorter and more contemporary than a discussion of Michelangelo's Sistine Chapel ceiling. However, ascertaining the cultural context that spawned each of these enterprises is equally important if the critic is to probe for the originator's motivation that lies below the surface attainment of money. Ben Stein's *The View from Sunset Boulevard,* for instance, explored how the insular, circumscribed world in which the Los Angeles creative community resides influences the design of the television programming digested by millions of people. That these creators were largely unaware of the impact of their residency on the character of their program output illustrates just how important the analysis of the originator function can be.

Television creators disagreed with some of Stein's theses about them; this disagreement between critic and originator always is to be expected. As was cautioned in the previous section on critic preparation, friendship between critic and creator is to be avoided. This is not to imply that hostility between the two need result, but it affirms criticism professor Hilary Cohen's observation that:

> The relationship between artist and critic has always been a love-hate affair. It's not surprising that artists loathe being publicly damned as much as they love being publicly praised. . . . Artists are uneasy in a relationship they can't quite dismiss because they recognize their dependency on the critics to make their work known, whether or not they recognize their desire for the critic's validation.[11]

Even should this tenuous relationship deteriorate into unbridled animosity, the critic who believes he or she has made a knowledgeable, carefully considered judgment should not be intimidated into abandoning an assessment of the originator as part of the assessment of the message.

The radio/television critic's legal right to conduct appraisals of mass communicators acting in their professional capacity was, in fact, expressly recognized in a recent U.S. Supreme Court action. In 1987, the high court let stand a California tribunal's determination that an allegedly libelous evaluation of a television producer by a newspaper writer was a constitutionally protected statement of opinion. Specifically, the case involved a sex-education documentary produced by KHJ–TV (Los Angeles) under the supervision of Walter Baker, the station's programming vice-president. *Los Angeles Herald Examiner* critic Peter Bunzel reviewed the program and wrote, as part of his evaluation, "My impression is that executive producer Walt Baker . . . told his writer . . . 'We've got a hot potato here—let's pour on titillating innuendo and as much bare flesh as we can get away with. Viewers will eat it up.'"[12] For his part, Baker maintained that a reviewer "has a right to attack the show but not me when [his remarks are] not true."[13] The Supreme Court, however, seemed to feel otherwise. Whether one agrees with reviewer Bunzel's mode of expression, the court's finding on his behalf clearly affirms a critic's right to make comments that focus on the creator as well as on the content of a message.

Certainly, the conducting of originator criticism seldom degenerates into judicial skirmishing. That is fortunate since legal proceedings, even with a critic-triumphant outcome, have a tendency both to inhibit the free practice of criticism and to make critic/creator relations more disputatious than they should be. As we have discussed, analysis of the originator function is important not only to consumer understanding of radio/television, but also to sensitizing creators to new possibilities and existing pitfalls. Actions on the part of either originator or critic that needlessly constrict communication between them can only serve to lessen the possibility of broadcast/cable content improvement.

The following radio review by Alan Bunce of *The Christian Science Monitor* demonstrates that originator criticism need not be negative to be legitimate. It also shows that radio/television critiquing can, when possible, isolate the contributions of creator (singular) as well as creators (collective). Given the fewer numbers of people required to mount an aural as compared to a visual production, it is probably easier to discuss individuals in a radio, than in a television, critique. Still, the reason for originator analysis remains the same in both media as the critic attempts to further consumer understanding of why the product is the way it is.

PUBLIC RADIO PROGRAM COVERS ARTS SCENE DAILY
by Alan Bunce

It has the familiar National Public Radio tone, all right—nicely inflected voices, smooth transitions, thoughtful topicality. But NPR's "Performance Today," which has begun airing in more than 50 stations around the country, is a distinctly different kind of show: a daily national radio program devoted to covering the arts.

Call it a thinking person's "Entertainment Tonight" or an arts-oriented alternative to "Morning Edition,"—the program offers a highly selective but skillfully integrated diet of classical music and arts features.

For example, an interview with modern composer Earl Kim the morning after the premiere of his new composition; a talk with bagpiper Nancy Krutcher Tunnicliffe; and an audio portrait of Clementine Hunter, the 101-year-old primitive folk artist.

Offered Monday through Friday from 8 to 10 A.M. (check local listings), "Performance Today" has a familiar classical deejay format, with host Kathryn Loomans sandwiching sprightly commentary between musical selections.

But it also adds a timely mix of interviews, on-location concerts, on-air phone talks with listeners, and other segments. These are usually related to music, but they also cover the other arts and add up to a continuing overview of the cultural scene.

"It's three-fourths music and the rest is information about the arts," said Wesley Horner, executive producer of "Performance Today," when we chatted while he was in Boston in connection with the show's area premiere on station WBUR–FM.

"The music is a combination of compact discs or performances that we've extracted from concerts that happened in very recent days or weeks," he notes.

"It includes information on all the arts—dance, theater, film, books."

Ms. Loomans, who was also in Boston for the occasion, said, "'Performance Today' is interested in the big national stories of concern to anyone who wants to know about the arts. But it's very important to me to reflect the arts in the small towns all over the country and not just in the major metropolitan centers, and I think we're well set up to do that. We have three features producers who are regionally assigned."

What part does Loomans play in preparing the material she reads on the air?

"To tell you the truth, at this point I write very little of it," she said. "But I've spent a lot of time reading newspapers and magazine clippings from all over the country to help contribute to what we might have on the air. The staff is very informed and they talk to me on an ongoing basis."

"I take a great care to go over the material, to do some rewriting, to make it my own. And I would expect that, down the road, I would be a little bit more involved in specific features, and then in the writing of those features."

On the air, Loomans strikes a tone that is just right for a music-listener who wants a host who has individuality without being assertive.

Loomans' clear voice and intelligent readings should wear very well in the months ahead. She is not a media "personality" but a communicator whose approach seems to say she's there to give arts lovers a chance to get their fill in a catchy but not obtrusive way.

But more than Loomans' style and the "Performance Today" content determine what listeners hear. Local stations are encouraged to customize the basic national program they receive from NPR. How much of this they do depends on the size and production capabilities of the station carrying the show.

"The program will not sound the same anywhere," Mr. Horner points out, "because every station will insert local information about the arts in their community and local features, and local performances if they like.

"We're providing a vehicle through which local stations can create a window on the national cultural world. It's very, very flexible. I suppose a station could carry as much as six hours of it and make it continuously different."

In fact, a few large, capable stations put so much of their own stamp on the program that listeners may not always be sure exactly where it's coming from:

"I'm Dennis Boyer with Kathryn Loomans on WBUR's 'Performance Today,'" says a Boston host in a local segment on one of those larger stations. In this case, the national and local identities of the program have merged so seamlessly that it's being called "WBUR's 'Performance Today'" and the names of the two hosts—one in Washington whose voice is being "fed" nationally, the second in Boston speaking in local inserts—are billed as being together.

This is just fine with NPR, according to Horner, since NPR has designed the show to allow such integration. He does hope, however, that local versions of "Performance Today" retain "some identity with NPR, because the bulk of the funding is coming through NPR to create the program in the first place."

"And in most places," he says, "the program would clearly have a stronger NPR identity than a local one. WBUR is contributing a lot of national material, and its local material is the reverse of the typical."

Steve Elman, WBUR's producer for "Performance Today," explains that "WBUR's objective is to produce pieces on our level and about Boston arts that will be just as good as the NPR pieces."

At the WBUR event, Mr. Elman stated, "Our style is one that has been used as a kind of model for other stations in the network. When 'Performance Today' was brought to network affiliates at a kind of convention a couple of months back, they asked us and a couple of other stations to produce our versions of what we would do with the program in a local fashion," and the results were played at the meeting.

In the weeks ahead, listeners can anticipate coverage of the Salzburg Festival on Jan. 23, Mozart's birthday on Jan. 27 (when celebrities will be asked to request their favorite Mozart compositions), and—on Jan. 28—a feature on Artur Rubinstein's birthday.

Mr. Bunce's piece delineates the originator function clearly and provides readers with the important revelation that this function is shared between network and local station creators—the more capable of the latter putting "so much of their own stamp on the program that listeners may not always be sure exactly where it's coming from." The reviewer further conveys the collective nature of *Performance Today* by citing "the familiar National Public Radio tone," the "three features producers who are regionally assigned," and the "informed staff." Bunce balances this group commentary with evaluation of host Kathryn Loomans's "clear voice and intelligent readings [that] should wear very well in the months ahead" and her functioning as communicator rather than personality. In this way, potential listeners have been given a frame of reference for comprehending the program—but one that did not rely on the "personality gossip" in which originators are publicized at the program's expense.

Message Criticism

Content evaluation is what most people think of when the subject of criticism is mentioned, and it is a principal topic of several subsequent sections in this book. (See especially Chapters 8, 9, 10, and 12.) Thus, the message aspect of the communications process needs less attention here than does our assessment of originator, medium, and receiver critiquing.

Still, it is important to mention at this juncture that, in the same way he used the term *historical criticism* to encompass originator-aimed analytical activity, Theodore Meyer Greene attaches the label of *re-creative criticism* to the procedure of examining messages. For Greene, "the special task of re-creative criticism is that of apprehending imaginatively, through sensitive artistic response, what the artist has actually succeeded in expressing in a specific work of art . . . to *re*-create a work of art is to apprehend the content which its author actually expressed in it, i.e., to interpret it correctly as a vehicle of communication."[14] For our purposes, this means that the critic, in scrutinizing the electronic media message, must be a decoder of artistic communication as well as an artistic communicator in his or her own right. The critique will thereby recall the original in such a way that the public can feel a part of the experience.

Notice how Bunce, in the *Performance Today* review, accomplished this sense of simulated involvement for his readers. He not only details the show's specific content, both current and upcoming, but he also characterizes the embodiment of that content in highly descriptive phraseology: "nicely inflected voices, smooth transitions, thoughtful topicality"; "highly selective but skillfully integrated diet of classical music and arts features"; "sandwiching sprightly commentary between musical selections." Bunce, therefore, as Greene would say, "apprehends imaginatively" the experiential essence of what he believes to be the NPR program's success.

Well-written message description such as this is often difficult to find in broadcast/cable criticism—not only because stylish writing is hard to achieve, but also because it is much easier to compose negative than positive content reviews. Critics who see themselves primarily as entertainers usually try to be funny, which is more easily attained in sarcasm than in commendation. This is probably the reason weaker programs are likely to be reviewed more often than stronger ones; a condition to which John Crosby, perhaps the first authentic radio/television critic, attested almost forty years ago:

> Some of the worst programs ever broadcast—many of them long since departed—are described in agonizing detail while some of the best programs are not mentioned. That's because bad programs make fairly entertaining copy.[15]

Message criticism, then, should not be the practice of picking off stragglers; instead, it should choose its targets based on their current or potential vitality for listeners and viewers. Whether this vitality is deserved then becomes a fair-game question for the message critique.

Medium Criticism

The ancient royal practice of killing the messenger who brought bad news has, in this century, been modernized into the pastime of attacking the mass medium that brings noxious content. Through such devices as TV set burnings, video abstinence crusades, Surgeon General's reports, and showcase Congressional hearings, some people have sought to disembowel an entire delivery system rather than to suture individual message lacerations. Such a blanket indictment of channel results from criticism that looks *only* at the medium and completely ignores the counterpart tasks of analyzing originator, message, and receiver.

An extreme example of such an orientation is the following 1964 pronouncement by Albert Hertzog, the videophobic South African Minister of

Posts and Telegraphs who was instrumental in delaying the introduction of television into his country until 1976:

> The overseas money power has used television as such a deadly weapon to undermine the morale of the white man and even to destroy great empires within 15 years that Mr. Oppenheimer [a South African industrialist] and his friends will do anything to use it here. They are certain that with this mighty weapon and with South African television largely dependent on British and American films, they will also succeed in a short time in encompassing the destruction of white South Africa.[16]

Radio also has not been immune to this brand of comprehensive condemnation. German theorist Gunter Anders once charged, for instance:

> Because the receiving sets speak in our place, they gradually deprive us of the power of speech, thus transforming us into passive dependents. . . . The pairs of lovers sauntering along the shores of the Hudson, the Thames or the Danube with a portable radio do not talk to each other but listen to a third person—the public, usually anonymous, voice of the program which they walk like a dog or, more accurately, which walks them like a pair of dogs. . . . Intimate conversation is eliminated in advance; and whatever intimate contacts take place between the lovers are introduced and stimulated not by them, but by that third party—the husky or crowing voice of the program which (for is that not the very meaning of "program"?) tells both lovers what and how to feel or do.[17]

Similar dread about the impact of the electronic media has often been expressed or implied in the attitudes of American clergy, members of Congress, and citizens groups. It is what we might call, with apologies to *Music Man* creator, the late Meredith Willson, the "Trouble-Right-Here-in-River-City Phenomenon." Now, it is not the pool table on Main Street whose effects we fear, but a multitude of plastic boxes that have insinuated themselves into our homes and automobiles. (That the closed car was itself roundly criticized on its introduction as a vehicle to promote mobile and illicit love-making by the nation's youth is a related, though separate, story.)

As early as 1948, eminent media scholars Paul Lazarsfeld and Robert Merton identified three key reasons that both followers and leaders fear the mass media.[18] In essence, they concluded that:

1. The pervasiveness of the media and its consequent power for manipulation lead people to believe they have no way of exercising control or restraint over these media (a concern that differs from earlier fears of pool tables and automobiles only in degree).

2. Economic interest groups may use the media to ensure continuance of an economic and social status quo that serves their interests. One result of this is the minimizing of social criticism and deterioration of the audience's critical thinking skills.

3. In catering to large audiences, the media will cause the deterioration of artistic tastes and cultural standards.

Though their purview included all of the mass media, Lazarsfeld and Merton seemed to recognize the special prominence of the electronic media by relying most often on radio in order to provide precise examples for their discussion. Again, it must be pointed out that the two authorities were talking, not about specific messages, but rather, about widespread attitudes toward the vehicles that carry these messages. Thus, Lazarsfeld and Merton were attempting to shed light exclusively on the dynamics of *medium criticism.*

Nothing we have said so far should be taken to mean that medium criticism is inherently wrong or defective. Our whole point here is simply that medium criticism provides, by itself, only one of four critical vantage points necessary to a comprehensive understanding of the radio/television experience. Unfortunately, when it is engaged in to the exclusion of the other orientations, medium criticism is more likely to constitute either a weapon to be aimed at broadcasting/cable or a platform for the expression of fears about it.

Television (the medium more than its messages) is especially vulnerable to such myopic critiquing today because of the pervasiveness factor Lazarsfeld and Merton isolated. "All the talk, criticism, concern and controversy that surrounds our industry today," asserts CBS/Broadcast Group President Gene Jankowski, "is taking place because of the important role that television plays every day for more than 200 million Americans."[19] Veteran critic Les Brown cites a further possible cause for the channel's ill-treatment when he claims that "the press still regards television as the enemy, as its chief competitor, and cannot get around its own bigotry towards this immensely popular medium that can produce, distribute and exhibit in a single process."[20]

Whether Brown's observation remains true today, the reasonable practice of criticism in general and medium criticism in particular requires that the critic approach the medium being analyzed with an open mind. As Robert Landry, one of the first true radio critics, observed, an individual worthy of the title of critic:

> cannot function in a temper of constant dislike of the medium, the mass mind, and advertising. That way lies the intellectualized wisecrack and the cliches of condescension. Such a critic can have no real contact with the radio audience. He cannot share or interpret its enthusiasms. Indeed one wonders if he can even tolerate these enthusiasms.[21]

The legitimate enthusiasm felt and interpreted by Alan Bunce in his *Christian Science Monitor* review of NPR proves that carefully considered medium criticism need neither fawn nor condescend. Bunce, for instance, balances his admiration for how "the national and local identities of the program have merged so seamlessly" with a caution that "listeners may not always be sure exactly where it's [*Performance Today's*] coming from." Readers of this review get a clear concept of how national and local media interact to produce this series and learn ways in which stations "customize the basic national program they receive from NPR" depending on their production capabilities. The fact that the "bulk of the funding is coming through NPR" is also revealed— and revealed as a rationale for why the station component of the medium should continue to promote the network component's identity with this program. In short, Bunce's reader is provided with information as to how the medium works in order that the character of the message and its originators can more accurately be apprehended. This constitutes medium criticism at its functional best.

Receiver Criticism

Directing one's sights at the receiver element in the communications process often involves attempting to determine the effect on the audience of an originator's message as presented over a given media structure. It can also involve speculating about the uses or gratifications listeners/viewers acquired or sought to acquire as well as assessing what kinds of people these listeners or viewers are. Finally, under certain circumstances, receiver criticism might even culminate in scolding the audience for failing to respond to a program or for responding positively to a show the critic perceives to be trash.

Knowing for whom a given program or commercial is intended helps the critic more insightfully evaluate the originator's message construction and choice of medium. It would be difficult to evaluate accurately the following commercial, for example, if one were ignorant of the fact that the spot is designed to lure eighteen to thirty-four-year-old single working women to First Federal and to reach them efficiently via radio stations whose formats perform well in attracting that demographic group.

AMANDA:	This morning I woke up and the clock said 8:35. I said oh no. I'm gonna be late for work.
ANNCR:	A day in the life of Amanda Clarke.
AMANDA:	And then I remembered, it was Saturday. Tonight I had a date with Steve. And a million things to do before then.
ANNCR:	A million and one.
AMANDA:	Right, the bank. I had to go to the bank and cash a check.
ANNCR:	And why do you suppose that was?
AMANDA:	Because Steve never has any money. He's nice, but broke. Broke, but nice. Way he is, that's all.

ANNCR: So Amanda went to First Federal Savings Bank of
            California.

AMANDA: It was Saturday. And it was open. What a startling
            concept.

ANNCR: First Federal is people friendly.

AMANDA: Who ever heard of a bank that caters to the needs of
            human beings?

ANNCR: You have.

AMANDA: I have.

ANNCR: You also have a date.

AMANDA: With Steve. He's not my prince. But he is convenient.

ANNCR: Like your bank.

AMANDA: So that was my day, first and last. First, First Federal.
            Last, Steve.

ANNCR: Did Steve last?

AMANDA: No, first things first. Last things last. No love lost.

ANNCR: First Federal Savings Bank of California. Open
            Saturdays, 9 'til 3. Very convenient.

AMANDA: Like Steve was.

ANNCR: But isn't now.

AMANDA: Not any more.

(Courtesy of Christine Love, Sarley/Cashman Creative Services)

Sometimes, informed receiver criticism is the only mechanism that can illuminate why a seemingly successful program entity has expired. The CBS detective show *Cannon*, which featured the corpulent William Conrad in the title role, went off the air, for instance, not because its raw ratings were deficient, but because the more and more elderly receivers who were attracted to it constituted unattractive targets for series' advertisers. The same thing happened to *The Lawrence Welk Show,* but that property was sustained when analysis of its receiver appeal led to the decision to continue production of the show for syndication directly to stations instead of continuing network airing. Selection of a different distribution system (functionally, a different *medium*) led the show to make more money as a syndicated show than it had as a prime-time network property. In short, receiver critiquing led to a shift of medium that allowed the same older consumers to be reached by advertisers in a more cost-effective environment.

Astute receiver criticism should never start by damning the public for the message/medium choices it makes. Instead, the critic must begin with an understanding of and sympathy for where that public is at the moment. Only by taking their current preferences into consideration can the critic hope to expand or shift those preferences to items he or she estimates to be of greater comparative value. On too many occasions, lamented then-FCC Commissioner Lee Loevinger, "when the public gets what it wants from the mass media this incurs the wrath of an intellectual elite and the slings and arrows of outraged critics who have been demanding service to the public—but who have been expecting their own rather than the public's views and tastes."[22]

On the other hand, a critic can also err in the practice of receiver criticism by assuming public taste to be less than it is. Syndicated columnist Ernie Kreiling recognized this when he stated: "Most of us critics are guilty of precisely the same sin of which we accuse broadcasting, namely underestimating the American public and catering to a lower common denominator of tastes than we should."[23] Certain writers betray a susceptibility to this attitude when they pander to their audience by superficially denying their own expertise. But, as Gilbert Seldes argues:

> The critic who so earnestly insists that he is no surer in judgment than the untrained public is failing in his job or being patronizing, in a sort of inverse snobbery, and a little hypocritical. He seems at times to be begging people to remain ignorant, threatening them with a loss of aesthetic virginity if they eat of the fruit that grows on the tree of knowledge.[24]

A knowledgeable critic, in other words, has a responsibility to demonstrate candidly that knowledge in making recommendations to an audience whose current tastes the critic has taken the trouble to fathom.

We can illustrate positive receiver criticism by returning once more to Bunce's review of *Performance Today*. He does not try to position the program as something for everyone or to indict it because of listeners it will not reach. Neither does he adopt a "your guess is as good as mine" attitude, even though he could easily do so when talking to an upscale readership. Instead, Bunce defines the show as "a thinking person's *Entertainment Tonight*" and as a product "to give arts lovers a chance to get their fill." This does not demean the comparative program so much as it lets his readers know that, with *Performance Today,* they will be challenged to serious exploration not just of music, but also of "stories of concern to anyone who wants to know about the arts." Bunce, therefore, combines a knowledge of his own receivers with an ascertainment of the receivers *Performance Today* is designed to attract. He then draws the authoritative conclusion that those of his readers who enjoy the arts will find a positive experience in the new NPR offering.

Before concluding this initial discussion of receiver criticism, we must raise one further caution about its application. We have maintained that understanding the receiver is of crucial importance in fashioning meaningful critiques. However, such understanding can turn to manipulation when the critic exploits it merely to increase his or her own popularity. This is most readily apparent in the pronouncements of writers who build a cult following through unrelenting attacks on the medium, its messages, and its practitioners—in short, who use insights gained through receiver criticism to blacken the character of agencies comprising the other constituent parts of the communications process. This may enhance the reputation of the alleged critic in certain quarters, but such unvaried naysaying can never produce media betterment. As Ralph Smith testifies, critics' "final aim is not to arouse violent antagonistic responses from the industry and strong partisan support from a handful of readers; it is to involve broadcasters and the public in a cooperative critical endeavor."[25]

Reputable criticism does not set the four components of the communications process against each other. Nor does it succeed by concentrating on one element of the process to the total neglect of the others. The parts of this systemic quartet are as interdependent to criticism as they are to the communication that facilitates the subject matter monitored by that criticism. In the words of aesthetician Eliseo Vivas:

Criticism seeks to reveal the aesthetic value of an object,	[message criticism]
to relate it to the structure that sustains it,	[medium criticism]
and to relate the object to the traditions to which it belongs,	[receiver criticism]
and define the intention of the artist.[26]	[originator criticism]

Notes

1. Robert Lewis Shayon, *Open to Criticism* (Boston: Beacon Press, 1971), 5.
2. Les Brown, "Remarks to the Iowa TV Critics Conference," *Critical Studies in Mass Communication* (December 1985): 392.
3. Ibid., 393.
4. William Henry, quoted in Mary Ann Watson, "Television Criticism in the Popular Press," *Critical Studies in Mass Communication* (March 1985): 71.
5. Samuel Singer, *Reviewing the Performing Arts* (New York: Richards Rosen Press, 1974), 142.
6. George Bullard, quoted in Watson, *Television Criticism*, 68.
7. Jeremy Tunstall, ed., *Media Sociology: A Reader* (Urbana: University of Illinois Press, 1970), 15.
8. Charles Wright, *Mass Communication: A Sociological Perspective*, 2nd ed. (New York: Random House, 1975), 60.
9. Eliseo Vivas, *Creation and Discovery* (New York: Noonday Press, 1955), 191.
10. Theodore Meyer Greene, *The Arts and the Art of Criticism* (Princeton: Princeton University Press, 1952), 370.
11. Hilary Cohen, quoted in Watson, *Television Criticism*, 68.

12. "Supreme Court Lets Press Rulings Stand," *Broadcasting* (January 19, 1987): 188.
13. Ibid.
14. Greene, *Arts and Art of Criticism,* 370–71.
15. John Crosby, *Out of the Blue* (New York: Simon and Schuster, 1952), x.
16. Albert Hertzog, quoted in *The New York Times,* 10 November 1964, p. 1.
17. Gunter Anders, "The Phantom World of TV," in Bernard Rosenberg and David Manning White, eds., *Mass Culture: The Popular Arts in America* (New York: The Free Press, 1957), 361.
18. Paul Lazarsfeld and Robert Merton, "Mass Comunication, Popular Taste and Organized Social Action," in Lyman Bryson, ed., *The Communication of Ideas* (New York: Harper and Brothers, 1948).
19. Gene Jankowski, "The Golden Age Revisited." Speech presented at the International Radio and Television Society, 19 March 1979, at New York.
20. Brown, "Remarks," 393.
21. Robert Landry, "The Improbability of Radio Criticism," *Hollywood Quarterly* (1946–47): 70.
22. Lee Loevinger, "The Ambiguous Mirror: The Reflective-Projective Theory of Broadcasting and Mass Communications," *Journal of Broadcasting* (Spring 1968): 112.
23. Ernie Kreiling, quoted in Gale Adkins, "Radio-Television Criticism in the Newspapers: Reflections on a Deficiency," *Journal of Broadcasting* (Summer 1983): 283.
24. Gilbert Seldes, *The Public Arts* (New York: Simon and Schuster, 1956), 292.
25. Ralph Lewis Smith, *A Study of the Professional Criticism of Broadcasting in the United States 1920–1955* (New York: Arno Press, 1979), 473.
26. Vivas, *Creation,* 201.

The Species of Criticism

Beyond merely presenting a broadcast schedule and the accompanying "news/notes" string of random blurbs (neither of which meet our definition of criticism), writing about radio and television generally coalesces into one of five forms:

1. The personality/gossip feature
2. The audience reaction column
3. The preview
4. The program review
5. The opinion essay

All of these forms can accommodate the practice of legitimate critiquing. All can be transmitted via either the print or electronic media, although print is used much more extensively. In fact, radio/television self-criticism is very limited because, with rare exceptions, broadcast/cable enterprises (1) remain understandably cool to the prospect of negative commentary about their own program product; (2) are honest enough to structure unabashedly positive comment about this product as promotional announcements (promos) ; and (3) try to avoid the mention of offerings by competitors.

Print media, on the other hand, have no vested interest in a given radio/television creation though, as Les Brown alluded to in Chapter 2, factions within the "press" may still regard the electronic media per se as the enemy. In any event, even though the quantity as well as the quality of broadcast/cable criticism varies widely depending on both the publishing source and the dexterity with which its critic executes a given critical species, the public seems tolerant of all of these critique categories as long as each is capable of providing an entertaining experience.

The Personality/Gossip Feature

The personality/gossip feature is a programming and publishing staple. If uninterrupted strings of human interest pieces can successfully sustain entire print and broadcast magazines, one or two such items can certainly help popularize a radio/television column. Many editors, and some writers, share this belief. As David Williams, TV critic/reporter for the *Arizona Daily Star,* recently revealed to a conference on television criticism,

> There are two TV critics in my market. Both of them used to be alike—they were both more interested in whether the local anchor girl was pregnant than anything else. When I got the job my editor hired the absolute opposite of that. . . . The funny thing is my editor is screaming at me to be more like the guy on the afternoon paper—"You missed the pregnancy story!"[1]

There are many occasions in the lives of radio/television personalities that their astute publicity agents can convert into desirable copy for a lazy critic. Pregnancy may even be one of these. Because (1) a large percentage of the public enjoys gossip, (2) broadcast/cable personalities' careers rise or fall based on their public exposure, and (3) their own publicists or station promotion departments are employed to enhance this exposure in a positive context, then the personality/gossip feature continues to be a ready space-filler for deadline-weary critics.

Under certain conditions, this category of writing can contribute to more than the reputations of star and critic. When the profile, for instance, goes beyond biographical nicety to provide background on media factors that determine individual success, it can help consumers better understand broadcast/cable industry workings. When the critic goes beyond the publicity handout to estimate the talent displayed by the personality, the public can acquire a keener appreciation for performance, newsgathering, or business acumen. The following sketch of a veteran local radio personality demonstrates both of these attributes. This Jim McFarlin column offers several insights into radio business ebb and flow and the format devices that fund it as well as an understanding of Bob Allison's resilience in adapting to the medium's shifts.

WHO'S BOB ALLISON? JUST ASK YOUR NEIGHBOR
by Jim McFarlin

Bob Allison may be a great broadcaster, but he's a lousy prophet.

After working three Indiana radio jobs in three years—changing cities each January—Allison went on the air at Detroit's WWJ in January, 1961. "I came here with the full intention of staying a minimum of one year, a maximum of two," says the former media nomad.

Wrong. It is now 1987. Allison is still here. "I just sort of fell in love with Detroit," he says.

Only months after his arrival, he was the No. 1 afternoon-drive disc jockey in town with a show called *The Bumper-to-Bumper Club.* An instant smash. Then, in February of 1962, Allison's boss told him he had been chosen to host a new talk show from 1 to 2 P.M., replacing a soap opera that was being dumped by the NBC Radio Network.

A chance to express his own opinions? To expound on weighty issues and current events? He practically leaped at the opportunity.

"I said, 'How's it going to work?'" Allison recalls. "They said, 'We're calling it *Ask Your Neighbor.* People will call in with questions about household hints and recipes, other people will call in with answers, and you will make it go.'"

Allison was appalled. "I said, 'Household hints and recipes? You guys have got to be nuts! I'm the only hip performer you've got, and you want to turn me into the poor man's Aunt Fanny? There's no way in the world I'm going to talk to little old ladies in tennis shoes about their favorite recipes!'"

Wrong again, Bob. On Feb. 5, 1962, thousands of Detroit housewives tuning in to hear the next episode of *My True Story* were shocked to hear a disc jockey asking them for helpful household advice.

Though he still hosted *The Bumper-to-Bumper Club,* he was less than enthralled with his added duties. "I went in and told them, 'This show can't last for a year, two years, max, that's it. This thing will never fly.'"

Strike three. Impressively—in fact, amazingly—Allison and *Ask Your Neighbor* have endured together through 25 years, five Metro Detroit radio stations and countless shifts in listeners, trends and tastes. Today the series celebrates its silver anniversary broadcast from 10-11:30 A.M. on WEXL-AM (1340) in Royal Oak, where it is now heard Monday through Friday. Heaven knows, Mr. Allison.

"It's not a record, but it's one hell of an average," smiles the 55-year-old Allison, now local radio's most recognizable baritone. "I thought, 'How could I possibly sit down and talk about household hints and recipes? I don't know anything about it.' But although the core is designed around that, it has never actually played that way.

"It's really people with people. We wind up talking about all kinds of things, very human things. The show turned out to be very interesting, though I didn't realize it at first. I suddenly realized how hard it is to be a housewife. It's a very lonely job, and our show has given people an avenue to feel better, to know that there's somebody else out there. Now we have a lot of people calling in from work, which surprises me."

From the very beginning, Allison molded *Ask Your Neighbor* in his own personality, which may be a key to its longevity. "They didn't want me to talk [at WWJ]," he says. "They wanted the listeners to call in and do all the talking, and I would just say "Uh-huh' and 'Yes, Ma'am.' I wouldn't do that. I got into conversations with these people and would expand my positions on certain topics, sort of open up and let them know who I was.

"They would call me into the office once a week and read me the riot act about how I wouldn't shut up and never cut people off. I know they were ready to fire me. But when the first ratings book came out, we were the No. 1 afternoon show in the market. Then they said, 'Well, he's not doing it like we want him to, but don't change a thing.'"

Ask Your Neighbor ran for 16 years at WWJ, proving so consistently successful that along the way it was moved to a morning slot, expanded to as long as five hours and once aired on both WWJ-AM and FM. But when WWJ made the decision to switch to an all-news format in 1978, the show was dropped. "I thought it was a little bit silly (to cancel it), but they were running the station," he says.

Allison was set to move to another Detroit station when he got a call from WIID-AM (now WCAR) in Garden City. "They asked me if I would like to come out there, buy my own air time and then sell it myself," he says. "I didn't think that was legal. But I got out the FCC rule books and sure enough, it was." In less than two hours Allison had called all his old *Ask Your Neighbor* advertisers, received enough assurances of commercial support to give him confidence, and agreed to WIID's offer.

He stayed at WIID/WCAR for four years, eventually simulcasting on WBRB in Mt. Clemens to compensate for WCAR's weak signal, then moved to the 50,000-watt power of religious station WLQV-AM. But when WLQV dropped religion for rock (it's now Top 40 WCZY-AM), *Ask Your Neighbor* went packing again. The show has been on WEXL since June, 1985.

Today *Ask Your Neighbor* is a pleasant little anachronism in this radio era of big-budget stations and split-second formats. (One show this week revolved around the search for a decent recipe for scones.) And because of its old-fashioned aura, there's a tendency to feel a bit sorry for Allison.

After all, his is one of the richest legacies in Detroit broadcasting. In addition to his radio stardom, he appeared on TV here as the Twin Pines Milkman for the last five years of the *Milky's Party Time* kids' show, and became host of the hugely successful *Bowling for Dollars,* one of the highest-rated local programs in Detroit history.

"We had almost a 50 share (of the audience), always around a 47 or 48," he says, "but I had a hefty advantage. Every morning I would go on *Ask Your Neighbor* and say, 'If you're not doing anything tonight, tune in *Bowling for Dollars.'* So I was able to bring that radio audience down to television."

Even so, he admits, "I truly hated doing that show. I disliked it. We taped all five shows in one day, and once you got past the second show, it was like being hit by a truck. I got to the point where I would wake up on Friday, realize what day it was, and get sick."

Like WLQV, WEXL broadcasts a religion-oriented format. The station is low-powered and not widely known, and Allison's listenership has diminished drastically from its 1960s heyday.

But save your pity: By purchasing his own airtime on WEXL and selling his own ads (with his personal sales manager, Al O'Neal, whom Allison would like to see take over the program someday), Allison claims he's now making more money than at the height of *Ask Your Neighbor*'s dominance, a six-figure gross income annually. He's even printing a monthly newsletter, the Menu Minder, which publishes all the on-air recipes of the previous month for a $16-a-year subscription.

Though his audience is smaller, Allison says it's intensely loyal: He knows many listeners who have been with him since that debut broadcast in 1962. Today's show was reserved for congratulatory calls from long-time listeners as well as state and local government officials and media celebrities. "I'd love to have a party with everybody who was there on that first day," he says. "I'll bet you we could fill a pretty good-sized room.

"Even though it has been surrounded by Christian broadcasting, the show is still *Ask Your Neighbor.* The reason it fits into the religious (format) is because fundamentally we do what religions talk about. We treat each other with great respect; we care for each other, and we help each other."

(Courtesy of Robert H. Giles, *The Detroit News*)

McFarlin's profile of Bob Allison demonstrates that the credible personality feature is not a mere reprint of the subject's professional biography. Rather, critics must filter the biography (or gossip) through their own experienced comprehension of radio/television's power structures and procedures to fashion a story that gives readers generalizable insights about the medium. To function effectively, the critic must have the ability to serve as independent assessor rather that as ignorant conduit.

The Audience Reaction Column

The audience reaction column gives writers and their consumers the chance to exchange opinions and responses in a public forum. Typically, the critic prints selected letters received from the citizenry and buffers these with personal commentary. These letters may ask a direct question of the critic or state an opinion to which the critic responds. On the whole, the question variety is the less beneficial because many queries are so narrow that they do little to orient the audience as a whole toward a clearer comprehension of radio/television. "Why is Channel 7 on the cable's Channel 8?" is a puzzle, the solution to which probably will be of interest to many people and will introduce them to the importance of signal harmonics. "Who played Roscoe on *77 Sunset Strip?*," on the other hand, can only be answered with uninsightful trivia.

Conversely, letters of opinion provide the critic with much more latitude and enable him or her to address a controversial subject with less personal risk. Public perception of a critic who writes an unsolicited piece on the propriety of condom commercials may be significantly less favorable, for example, than if the critic is seen as responding to "an average viewer's" opinion on the subject. In both cases, the issue gets addressed, but in the latter case, the citizen rather than the critic receives much of any subsequent blame for raising the topic in mixed company.

Letters on a certain subject may be requested by a critic, or the critic can rely on what randomly arrives through the mail. A critic who invites letters on a given topic, of course, cannot then escape the blame if that subject is too volatile and further ensures a special (and unfulfillable) obligation to publicize every letter received. Still, this technique does provide an opportunity for gauging public opinion on an issue the critic deems important. It also surrounds the critic's column with the aura of a participatory town meeting rather like that of a talk radio program. The difference, of course, is that many more individuals can be featured on the air than can be accommodated within a few paragraphs of print.

A variation on the letter approach involves the critic or a subordinate in face-to-face interviews as another means of sampling public reaction. This scheme has several comparative advantages: (1) listener/viewer attitude can be ascertained much more quickly than by waiting for the mail; (2) because the request for opinion is made face-to-face rather than through the column, the critic has not had to divulge to the readership before an interest in the topic. If public reaction is bland or indifferent, that topic simply can be abandoned without readers' having been led to expect a piece about it; (3) it is much easier to gather a true cross-section of audience opinion orally because the greater proportion of people will not or cannot express themselves in writing.

An adept execution of the interview technique is shown in the following article by *The Detroit News*'s Marc Gunther. Notice how Gunther provides substantive background on the show in question before excerpting local comment. This format provides Gunther's reader with a frame of reference that invests local reaction with a greater sense of significance.

'AMERIKA' VIEWERS SHOWING SIGNS OF RETREAT
by Marc Gunther

Amerika did not win over America. So there's kause for koncern at Cap Cities/ABC.

Ratings for Sunday's opening episode of the seven-night mini-series about the United States under Soviet rule were strong, but they did not approach blockbuster levels.

The numbers further suggest that the high tune-in for the program was followed by a significant tune-out.

ABC estimates that about 70 million viewers tuned in to Sunday's installment. National ratings won't be available until today, but A.C. Nielsen Co.'s 13-city overnight survey gave *Amerika* a 27.9 rating and 43 share. Arbitron surveyed 11 cities and gave the show a 23.5/39.

In Detroit, Nielsen gave the show a 33.7 rating and a 50 share, while Arbitron gave it a 25/38. Each rating point equals 1 percent of all households with TV, while each share point equals 1 percent of the homes using TV.

Those numbers exceed ABC's estimate of a 35 share for all $14\frac{1}{2}$ hours of *Amerika.* But a closer look at the numbers, coupled with a sampling of viewer opinion in Detroit, suggests that the audience levels are about to slide. The numbers also pale in comparison to past mega-hits. *Amerika,* for example, didn't reach nearly as many people on Sunday as *The Day After* did on Sunday, Nov. 20, 1983. The ABC movie about nuclear war, which indirectly led to *Amerika,* drew a 46.0 rating and a 62 share.

Amerika's ratings also came in well below the 40-plus levels for *The Thorn Birds, Winds of War* and *Roots.* There's even a good chance that *Amerika* won't be the most watched program of the week. NBC's Thursday night sitcoms, *Cosby* and *Family Ties,* typically score ratings above 30 and shares in the high 40s.

What's most revealing about the *Amerika* numbers is that they show viewers turning away from the program. In Detroit, for example, Arbitron reports that the ratings declined for each quarter hour the show was on—from an initial tune-in of 29.1 to a low of 23.4 during the last quarter hour before 11 P.M.

Several Detroit viewers interviewed at downtown locations say they watched some of the show but then tuned out.

"I watched for 20 minutes and then I fell asleep." says Ann Tobin, a Detroit lawyer.

Kevin Kenehan, a freshman at Hope College, says he felt that the opening hour was slow and confusing but that the program improved.

"They introduced too many characters too soon," he says. But, he adds, "Overall, I really enjoyed it. I plan to keep up with it."

Max Rippstein, a 78-year-old retiree, says he is reserving judgment until seeing the rest of the mini-series. "Some segments were excellent," he says. "Some were for the birds."

Certainly the show continues to spark political debate, as it has since it was conceived late in 1983.

Jim Coleman, a Vietnam veteran from Detroit, notes that ABC's view of a Soviet-run *Amerika* looks suspiciously like present-day America, with its pictures of poverty, the homeless and drug abuse. He comments, "Who was it who said, 'We have met the enemy and it is us?'"

Marilyn Wilson, a Detroit spokesman for the Revolutionary Communist Party, attacks the show for promoting "blind obedience" and "unquestioning allegiance" to the United States.

While a handful of members of left-wing groups picketed Channel 7 on Sunday, the station reports receiving only a few calls objecting to the show.

ABC's switchboard received "hundreds of calls," UPI reported, adding that demonstrators picketed ABC television stations around the country, shouting, "Better dead than Red," in favor of the show and "World War III brought to you by ABC" against it.

Jeff Cohen, the Detroit native who directs a group called Fairness and Accuracy in Media, again denounced ABC for refusing to provide air time for responses to *Amerika,* as it did for *The Day After.*

"I think it shows a tilt to the right at ABC that's quite marked," he says.

(Courtesy of Robert H. Giles, *The Detroit News*)

The Preview

Previews, unlike other critique species, have the distinct benefit of alerting the audience to listening and viewing opportunities before their airing. Such articles thus can influence program choice in a more substantial manner. In the past, however, previews were often deservedly distrusted. This was because many critics lacked the machinery to experience the program in advance of its premiering to the general public and so relied on a studio press kit or wire service report in filing their story. This lack of firsthand knowledge made the critic little more knowledgeable than the general audience and often reduced writers to serving as shills for studio public relations departments.

Fortunately, advances in technology have freed the preview critic from this press-release bondage. Audio and video cassettes make it possible to pre-screen a show before its public exposure. If time is short, program content can be delivered by satellite either for direct closed-circuit viewing or for regional recording of cassettes that can then be locally hand-delivered. With an audio cassette player and a VCR, the local critic now has access to material formerly available only to writers who could attend New York or Los Angeles screenings. The preview, thus has become much more widely used as a vehicle for listener/viewer guidance.

Despite the new technology, some alleged preview critiques still remain functionally no more than carnival barkers for the programs they identify. The likelihood that a preview is, in fact, a studio or station press release increases as the preview gets shorter and the reporter's byline becomes more difficult to find. One-paragraph, unsigned blurbs are, more often than not, the children of publicists rather than critics. The more they try to make miniature evaluative judgments of a congratulatory nature rather than restricting themselves to time/channel information, the less they should be accepted as valid criticism.

The following piece by Marc Gunther is signed, is extensive, and shows that the same critic can, from day to day, shift from one critique species to another (in this case, from audience reaction column to preview) in meeting the perceived needs of his audience. This Gunther piece is also notable because it is thematic. Instead of devoting an entire column to previewing a single show, this *Detroit News* article takes the theme of love between man and woman and discusses how that subject will be treated on two competing programs. Gunther thereby provides his reader with a prominent benchmark by which the evening's viewing can be planned—the fundamental duty of any broadcast/cable preview. Readers who are seeking a love story to watch have substantial information on which to base their choice, and those not interested in romance have been alerted to seek out a third viewing alternative.

A MAN AND A WOMAN—2 DIFFERENT VIEWS
by Marc Gunther

ABC's *The Last Fling* and PBS' *Smooth Talk* both tell a story about a man and a woman who meet and fall in love. Both movies will be shown at 9 P.M. tonight, *The Last Fling* on Channel 7 and *Smooth Talk* on Channel 56. Beyond that, they could not be more different.

The Last Fling is an easygoing film featuring a couple of TV names—John Ritter and Connie Selleca—in a trifle of a story that is at best mildly entertaining. Ritter is always a pleasure to watch, but he deserves better material.

Smooth Talk is a quirky, sometimes disturbing film that will not be quickly forgotten. Laura Dern stars as a sensuous California teen who becomes involved with a dangerous stranger, played by Treat Williams.

In *The Last Fling*, Phil (Ritter) is a swinging divorce lawyer who is ready to settle down. He says things like, "I just keep thinking, what if my Miss Right has run off with Mr. Close Enough?"

The moment he meets Gloria (Selleca) at the zoo, we know they're meant for each other. Just in case anyone isn't paying attention, Phil asks her, "Have you ever seen someone or heard someone's voice and you know, you just know?"

However, Gloria's about to marry another man who seems to be Mr. Right. Actually, he's Mr. Uptight. He even instructs her on the proper way to put dishes in the dishwasher. Nothing about this movie is subtle.

Still, since *The Last Fling* is designed as nothing more than a lark, there's no sense faulting it on that score. Nor is the problem that we've seen this story before. Done right, it would be worth seeing again.

What's wrong with *The Last Fling*, aside from painfully bad writing, is that the movie just isn't enough fun. Just when we're ready for some inspired silliness, the characters start spouting pop psychology.

"Men use intimacy to get sex. Women use sex to get intimacy," one says. People don't talk that way, and when they do they should be told to shut up.

The conversation is much better in *Smooth Talk*, a 1986 theatrical release that was funded by and produced by *American Playhouse*. Based on a short story by Joyce Carol Oates, the movie marks the feature film debut for director Joyce Chopra, an acclaimed producer and director of documentaries.

Smooth Talk is delightfully unpredictable, sweet and funny until Connie (Dern) meets up with the ironically named smooth talker Arnold Friend (Williams). Unlike *The Last Fling,* where nothing has any reference point in the everyday world, *Smooth Talk* unfolds in real places, the drive-in restaurants and malls where teen-agers hang out.

The performances, especially Dern's are wonderful. Connie is a memorable character, a teen-ager on the brink of becoming a woman—awkward, inarticulate, self-centered, vaguely angry and yearning for excitement. She's not a typical character, and this isn't a typical television film.

(Courtesy of Robert H. Giles, *The Detroit News*)

The Program Review

The fourth species of broadcast/cable criticism, the program review, constituted the most often used critique format until technology made reputable previewing widely feasible. Now, in examining a program after its airplay, the review would seem to be relatively worthless. Why evaluate the circus when the circus has left town? Still, the review-after-the-fact remains valuable for two key reasons. First, in discussing the already-aired show, the critic can give the public elements to look for in future offerings of a similar type. (What do I look for in a circus the next time one arrives?) Second, because many reviews are of program series rather than of a one-time event, critical dissection of departed episodes can help us know what to expect in future ones—or can provide rationale for avoiding the series in its entirety.

Both the Don Merrill *L.A. Law* piece in Chapter 1 and the Alan Bunce *Performance Today* article in Chapter 2 are examples of the continued utility of reviews. Though we may have missed some of the firm's previous cases, Merrill made clear to us the players and elements likely to be involved in those still to be litigated. Though *Performance Today* had already premiered, Bunce revealed the ongoing character of the show and even concluded with examples of specific upcoming features. Both reviews thereby extended their spheres of influence. Further, as Professor Jules Rossman states:

> Some program reviews can be important if looked at not necessarily as an attempt to affect program viewing but as an attempt to educate viewers in recognizing criteria by which critics determine whether they enjoy a particular program. Review can also serve to give the program's creative and performing artists a professional evaluation of the quality of their effort regardless of viewer opinion as reflected in ratings.[2]

One special caution must be raised about the focus of series reviews. Some critics, when evaluating an on-going program, will use that program's pilot episode to gauge its effectiveness. This tendency is encouraged by the show's producers, who make certain the pilot is readily available for reviewing or previewing. Yet, as any producer will testify, the pilot is not a typical installment. Because it is the pilot that sells the concept to networks, advertisers, and corporate underwriters, this premiere or centerpiece episode has a much longer gestation period than the episodes that will follow it. The TV pilot may take eight or ten weeks to produce, whereas each regular installment will be cranked out in about five days. The radio feature or format may have been under substantive development for months, but it will have to be executed on a daily basis. The radio/television critic who evaluates pilots is thus like the *Car and Driver* reporter who gets behind the wheel of an experimental prototype in an attempt to appraise the production model's quality. In both cases, the hand-built entity is not a true guide to what eventually will roll off the assembly line. A critic who has reviewed a pilot should reveal this fact, and its implications, to prospective viewers.

The Opinion Essay

"Reviewing," writes John Cawelti, "essentially predicts how much it's worthwhile to turn on the set or change the channel."[3] Because of that topical emphasis on a single program, the review and preview are not forms that encompass the great questions surrounding the electronic media's merit. The opinion essay or think piece, on the other hand, can afford to survey the larger landscape. This fifth and final species of criticism is practiced most often in magazines in which both time and space permit a more contemplative approach to the products of radio and television. Because of their more specialized audiences, these magazines can profit from a critical purview that examines a subject more attuned to the specific cultural interests or ideological preferences of their readership. For the same reasons, think pieces are also found in certain news and public affairs programming that attracts the upscale audience thought to prefer such features.

Through whatever vehicle, opinion essays attempt to put the electronic media in a broader context. They may analyze program content as to how it reflects its parent society, chart the rise and fall of political fortunes in terms of media coverage, or explore the aggregate workings and impact of radio/television business decisions. Such think pieces and the issues they raise are seen as mooring masts to which can be anchored the shorter and more transitory personality and audience reaction columns—previews and reviews.

Perhaps because of their comparatively lengthy and thoughtful constitution, opinion essays are one of the least used critique species. Yet, the inherent importance of their subject matter makes them the most valuable in illuminating and debating long-term media trends and effects. Another reason for the relative absence of these commentaries may be that, because critics minimize their ability to stimulate government and industry decision-makers, they neglect the critical vehicle whose greatest value would seem to lie in its potential for triggering such stimulation. This chicken-and-egg situation was isolated in a study by Jules Rossman, who, in 1975, concluded:

> While critics doubt their influence on programmers, government decision makers, or viewers, their columns still do not emphasize the kind of content which *could*

influence. . . . Leading critics should devote much more space to opinion and comment on issues and programming and less space to program review and other content. Their daily columns to a large degree do not constitute enough of the significant content of which influence is made.[4]

Because of the mass audience's preoccupation with immediate listening/viewing choices, it is doubtful that the more reflective think piece will ever approach the popularity of the other four species of criticism. However, this does not mean that opinion essays are obsolete, ornate, or sterile. The following *New Republic* article, for example, is the epitome of the sleek, contemporary think piece. In it, writer Janet Maslin delineates an entire radio/television commercial category and the assumptions that the purveyors of this category make about their "up-and-coming young somebody" targets. Readers of the Maslin article thus are sensitized not only to cereal advertising, but also to an insightful chronicle of the marketing theory and social presumptions that spawned this advertising. The resulting broadened perspective on the relationship between commercial content and public attitude is indicative of the type of substantive harvest that opinion essays are capable of yielding.

PRIME TIME CEREAL
by Janet Maslin

Perhaps you saw him, the man built like a tree trunk delivering the cold, hard facts about breakfast cereal. "I'm only 35," he announced, with an unfriendly stare that smacked of defiance. So when he learned about the possible link between bran eating and cancer prevention, he "didn't exactly jump." Then he thought about All-Bran. He reasoned that the bran itself might be a smart buy. And when he "found out I could get apples and raisins in the bargain," that clinched it. His breakfast deal was made.

Breakfast, we have lately been learning, is the meal at which today's tough customers test their mettle. It's the proving ground, the crucible, the occasion for finding out whether they are indeed good enough for Grape Nuts. It's the hour that finds John Denver welcoming you to his morning in a mountain setting (is this his backyard, or a national park?), offering a bowl of Raisin Bran as big as all outdoors. It's the time when a lone, handsome male in pajama bottoms, showing off a finely tuned torso, wakes up at his weekend house to savor the solitary benefits of "an honest, nutty crunch." The emphasis is on pure, healthful, no-frills nutrition, ingested by people whose only interest is in doing what's best. Of course, the underlying idea is that they would much rather be eating Kix.

In case there's any doubt as to just whom these messages target, consider the case of Eric and Alice, for whom a breakfast cereal plays Cupid. Alice arrives at Eric's one morning, wearing a business suit, tiny necktie, and (we can't see them but we know they're there) running shoes. She chides Eric, in a bashful tone she probably never uses in the boardroom, about his eating habits. He's 43 years old, Alice says, and he's still eating cold pizza for breakfast. Eric hangs his head. Alice offers him a box of cereal and scuttles off to work. "Does this mean you . . . love me?" Eric asks, cued by "Dedicated to the One I Love," which is the cereal's theme song. Believe it or not, it does.

Not everyone in the new generation of breakfast-eaters is as easygoing as this; the majority are a good deal more demanding. There is the young woman on the boat, for instance, whose male companion makes the mistake of offering her some coffee. Not so fast, she warns him; she's not about to drink a whole cup of *anything* until they make a coffee that meets her exacting standards.

The aggressiveness of such tactics may be novel, but the focus on breakfast is not: breakfast, in the minds of America's advertisers as well as its nutritionists, has always been the day's most important meal. In terms of energy, ambition, fastidiousness, and even class distinctions, it sets a certain standard. This goes back to the days, in the 1920s and 1930s, when sauerkraut and Parkelp (containing "natural minerals from the sea") were being marketed as plausible alternatives to cereal, and when cereal was itself being put forth as a remedy for the constipation that might make workers too weary to do their jobs well. *Fit for America,* Harvey Green's fascinating compendium of health- and nutrition-related minutiae, reveals that in 1927 a Post's Bran Flakes advertisement depicted a woman who "*could* be beautiful" but was "never quite up to par" because of "lack of natural bulk." And All-Bran that same year was taking "a somewhat menacing tone, emblematic of the fears of failure that were steadily increasing among white-collar workers in the 1920s."

"From the outset," Green points out, the primary targets for advertisers of break-fast cereals and other health foods were the middle class and the elite. It was a safe and shrewd maneuver, since the working class often shared the same success aspirations implicit in the litany of advertisements warning of the failure of advance because of being "worn out."

So, in a sense, not much has really changed. But today's hardball, upscale sales approach is a far cry from such obvious scare tactics, let alone from the joyful lip smacking that used to sell cereal a mere decade ago, or the simple promises of early-morning wakefulness that made coffee so appealing. This new breed of commercials is geared to a truly different state of mind. For the over-achieving young ascetics at whom the new breakfast pitch is aimed, the enjoyment of breakfast qua breakfast would be unthinkable. What is being sold isn't health, well-being, or pleasure. It's power, the kind that comes from hard work and rigorous discipline and, yes, from eating bran. It's the power to emerge from the cave trim and fit and fully in command, ready to leap full-blast into the business day.

That, of course, is the reason these serious new cereals are aimed so emphatically at this particular crowd. For them, breakfast is the make-or-break meal, all that talk about restaurants-as-nightlife notwithstanding. If the dinner hour is for relaxing, there's no point in pitching it to these people, for whom rest is anathema. What can you sell them at dinnertime except some tasteless, listless variant on Lean Cuisine? (Though for advertising acumen and snob appeal, there's no beating the frozen dinner touted as "Perhaps the only ten-minute dinner that goes with ten-year-old wine.")

Breakfast surely does set a tone for one's day. Skipping breakfast suggest indifference, or a dangerous inability to treat one's body as the superb, well-cared-for instrument one knows it to be. Too much breakfast, on the other hand, falls within the purview of fat, lazy souls without worlds to conquer (unless they've already conquered them). Ditto Pop-Tarts, or any other such habits a newly solemn executive type would like to forget. For such a corporate hopeful, the only proper breakfast route is the life-preserving, cancer-daunting, palate-numbing route of bran.

Of course, one is free to eat what one likes, but the underlying elitism and fussiness in these messages is a lot more disturbing than the questionable 1904 claim that Shredded Wheat "can be prepared in over 250 different ways." More often than not, the early morning gourmet is depicted in solitude, actually looking a little peevish if someone else wanders onto the same trail. There is a superior, proprietary quality to these people, even in the great outdoors. Although the notion of prosperity is never made explicit, it can't help but come to mind with the image of someone who's apparently master of all he surveys. Eating right is presented not simply as healthful or preventative, but also as a means of separating oneself from the workaday hordes.

And the high epicurean standards suggested by these messages seem particularly absurd when applied to products that nobody has the temerity to call tasty. The idea seems to be that an up-and-coming young somebody should always think twice about what is ingested, not only to avoid the risk of strychnine, but to make sure that this food actually deserves his or her high-caliber attention. In times gone by, it was the diner who supposedly cried "Mm-mm-good!" over a nice bowl of Campbell's. Nowadays, it's the soup that can consider itself lucky if a fast-moving young executive deigns to dig in.

The people who plot these cereal strategies know a thing or two about insecurities. They know that most back yards don't look anything like Yosemite, and that even if they did, few of us would ever stagger out there any sooner than was absolutely necessary. They know that some backsliders are in fact asleep as the dawn breaks, and may head for work without a single nutritious molecule anywhere in their digestive tracts. They are aware that the attitudes being advanced in these advertisements, aside from being selfish, snobbish, and anhedonic, are also largely unattainable. And they know that while at any other time such qualities would hardly seem attractive, at this moment ruthlessness is widely perceived as a virtue. But they don't always take recidivism into account. To be sure, there's a lot to be said for purity and discipline, for rising with the birds to meet a nutritional challenge. But there's also something to be said for sleeping late. And for Cheerios.

(Reprinted by permission of *The New Republic,* ©1986, The New Republic, Inc.)

Conclusion

Personality/gossip features, audience reaction columns, previews, reviews, and opinion essays are all, in their own rights, serviceable forms of broadcast/cable criticism. Though the opinion essay may have the capacity for the greatest long-term influence, a well-focused personality piece can also provide key insights.

In the final analysis, the species of the critique is not as important as is the requisite that it be produced by a knowledgeable critic exercising independent and reasoned judgment; one who keeps the needs and interests of the audience uppermost in mind. With their different points of emphasis, all five critique varieties are singularly and collectively necessary, because the subject on which they focus is so multifaceted. As Robert Lewis Shayon declares,

> Mass media criticism must, with modesty but with courage and daring, touch all the human bases that it can possibly use. For television and radio today everywhere in the world are the total human environment, the mental ecological field where mankind's destiny is being shaped. Let the intellectual who despises and scorns television and radio as the pablum of the comic-strip masses, ignore them as he will and fix his gaze on more noble objects of attention—yet the commonalties as well as the peculiarities of his life are impinged upon by the mercurial power of these media.[5]

Notes
1. David Williams, quoted in Mary Ann Watson, "Television Criticism in the Popular Press," *Critical Studies in Mass Communication* (March 1985): 69.
2. Jules Rossman, "The TV Critic Column: Is It Influential?" *Journal of Broadcasting* (Fall 1975): 403.
3. John Cawelti, "With the Benefit of Hindsight: Popular Culture Criticism," *Critical Studies in Mass Communication* (December 1985): 375.
4. Rossman, *TV Critic Column,* 410.
5. Robert Lewis Shayon, *Open to Criticism* (Boston: Beacon Press, 1971), 47–48.

Knowledge Processing

So far, we have examined the key attributes of criticism, critics, communications, and critiques. We looked at the various forms a radio/television critique can take, dissected the communications process, and chronicled how broadcast/cable critics and criticism evolved to their current state. In this chapter, we amplify our discussion by exploring, in more detail, the process by which the critics, and the electronic media audiences, acquire knowledge.

Empirical and Normative Perspectives

In seeking to understand and to judge phenomena, any individual must choose between or attempt to reconcile two divergent orientations: the empirical and the normative.

Empiricism

Empirical methodology is, at heart, descriptive. Relying on observation, the empiricist attempts to apprehend as much relevant detail as possible and then seeks to explain it by discovering how the facts are in harmony with each other.

We observe, for instance, that radio station KURP consistently plays fifty-five minutes of music in an hour, whereas its closest competitor, airing a similar format, plays only forty-one minutes. We also ascertain that neither station offers any newscast except in morning drivetime, and neither uses "talky" disc jockeys. On further observation, we identify the main source of their quantitative music difference: KURP transmits only three minutes of commercials per hour whereas the competition advertises for fourteen! Having garnered all these details, we, as empiricists, must then attempt to explain them. KURP tells its listeners that it "plays more music because we want to be your music station." To the public, this may seem a plausible explanation, but conscientious empiricists/critics will not accept it at face value; they survey further to find out if other factors might be present.

It subsequently comes to light that KURP is able to attract less than one-third the number of listeners who tune to its competitor. Because of this, even though it charges significantly less for its airtime, KURP is hard pressed to sell even three minutes per hour, whereas the opponent station has no trouble finding advertisers for its fourteen minutes. In short, KURP plays more music not because it has any special love for its listeners, but because the tunes are filling time the station cannot sell to sponsors. As incisive empiricist/critics, then, we have neither stopped at observation of what the station is airing nor been satisfied with unqualified acceptance of KURP's public explanation. Instead, we applied more extensive scrutiny in order to obtain comprehension of the situation that might then be passed on to the public as guidance.

Any good critic is, at least in part, an empiricist who probes below the surface as one means of reaching a carefully considered judgment. Description is certainly a part of the empirical perspective. But description alone has little purpose without associated unveiling of the determinant facts that have caused the described entity to be what it is. Unequivocal acceptance of KURP's "more music" as a listener-serving kindness will not disclose the reality of the station's continuing unpopularity or set us on the path toward discovering what has caused that unpopularity in the first place. Is the format poorly executed with harsh transitions between elements? Is the station signal weak? Is it located on a remote place on the dial or, as is increasingly the case with AM music stations, on the less preferable dial altogether? These and other questions can and *should* be asked by critics interested in conveying more than distortive superficialities to their public.

As Robert Lewis Shayon argues, the critic "must talk to himself, self-deprecate, needle, challenge, scorn and provoke. He must stimulate, repudiate, query, refuse, oppose—in a phrase, he must continually say to himself: 'So what?'"[1] Even though he was referring to criticism of older art forms, Theodore Meyer Greene made the same point when he observed:

> From Greek and Roman times, through the Middle Ages and the Renaissance, and down to the modern period most of the critics who have achieved distinction and whose names have endured have been those who were not content to bask in the pleasing "aesthetic surface" of art, but who sought rather to delve beneath this surface to the interpretations of human life and objective reality.[2]

The surface reality of KURP's musical format, then, may or may not be pleasing in itself; but in either case, the critic must dig deeper. If the station sound is pleasing to the critic, why do so few listeners patronize it? And if it is not pleasing, what needs to be changed and why hasn't this change already occurred? Sustained empirical observation and search for explanations of what is perceived must follow in tandem if critics are accurately to meet their knowledge processing responsibilities. Imagine for a moment the disservice that the following ill-conceived critique might render to the listener and the radio industry:

GET YOUR KICKS ON KURP
by Johnny Rubato

This Radio Ranger has been scouring the spectrum and has found a real jewel. The jewel is KURP. KURP should be congratulated for its apparent decision to decommercialize the radio scene. The station is the first in town to consistently deliver 55 minutes of tunes per hour. While other outlets seem to pride themselves on how many advertisements they can fire off, KURP proves that it puts listeners' interests first. For ears who'd rather hear song than sell in an adult music format, AM 850 is a good bet. If you're a contemporary music fan, you should check out KURP. When enough listeners do, maybe we'll have fewer commercials and more melodies to enjoy all across those digital dials of ours.

J. R.

Clearly, Mr. Rubato's empiricism ceases at the boundaries of whatever first impression he gathers. He has accepted at face value the station's explanation for its main claim to fame and conveys this claim without searching for other facts or explanations. He unknowingly urges his readers to patronize a station because of a condition that accrues from its failure rather than its success and then tries to inflict that same defective procedure on other outlets in the market. Notice, too, that this critic said nothing about either the quality of the music played on KURP or the arrangement and flow of those selections. The reader learns only that there is "more" music in a quantitative sense but receives no evaluation of a qualitative dimension. To Rubato, less advertising automatically means better programming, but he appears not to have analyzed the KURP situation enough to ascertain whether it harmonizes with his general belief. If, on the other hand, he did conduct such an analysis, he has failed to convey the specifics of his findings to his audience.

Let us assume that Rubato's column has clout. What might be the effects of this piece? First, more people would check out KURP. If the station is adroitly programmed and they like what they hear, these people will listen more often. This will boost the station's shares and ratings and cause it to take one of two courses of action: either to add more commercials per hour or substantially raise its rates for the three minutes it currently sells. The first course of action would cause KURP to abandon the very characteristic that attracted those new listeners. They may well, in turn, abandon the station. On the other hand, raising time prices to the point at which three minutes of spots generates the same revenue as twelve or fourteen will put the station's rate card out of the reach of many potential advertisers with the time thus being more difficult to sell than it was before! This might further put pressure on other local stations to inflate their rates in order to reassert their comparative value to advertisers—a move that could drive some local sponsors out of radio entirely and into competing media.

But what if KURP is not skillfully programmed? What if its music selection is haphazard with harsh or dissonant transitions between format elements? In this case, Rubato has guided his public to an event of lesser value for no other reason than that they will experience this poor quality with fewer interruptions! The more astute music listeners will detect this bad bargain on their own and will seek out other outlets. But the less astute—the people who could benefit the most from initial guidance—may accept KURP on its own terms and miss the opportunity for more pleasing service on other stations. Rubato neither fully observed nor fully analyzed his data and thus has failed as a critic in general and as an empiricist in particular.

Genuine empiricism helps the critic achieve that knowledgeable comprehension and carefully considered judgment that are the requisites of true criticism as we have consistently defined it. Absence of the empirical approach or superficial allegiance to it, on the other hand, can deceive the public and thus distort their valuation of radio and television.

The Normative View

Empiricism's counterpart, the *normative* perspective, seeks to erect norms or standards by which to make an evaluation or judgment. In a sense, Rubato implicitly demonstrates this perspective in his assumption that a radio format's value is directly proportional to how few commercials are contained within it. That Rubato neither states this position directly nor provides rationale for it, however, makes his normative stance as defective as his empirical performance.

Whatever the standard to be used (and we touch on several types of standards in our final eight chapters), it can be applied only after the critic has fully engaged the empirical perspective in order to acquire sufficient understanding of the object in question. Former FCC Commissioner Lee Loevinger advanced an analogy that illustrates the limits of the normative perspective when he wrote:

> It is silly to condemn a camel for having a hump and praise a horse for having a straight back, or condemn a horse for requiring frequent drinks of water and praise a camel for his ability to travel without water. These characteristics are simple facts of existence and are not rationally the basis for either praise or blame. These are things for which normative standards are irrelevant and the only reasonable course is to observe and understand. Once we observe and understand [empiricism] the nature of camels and horses we can then decide the use to which each is best put.[3]

When Rubato demeaned commercial radio for being commercial, he was indulging in the same sort of irrational behavior that Loevinger's camels and horses example isolates. In effect, he was censuring the camel for its hump despite the fact that it is this hump that allows the camel to function efficiently. From our discussion in Chapter 1, you may recall that Charles Siepmann's contribution to the FCC's "Blue Book" was impugned for the same reason: Siepmann's past involvement with the British Broadcasting Corporation's non-commercial "horse" made his critiquing of American radio's commercial "camel" inherently illogical. At least, that was what U.S. broadcasters charged.

Years ago, the marketing director for a photocopy machine manufacturer had a similar, though more positive encounter with solely normative thinking. His company had sponsored a number of cultural specials on television: documentaries, Shakespearean plays, and ballets. For its efforts, the company received many awards from the intellectual establishment—and many unsolicited proposals for programs dealing with such arcane topics as Lithuanian folk ballet. While he welcomed the former, the executive was understandably irritated by the latter because it reflected a belief that he would sponsor anything possessing narrow, esoteric appeal.

The truth was, of course, that the documentaries and the Shakespeare attracted the people the marketer was paid to reach: upscale decision-makers who, at the stroke of a pen, had the power to lease photocopiers by the dozens. Were downscale shows of the time, such as *The Beverly Hillbillies* or *Petticoat Junction*, able to deliver this target with similar cost efficiency, he would have been just as likely to sponsor them. That the purely normative intellectuals and program purveyors failed to understand this empirical reality only made the marketer's life more cluttered.

Make no mistake, the normative perspective is vital to the critic's task of reasonably estimating a work's value. Valuation can be derived only via the application of some yardstick, whether that yardstick is artistic, philosophical, sociological, or financial. Nevertheless, until the empirical perspective is mobilized to achieve understanding of the work and its dynamics, our valuation is irrelevant because we have no comprehension of what that work is striving to be. Mr. Rubato's valuation of KURP was wrong because he believed the station was seeking to diminish commercials when instead, it was desperately striving for more listeners to generate improved advertising revenue. The intellectuals' appraisal of the photocopier manufacturer's program packaging was defective because they thought the company was seeking to raise the cultural level of television. It was instead simply trying to lease a multitude of machines. In both episodes the yardsticks selected by the outside evaluators were chosen through ignorance, not comprehension, of program originator goals.

It is true, as Ralph Smith asserts, that "critics are inclined to be moralists, unafraid to preach standards, and idealists, untiring in their efforts to bring commercially subsidized mass arts into closer relationship with traditional arts."[4] However, this tendency can be tolerated only to the extent that the standards preached are functionally relevant to the environment in which the scrutinized programmatic entity must exist. In other words, the critic's normative conclusions are justified or repudiated in direct proportion to the depth of that same critic's empirically derived industry knowledge.

The Four Ways of Knowing

All knowledge, empirical and otherwise, can be accumulated in a variety of ways. In his incisive *Beyond the Wasteland,* Robert Rutherford Smith argues that the critic's knowledge is the amalgamation of another three orientations, which he entitles "the ways of knowing."[5]

The Scientist

The first of Smith's ways of knowing, the way of the scientist, is entirely empirical and involves the gathering and explanation of data. The scientist seeks evidence—ideally, quantifiable evidence—as a means of establishing fact. In radio/television for instance, a rating is supposedly an objective, empirical measurement of program or station popularity at a given time, as distinguished from the popularity of all other pursuits to which a listener/viewer might otherwise attend. A share, however, is a measure of that popularity compared only to competing programs or stations on the same medium. It is the portion of the actual broadcast audience at the time that has chosen your station over the others. The scientific formulae for ratings and shares thus are expressed this way:

$$\text{Rating} = \frac{\text{people or homes in using your station/program}}{\text{total people or homes in survey}}$$

$$\text{Share} = \frac{\text{people or homes using your station/program}}{\text{people or homes using the medium}}$$

Currently, radio tends to be measured in terms of individual listeners, and television has been concerned with homes using television (called HUTs). Newer survey devices such as "people meters," however, are now also moving television measurement toward expression of individual rather than household use preferences.

To illustrate further how this scientific knowing scheme functions in the electronic media, let us assume we have a television sample size of 550 people that has been statistically selected to represent a regional population mass of 7 million. In conducting our survey by whatever means (telephone, electronic meter attached to television sets, or written diary that they fill out) we find that 396 of the sample are watching TV at the time our game show, *Spittin' Distance,* is aired. Of these 396, exactly 99 indicate they tuned to *Spittin' Distance.* Dividing 99 (the number of people watching us) by 550 (the total number of people in the sample) we find that the show has a rating of 18:

$$\frac{99}{550} = .18$$

In other words, 18 percent of the total population is watching *Spittin' Distance*. To compute the share, we divide that same 99 by 396 (the sample's active viewing audience) to achieve a share of 25:

$$\frac{99}{396} = .25$$

Thus, one quarter (25 percent) of all actual viewers in our survey report that they watched our game show.

Assuming that the composition of our sample statistically mirrors the make up of that total population of 7 million, we infer from all this that, since 72 percent (396 divided by 550) of our sample is watching television at the time, this translates into an active viewership of 5,040,000 (7 million multiplied by .72). We would further conclude—and inform our advertisers—that 1,260,000 people (7 million multiplied by our rating of 18 or, .18) are reached by *Spittin' Distance*.

These advertisers could then divide whatever it costs them for a commercial on *Spittin' Distance* by 1,260,000 to see how much they are spending to reach each viewer. But since this computation would result in a tiny decimal, in actual practice sponsors would first divide that total audience by 1,000 before dividing the cost of the airtime by the result. This calculation gives them a CPM or *cost-per-thousand* figure. (The abbreviation is CPM and not CPT because *M* is the Roman numeral designation for 1,000—who says broadcasters can't be classicists?!)

The legendary bottom line for advertisers on our program thus would be computed as follows, assuming that a thirty-second commercial on *Spittin' Distance* costs $1,900:

$$\frac{1,260,000}{1,000} = \begin{array}{l}1,260 \text{ groups of one} \\ \text{thousand people each}\end{array}$$

$$\frac{\$1,900}{1,260} = \begin{array}{l}\$1.5079 \text{ or a cost per thousand} \\ \text{(CPM) of about } \$1.50\end{array}$$

It thus costs an advertiser approximately $1.50 to reach a thousand people through one commercial on *Spittin' Distance*. In most instances this would be considered a bargain since it is less than half the cost an advertiser currently would expect to incur in using broadcast television to reach consumers. As we discuss in Chapter 6 this is, however, a simplification since we do not yet know whether those 1.2 million viewers are the kind of people likely to buy the type of product a given advertiser is marketing.

Notice that in all of these empirical, scientific calculations, we have not determined *why* those 1.2 million people chose to watch *Spittin' Distance*.

We are just inferring that they did watch, based on extrapolation of the data from our 550-person sample. In fact, there is rapidly accumulating scientific data to show that ratings-derived watching reports are not true measures of actual cognition. M.I.T. researcher Russell Neuman has written that, "a decade ago, researchers found the average viewer's eyes on the set only 65 percent of the time under normal conditions. More recent research confirms that competing activities—eating, talking on the telephone, reading, playing—go on during 30 to 50 percent of 'viewing' time."[6]

Radio/television's use of scientific empiricism, then, can generate mounds of quantified conclusions, which are then modified by other mounds of data. Data explanation becomes ever more refined while our conclusions about broadcast/cable impact become ever more tentative. Even so, empirically derived ratings indexes are still a prime normative and scientific scale by which program or format success and failure are measured.

The Mystic

The scientific way of knowing proceeds empirically (even though the results of this process can be applied normatively). In contrast, Robert Smith's second way of knowing, the way of the mystic, operates from a fundamentally normative perspective. To the mystic, truth rather than data assimilation is all-important. If this truth can be verified by empirical data, so much the better. But such evidence, in the mystic's view, is not superior to such unquantifiable powers as faith, belief, and vision. Science thus becomes incapable of resolving values conflicts, and the citation of empirical data, no matter how unequivocal, will not dislodge the mystic from a stance he or she knows to be righteous.

Johnny Rubato's belief that KURP was a "better" station because it ran fewer commercials seems to contradict the ratings that showed the station's prime competitor to attract more than three times as many listeners. This is a values determination that clashes with empirical data. Perhaps if he had bothered to analyze the situation empirically, Rubato could have ascertained a reason for this discrepancy. It might be that KURP is suffering from a smaller coverage pattern or an inadequate promotions budget. But if his way of knowing is solely mystical—if it embraces the unequivocal conviction that fewer commercials mean better programs—Rubato would not see the need to find, or even to search for, any such explanations. Nor, to cite another example, would mystics feel compelled to establish a causal link between television's plot-action use of firearms and the actual incidence of armed robberies. They somehow "know" that the latter is caused by the former, and no numerical chronicle will convince them otherwise.

Our citing of these examples was not meant to suggest that the mystical perspective is nothing more than an unverifiable weapon with which to attack the electronic media and their advertisers. Actually, the radio, television, and advertising industries themselves frequently exploit the way of the mystic as a means of appealing to audiences. Thus, the following radio commercial skillfully conveys the vision of an automobile as a mystical symbol of personal philosophy rather than as a validated method of transportation. Little in this spot can be proven or disproven in a scientific sense, but extensively articulated is the normative belief structure that prizes a car on the basis of the individual freedom it bestows.

ANNCR: As a famous philosopher once observed, "Freedom is nothing else but a chance to be better." And that's what's so puzzling about the way so many people choose their cars. They seem to deliberately choose an albatross; an overpriced, underpowered assemblage of spare parts that finally breaks down. Because it's made to break down. So, what price freedom? The price of a new Lotus Esprit Turbo from Krone, Limited. As <u>Motor Trend Magazine</u> put it: "This is a vehicle with creature comforts and safety considered. But make no mistake, this surface-to-surface missile is for getting from Point A to Point B in the shortest possible time." "Driving the Lotus Esprit Turbo," according to <u>Motor Trend</u>, "is a promise fulfilled." And buying a Lotus Esprit Turbo from Krone, Limited, is a promise insured. The promise of ultimate service, advice, courtesy and performance. In a word, <u>freedom</u> . To be better. The Lotus Esprit Turbo, only from Krone, Limited. North Carolina's only factory-authorized Lotus dealer. 200—A Pomona Drive, in Greensboro. Not for everyone. But quite possibly, for you.

(Courtesy of Bernard Mann, Mann Media)

Noncommercial interests can mobilize a mystical approach as well. In the television PSA (public service announcement) below, it is empirically preposterous that the arts in Oregon are in literal danger of drowning—or that donations would hold back the waves if they were. Yet, faith in fine arts as the buffers against bleakness is visually certified and mystically affirmed.

<u>VIDEO</u>	<u>AUDIO</u>
LOCATION: THE OREGON COAST, A DESERTED BEACH. WE OPEN ON LONG SHOT OF YET UNIDENTIFIED FIGURE. THE DAY IS GREY, CLOUDY.	SFX: WAVES, BLENDING WITH SLIGHTLY MELANCHOLY <u>MUSIC OF SINGLE FRENCH HORN</u> .

VIDEO	AUDIO
WE PULL IN SLOWLY AND FIGURE BECOMES RECOGNIZABLE. A MAN, BETWEEN 30 AND 40, WEARING A TUXEDO, PLAYING A FRENCH HORN. HIS PANTS LEGS ARE ROLLED UP AND WATER IS BUBBLING IN THE SAND AROUND HIS BARE FEET.	ANNCR: (VOICEOVER) If there was no place to perform, what would become of the arts in Oregon? (SFX: WAVES, GULLS) So that local arts organizations can build and renovate concert halls, theaters and galleries, the Oregon Arts Commission needs your help.
VARIOUS CUTS OF HIM SERENADING THE BREAKERS.	You can contribute simply by checking the box near the bottom of your state tax form. Do it for <u>all</u> the arts.
MED-TO-LONG SHOT SHOWS HIM CONTINUING TO PLAY AS A LARGE WAVE SLOWLY FORMS AND BEGINS TO BREAK IN FRONT OF HIM.	
ON ITS WAY DOWN, AS IT LOOKS AS IF THE WAVE MAY OVERTAKE HIM, WE FREEZE FRAME.	(SFX OF WAVE BEGINS TO OVERPOWER <u>HORN</u>) And for the music that, without your help, no one may ever hear.
FADE TO BLACK	
UP ON OAC LOGO	(WAVE CRASHES AS <u>HORN FADES OUT</u>, GULL)

SUPER: <u>CHECK OFF FOR OREGON'S ARTS SO WE'LL ALWAYS HEAR THE MUSIC</u>.

(Courtesy of Leslie Ann Butler, Whitman Advertising and Public Relations)

Clearly, the way of the mystic involves the deep-seated holding to, and application of, personal or philosophical values. That the objective truth of these values cannot be proven in an empirical way makes them no less real or profound for the people who hold them. In Chapter 8 we analyze more fully the values found in radio/television content.

The Rhetorician

The way of the mystic is normative-based, and the way of the scientist is grounded in empiricism; Robert Smith's third knowledge processor, the way of the rhetorician, is both empirical and normative and centers on the winning of arguments. These arguments may be won on the basis of a belief structure as easily as on a quantified product of scientific research. Whatever the case, the important thing to rhetoricians is that a decision in their favor is arrived at— hopefully by reputable means. Specifically, rhetoric is defined by professors

Young, Becker, and Pike as being "concerned primarily with a creative process that includes all the choices a writer makes from his earliest tentative explorations of a problem . . . through choices in arrangement and strategy for a particular audience, to the final editing of the final draft."[7] Even though this definition refers to written products, it can apply as well to oral communication whether or not that communication passes through an intermediate written form.

The "creative choice process" to which Young, Becker, and Pike point involves weighing the comparative strengths of scientific and mystical approaches as to which will be more effective in persuading a given group of people (a given *universe,* as we say in mass communications). How these arguments are structured and presented is just as important as is their selection in terms of the gaining of a decision. In reality, the rhetorician is an eclectic who borrows from the empirical as well as the normative to package in an imaginative fashion the most advantageous discourse possible.

Advertising frequently practices the way of the rhetorician in composing its pitches, as do the writers of programs as a means of advancing the themes that hold their shows together. Any program, like any commercial, has an implicit or explicit point of view, and rhetorical knowledge processing affords the greatest flexibility as to how that view is promoted. Since, however, the rhetorical way is most easily isolated in the concise world of the spot, let us examine the following sixty-second radio advertisement that was delivered by comedian Martin Mull:

MULL: Ever hear of "Nictophobia"? No, this doesn't mean you're terrified by unfiltered cigarettes: Nictophobia is simply an irrational or excessive fear of the dark.

Now, keeping your bedroom light on because of that slobbering one-eyed slime thing under your bed does not necessarily qualify you as a nictophobe. Oh, a little strange, yes. However, being afraid of dark beer is textbook nictophobia, because this fear simply does not make logical sense when you consider Michelob Classic Dark.

Why don't you try this: Gather an encounter group over a few Michelob Classic Darks and confront your fears directly. You'll find Classic Dark has full-bodied flavor that's remarkably smooth. There's no dark beer bite, there is nothing to be afraid of.

There! That was painless, wasn't it? You've made your first step along the road to recovery. You've discovered a rich new flavor. And you've saved a bundle on therapy. My fee? No, no, no, no. Knowing I did my part to help is

reward enough. Just try Michelob Classic Dark. And don't
be afraid of the Dark.

ANNCR: Anheuser-Busch, St. Louis, Missouri.

(Courtesy of Tony Sciolla, DDB Needham Worldwide)

This commercial attacks head-on the normative belief structure that the
darker a beer's color, the more bitter its taste. But it mounts this attack
obliquely by first linking it to an irrational (in other words, childish) fear of dark
places. Both mystical fears are thus collectively negated as excessive and are
replaced by the logical sense of a seemingly scientific group taste test in which
Classic Dark is empirically determined to be "full-bodied," "remarkably
smooth," and with no "dark beer bite." Because the ad is aimed at adults who
would consider themselves to be level-headed, this tongue-in-cheek dismissal
of their outgrown beliefs is rhetorically persuasive without seeming to be argu-
mentative. Scientific observation triumphs over mystical misbelief in this creative arrangement that is well-suited to the self concepts of its audience. The
same basic strategy is evidenced by the television spot reproduced as a photoboard in Figure 4–1—with the added argument that people who really are in
search of dark, bitter drinks should try soy sauce instead! Since it borrows
from both scientific and mystical approaches, the way of rhetorician is, as a
design for knowing, significantly more complex than either. Yet, this third
method thereby acquires the greater flexibility in unveiling information in a way
most likely to engage the favorable understanding of a particular audience.

The Critic

Rhetoricians, however, are not the most profuse borrowers. Instead, that distinction must be awarded to those practicing the fourth way of knowing: the
way of the critic. Critics are as likely to accept rhetorical argument as they are
to prize scientific evidence or mystical truth in arriving at their evaluation. Conscientious critics consider all opinions and exercise all options in attempting to
fulfill their comprehensive role that was described in Chapter 1. "Although," as
Robert Smith cautions, "critics should be fair and accurate in using sources,
there is no arbitrary limit upon the kinds of support they can use to inform a
critical judgement."[8]

The following critique by *The Washington Post*'s David Remnick demonstrates how the scientist's need for empirical explanation, the mystic's focus
on truth, the rhetorician's engrossment with argument, and the critic's requisite for evaluation all can be intertwined in even a relatively brief composition.

MISSING THE TOUGH SHOTS: UNFULFILLED PROMISE OF 'PLAYGROUND PROS'
by David Remnick

Playground basketball is a rich subject, for it goes beyond the sport to the dreams of
children and adolescents. The game, with its strange combination of subtlety and

 **MICHELOB** *Classic* **DARK.** BEER

"SOY SAUCE" :30

ANHEUSER-BUSCH INC., ST. LOUIS, MO.
AUMD-3718
DDB NEEDHAM WORLDWIDE, INC.

MULL: The dark, can give you the willies.

Everything looks different. (SFX: THUNDER)

Woo! boy...

Now, take Michelob Dark.

You might ask, "Whatcha do, burn it? Have a little mishap down at the brewery?" Ha, ha, ha, ha--

NO.

Michelob Dark is meant to be

a richer, smoother, and yes, darker beer.

Now, of course, there are some of you that like a dark and bitter drink--

that's why I keep the soy sauce.

Try Michelob Dark.

Don't be afraid of the Dark. (SFX: THUNDER)

Figure 4–1 Michelob Classic Dark "Soy Sauce" Photoboard (Courtesy of Tony Sciolla, DDB Needham Worldwide)

61

strength, can take possession of a kid and can lead him or her to a few conclusions about life itself.

David Johnson's documentary, produced locally by the Workshop for the Visual and Performing Arts and airing tonight at 8:30 on Channel 32, focuses on the youth basketball program at the 3rd District Metropolitan Boys and Girls Club at 14th and Clifton streets NW. Johnson means to talk about the virtues of that program, its emphasis on teamwork, discipline and sportsmanship. One hoped that he could match on video what, say, Pete Axhelm did for New York playgrounds in his book "The City Game."

But for all its good intentions, "Playground Pros" fails to come alive, visually or even educationally. Johnson does not use a narrator. Instead he tries to let his pictures and talking heads do all the work, and they are not up to the task.

For minutes at a time we watch Coach Edward Hill shout on the sidelines as his 11-year-olds struggle on the court. "Defense!" he will scream, typically. Or "Pressure!" Or "Where's the foul?" Other than to measure the timbre of Hill's voice—which is considerable and, by all reports, inspiring—it is hard to see what we are to learn from all the shouting.

The neighborhood the program draws on for its players is, the film says, "a drug corridor," while the basketball court is "an oasis in the desert." But the shots of street life are static, never showing much more than traffic. One is grateful when the film turns back to the court, dribbling guards being more interesting than coasting Buicks.

More troubling than the images, however, are some of the implicit messages of "Playground Pros." Even while the proper virtues are announced and reannounced, there is a disturbing sense that too much air is being pumped into the basketball, too much stress being placed on the game as a singular alternative to a wasted life.

Hill quite properly says that he doesn't want his players to think "that basketball is the be-all and end-all . . . [lest] they become one-dimensional." He says that basketball "gives them that sense of identity . . . they can walk with their chest stuck out." He even admits that he sometimes invites losing so that his kids can learn from it.

And yet, minutes later, there is the same coach telling his players that the upcoming tournament will be "just like a war."

Missing in "Playground Pros" is a point of view, a documentary filmmaker who not only celebrates a world but also asks tough questions of it. Such as: How can we help kids get as enthusiastic about school as they are about sports? Is it possible that there is too much emphasis on sports as an escape hatch from poverty? How do the lessons of the court carry over into the more important realms of life?

The only conclusion of "Playground Pros" is a good luck wish on the team's upcoming tournament. This is just not enough.

(© *The Washington Post*)

Remnick has gathered a number of pieces of observable data. Through Remnick's writing, we know that the documentarist "does not use a narrator. Instead he tries to let his pictures and talking heads do all the work." There is also empirical evidence that the featured coach possesses a voice of "considerable" timbre though the viewer is unable to measure the impact of this voice since the camera apparently focuses mainly on the coach rather than on his players. The street scenes shown prove that there is traffic in the neighborhood—but not that there are drugs. In this case, then, the way of the scientist would seem to conclude that the data gathered did not explain or ratify the program producer's premise for including it.

Columnist Remnick clearly retains a belief structure that helps orient him in a normative way to his subject. Basketball, he maintains, is something of which children's dreams are made and that can lead a child "to a few conclusions about life itself." Still, this faith in the activity is qualified by a mystical "sense" that there is "too much stress being placed on the game as a singular alternative to a wasted life." Basketball, in short, is losing its virtue as a teacher because it is forced to assume the role of savior. Therefore, affirms the critic, we need "to help kids get as enthusiastic about school as they are about sports." These are clearly Remnick's values, and his candid articulation of them helps the reader understand the normative goggles through which he is viewing *Playground Pros.*

Rhetorically, the critique then argues that the program does not live up to its own (or the critic's) values because there seems to be discord between "announced and reannounced" "proper virtues" and the "implicit messages" the documentarist has allowed to surface. Is basketball something "kids can learn from" or "just like war"? The absence of a clear "point of view" on this central issue is of great concern to the reviewer, and he strategically focuses this concern in the climactic conclusion to his piece.

The critical evaluation that results from the contributions of the other three ways of knowing is that *"Playground Pros"* fails to come alive, visually or even educationally." The producer's methods are "not up to the task," and we lack here "a documentary filmmaker who not only celebrates a world but also asks tough questions of it." "This," in Remnick's final words, "is not enough." Thus, his evaluative conclusion (the way of the critic) becomes the clear and inevitable result of what he observed in the program (the way of the scientist), his own values and beliefs (the way of the mystic), and the arguments raised not only within the show but also those clashes arising from the differing subject matter visions of producer and critic (the way of the rhetorician).

Fundamentally, the four ways of knowing resemble the points of view that might be found in a courtroom during a murder trial. A forensic pathologist is called on to establish probable time and a cause of death. Less unequivocally, one or more psychiatrists might be asked for their professional evaluations of the defendant's psychological state and capabilities. Such activity is, of course, the way of scientists. The defendant's boss and fourth-grade teacher are character witnesses to the fact that, in their beliefs, this man is incapable of such a heinous crime, while the accused's ex-wife sees him as all too capable. That these beliefs contradict each other does not make the verdict easier, but it does represent the often unprovable nature of the way of the mystic. Meanwhile, as well-trained rhetoricians, the prosecuting and defense attorneys do their best to arrange all this fact and faith into a pattern that is most advantageous in securing the decision each is being paid to win. Finally, the judge and jury must weigh evidence, belief, and argument in reaching an evaluative pronouncement that will serve justice and stand the critical scrutiny of appellate review.

For the radio/television critic, this appellate review is ultimately conducted by listeners and viewers, each of whom determines how much or how little that critic's findings have furthered the attainment of satisfying programmatic outcomes.

The Perceptual Triad

Another approach to knowledge processing focuses not on methodologies or techniques for critical message comprehension but rather, on divining the level at which the receiver apprehends the message. The celebrated American composer Aaron Copland embraced this receiver-oriented procedure in his analysis of the three musical planes to which a listener might attend: "(1) the sensuous plane, (2) the expressive plane, (3) the sheerly musical plane."[9] If we broaden Copland's perspective to include visual and linguistic as well as tonal and rhythmical intake, this same schema also can be used to understand how broadcast/cable messages are absorbed.

The Sensuous Plane

The sensuous plane involves seeking out a stimulus for the pleasure of the sound or sight itself. The perceivers lose themselves in the phenomenon "without," as Copland says, "thinking, without considering it in any way. One turns on the radio while doing something else and absent-mindedly bathes in the sound. A kind of brainless but attractive state of mind in engendered."[10] Obviously, the goal associated with this plane is escape—to flee the boring or painful condition of reality and uncritically bask in the conscious fantasy or semiconscious reverie. When, for example, we refer to some radio formats as "background music" we are also citing their tendency for absorption as sensuous rather than expressive events. However popular such a format might be, it poses special problems for commercial copywriters who must break through the fog to secure fully conscious attention toward their product. "Foreground" formats such as "news/talk" or "country" (with the latter's storyline-dominant lyrics), may more fully engage listener heed but trigger attentive recess when the ads come on.

Certain television programs are also said to be "sensuous plane oriented," although that Coplandesque phrase is not specifically used. Music videos as a class are most prominently mentioned in this regard, but so too are the action/ adventure series in which chase-and-carnage sequences predominate or situation comedies in which visual slapstick supplants character insight.

This does not mean that all sensuous-oriented content is inevitably low brow or that content gravitating more to the other two planes is automatically high brow. The near hypnotic appeal of a Balanchine ballet on PBS is, although highly sensuous for dance lovers, certainly not crass. Likewise, the seemingly intellectual question format of a *Family Feud* or *Hollywood Squares* is hardly the stuff of which Rhodes Scholars are made. The quality of an electronic media product, in other words, is not measured by how much sensuous-plane stimuli are curtailed but by how well their use furthers and supports the work's goal and value transmission to the audience.

The Celentano television spot featured in Figure 4–2 demonstrates effective and candid exploitation of the sensuous plane. Sparse copy lets viewers supply their own verbal evaluations of the entrees being shown, and the tomato in frame 3 helps suggest the sensual essence of Italian cooking. Even the red rods in the background grid help submerge the perceiver in a crisp contemporary restyling of the traditional red-checked tablecloth so closely associated with viscerally stimulating Italian dining.

The Expressive Plane

Copland's second plane, the expressive, deals with the complex world of intellectual meaning—for him, "the meaning behind the notes." In terms of radio/television, it is the meaning behind the electronic patterns and productional manipulations that constitutes the focus of the expressive plane's attention. We are thus moving beyond the sensuous in an attempt to see if the work in question offers long-term insight instead of, or in addition to, short-term gratification. As aesthetics scholar Theodore Meyer Greene would put it:

> The less reflective the agent, the more will his evaluations be determined by the poignancy of each immediate experience; the more thoughtful he is, the more will he tend to evaluate his experiences and their objects in a wider frame of reference, i.e., in terms of their more ultimate import for himself and his fellow men. *Both* emotion and reflection are requisite to *adequate* evaluation.[11]

Since the mass audiences of the electronic media tend to be made up of people who lack the training for "more thoughtful" comprehension of radio/television (recall the "Why is Radio/Television Criticism Needed?" section of Chapter 1), the critic's role in helping delineate the expressive plane becomes crucial. Even though the least reflective consumers need no guidance to experience a sensual electronic stimulus, expressive plane comprehension requires more acuity than many people are prepared to bring to the sound box or picture tube.

It is the meaning of a program or series, then, rather than its surface sense-appealing factors, that usually demands more of a credible critic's attention. A hack reviewer, for instance, may be content merely to retell a situation comedy episode's key jokes. A conscientious critic, in contrast, would strive to ascertain the quips' thematic relevancy/irrelevancy, structural role, and dramatic or social impact. To examine this distinction in miniature, let us consider the following radio commercial as the subject for a hypothetical critique:

CELENTANO®

MUSIC (instrumental)
ANNCR VO: Have you ever
seen Italians like these before?

Celentano Italian Entrees.

Lasagne Primavera.

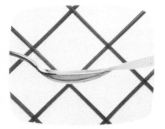

Chicken Primavera.

All natural

and delicious!

Celentano.

The New Italians.

Celentano, Inc., 225 Bloomfield Avenue, Verona, New Jersey 07044. (201) 239-8444.

Figure 4–2 Celentano "New Italians" Photoboard (Courtesy of Jane Adamo,
Margeotes Fertitta & Weiss, Inc.)

(MUSIC: <u>HARP EFFECT</u>)

ST. PETE: Name?

SLEAZ: Call me Ralph, Sweetheart.

ST. PETE: And what did you do on earth, Mr. Sweetheart?

SLEAZ: I sold cars. I can make you a good deal on a great—

ST. PETE: Uh, excuse me, may I borrow your sunglasses, Mr. Sweetheart? I can't look directly at your—sports jacket.

SLEAZ: Wanna buy it? I can make you a good deal on this—

ST. PETE: I'm afraid we can't open the pearly gates at this time, mister, uh—next?

MAN: Ah, that's me, sir.

ST. PETE: Earthly occupation?

MAN: I sold cars for O'Mara Pontiac-Toyota.

ST. PETE: For who?

MAN: O'Mara Pontiac-Toyota.

ST. PETE: Oooohh—Isn't that the place where everyone is so courteous and there's no pressure or hype?

MAN: Right, O'Mara Pontiac-Toyota is just a friendly, relaxed place.

ST. PETE: Oh, wait until the guys meet you!

MAN: You mean, it's O.K. to go in?

ST. PETE: Heaven's, yes. We don't see many like you. Just go right in. Pick out a cloud and a pair of wings, I'll get your halo size, and we'll—

SLEAZ: Hey, did I tell you I worked for them guys too?

ST. PETE: Are you sure?

SLEAZ: If I ain't tellin' the truth, may lightning stri—

(SFX: <u>LIGHTNING BOLT</u>)

SLEAZ: I'll just wait out here, O.K.?

ANNCR: Let the dealer that delivers—deliver yours today. O'Mara Pontiac Toyota. 1200 East 30th, Hutchinson.

(Courtesy of Fran Sax, FirstCom)

The cursory critic might talk about the clever portrayal of the knavish car salesman, chuckle at the man's loud jacket and abortive attempt to con even St. Peter, and regale his audience with commentary as to how one goes about getting fitted for a halo. This critic might then ask readers if they've run into a sleaz like the one the commercial depicts and even offer to print the best auto pusher story received from a reader. The entire review, then, simply mirrors the production's sensuous plane, which, in this case, is embodied in humor. The supposed critic merely offers the public more of the same instead of deepening an understanding of the broadcast/cable creation he was supposedly analyzing.

Conversely, a more conscientious reviewer seeking to widen the public's expressive perceptions might make the observation that even in commercials, it is now possible to create lighthearted commentary on things religious without having a public outcry about sacrilege. The critic could also choose to discuss the strategic reasons a car dealer would deliberately dramatize his industry's negative stereotype and what this may imply about contemporary consumer attitudes. Perhaps the economic reality of American auto dealers now co-affiliating with foreign manufacturers would also be explored, with special attention to O'Mara's promoting of personnel deportment rather than either one of his product lines. A socially conscious critic might even discuss why the offer of courtesy and friendliness seems so attractive in a cold and manipulative world. Whatever the specific orientation, critical attention to the expressive plane allows an audience to comprehend the more substantial ramifications implicit to some degree in even the most frivolous of media content.

The Productional/Technical Plane

Copland's third—and "sheerly musical"—plane is, in the case of radio/television, the total productional vantage point. As detailed in Chapter 5, this includes not just the recording and manipulation of sound, illumination, and substance, but also the skills and techniques that writers, actors, directors, and technicians bring to the program property. The most adroit of these manipulations will not even be noticed by the audience, but their absence or mishandling would be widely felt. It is said that broadcast/cable professionals, like professional musicians, can never fully enjoy one of their art's performances since their sensitivity to technique overshadows for them the expressiveness and stimulation that the work as a whole emotes. As Copland says of musicians, "They often fall into the error of becoming so engrossed with their arpeggios and staccatos that they forget the deeper aspects of the music."[12]

The Planes Combined

It thus is the critic's job to help both creators and their publics achieve a fuller comprehension of the work's totality. For consumers of the art, this may require more attention to the productional and expressive planes; and to service the artists themselves, greater emphasis may need to be placed on the expressive and sensuous planes—on taking a step back from the nuts and bolts in order to experience the total mechanism. All three planes, of course, exist simultaneously, and no one can ever equally experience all three at a given moment. The thoroughgoing critic, nonetheless, will try as much as possible to raise the perceptual levels of both amateur and professional so that a cognizance of all three planes can be consecutively if not concurrently mobilized. In this way, the utility of the critic's evaluation, and the evaluative capabilities of the critic's audience, are equally enhanced.

In this piece written by Tom Shales of *The Washington Post,* elements of all three planes are introduced and interwoven.

'YEAR': TRIED AND TRUE CHARMS
by Tom Shales

Many scenes in the three-part NBC mini-series "A Year in the Life" ring true—some even clang true—but perhaps the one that rings truest finds the fictional Gardner family of Seattle, gathered around the family television set in happy harmony. That's because all of them are asleep.

Here we have a true American ritual, though one not likely to be enacted in many homes watching "A Year in the Life"—not because the film is fresh and original, which it isn't, but because its frequent lunges for the old heart strings do result in copious, melodious plucking.

"Year," which follows life with and among the Gardners from one Christmas to the next, airs tonight, tomorrow and Wednesday at 9 each night on Channel 4.

Those who made "Year" knew what they were doing, in part because much of it has already been done. Scene after scene seems ragingly familiar because we know we've seen it in some other film. The achievement of the production is in bringing all these clichéd domestic scenarios together under the same figurative and literal roof and putting them over with captivating oomph.

You may feel, though, as if you're watching a "That's Entertainment" compilation of movie-family crises, or that you're having fits of *déjà vu.* For instance, one of the Gardner sons has grown up to be something of a n'er-do-well, but he once had dreams of playing pro baseball. So one night, alone, he silently runs the bases in an empty ballpark.

Hmmm. The question is not so much which movie that's from as how many movies it's from. Meanwhile, a chipper young lad is trying to lift his mourning grandpa's spirits by getting him out of his house on a bicycle, with hopes of entering him in a 25-mile bike race. Grandpa goes out a few times, but then widower's depression gets the better of him and he tells the grandson he doesn't have the stamina to continue.

This leads directly to dramatic confrontation No. 426-A. "So, that's it?" the tearful grandson says. "You're just quitting, just like that? You're not even going to try?"

So does Grandpa get back on his bike after that little talking-to? In a word, *oui.* And when a little later, the lovesick and moonstruck 23-year-old son tells the girl he's strenuously but unsuccessfully been wooing that he can't stand to be rebuffed by her anymore and so he's running away on a ferry to Vancouver, does she show up at the dock to stop him just before the ferry leaves?

Are you kidding? What do you think—that he gets on the ferry and it blows up when it hits an old Japanese mine still bobbing around from World War II? No, no, you could never write a television script for a mini-series like this!

However, it's important to remember that derivativeness is no curse in television and can be an asset. Even though producers Joshua Brand and John Falsey and writer Stu Krieger give the impression they hooked a word processor up to a computer that had seen lots and lots of sentimental Hollywood movies, all the trite or pat elements, plus a few relatively new ones, come together in salutary synthesis.

As hackneyed and homogenized as some of the Gardner family's tribulations and misadventures may be, they're rendered here in a highly flavorful way, and being terribly sophisticated about the manipulations going on may be no real defense against them. Sitting back and going along with it seem just the things to do.

The cast is largely responsible for putting the movie over, and, with the exception of the two leads, it is an admirable, hard-working troupe. The two leads are Richard Kiley, far too theatrical and dulcet as 64-year-old patriarch Joe Gardner (owner of a plastics factory), and Eva Marie Saint, wispy and vague as wife Ruth. She lasts only through the first third of the show, which is just as well. Comes one of those rainy Seattle nights, the dog has to be rushed to the vet and—oh, no!

Kiley and Saint are outdone handily by the younger actors, those playing Gardner offspring and their spouses. Wendy Phillips has a vital, simmering energy as Anne Gardner Maxwell, oldest of the daughters, who has married an out-and-out louse, Glen Maxwell, played by Scott Paulin. Paulin and Phillips are husband and wife in real life.

They share what is, for television, a fairly explicit sex scene in Part 2. Discovered huffing and puffing in bed, they lie back in exhaustion and he asks, "Like that?" She replies, "I love everything you do to me." Earlier they had discussed the fact that she became pregnant even though she'd been using a diaphragm. "Maybe once I forgot to put it in," she says.

Happier in marriage are Jayne Atkinson as daughter Lindley and the immensely likable Adam Arkin as a modestly ambitious Jewish inventor. Atkinson's earthy charm is an enormous asset to the film; she glows without trying. In Part 3, having had a child in Part 2, the two engage in a discussion of how breast-feeding a baby affects a mother's nipples, a word rarely heard in prime time. The film does have its blunt moments.

The mantle of star-crossed lover falls heavily on the shoulders of David Oliver as Sam Gardner, sexually inexperienced and sleeping with his fiancée (something that everyone in the family takes in stride). Then one day he meets this fabulous kooky girl, played by Sarah Jessica Parker (a bright star of the failed sitcom "Square Pegs") and something goes boing in his head. Oliver could become TV's new reigning WASP dreamboat. Parker has a warm sort of sparkle.

This group is what the producers feel to be typical of an American family in the 1980's. Interestingly, religion plays almost no role in their lives. They go to church for weddings and funerals and Christmas. Anne tells her husband she'll think seriously about converting to Judaism but that she "never really felt strongly about organized religion."

Does this tell us something about the typical American family or about typical Hollywood producers?

Here and there the drama is brightened by a flash of style. A dark night of the soul for young Sam, circa 4:18 A.M., becomes a montage set to the Percy Sledge classic "When a Man Loves a Woman," and does he ever. The n'er-do-well, played believably by Morgan Stevens, does his nocturnal base running to an infectious, uncredited piano piece.

The producers wanted to make a movie about a family whose problems were ordinary, a household not attacked by terminal illness or lethal substance abuse. They also felt a Capraesque urge to celebrate the joys and sorrows of everyday life. In "Year," someone dies, someone is born, someone marries, someone divorces. Nothing ever happens at Grand Hotel, maybe, but just enough goes on at the Gardner place.

Coproducer Falsey (who with Brand brought "St. Elsewhere" into existence) said from Hollywood last week that "A Year in the Life" is a candidate to become a series; then it would be like "Family" (ABC, 1976–80), he said, but more realistic and with a harder edge.

"What we hope to show is that you don't have to have Moldavia and oil barons to make something entertaining," Falsey said. That mission was accomplished, even if they did have to borrow from umpteen Hollywood movies that came before. Trite and tear-jerky though it may often be, "A Year in the Life" runs the bases wisely and well.

(© *The Washington Post*)

According to Shales, the sensuous plane of this mini-series is saturated with moist melodrama that "lunges for the old heart strings" with a grandson urging his grandfather to bike away from depression, a spurned lover being intercepted at the docks by the object of his affection, and with the poignant running of base paths that are beyond one's grasp. Together with some "blunt" (for television) sexual material, *A Year in the Life* is a program for which "being terribly sophisticated about the manipulations going on may be no real defense against them. Sitting back and going along with it seem just the thing to do." In other words, Shales feels that the sensuous plane should be allowed to predominate over the expressive one in the viewing of this particular show because, "Trite and tear-jerky though it may often be," it stimulates that entertaining sobbing "wisely and well."

From a purely expressive standpoint, Shales's reader learns that *A Year in the Life* is permeated with "clichéd domestic scenarios" that owe their origins to a "compilation of movie-family crises" in "lots and lots of sentimental Hollywood movies." However, cautions the critic, "it's important to remember that derivativeness is no curse in television and can be an asset." The search for the new and untried in network prime time may succeed in originality—and fail as television during those evening mass viewing hours when tonnage ratings are required. Sociologically, this mini-series asserts that "religion plays almost no role" in the life of the contemporary American family, but, argues Shales, this may tell us more "about typical Hollywood producers" than it does about the nation's typical families—a possible meaning that viewers need to consider.

In the case of the third plane (Copland's "sheerly musical" and radio/television's "productional" level), the critic focuses extensively on the element of on-camera performance because, in his view, "the cast is largely responsible for putting the movie over." This statement by itself strongly implies that other productional aspects (writing, directing, cinematography) are, as far as *A Year in the Life* is concerned, clearly subservient to the contributions made by the actors "with the exception of the two leads." Still, the audio-visual implementation of the program is occasionally "brightened by a flash of style," such as the musical/visual montage Shales takes pain to detail. Finally, in a behind-the-scenes bit of calculated industry comparison, the reader learns that this mini-series is striving to be a continuing series by resembling an earlier network property but "more realistic and with a harder edge."

Shales's critique embraces all three planes but blends them together in the overall evaluation that says, Here is a derivative melodrama which largely succeeds with its clichés because they further its premise of the honestly ordinary rather than the terminally bizarre. There are no "Moldavia and oil barons," only the "urge to celebrate the joys and sorrows of everyday life," an urge largely realized through the efforts of a talented cast.

Copland's three planes, Robert Smith's four ways of knowing, and the associated empirical and normative perspectives are systems that attempt to discern how knowledge about any object or experience is gathered and evaluated. Since radio/television critics must gather and evaluate not only for themselves, but also for their audiences, it is vital that they have some understanding of how perceptions are harvested. Critics who are cognizant of the divergent ways in which the broadcast/cable audience apprehends are in a much better position to communicate successfully their insights in that audience's terms. As media scholar Samuel Becker observes, "Sophistication in more than one approach to knowing can stimulate the development and persuasive testing of imaginative solutions to problems."[13]

Notes

1. Robert Lewis Shayon, *Open to Criticism* (Boston: Beacon Press, 1971), 33.
2. Theodore Meyer Greene, *The Arts and the Art of Criticism* (Princeton: Princeton University Press, 1952), 233.
3. Lee Loevinger, "The Ambiguous Mirror: The Reflective-Projective Theory of Broadcasting and Mass Communication," *Journal of Broadcasting* (Spring 1968): 113.
4. Ralph Smith, *A Study of the Professional Criticism of Broadcasting in the United States 1920–1955* (New York: Arno Press, 1978), viii.
5. Robert Rutherford Smith, *Beyond the Wasteland: The Criticism of Broadcasting*, rev. ed. (Annandale, Va.: Speech Communication Association, 1980), 3–4.
6. Russell Neuman, "Finding the Quality Time in TV Viewing," *Adweek Television 1984 Special Issue* (August 1984): 32.
7. Richard Young, Alton Becker, and Kenneth Pike, *Rhetoric: Discovery and Change* (New York: Harcourt, Brace & World, 1970), xii.
8. Robert Smith, *Beyond the Wasteland*, 4.
9. Aaron Copland, *What to Listen for in Music,* rev. ed. (New York: Mentor Books, 1957), 18.
10. Ibid.
11. Greene, *Art of Criticism*, 462–63.
12. Copland, *What to Listen For*, 21.
13. Samuel Becker, "Critical Studies: A Multidimensional Movement," *Feedback* (Fall 1985): 24.

5

Productional Ingredients

We concluded the previous chapter with a discussion of the last of Aaron Copland's three musically derived perceptual planes—the "sheerly musical" or, as we applied it to radio/television, "sheerly productional" vantage point. This encompasses what we refer to as the musical, on-stage skill, and stage-molding ingredients. Since these three productional elements and their arrangement are what most obviously distinguish electronic media creations from other communicative arts, it is important to examine such elements critically before proceeding. We begin by looking at music, which, for us, is an intermediate ingredient rather than an artistic end product.

The Musical Ingredient

One difficulty of critiquing the use of music as a programmatic tool is the same difficulty encountered by people who critique music itself. The problem is that music, as composer Richard Wagner observed, "begins where speech leaves off." Therefore, the use of mere words to evaluate tones seems a highly questionable enterprise. "To be sure," wrote aesthetics scholar DeWitt Parker, "music is a language which we all understand because it expresses the basic mold of all emotion and striving; yet it is a language which no two people understand in the same way, because each pours into that mold his own unique experience."[1] Roy Dickinson Welch adds, "Though the emotions suggested by a given composition may be apparent to most men, it is well-nigh impossible to describe them in words acceptable to all men."[2] If aesthetics experts find

73

themselves in this quandary, what is the electronic media reviewer to do?

Fortunately, radio/television critics need only realize that they are not in the business of critiquing music for itself but rather must evaluate music's contextual effectiveness within a certain broadcast/cable framework. Once we have ascertained this framework, we can try to determine whether some other musical treatment or even a completely nonmusical element would have been more effective in the programmatic case at hand.

We are not demeaning music's power by conceiving of it as only one of many content devices at our disposal. We are simply recognizing that radio/television is no more analogous to the art of music than it is to the literary, visual, or dramatic arts. Instead, the electronic media borrow from and amalgamate some or all of these arts in the process of creating programmatic and continuity product.

Clearly, music possesses certain properties and characteristics that give it a special communicative potential. Whether that potential has been achieved or wasted is a fair and appropriate determination for the broadcast/cable critic to make. Aesthetics scholar Theodore Meyer Greene points out that, in and of itself, "music is the most 'artificial' of the arts because its primary medium, i.e., the system of tones based on any given scale, as well as its generic forms, have meaning only in a musical context. That is, this meaning attaches to them only by association and convention."[3] Greene's observation is also valid in a much broader sense: music over the media usually acquires meaning not for itself, but for the associative role it plays in conjunction with other productional elements. Even a live broadcast concert is not the presentation only of music but is, instead, a remote performance event encased in a series of announcements and generally designed to showcase the star musicians involved, be they the Toronto Symphony or Twisted Sister.

Since media critics therefore are reprieved from the awesome task of attempting to critique music as music, they can concentrate on whether the musical choices made in a given programmatic context are optimal ones. Specifically, this task calls for scrutiny of four interdependent attributes: clarity, execution, continuity, and aptness of task.

Clarity

By clarity we are referring to the acoustic integrity of the music's electromechanical capturing and transmission. This is impacted by such technical considerations as the type of microphones, speakers, recorders, mixers, turntables, cartridge machines, and compact disc players that pick up, store, and reproduce the musical content. Clarity further involves such arcane conditions as transmitters, towers and antennas, and/or satellite uplinks, downlinks, and transponders. These pieces of equipment affect the quality of any radio/television message; they are especially important in carriage of the continuous tones and timbres of music where distortion and constriction are much more noticeable than in the conveyance of harmonically forgiving speech. The superior fidelity of FM over AM broadcasting figures prominently in this regard, as the flight of music-heavy formats to the FM band attests. Even though AM stereo may somewhat mitigate the trend, the older service is increasingly preoccupied with news, talk, and nostalgia music formats, on which the quality of the sound is itself nostalgic. (A discussion of nostalgia is included in Chapter 7.)

Critics concerned only with clarity probably would choose to write for consumer electronics or broadcast engineering trade publications. Thus, their orientation would be much like that of the hobbyist reviewers of the 1920s mentioned in Chapter 1. Today's more mainstream reviewers also are cognizant of clarity. However, the largely trouble-free world of solid state electronics together with broadcasters' recognition of the competitive importance of signal quality usually mean there is little distinction between stations, and thus little to comment on in this regard. When one music outlet in a market switches to a compact disc playback system or when a television station converts to stereo, most of its rivals will feel the marketing necessity to do the same—even if the difference in quality of reproduction is unnoticeable by most listeners.

Execution

Execution, the second element of broadcast/cable music criticism, is concerned with whether the performers and presenters involved seem to know what they are doing. Listeners and viewers do not need an extensive background in music theory to be sensitive to execution any more than they require classes in playwriting before understanding dramatic dialogue. The record spinners who know little about the genre they play and the cover versions of top group hits by those of lesser talent are defects that a critic may need to explain but seldom has to point out. Certainly, as David Altheide and Robert Snow affirm, "Talent and skill are judged differently by different listeners, but every music aficionado can recognize the presence or absence of those qualities. Radio stations occasionally try to 'hype' a performer of dubious talent, but this is rarely successful. Even established stars who sluff-off or 'lose it' are quickly dropped by a listening audience."[4]

At the other extreme is the radio/television execution that is too immaculate. In the case of musical recordings, veteran reviewer Samuel Singer points out that "The technical perfection achieved through careful tape editing [video as well as audio] may sometimes rob a performance of spontaneity and urgency."[5] The same can be said for the prepackaged syndicated music service which, through too much slickness, makes a local station seem mechanistic, bloodless, and remote. Everything is done so flawlessly that the receiver fails to sense the sort of human intimacy that distinguishes the truly communicative music outlet.

Music programming, therefore, must not sound robotically executed. Instead, it should take advantage of the fact that its evocative content, even more than the seeming intimacy of talk shows, can offer a degree of continuous personal preference ministration that is virtually impossible to find else-where on the media landscape.

This potential exists more in the musical than the verbal transmission be-cause, as DeWitt Parker once observed, "Words are means of communication as well as expression; they therefore embody of any experience only as much as can be passed from speaker to hearer; but in music the full personal reso-nance of experience is retained. In music we get so close to ourselves that at times it is almost frightening."[6] The perceptive critic thus will carefully monitor the music transmission's sense of personalized execution as a means of evalu-ating what we might call its spontaneous competence. That is, the execution should sound well-captured but not quick-frozen.

To illustrate how execution can be commented on within a multifaceted critique, let us examine the following article written by *The Washington Post's* Lon Tuck. Notice that because radio tends to be format-based rather than program-based like television, Tuck's review encompasses WGMS's schedule as a whole.

THE PRIME OF WGMS
by Lon Tuck

Would that all of us reach, or had reached, the daunting divide of 40 years with the un-expected poise and prosperity that WGMS, Washington's primary purveyor of the clas-sical music arts, will bring to it tomorrow.

The station's big DO will include a three-hour broadcast starting at 4 P.M. from the Kennedy Center Grand Foyer, at which such loyal listeners as Mstislav Rostropovich, André Watts and James McCracken are scheduled to give their blessings.

Lots of cultural institutions reach 40, but rarely like that.

Only 14 years ago, WGMS' owner, RKO General Inc., pretty much wrote it off as a profit-making enterprise, and decided to convert its AM outlet to rock n' roll.

The firestorm of protest that greeted and ultimately reversed that decision of 1972 resulted in several surprises.

One was the discovery that the audience cared so much. "Nobody anticipated that all hell would break loose," recalled vice president and general manager Michael Ferrel. There was an unprecedented outflow of editorializing from the papers (which were then more numerous than now), many letters to the editor, a drive in Congress and a peti-tion signed by 15,000 listeners.

A spokesman for WGMS maintains in a press release on this anniversary: "No other Washington station has ever received this much attention by the press and prob-ably would never under similar circumstances."

RKO General agreed to save WGMS–AM as a classical outlet in return for Federal Communications Commission suspension of a rule then in force forbidding exact simulcasts by a station on its AM and FM channels (570 and 103.5 respectively).

There were two other consequences of the 1972 flap almost as interesting as the station's survival.

One was that for the first time, WGMS started making a substantial amount of money, due in part to more aggressive marketing. "We have gone from almost nowhere," said Ferrel, "to being one of the most profitable classical stations in America. We are in line behind Los Angeles, but I think we are ahead of everybody else," includ-ing New York's much esteemed, and older, WQXR.

The estimated current WGMS audience hovers around a quarter of a million. Ferrel grants that that is not as big as WMAL–AM (630) or WKYS–FM (93.9), but it is awfully substantial for a classical music station—and growing (it rose more than 100 percent the year after the furor alone). Another thing that the station learned from the programming incident was that its audience felt more passionately about the station's individual way of doing things than was realized. One of WGMS' great strengths with its audience, it was disovered, was its deliberate cultivation of personality on the air—a characteristic rare among classical stations. Since then the program hosts have been encouraged to chat things up, at times approaching in their collective folksiness a gaggle of erudite Willard Scotts. The hosts even do their own programming, a concept unheard-of on most classical stations. Observes program director Paul Teare: "We have to allow that kind of independence to get the kind of people we want."

There are certain things WGMS listeners have come to count on.

The morning rush hour would hardly be the same without the mellifluous baritone of Dennis Owens, spiced as it is by his occasional crotchety commentary on the news and the morning papers. Of WGMS's full-time program hosts, Owens is the senior figure, a veteran of 20 years.

Tending the homebound drivers is Renee Chaney, with her breathy contralto and insinuating air, which she says were designed "to soothe people through the evening rush hour." As a student at American University, Chaney failed her first audition at WGMS. Now she's a Washington institution.

The weekend star is Judy Gruber, a fairly recent recruit from the Washington Opera, where she directed public relations. As a broadcast personality she comes across somewhat in the Chaney mold, with programming particularly strong in Italian opera.

However, the dean of opera on Washington radio remains former *Washington Post* music critic Paul Hume, who among other things presides over WGMS' Saturday opera programs on weeks when the Metropolitan Opera is not broadcasting.

One thing members of the WGMS team—that includes Bob Davis, Win Clearwater, John Chester and Eric Freud—seem to have in common is the injunction in Owens's words, "to go in the studio and be yourself." By contrast with most of the country's several hundred classical deejays, WGMS people, he adds "try to be communicators, not just announcers."

It's a different philosophy, said Teare, from that at such respected stations as Chicago's more formal WFMT.

As with many such stations WGMS carries live broadcasts (like the Met and the Sunday evening concerts at the National Gallery of Art) and syndicated features (like Karl Haas on weekday afternoons or that addictive Thursday evening showcase for new recordings called "First Hearing.")

The focus of the programming shifts with the hour. "At night we are after the true music lover," said Teare, "but during drive time we shift and address the person who may have taken Music 101, or just some piano lessons."

General manager Ferrel was asked what it is, in his opinion, that makes WGMS "different." He came up with an anecdote:

"I was driving a company car one day a couple of years ago in Georgetown. It had WGMS painted all over it—the most conspicuous thing in the city. I was waiting to turn left from a side street onto M Street. The light was green, and the traffic was coming toward me. Then it turned amber, and I made the turn."

"A motorcycle policeman came behind me and immediately turned on the siren, and I thought, 'Oh. Good Lord.' I rolled down the window, and he said, 'I'd like to get a signed photograph of Renee Chaney.'"

"I think that illustrates a lot of the listenership that is out there. i don't think we could be what we are if we were just dealing with academics."

And though the station's listeners are concentrated in the upper middle income brackets, with special strength in Northwest Washington, and Fairfax and Montgomery counties, Owens said, "we long ago overcame the reputation of being just a station for a Cadillac-driving, adult audience in Chevy Chase."

(© 1987 *The Washington Post*)

Clearly, Tuck's assessment of WGMS's execution is a very positive one. The station consistently adheres to "deliberate cultivation of personality on the air—a characteristic rare among classical stations." Its staff "try to be communicators, not just announcers," and these "hosts even do their own programming, a concept unheard of on most classical stations." Because of this independence, it is the WGMS program director's belief—and Tuck's separate evaluation—that the station is able to attract better people onto its payroll. It would certainly seem, therefore, that WGMS has attained that quality of spontaneous competence that we previously isolated.

Musical execution is also a concern in the video arena, of course, where it is most frequently interwoven with an analysis of the way camera shots and visual action were realized. Nowhere is this more apparent than in the production and knowledge processing of music videos, where, as Charles Turner reports, "pop musicians and their fans entered the 1980s with a *new perceptual agenda,* a joint readiness for watching instead of listening, for sharing the music in pictorial bits and bytes."[7] Thus, although questions of musical execution are as of as much importance to the critic of MTV as they are to the critic of WGMS, they tend to be subsumed in a preoccupation with the predominating watching elements of lighting, videographic technique, and the nonverbal expressiveness of the performer.

Continuity

The third element of radio/television music criticism is continuity, or how the individual musical elements are programmed to establish linkages with each other and, perhaps, with the time of day. Obviously, there are infinite numbers of ways to string music videos or audio selections together, but something more than random chance must determine what comes first, what comes last, and the order of elements in between. This something more is the execution skill of the video service's producer or the radio station's program director. An abrupt clash of musical keys, genres, or stylings may disorient the audience to the extent that their sensuous and even expressive plane pleasures are derailed. As a result, the casual perceiver's immersion in the sound or sound/picture and the serious/expert perceiver's interest in the meaning of the event are both, to some degree, inhibited.

Skillful continuity, conversely, will extend this immersion or this interest so that the consumer stays with the medium longer. The progression of this music will coalesce so well with the listener/viewer attention cycle that their ebb and flow are as one. "Life begins," remarked composer Roger Sessions, "with an up-beat, the first breath of the new born child corresponding to the preparatory anacrusis of a musical statement, and ends, like the most natural and satisfying rhythm, with a down-beat."[8] In the same way, a broadcast/cable program or format will attempt to arrange its musical sequence to match the life beats of its target public. This is most noticeable in radio, where, as Altheide and Snow discovered. "This rhythmic variation provides a sense of balance within the general tempos of a time segment. Developing this rhythmic balance has become such a sophisticated operation that many stations now employ computer technology to insure appropriate music scheduling."[9]

If we return to Tuck's review of WGMS, the station's and the critic's attention to continuity come through quite clearly. On WGMS, Tuck finds "the focus of the programming shifts with the hour." The "occasional crotchety commentary" that breaks up the music in morning drivetime (when the listeners themselves might be crotchety) gives way to the soothing nature of selections buffered by a "breathy contralto and insinuating air" as the evening drivetime winds down. Daytime listening, when hearers are partially preoccupied with commute and commerce, uses less imposing musical elements suitable for digestion even by musical novices who have experienced only "Music 101, or just some piano lessons." In the evening, by contrast, when people's schedules permit less fragmented listening, compositions to attract "the true music lover" are highlighted. Through such careful construction of continuity, the programmer can exploit the fact that, as Rose Goldsen, affirmed, "Music synchronizes groups. Each member of the group feels the same rhythms, the same beats, the same pulses, the same timings, and in this way the conditions for empathy and mutual awareness are created."[10]

Aptness of Task

Aptness of task is the fourth musical attribute that the broadcast/cable reviewer can critique. The question here is whether music has been asked to perform functions in keeping with its capabilities. Task-assigning to music certainly is not new; as Rudolf Arnheim discovered, no less a personage than Plato "recommended music for the education of heroes because it made human beings partake in the mathematical order and harmony of the cosmos, located beyond the reach of the senses; whereas the arts, and particularly painting, were to be treated with caution because they strengthened man's dependence on illusory images."[11] It thus seems that Plato would value radio's music more than that of the "illusory-image"-filled music video—but this is not our point here. Rather, the radio/television critic wants to ascertain whether music is equal to and appropriate for an electronic media production chore for which it has been designated. (Plato, in fact, saw music as capable of performing negative as well as positive labors, and so he would admit to his Republic only "rhythms appropriate to a life of courage and self-control"[12] while barring compositions that expressed "drunkenness, effeminancy, and inactivity."[13])

Aptness/inaptness of task is easily comprehended in the case of the television program soundtrack in which music can be called on either as a legitimate heightener of audience involvement or as a sleazy apologist for dull dialogue or ponderous plot. A good example of the legitimate use of music is found in Tom Shales's review of *A Year in the Life,* presented in Chapter 4:

> Here and there the drama is brightened by a flash of style. A dark night of the soul for young Sam, circa 4:18 A.M., becomes a montage set to the Percy Sledge classic "When a Man Loves a Woman," and does he ever. The n'er-do-well, played believably by Morgan Stevens, does his base running to an infectious, uncredited piano piece.

An intimation of music's use as an extraneous bilker of audience emotions, on the other hand, is contained in Robert MacKenzie's *TV Guide* review of *Highway to Heaven,* where he begins his critique by observing that "this weekly NBC hour—about an angel on earth—is providing a lot of work for violinists" and concludes by reiterating, "If it makes viewers feel better about life instead of worse, and puts all those string musicians back to work, I suppose it must be OK."[14]

Commercials also are heavy users of music and, as in the case of the program they sponsor, evidence both its proper and improper recruitment. In general, when music is called on to enhance a strong, clear creative concept by mirroring the personality of the product or the imagined product use environment, the critic would say its task is apt. When, however, the music is expected to cover for imprecise dialogue or substitute for a clear selling benefit, one is expecting too much explicitness from an inherently implicit instrument. Music, as Theodore Meyer Greene avows, "does not lend itself readily to the representation of perceptual objects, scenes or events."[15]

The radio commercial that follows makes no such inapt demands of its music. Sung to the Dixieland standard "Sweet Georgia Brown," this Canadian spot positions its product, Newcastle Brown Ale, as the real English pub beer to reflect the growing trend toward pubs in the Toronto area. The fun-loving, North American derivative tune deftly bridges the gap between the English and Canadian environments to capitalize on the product's heritage without making it seem stodgy.

CHARACTER #1:   Gimme an 'A', mates!

ALL: "A"

CHARACTER #1:   Shove off!

HE SINGS: When me mates go out at night it's
                       Newscastle Brown.
                       When the bloke says 'Last call, Mike' it's

Newcastle Brown.
When me bird says 'that's all right'
By romantic candle-light
That's the time to hold on tight to
Newscastle Brown!

HE SPEAKS: Whether you're out with your mates or out on a
date, consider partakin' of the high-class taste of
Newcastle Brown. It is just a little bitter—just a
little sweet. The taste is rich and quite satisfying.
It's the biggest selling bottled ale in Britain.

HE SINGS: Wif me steak and kidney pie
Specially when 'er mum drops by
On me yacht wif Princess Di it's
Newcastle Brown!
Newcastle Brown!

HE SPEAKS: Also available in liquor stores and on draught in
friendly pubs.

CHARACTER #2:   —and I hope we passed the audition.

(Courtesy of Barry Base, Base Brown & Partners Limited)

The musical task was apt here because the tune's character and style were relevant underpinnings to the copy and marketing approach. On the other hand,
imagine for a moment what would happen if this song were added to the
Michelob Classic Dark radio spot printed in Chapter 4. Not only would the music intrude on the comic presence of Martin Mull, but it would also clash badly
with his psuedohipness approach to fear and the accompanying dare to try
something different.

For a final illustration of musical aptness of task, let us return to critic Lon
Tuck's WGMS piece. To a business enterprise, making money is a top priority,
and Tuck's analysis shows that even a classical format can be appropriately
enlisted toward this goal if accompanied by "more aggressive marketing." In
fact, we learn that WGMS "is one of the most profitable classical stations in
America." The station's programming to specific dayparts, which was commented on in conjunction with continuity, can also be considered an "aptness
of task" element with its use of heavier material on the evenings and weekends
and less challenging listening during the day. People are thus given a fuller
diet at those times when they have the opportunity to listen more intently while
served lighter, more staple fare to accompany the hassles of the workday and
a Washington, D.C., commute. That this musical strategy has been appropriate to audience maintenance and audience growth is evidenced by the fact
that WGMS is now patronized by traffic cops as well as academics and, as

Tuck's critique concludes, is no longer "just a station for a Cadillac-driving, adult audience in Chevy Chase."

A Musical Summary

Clarity, execution, continuity, and aptness of task constitute a criteria quartet by which even the nonmusically trained critic can comprehend, consider, and evaluate radio/television's musical ingredient on behalf of both the musicians and nonmusicians in that critic's audience. It is important that the broadcast/ cable reviewer not shy away from mention, and where appropriate, real analysis of the subject. Music's positive or negative contribution to electronic media content is substantial because, even though its powerful impact is universal, it is also highly personal. As scholar DeWitt Parker recognized, "We fill in the impersonal form of musical feeling with the concrete emotions of our own lives; it is our strivings, our hopes and fears which music expresses. . . . As we listen to the music, we shall see the things we hope for or fear or desire; or else transport ourselves among purely fanciful objects and events."[16] In fulfilling their mandate, broadcast/cable critics need to be aware of the latent power of this musical ingredient and to help their public be aware of it also.

The On-Stage Skill Ingredient

Depending on the programming context, music's presence can be either overt or subtle. What we call the *on-stage skill ingredient,* however, is always front and center in the consumer's perception. This phrase, of course, signifies the announcers, disc jockeys, reporters, hosts, and actors and actresses who, via tube or speaker, establish what they hope will be perceived as direct audience contact. How they do their jobs is an obvious if not overemphasized subject of critical attention. Our aim here, consequently, is to highlight what should be the key components of any critic's estimation.

Radio People

Looking at the format-preeminent world of radio first, it becomes clear that program hosts (disc jockeys and talk show mentors, for example) must accomplish two main objectives: (1) they must establish a sense of personal communication, even personal intimacy with the listener; and (2) they must maximally exploit and blend in with all the elements of the format in which they work. Some hosts, for example, know a great deal about their subject, be it jazz, mental hygiene, or pork bellies, but are unable to engender a sense of conversation between themselves and the listeners. Other hosts possess a keen ability to stimulate listener dialogue but are so ignorant of the mechanics or subject matter of their format that their communicative powers seem just vacuous veneer. This is why format changes at a station usually also involve wholesale on-air personnel changes.

For better or worse, in the packaged totality of today's radio service, the communicator and the format substance must be not merely compatible but perfectly synchronized. Nationally prominent radio consultant Tim Moore sees this personality dimension as vital to the successful positioning of a station in its market; he condenses it into two functional qualities: the correct amount of talk required to lubricate the format and the sense of control the on-air host seems to bring to and through the microphone.[17] In reviewing critiques previously printed in this book, we find several instances in which critics have taken note of this phenomenon. Alan Bunce's coverage in Chapter 2 of *Performance Today* host Kathryn Loomans, for instance, includes the following comments:

> On the air, Loomans strikes a tone that is just right for a music-listener who wants a host who has individuality without being assertive.
> Loomans' clear voice and intelligent readings should wear very well in the months ahead. She is not a media "personality" but a communicator whose approach seems to say she's there to give arts lovers chance to get their fill in a catchy but not obtrusive way.

Bunce amplifies this content/communicator consonance with a relevant quote from Loomans herself: "I take great care to go over the material, to do some rewriting, to make it my own."

That a keenly communicative host can grow into a format shift was demonstrated in Jim McFarlin's personality profile of Bob Allison in Chapter 3. Allison moved from "hip performer" to household hints facilitator by management fiat, but he was astute enough to see that partially molding the format to his own style and refocusing his own style to the format would be mutually beneficial. As the critic let his subject describe it:

> "They didn't want me to talk. They wanted the listeners to call in and do all the talking. . . . I wouldn't do that. I got into conversations with these people. . . . They would call me into the office once a week and read me the riot act about how I wouldn't shut up and never cut people off. I know they were ready to fire me. But when the first ratings book came out, we were the No. 1 afternoon show in the market."

On the other hand, McFarlin's article also demonstrates that, having made *Ask Your Neighbor* inextricable from his own personality, Allison *and* his show were forced to migrate from station to station as format changes rendered his property incompatible with the rest of the station landscape. As a final example of a critic's grasp of the radio personality/format dimension, reread the WGMS piece by Lon Tuck earlier in this chapter for another cogent dissection of this vital radio dynamic.

Even though he was referring to artists in general, aesthetician DeWitt Parker may have articulated the most incisive description of the aural on-stage ingredient when he wrote: "The artist must be able to create, in the external world, something to charm the senses as well as to speak the mind. . . . His work remains a show, a make-believe, to the end; or rather it makes of reality itself a show."[18]

Electronic Newspersons

Even in radio/television journalism, one finds more criteria similarities than differences between news talent and successful radio hosts. Because broadcast/cable journalism is subsumed within an entertainment-based format, news presenters are generally thought to need pleasing visual and/or aural appearance in order to make inherently unpleasant events palatable for the public. While he was speaking only of male network personnel, Dan Menaker's 1972 observation today applies equally to both sexes of local practitioners:

> Most of the players in the three troupes are physically attractive and aurally elegant. An obese, ugly, or squeaky-voiced newsman, though he might be professionally qualified, could not meet the non-journalistic requirements of a network correspondent's job. The competition for ratings, one assumes, must lead the three organizations to seek reporters with stage appeal.[19]

In addition, like the format-congruous radio host, these reporters must be skillful and even entertaining packagers of the stories in which they wrap themselves. This is not to say that the broadcast/cable reporter should be a newsmaker, but instead, suggests that listeners or viewers should believe the reporter to be a proximate, knowledgeable, on-scene observer. As media scholars Dennis Davis and Stanley Baran put it:

> Local television newspeople claim to be "eyewitnesses" and implicitly assure us that getting news from them is like "hearing it from a friend." The informal or happy news format assures us that newscasters are friendly people, that the news genre simulates everyday communication. This local news genre is especially attractive to those viewers who want to frame the news as they would frame gossip. It assures them that they are getting the news straight from trustworthy friends, not from professional newspeople working for a remote media bureaucracy.[20]

This sense of involved immediacy is vital for broadcast/cable news because it helps to distinguish it from and, in some people's minds makes it *superior to,* the world of print. Radio learned the commercial advantage of this distinction in the thirties, and it is an advantage that on-stage news presenters are rigorously trained to exploit. The benefit attendant on this immediacy is recognized even by scholars outside the communications discipline. Thus, more than forty years ago, aesthetics authority Theodore Meyer Greene fathomed the fact that

> in a written description of a contemporary event some time must necessarily elapse between the actual occurrence of the event described and its verbal portrayal, and an additional period of time must elapse between the writing of the text and its perusal by the reader. From the reader's point of view, the historical

present, as portrayed, has already been pushed back twice over into the historical past, whereas the radio announcer can not only describe what is occurring in his own present, but is able to convey to the listener a vivid sense of actual participation in events which are just as contemporaneous to him.[21]

Other Television Personalities

We cannot conclude our scrutiny of the on-stage skill ingredient, of course, without some examination of the evolved and crucial qualities of game show hosts and television actors. The former can be discussed relatively briefly—not because there is a shortage of such positions but because the characteristics by which they are critiqued are so similar to those of the radio talent and broadcast/cable news personnel previously discussed. Thus, these contest mentors also must establish a strong sense of personal communication. In their case, however, this communication must be attained not only with the at-home perceiver, but with on-stage contestants and a studio audience as well. Game show hosts must also insinuate themselves into the program's fabric and pacing so that contest and coordinator accelerate in tandem toward whatever installment climax the game's format entails. These personally and tele-genically winsome M.C.s therefore control the pacing of the game by regulating contestant responses. Above all, they strive to bring the same sense of immediacy to their televised tournament as anchors and reporters inject in their newscasts—and for the same audience-involving reasons. In his review of the immensely popular *Wheel of Fortune, TV Guide's* Don Merrill isolated what he believed to be the perfect attributes for a game show ringmaster when he reported:

> The host is Pat Sajak, a former television weatherman and public-affairs show moderator. A smooth operator, he is pleasant enough, asks the contestants where they're from and what they do without getting in the way of the game. . . . As game-show hosts go, he's as good as they come and well worth the half million a year he is paid.[22]

Some television actors, of course, can command a good deal more in salary than a game show host like Sajak, who, in addition, may sometimes be required to tape up to five shows in a single day. But while the salaries and working conditions may vary, visual impact remains of the utmost importance to actors, contest conductors, and video news personnel alike. For actors, this impact need not be pleasant or comely as long as it is emotionally and physically believable in terms of the role to be played. The intimate nature of the television camera and picture tube will magnify any awkward contrivance and expose any slippage of characterization. Under such a microscope, wrote Russian filmmaker V. I. Pudovkin, performers would do well "to exercise the finest shading of voice and gesture."[23]

As a film creator, Pudovkin's comments have a great deal of relevance to the television arena, but for the actor, there are also some differences between the two media. Actor-director John Houseman, who has worked in both, discovered that:

> Television puts more emphasis on the spoken word; it lessens the importance and effectiveness of the reaction shot, which is the most basic element of most film performances; it encourages a more naturalistic mode of acting; its emotional curves tend to be shorter, intended for a more direct and immediate effect on the viewer.[24]

To involve viewers in the doings on the small screen, and to involve them in spite of the inherent distractions of their domiciles and the comparative brevity of most television programs, presents a tremendous focusing challenge for actors. For, as media scholar Horace Newcomb observed, "Even when landscape and chase become part of the plot, our attention is drawn to the intensely individual problems encountered, and the central issue becomes the relationships among individuals."[25]

Under such conditions, performer believability becomes a function of not just physical appearance but also of concentration and controlled nonverbal embellishment. Concentration is an inherent part of any actor's trade that must be especially tightened in television. Director George Schaefer, for example, knows that theatrical actors communicate beyond the footlights to get unanimity of reaction on the part of their audience. In creating television, however, Schaefer finds he must convince his actors to ignore what's out there in the darkness if they are to sculpt their performances properly.[26] Even in the case of live-studio-audience situation comedies, performers cannot play *to* that audience but can only use it as a partial guide in deriving the timing of their delivery for the camera. Add to this the breakneck production schedule of television as opposed to film or stage work and it becomes clear how rigorously distilled the process of video acting must be. "You don't have time to do your scenes," states veteran series actor (*Dynasty, The Colbys*) Ken Howard. "You have to be ready in two takes. That can be an incredible burden. I think many good feature-film actors would be crushed on TV."[27]

Controlled nonverbal embellishment, the third component of television acting's believability, is, in a sense, the creation as well as the requisite of video performance. "Until the advent of modern visual and aural recording techniques," posits John Cawelti, "these [nonverbal] aspects of performance were largely ephemeral. . . . Now, however, performances can be recorded, filmed or taped. Thus, modern communications technology has given the nonverbal aspects of performance an even greater importance."[28]

Though much more esoteric, the principles of modern Gestalt psychology also help undergird this attention to the nonverbal. The Gestalt hypothesis, writes Rudolf Arnheim, "means that if the forces that determine bodily behavior are structurally similar to those that characterize the corresponding mental states, it may become understandable why psychical meaning can be read off directly from a person's appearance and conduct."[29] Whether or not this

Gestalt view is recognized by or reflective of television audience behavior, it is certainly true that the time-constricted productions on the small screen require that even the most intimate action be marshalled in the quick registration of character.

To sum up the subject of actor believability, notice how this function is comprehended, judged, and valued in these excerpts from Don Merrill's review of the show *227:*

> The star and sparkplug is Marla Gibbs, an accomplished singer and comedienne who can do more with her eyes than most actresses can do with their entire bodies. . . .
>
> Jackee Harry plays Sandra broadly, sexily and brilliantly. She walks funny, talks funny, makes funny noises and is a complete delight. . . .
>
> Sandra is big on innuendo, and while what she says is merely blue, some of her glances and stares are worthy of an "R" rating.[30]

Even though, by its nature, a situation comedy like *227* can be delivered more expansively than a drama, Merrill's comments indicate that in the case of sit-coms too, nonverbal reactions that fill the screen would scarcely be noticed in the theatre.

The Stage-Molding Ingredient

The performances of radio/television talent, of course, are only apprehended by the audience after they have been filtered through microphone and camera. These stage-molding elements, and the people who manipulate them, constitute the technological definers of the broadcast/cable use experience.

The enforced intimacies of the television camera were introduced in the previous section as a central determiner of performer style. In their study of television drama, Alan Wurtzel and Joseph Dominick found that:

> The broad, expansive style of acting associated with the stage suffers when shown with close-ups. Conversely, with medium shots giving more of a theatrical perspective, stage-acting seems to be given a favorable evaluation. Television acting is rated less positively when deprived of the intimacy provided by close-ups.[31]

In other words, acting style can become more spacious as the shot widens, but TV viewers are not conditioned to appreciate a preponderance of such panoramic views as framed by the uncompromising edge of their picture tubes. "There is a world of difference," maintains John Houseman, "between the collective reaction of an audience assembled in a darkened auditorium, staring up at a huge screen under hypnotic concentration and the reactions of a fragmented and scattered audience following on a small screen an action that must compete with all kinds of domestic and social concerns."[32]

Scores of books and articles have been written about the so-called productional rhetoric of this small screen with little if any unanimity as to the unequivocal meaning for the viewer of any of this screen's visual devices. Our concern here, then, can only be to inventory such tools in order to anticipate their inclusion or detect their omission in a given critic's pronouncements.

Light and Shadow

Light and shadow are perhaps the most primary of television's implements since without light, we could have no picture. At its most fundamental, then, one could consider light to be a purely technical requirement for proper camera operation. Herbert Zettl refers to this property of lighting as Notan, or "lighting for simple visibility. Flat lighting has no particular aesthetic function; its basic function is that of illumination. Flat lighting is emotionally flat, too."[33] Obviously, then, the use of this approach will make lighting play only a passive and objective role in a production, with the other on-stage and stage-molding elements assuming the preponderant burden for establishing meaning and mood. Notan lighting reinforces the two-dimensionality of the television screen, and scene sculpting and emphasis become the tasks of character and camera shot selection alone.

Chiaroscuro lighting, on the other hand, is concerned not only with illumination but also with the way it can determine and contrast with shadow. Using this approach, says Zettl, "The basic aim is to articulate space . . . to clarify and intensify the three-dimensional property of things and the space that surrounds them, to give the scene an expressive quality."[34] Chiaroscuro lighting thus becomes an important instrument for pictorial composition and mood enhancement. As aesthetics scholar DeWitt Parker observed:

> We know that light has a direct quickening and darkness a direct quieting effect upon mental processes; that in the light men feel relatively secure and at home, while in the dark they are uneasy and afraid; and we know that these feelings vary with the intensity of light or darkness and the time of day.[35]

We can easily illustrate the importance of lighting and shadow by examining a television commercial that promotes illumination. Note how the shadows in Figure 5–1 seem virtually to swallow up the actors. They are totally consumed by frame 7 until the illuminative dominance of the Philips light bulb takes over the foreground in frames 8 and 9 to bring a more positive end to our—if not their—experience. Were the commercial's first six frames fully illuminated (Notan-lit), the psuedosinister build-up to the product solution could not have been accomplished.

As the theme is similarly lighting-centered, you may also wish to turn back to the Michelob Classic Dark commercial in the previous chapter (Figure 4–1). Note especially frame 5, in which shadow dominates and subtly contradicts what the character is saying.

NORTH AMERICAN
PHILIPS LIGHTING

CABIN :30

(SFX: GROWLING/RUSTLING NOISES)

1st MAN: What was that?

2nd MAN: The Boogie Man...from the Black Lagoon!

1st MAN: There's something out there.

2nd MAN: Don't worry. As long as the lights are on, we're fine.

(SFX: LIGHT BULB BLOWS)

1st MAN: What do we do now?
(SFX: GROWLING NOISE)
2nd MAN: Run for your life!

ANNCR (VO): It's time to change your light bulb.

Philips Longer Life square bulbs last 33% longer than ordinary round bulbs.

Figure 5–1 Philips Lighting "Cabin" Photoboard (Courtesy of Arthur Bijur, DFS– Dorland)

We cannot leave the subject of lighting without mentioning the more abstract subject of the TV screen itself as source of illumination. Video artist Frank Gillette has pointed out that with television, "you look *into* the source of light, with film you look *with* the source of light. In television, the source of light and the source of information are one."[36] Because of this, infers Peter Crown, sitting in front of a TV set is like sitting in front of a fireplace and "television's hypnotic effect can create a strange rapport between viewer and screen that is totally unrelated to program content."[37] Certainly, the average reviewer will find little reason to explore this speculative illumination property, but those writing deep commentary on the nature of the medium may find its ramifications occasionally relevant.

Horizontal and Vertical Camera Planes

Our second stage-molding ingredient consists of the horizontal and vertical camera planes. Essentially, the horizontal camera plane is the type of shot used, from the screen-filling intimacy of the extreme close-up (ECU) to the panoramic cover shot (CS) or full shot (FS) that surveys the entire scene. In between, as illustrated on the continuum in Figure 5–2, are several other gradations. Long shots (LS) or wide shots (WS) may, in shooting interior scenes, be interchangeably referred to as full shots. At the minimum, they would show a character from head to toe. Medium shots (MS) can vary widely depending on the scope of the scene, but they are generally thought of as framing only the upper two-thirds of a standing character with minimal additional revelation of the set behind. When two or three characters are featured, a medium two-shot (M2S) or medium three-shot (M3S) can be specified. For more definitive designation, the terms *medium long shot* (MLS) and *medium close-up* (MCU) also refer to each end of the medium shot spectrum. Finally, in the close-up, the specific character or prop fills most of the screen so that, for example, only the head and shoulders of a person would be seen while the aforementioned ECU could devote its entire attention to a nose, mouth, or hand.

To illustrate these horizontal camera plane variations further, we can again refer to the Philips photoboard in Figure 5–1. In this commercial treatment, frame 1 is a cover/full shot, frames 2, 3, 5, and 6 are medium two-shots, and frames 4, 8, and 9 are close-ups. (Frame 7 is whatever you conceive it to be, thereby adding to viewer involvement in story-building.)

As Wurtzel and Dominick tell us, this battery of shot types ensures that "The viewer, as represented by the camera, does not remain in one viewing

Figure 5–2 TV Shot Continuum

position. He sees the action from both close-range and at a distance, depending on the director."[38] The director's main concern in this regard, maintains Robert Williams, is

> how to maximize attention and minimize interference. . . . He is the person who selects the type of shot to which the viewer will be exposed. He may select a close-up which may or may not direct attention. Another possibility is that he may select a loose-shot which may expose extraneous objects or materials to the viewers. This may prove to be a distraction which would serve as interference since the audience would then be required to select and evaluate the entire body of information presented to it.[39]

What we are allowed to see as viewers and what we are prohibited from seeing are crucial determiners of the involvement we feel with the developing televised narrative. As in the apprehension of any art form, it is not important that we always see the entire scene for, as art scholar Stephen Pepper understood, "Literally one can never see the whole picture in all its detail in focus at one time. But one can feel the whole picture in all its detail in a funded consciousness with certain details in clear focus and the rest fused into these as memories of their character and interrelationships."[40] By encouraging this active and immediate memory-building, a skilled director facilitates more in-depth viewer participation. In the words of leading television analyst Gilbert Seldes, "It is the *mind,* not the eye, that creates long shots and medium shots and closeups; and the well-handled camera satisfies us by being true to our thoughts and, when it acts for the heart, to our desires."[41]

Working especially with the horizontal camera plane's tighter shots (from medium shot to close-up), the vertical camera plane gives the viewer the feeling of looking up at, or down on, a character or object. Most, but not all authorities see these angles as thereby conferring implications of dominance or submissiveness on the pictorially featured subjects. The technique was pioneered in film and is explained by film expert Donald Livingston in this manner:

> The angle of a shot has a marked influence on the audience's psychological reaction to the subject matter photographed. As demonstrated in *The Fallen Idol,* angles shooting upward cause the subject matter to appear stronger, more powerful than the audience. Angles shooting downward give the audience a feeling of strength and make the subject appear weaker.[42]

This assertion has never been unequivocally proven by communications researchers and is certainly subject to qualifications. McCain, Chilberg, and Wakshlag, for example, found that, "High and low angle shots have different effects depending on how they are employed in the context of a sequence of shots."[43] These same researchers further discovered that, if the viewer does infer dominance from camera angle, a negative implication may result:

> A camera shooting upward toward a televised or film performer may increase the perceived power that he or she has over individual audience members. Camera angles which present figures to receivers as bigger than life and wielding some sort of dominance over them are not the types of people with whom audiences can easily relate.[44]

In other words, assuming upward angles do confer dominance, viewers may be turned off to the characters so shown. This may be an appropriate reaction in the portrayal of fictional villains, but it is hardly the attitude a station would chance to be directed at its newscasters, so low-angle views of them are studiously avoided.

Camera/Character Arrangement

Camera/ character arrangement, the third stage-molding ingredient, deals with the physical relationship of the camera to the performer's field of focus. Does the lens convey a primarily head-on view of the character or does it look in modified profile or even behind? Some action/drama programs like to place the viewer within the psychological fabric of events by showing characters and their encounters from a variety of vantagepoints (including the direct frontal addressing of the camera/viewer); many situation comedies, however, provide an essentially detached view. This view reassures consumers that they can eavesdrop on, rather than stumble into, the comic episode and its often participant-disparaging interactions. The audience wishes to laugh at the condition—not seem to be the cause/recipient of it.

Painters, in their creation of what is essentially a single-shot experience, have long created in accordance with this general point-of-view principle. To cite Gilbert Seldes again:

> The ways in which the Last Supper has been treated pictorially is a prime example. The earliest representations show the disciples facing us, and the stress is on the sacrament, not the prediction of treachery. In Leonardo the dramatic interaction of all the disciples is conveyed by the direction in which they are looking—at one another or at Jesus, not at us. The lesson is clear: when we want to hypnotize the audience (to sell them something), the direct gaze into the camera is correct; for drama, people face one another, not us.[45]

For the critic, then, the crux of the matter is whether the director's choices have led the viewer to what Pepper has called "the point of optimum receptivity":

> Where is the best point to see a picture, or to listen to a piano? One has to move around in the consummatory area and find out. Nevertheless, that point is settled by the very structure of the field. It is a dispositional property of the situation. For the organism moving about in the field it is the ideal and norm of correctness of all his actions in the field. It is the place where he ought to be.[46]

Camera in Motion

Because television viewers cannot actually "move around" in the picture-tube field, our fourth stage-molding ingredient, the camera-in-motion, must accomplish this effect on the viewers' behalf. In horizontal plane shot variations, the audience's basic perspective does not change because the camera remains stationary while the optics of its lens are manipulated. Items consequently become larger or smaller, but the angle of view on them does not shift.

With the camera-in-motion, however, the spatial relationship among objects in the frame is actually modified to give viewers the impression that they are entering the picture. Therefore, as Philip Kipper found in a recent study, "the moving camera provides viewers with more information about the physical form of objects and about the three-dimensional layout of a television scene. . . . The viewer comes along for the ride, so to speak, entering the physical world on the screen, but also, perhaps penetrating the emotional or dramatic reality as well."[47] It should not be surprising, then, that the camera-in-motion is a hallmark of such gritty MTM dramas as *Hill Street Blues* and *St. Elsewhere.* Writing of the latter, *TV Guide's* Robert MacKenzie captured the essence of the technique with this observation:

> This time those dollying cameras are weaving through the clattering corridors of an old hospital instead of the noisy confines of an old police station. But *Hill Street* fans will recognize the style: the moving camera that catches snatches of interrupted dialogue . . . to resemble the jumbled rhythms of real life.[48]

Reaction Shots and Reverse Angles

Real-life rhythms can also be enhanced by using reaction shots and reverse angles—devices we are grouping together here as the fifth stage-molding ingredient. Reaction shots focus on the nonverbal commentary displayed by one character in response to the words and/or actions of another character or event that is momentarily off-screen. Thus, they allow the viewer to detect a character attitude that the writer may not wish revealed to the other people in the scene. When carefully planned, reaction shots can become just as much a part of the narrative as is dialogue and may, in fact, be more revealing of motivation and frame of mind.

Reverse angles allow viewers to look with instead of just at a character and so bring the camera directly into the action's proscenium (active stage area). The audience might, for example, see a character deliver a line and then, through use of a reverse angle, watch through that same character's eyes as the line makes its impact. In this case, the reverse angle constitutes a type of reaction shot, but it can also be used while the person whose view it adopts is still speaking or in motion. Often used as a POV shot (point-of-view), the reverse angle seems virtually to implant the audience within a depicted character's mind's eye and, when the shot is deliberately defocused or wobbly, can even convey the feeling of physical or mental infirmity.

Shot Transition and Duration

How one is propelled from one shot to the next and the time spent in each shot are the sixth ingredients of stage-molding. Shot transition and duration, more than any other factor complex, determine the pacing of a visually experienced sequence. The cut, or instantaneous take from one picture to another, is the simplest and quickest transition. A series of quick cuts can make for a rapid-fire progression, which, if properly motivated, compels each viewer to assemble the individual shots into meaning. Dissolves, in which one picture gradually replaces the other are, by contrast, softer and more fluid. If very slow, they can suggest passage of time or even engagement of remembrance. Fades are nothing more than dissolves into or out of the limbo of blackness.

Some theorists argue that television, to encourage continuous viewing within the distractions or languor of the household environment, usually embraces the dissolve at the expense of the more dynamic intercutting that film pioneered. As artist/critic David Antin sees it, television's

> endless, silken adjustments, encouraged and sometimes specifically called for by the director and usually built into the cameraman's training, tend to blur the edges of what the film director would normally consider a shot. To this we can add the widespread use of fade-ins and fade-outs and dissolves to effect temporal and spatial transitions, and the director's regular habit of cutting on movement to cushion the switch from one camera to another. This whole arsenal of techniques has a single function—to soften all shocks of transition. Naturally the different apparent functions of various genres of program or commercial will alter the degree of softening, so a news program will maintain a sense of urgency through its use of cuts, soft though they may be, while the soap opera constantly melts together its various close shots with liquid adjustment and blends scene to scene in recurrent dissolves and fades.[49]

The way in which shots are strung together thus is important in shaping audience comprehension, even though some print-bound critics fail to recognize, or at least fail to comment on, this aspect of a television work. In counteracting such neglect, television expert Michael Arlen argues that "The real power is the power of men and women who control the montage effects, the technologists who instinctively understand the truth of [film pioneer Sergei] Eisenstein's statement: 'The basic fact was true, and remains true to this day, that the juxtaposition of two separate shots by splicing them together resembles not so much a simple sum of one shot plus another shot as it does a creation.'"[50]

Duration, shot transition's counterpart, is what extends this creation in time. How long a given shot should be held has been a question that has divided television theorists as well as practitioners almost from the time of the medium's birth. The two fundamental schools of thought on the topic were well sketched by Robert Williams more than twenty years ago, when he recounted that "One group seems to feel that camera position should not be changed unless there is a reason for it and this reason is usually apart from that of changing it for the sake of variety and interest. The other group, larger in number, feels that if a shot is held too long, attention will be lost."[51]

Certainly, character blocking has a role to play in this issue since people in motion can maintain visual "variety and interest" without the necessity for a shot change. The shooting of a stationary person, however, whether on a newsroom stool, a sitcom sofa, or a soap opera bed, requires the director to face the question of duration squarely. The two contrary orientations Williams mentioned have not merged in the decades since he wrote this statement. If anything, they have acquired even greater distinctiveness as newer rationales for one or the other approach are developed.

Robert Pittman, the MTV Networks's former chief operating officer, for example, would infer that duration depends on the age of the target audience. To Pittman, the over-thirty-five or over-forty generation "thinks of TV as a replacement for other forms of entertainment, such as books, movies or conversation. Therefore, they respond to traditional forms on TV. This one-thing-at-a-time generation (pre-TV adults) grew up on trains of thought that made all the stops—ideas that progress in a sequential mode."[52] It follows that this sequential mode is better served by shot durations that correspond to paragraphs rather than phrases. The younger TV generation, on the other hand, "processed information in a nonlinear manner," says Pittman, so these viewers readily respond to a "quick burst of information format" that moves "very quickly with quick cuts, no transitions."[53] Since, in other words, TV is TV and not a print substitute as far as these younger viewers are concerned, they have grown up with, understand, and have come to expect terseness and brevity in the shots to which they attend.

Whether one embraces Pittman's or any other theory about shot duration and transition is much less important than that critics come to recognize these elements for the substantial if debatable role they can play in a viewer's perception. The pacing and progression of television images may be as significant as the content of those images in shaping the audience's cognitions and preferences. This the critic must consider and appraise in putting a television creation into real time perspective for the public.

Aural Transitions and Volume

We cannot leave the subject of stage-molding without examining its twin auditory ingredients: aural transitions and volume. How we shift from one sound to another is as consequential for radio as is television's shot sequencing. A pause between sound elements can create suspense, but too long a pause or one inappropriately placed is asking for listener tune-out. A seamless segue from one aural element to another may propel the hearer effortless along with the flow, but a clash of musical keys or voice qualities becomes much more jarring because of this proximity. Fading in one event while fading out another may help redirect audience attention but may also cause intervening moments when nothing is distinct. In short, radio transitions carry the same inherent risks as do their visual counterparts, with every situation having one right and several varying degrees of wrong applications.

Audio transitions have recently acquired expanded possibilities in television, where it was long assumed that one simply faded in sound and picture together. Now however, producers of dramatic programs have begun to stagger the entry of these two stimuli to simulate certain physiological or psychological effects. The audio of a *Hill Street Blues* roll call, for example, typically preceded any visual cue save for a digital-like time indication on a black screen. It is as though we are waking up to the situation, with our ears generally anticipating our eyes in the inadvertent return to consciousness. In contrast, the killing of audio at the end of a newscast while the anchors are still seen conversing seems to suggest that they continue on in their duties even though their sharing with us is temporarily suspended.

Volume in these and the much more conventional uses of television sound tends to be at a relatively constant level, but varied volume is the spotlight for the radio medium. Without access to visual close-ups and long shots, radio manipulates sound intensity to bring us toward or away from the objects of its attention. Gradations in volume block out the action on the radio stage and permit the easily followed shift from one scene to the next. This is as true for music or sound effects as it is for words. A fade-down allows one tune to recede while a fade-up rotates the next to the center of our perception like the shift of scene on a revolving stage. Different formats will spin this stage at different speeds, but the objective of simultaneously holding and redirecting listener attention is always the same.

Stage-Molding Summation

Aural volume and transitions, like visual transition and duration, reaction shots and reverse angles, camera-in-motion, camera/character arrangement, horizontal and vertical camera planes, and light and shadow, are all techniques to construct a persuasive stage picture out of elusive electromagnetic impulses. When effectively planned and executed, these stage-molding ingredients, in consort with the on-stage skills of performers and the multifaceted use of music, can make the radio/television experience a pleasing, involving, and, on occasion, even enlightening one. It is the critic's job to remind the public that these productional considerations are just that—executional elements in the service of a conceptual mass we call content.

No matter how slick the cadences, performances, and electronic manipulations, they can be judged only in terms of their appropriateness and value to the message complex being transmitted. That is why we have not considered writing in this section but instead implicitly examine its contribution in several subsequent chapters. Communicative writing is conception, and production is execution. The discerning critic will never confuse one with the other but rather will examine the concept for its clarity, strength, and validity and then seek to help the audience discover whether that concept was appropriately and skillfully consummated. The extravagance and glossiness of the production notwithstanding, the critic must always end up by appraising, in the words of an advertising industry caution, "whether all that pucker led to a kiss."

Notes

1. DeWitt Parker, *The Principles of Aesthetics,* 2nd ed. (Westport, Conn.: Greenwood Press, 1976), 143.
2. Roy Dickinson Welch, "A Discussion of the Expressed Content of Beethoven's Third Symphony," in Theodore Meyer Greene, *The Arts and The Art of Criticism* (Princeton: Princeton University Press, 1952), 488.
3. Greene, *Art of Criticism,* 322.
4. David Altheide and Robert Snow, *Media Logic* (Beverly Hills, Calif.: Sage Publications, 1979), p. 29.
5. Samuel Singer, *Reviewing the Performing Arts* (New York: Richards Rosen Press, 1974), 126.
6. Parker, *Principles,* 146.
7. Charles Turner, "Music Videos and the Iconic Data Base," in Gary Gumpert and Robert Cathcart, eds., *Intermedia,* 3rd ed. (New York: Oxford University Press, 1986), 382.
8. Roger Sessions, "The Composer and His Message," in Melvin Rader, ed., *A Modern Book of Esthetics,* 5th ed. (New York: Holt, Rinehart and Winston, 1979), 255.
9. Altheide and Snow, *Media Logic,* 25–26.
10. Rose Goldsen, *The Show and Tell Machine* (New York: The Dial Press, 1977), 87.
11. Rudolf Arnheim, *Visual Thinking* (Berkeley: University of California Press, 1969), 2.
12. Plato, *The Republic,* trans. by Francis Cornford (New York: Oxford University Press, 1950), 88.
13. Ibid., 86.
14. Robert MacKenzie, "Highway to Heaven," *TV Guide* (December 29, 1984): 40.
15. Greene, *Art of Criticism,* 47.
16. Parker, *Principles*, 143.
17. Tim Moore, "Producing the Image." Speech presented at the Great Lakes Radio Conference, 25 April 1981, at Mt. Pleasant, Mich.
18. DeWitt Parker, *The Analysis of Art* (New Haven: Yale University Press, 1926), 21.
19. Dan Menaker, "Art and Artifice in Network News," *Harper's* (October 1972): 47.
20. Dennis Davis and Stanley Baran, *Mass Communication and Everyday Life* (Belmont, Calif.: Wadsworth, 1981), 100.
21. Greene, *Art of Criticism,* 187.
22. Don Merrill, "Wheel of Fortune," *TV Guide* (October 5, 1985): 1.
23. V. I. Pudovkin, *Film Production and Film Acting* (New York: Grove Press, 1970), 234.
24. John Houseman, "Is TV-Acting Inferior?" *TV Guide* (September 1, 1979): 25.
25. Horace Newcomb, *TV: The Most Popular Art* (Garden City, N.Y.: Anchor Books, 1974), 249.
26. George Schaefer, comments in *Television Makers,* Newton E. Meltzer-produced televised PBS documentary, 1986.
27. Ken Howard, "Why I Left Prime-Time TV for Harvard," *TV Guide* (February 21, 1987): 6.

28. John Cawelti, "With the Benefit of Hindsight: Popular Culture Criticism," *Critical Studies in Mass Communication* (December 1985): 370.
29. Rudolf Arnheim, *Toward a Psychology of Art* (Berkeley: University of California Press, 1967), 58.
30. Don Merrill, "227," *TV Guide* (June 7, 1986): 47.
31. Alan Wurtzel and Joseph Dominick, "Evolution of Television Drama: Interaction of Acting Styles and Shot Selection," *Journal of Broadcasting* (Winter 1971–72): 109.
32. Houseman, "TV-Acting," 25.
33. Herbert Zettl, *Sight, Sound, Motion: Applied Media Aesthetics* (Belmont, Calif: Wadsworth, 1973), 44.
34. Ibid., 38.
35. Parker, *Analysis of Art,* 82.
36. Frank Gillette, *Frank Gillette Video: Process and Metaprocess,* Jodson Rosenbush, ed. (Syracuse, N.Y.: Everson Museum of Art, 1973), 21.
37. Peter Crown, "The Electronic Fireplace," *Videography* (March 1977): 17.
38. Wurtzel and Dominick, "Evolution," 104.
39. Robert Williams, "On the Value of Varying TV Shots," *Journal of Broadcasting* (Winter 1964–65): 34.
40. Stephen Pepper, *The Work of Art* (Bloomington: Indiana University Press, 1955), 28.
41. Gilbert Seldes, *The Public Arts* (New York: Simon and Schuster, 1956), 12.
42. Donald Livingston, *Film and the Director* (New York: Macmillan, 1958), 52.
43. Thomas McCain, Joseph Chilberg, and Jacaob Wakshlag, "The Effect of Camera Angle on Source Credibility and Attraction," *Journal of Broadcasting* (Winter 1977): 43.
44. Ibid., 44.
45. Seldes, *Public Arts,* 187.
46. Pepper, *Work of Art,* 54.
47. Philip Kipper, "Television Camera Movement As a Source of Perceptual Information," *Journal of Broadcasting & Electronic Media* (Summer 1986): 304–305.
48. Robert MacKenzie, "St. Elsewhere," *TV Guide* (January 15, 1983): 22.
49. David Antin, "Video: The Distinctive Features of the Medium," in John Hanhardt, ed., *Video Culture: A Critical Investigation* (Rochester, N.Y.: Visual Studies Workshop, 1986), 160.
50. Michael Arlen, *The Camera Age* (New York: Farrar, Straus & Giroux, 1981), 79.
51. Williams, "Varying TV Shots," 35.
52. Robert Pittman, "MTV's Lesson: We Want What We Want Immediately," *Adweek* (May 27, 1985): 34.
53. Ibid.

6

Business Gratifications

In Chapter 5, we examined the productional ingredients on which broadcast/cable content can draw to create the pucker that hopefully motivates a kiss. In this chapter and in Chapter 7, we attempt to dissect the dynamics of that kiss—the goals and satisfactions that senders and receivers seek to derive from embracing radio or television. Like any judicious critic, we begin by scrutinizing the sender or business side of the exchange because in the United States, this is the party that governs the engagement's direction.

People who would object to giving marketplace forces such critical notice must realize that, as art critic George Boas observed, "Works of art have always been a commodity and critics would do well to observe not only how artistry changes in response to economic demand but how works of art themselves change."[1] Michelangelo had his Pope Julius and Mozart his Emperor Joseph; and even though each artist was thus creating, in a sense, for a market of one, it was still a market, and the failure adequately to assess that market's less discerning tastes caused both geniuses great stress.

"The reconciliation of art and business is never an easy thing," said scholar Carl Grabo, "nor has it been too well achieved in the past."[2] Yet, the electronic media critic must achieve this reconciliation or, at least, explain to the public why such reconciliation, in a given case, is not possible. Radio/television stations, networks, and cable systems are such expensive enterprises to mount and maintain that without a huge government subsidy, they must rely on the profit motive to assure their continuance. To ignore this commercial factor is to ignore a fundamental reality with which all art, in varying degrees, must come to grips.

Bottom-Line Preeminence

Once upon a time, as all good fairy tales start, American broadcasting was regarded as a psuedo–public-service calling that would magically sustain itself by offering programming in the public interest and over the public airwaves. Everyone's idea of what constituted the public interest differed from everyone else's, but a common theme seemed to be that there should only be enough selling to keep the transmitter warm. Like mainline newspapers, stations (and therefore their owners and operators) were seen as serving some calling higher than other business ventures. This demanded a special willingness to forego any commercial excess likely to widen the profit margin. Stations, in fact, were held to even a higher standard than newspapers because they operated on an electromagnetic spectrum that, in theory, belonged to the citizenry at large.

A substantial number of broadcasters did take this responsibility to heart and acquiesced to the genuine assumption that running a station was not like running a furniture store or a bowling alley. They thereby adopted what veteran network news executive Richard Wald called the bifocal view of broadcasting in which what you see up close is profit and loss and what you see farther away is "doing good."[3] Even though they were close readers most of the time, the electronic media managers needed only to glance up to see the other vision staring them in the face.

Even though that vision may still be shimmering on the horizon, it is a horizon that has become more and more distant in the face of corporate takeovers that have brought nonmedia business interests into control of many broadcast and cable properties. Increasingly, veteran radio and television executives have looked through their bifocals to find themselves out of the industry entirely or peering upward at new management structures and myopic investor boards whose sole concern is the quarterly dividend. It is this new possibility that radio/television critics must consider in evaluating both what is and what might be. They need also to share this accounting with their public in order to increase not only understanding how the broadcast/cable business works but also admiration for the qualitative enterprises that have managed to surmount the heightened fiscal preoccupations.

A natural tension between creators and their monied masters has always existed; in this regard, Michelangelo and Mozart were no different than the artists, major and minor, who labor on the precarious scaffolding of radio and in the intrigue-filled halls of television. The intensified bottom-line pressures associated with the take-over of broadcast/cable operations by nonbroadcast entrepreneurs has only heightened this tension and made critical successes more worthy of critical encouragement. As Ben Stein found in his study of the Hollywood creative community, the TV writer

> is actually selling his labor to brutally callous businessmen. One actually has to go through the experience of writing for money in Hollywood or anywhere else to real-

ize just how unpleasant it is. Most of the pain comes from dealings with business people, such as agents or business affairs officers of production companies and networks. The number of calamities that can and do happen can hardly be believed unless they are experienced. The TV writer is not an honored guest at a meeting of businessmen at the Greenbriar [a posh conference center]. He is actually down there in the pit with the clawing agents and businessmen, and he often has reason to feel that he has been shortchanged, to say the least.[4]

"If I have some work printed or engraved," Mozart once wrote his father, "how can I protect myself from being cheated by the engraver? . . . I almost feel inclined not to sell any more of my compositions to any engraver, but to have them printed or engraved by subscription at my own expense."[5] The creator for today's electronic media faces the same quandary. Unless he or she becomes, like a Norman Lear or Grant Tinker, wealthy enough to own an "engraving company" (a production house), there is an uncontrollable dependency on the people who do possess this capability. Further, even the production house's ability to "engrave" on tape or film is useless if the financial interests who control the means of transmission cannot be persuaded to carry that celluloid or electromagnetic engraving to the public.

Obviously, radio/television's shifting ownership trends make the situation even more acute as the number of modern 'engravers' is compressed by mergers and the cost of such mergers (or of staving them off) puts more and more pressure on that profit-and-loss statement's terminal sum. Les Brown, editor-in-chief of *Channels of Communications,* sees the effects of this shift to be so sweeping as to constitute what he labels a "new morality" in electronic media ownership. The "big money" investors who have entered broadcasting and cable recently are, Brown warns, "coming without any passion for the industry at all, with passion for the bottom line."[6] This condition, in turn, has precipitated in academic media critics what Professor Samuel Becker sees as "the growing distrust of big business by many scholars, fueled by the growing dominance of a relatively few trans-national telecommunications industries, the continuing conglomerization of the media industries within the United States and, at the same time, the trend within this country to reduce government pressure on the broadcasting industries to serve public as well as shareholder interests."[7]

The conscientious critic, academic as well as nonacademic, must recognize this dynamic but must take care not to succumb to it lest a depressing grumbling sets in that would be the antithesis of reasonable criticism as we have defined it. Broadcasting/cable activities probably are, as Joseph Russin said of radio stations, "businesses first and beacons of truth and justice second."[8] But this only makes them commercial; it does not make them inherently evil or lacking in value. Bottom-line supremacy may modify the focus of radio and television, but it does not make their products any less significant in the public mind.

Ratings, Shares, and Tonnage

In the electronic media, bottom-line concerns translate most directly into how many and what kind of people are reached by a given outlet and a given content. From a business gratification standpoint, radio and television are *not* fundamentally in the enterprise of delivering programming to audiences. Rather, they are in the profession of delivering audiences to advertisers. The programming is the bait that attracts listeners and viewers and the glue that holds them together long enough for an adjacent advertiser to make contact. Any marketer or station executive who does not appreciate this dynamic is doomed to failure as a mass communicator and is like those dinosaur railroad managers who thought they were in the train business rather than the transportation business. Any critics who miss this reality will ask the impossible of the media they review and consequently mislead the public while being ignored by the producers.

CBS/Broadcast Group President Gene Jankowski argues that there is more to his business than the simple selling of audiences to advertisers and expresses doubt that his industry "could long survive if that were what we were all about. Broadcasters face the same clear, but by no means simple, challenge that every business faces: Either they satisfy the public or they do not. In that way, and that way alone, they succeed or fail. That's all there is to it."[9] Still, broadcasters have two publics and, Jankowski's statement notwithstanding, the one remains the means by which the other's business ends are achieved.

The delivery of audience as measured by rating, share, and cost-per-thousand points is mathematically delineated in Chapter 4. The rise and fall of these numbers are direct indices of business gratifications or gratification absence and are the making or breaking of programs, formats, and careers. Nowhere is the quest for big numbers more apparent than in prime-time network television, where the costs of program creation and delivery still make for a true tonnage environment. Tonnage is an industry term for the delivery of large, even massive audiences in which the sheer numbers of people reached take on a greater importance than who these people are. Thus, the typical daily newspaper is a tonnage medium constantly seeking to increase numbers of copies sold, whereas a magazine is typically nontonnage or qualitative and strives to deliver a precisely defined category of consumers (target audience) to its advertisers. Prime-time network television, in this sense, is like the newspaper, and most radio station formats attempt the audience delivery precision of a magazine.

A tonnage orientation is most likely to occur where the number of same-service competitors is small and the cost of production is high. Most daily newspapers are costly enterprises but must face no more than one competitor in their local markets. In fact, most U.S. dailies are monopolies with no rival for local readership or advertising. Even with its regional printing, the entry of *USA Today* cannot directly compete for the local consumer's demand for a locally oriented gazette. Thus, the territorial newspaper continues its quest to be the omnibus (something for everyone) medium in which how many are reading becomes a more appropriate concern than targeting to any single de-mographic group.

Network television formerly enjoyed a truly analogous position. Until the midseventies advent of satellite-delivered cable services and the growth in multichanneled cable penetration that this technology made possible, the TV landscape was typically three network-affiliated stations with perhaps a single struggling independent facility and noncompeting public station thrown in. During evening prime time, when the great bulk of homes using television (HUTs) were activated, the combined network share of audience was fre-quently 90 percent or more with 75 percent to 80 percent of the entire country tuned in to network programming for at least part of the evening. The three networks thus were in almost the same preeminent position as local newspa-pers. This was the era that spawned network executive Paul Klein's LOP (Least Objectional Program) Theory in which viewers were forced to choose what they least disliked from a three-item menu.

Today, of course, the pattern has changed markedly with literally dozens of choices available—network affiliate, local independent, distant independent, and cable-only services. In prime time, the networks still collectively command the majority of viewing choices; and their comparatively massive clout still in-curs programming costs to them, and compensatory time costs to their adver-tisers, which continues to motivate a tonnage environment. Yet, even here, the pattern is changing as more and more cable-wise younger viewers hook up. As David Poltrack, CBS/Broadcast Group vice-president recently stated at an industry/academic seminar, the networks can no longer afford to develop "broad-scale programming to attract everyone. We just can't attract everyone. There are too many alternatives out there."[10]

To many critics, the post-LOP era offers more positive possibilities than perils. "Prime time television, plain and simply, is getting better," *Channels of Communication* editor Les Brown told the Broadcast Education Association. "Maybe it's because you don't need as high a rating today to succeed with a television show."[11] Because of this, CBS's Poltrack reveals, "We have to move from the broadly drawn, exaggerated characters of the past to finely drawn, empathetic characters."[12]

This precarious balancing of the old tonnage assumptions and the newer content requirements of the multiple-alternative viewing environment is well il-lustrated in the following mini-series critique from the commercial trade publi-cation *Broadcasting*. Certainly, the crusade for "impressive ratings" and "substantial shares" remains dominant. Still, one also detects, even in this business publication article, a subtle if not automatically successful shift to more serious issues and executions in a publicity enhanced attempt to shore up viewing levels and combat audience fragmentation.

ABC's 'AMERIKA' LESS THAN BEAUTIFUL

Amerika is the kind of special network project that ABC pioneered a decade ago. *Roots* was the first in a string of highly promoted "big event" mini-series with which ABC was able to capture the hearts and eyes of viewers. That was followed by *Roots II:*

The Next Generation, and others, such as *Winds of War* and *Thorn Birds.* All generated lots of press attention, a good amount of critical acclaim and impressive ratings. The network strategy with *Amerika* was in the tradition—develop a sweeping big event, promote it extensively, and hope it draws legions of curious viewers.

But, in the view of many, the strategy backfired last week for one essential reason—poor execution. The program, most critics said, was long, drawn out, somber, overly serious—in a word, boring. The proof, critics were saying last week, was in the ratings, which steadily declined after a solid sampling in the first episode. The two-hour-and-20-minute opening episode on Sunday, Feb. 15, averaged a 24.5 rating and a 38 share. But after the first four episodes (Sunday, Feb. 15–Wednesday, Feb. 18), the program averaged a 20.2/31. By Wednesday, part IV was down to a 17.8/28.

In response to the ratings drop, ABC put out a statement that read in part: "The initial ratings were encouraging. The mid-week audience drop-off has been disappointing." The network also noted correctly that although the mini-series was not commanding the towering ratings of earlier special projects, it was pulling in a "substantial" share of the audience, taking three of the first four nights, losing only to CBS's *Miss USA Pageant* on Tuesday evening (Feb. 17). "We hope," the network concluded, "that the audience will build again on Friday and Sunday nights [Feb. 20 and 22] as *Amerika* reaches its dramatic conclusion." However, last week network officials were predicting ABC would come in second for the week, with NBC first and CBS third.

As for the program's impact, outside observers were more likely to see a profound and negative one on the mini-series program form, while executives inside the industry saw *Amerika* more as one program that simply didn't measure up.

Tom Shales, television critic for the *Washington Post,* said last week that *Amerika's* apparent failure to sustain a huge share of audience may spell the end of efforts by the networks to attempt to address serious ideas in the mini-series form. "I think you'll see more hokey, glitzy, frivolous stuff," he said, such as CBS's upcoming *I'll Take Manhattan,* a mini based on the Judith Krantz novel, scheduled for early March. "If it had only been better done and more successful," said Shales of *Amerika,* "it might have augured well for the ability of mini-series to address serious kinds of issues. I blame ABC and [Donald] Wrye [the program's writer/producer/director] for the failure. From a viewer standpoint it was unapproachable in that it drove people away after the first night."

But whatever the final outcome of ABC's *Amerika* experience, the network will try its hand at one more big mini-series project before settling in to the four-to-eight-hour projects that the other two networks seems comfortable with—*War and Remembrance,* the 30-hour World War II saga and sequel to the 1984 hit, *Winds of War,* both based on novels from Herman Wouk. Shooting for that project is close to completion, a network spokesman said last week, and there's no indication ABC has plans of scaling back the ambitious project. Last week Shales said he believed the Wouk sequel should perform on a par with *Winds* because the plot and character development will prove more entertaining and there will be the payoff of a happy ending. "After all, we did win the war," he said.

But while *Amerika* is not seen as an overwhelming success, it hasn't been a complete bomb either. "I don't know what people were expecting," said CBS Entertainment President Bud Grant last week. "It's been giving them better numbers than they've been getting all season. In terms of circulation, ABC is probably happy with it." Whether that is accurate remains a secret, because ABC executives last week refused to discuss any aspect of the mini-series. But, with the exception of Tuesday night, it did appear that the first five parts were bringing in higher numbers than its regular series programming this season.

As for the show's long-term impact, on the mini-series form, or on television generally, Grant doesn't see any. "I don't think that experience tells you anything [about the future of mini-series] one way or the other." Such generalities, he added, are "ill founded." As for his own thoughts on the form, "there is an important place for mini-series on television. As an event, it attracts attention and breaks up the predictability of television." At CBS, he said, eight hours is about as long as any mini-series will be. Any more than that, he said, "is too much of a risk. They are very expensive and not particularly good business."

Amerika certainly has not been good business for ABC. It will lose money on the production; how much depends on how the books are kept. The program had originally been pegged to cost about $32 million to produce, but ended up costing closer to $40 million. At best, gross advertising sales for the show would have totaled $32 million, and that was before the Chrysler pull-out (*Broadcasting*, Feb. 2). Replacement advertisers were paying prices lower than Chrysler and a handful of other advertisers who pulled out paid, although network executives have said the defectors will pay premiums for advertising in other programs to make up the difference. Still, net advertising revenues from the show will total less than $30 million, which would appear to guarantee at least a $10-million shortfall.

Normally, networks like to see their special events generate the kind of publicity *Amerika* did, accepting the bad along with the good. But in this case, the balance of coverage was decidedly negative, coming from both left- and right-wing critics as well as the United Nations which complained that the image of its peacekeeping troops was being unjustifiably bruised by their portrayal in the program. Many wondered last week whether all the free press did more harm than good.

The *Post*'s Shales was kinder than most—he at least said the program was worth "enduring" despite problems. "Its script is uneven, its direction is arch, it succumbs too frequently to stupefying lulls and its leading man gives a performance so wooden you could make a coffee table out of it," he wrote. John O'Connor of the *New York Times* called the show a "staggering muddle, a fill-in-the-blanks hodge podge." He said that ABC was, with good reason, being forced to fend off charges that the project represents a cave-in to right-wing interests which loudly objected to the antinuclear message of ABC's *The Day After.*

TV critics and ideologues were not the only ones sounding off about *Amerika*. John Mack, director of a psychology center associated with Harvard Medical School, wrote of the need for the media to develop "more realistic images" of how Russians and Americans are portrayed in each others' mass media. Under the "Topics" section of its editorial page, *The New York Times* said "*Amerika* seems designed to grab headlines and pump up ratings," an observation ABC probably would not disagree with.

ABC may have been too successful in grabbing headlines, a concern expressed publicly by ABC Vice President Robert Wright two weeks ago. He told *USA Today* that "People won't simply be tuning in to see a film, I'm afraid. There is so much hoopla, I don't know what people will expect. The Second Coming perhaps."

(Courtesy of David Whitcombe, *Broadcasting*)

In non–prime-time dayparts, TV tonnage preoccupations have ebbed much less resistantly and much more gradually due to the traditionally much lower viewing levels and consequent less awe-inspiring rate-card prices charged advertisers. These factors, in turn, mean much lower network production budgets with which the syndicated programming on independent stations and cable network offerings can much more easily compete. When combined with the FCC's Prime Time Access Rule that, in essence, removed the networks from programming the first hour of evening programming since the early seventies, the robust competition that marks non–prime-time television demonstrates greater and greater attention to more precise audience targeting. In other words, programming is produced and selected to appeal to specific demographic groups who are seemingly unserved or ill-served by the offerings on other channels. The soap opera, talk, or game show that is ground out on a five-episode per-week basis entails only a fraction of the production cost of the prime-time sitcom and can thus afford to price itself within a range acceptable to advertisers seeking a significantly smaller but also more specific body of viewers.

Taken as a whole, the magazine industry made the shift from tonnage to demographic specifics in the fifties when, in the face of television, advertisers were no longer willing to pay premium rates to reach a broad and undelineated audience. The general circulation dinosaurs such as *Look, Collier's,* and the original *Life* thus met their demise, to be replaced by publications that offered a much smaller but also much more homogeneous readership to advertisers marketing precisely targeted products. The same thing was happening to radio at the same time as the new television preempted the "old" national radio's tonnage expectations and converted the elder electronic medium to a locally programmed entity in which the universe-selecting format became the mark of success. Later, when FM came to parity with and then surpassed AM's popularity, the number of competing stations functionally doubled and made narrowcasting to population slivers the only feasible path to fiscal stability. In the words of broadcast consultant and professor Charles Warner, "Delineating yourself becomes essential when every station is moving to a 4 share."[13]

Radio stations, of course, are format-specific, whereas television outlets are program-specific. That is, people turn to a radio outlet for a definite kind of service (gratification) that they, in general, expect to be there regardless of time of day. Even though the on-air presenters change, the general nature of the radio transmission is assumed to remain a predictable constant. In television, however, consumers tend to move from program to program. They select shows rather than methods of transmission. Once the cable is attached to the set, a UHF superstation some four states away or a cable network uplinked from New York becomes as easy to tune to as the VHF network affiliate located a mile down the street. How one gets the signal is no longer important (if, indeed, it ever was); the sole concern is what is retrieved. A viewer in search of a sporting event or a sitcom will find it without regard for, or even awareness of, the transmission entity supplying it. The economics of cablecasting now even make it possible for some entities such as MTV or CNN to take a page out of radio's book and air one format exclusively. Like radio, advertisers know precisely the kind of viewer they are getting without wasted circulation—without paying to reach a substantial number of people who do not comprise their target market. Even though cable audience measurement is still in its infancy, the medium's attractive advertising rates have lessened the gamble video sponsors must take and are further eroding the concept of television as a tonnage buy.

Critics who review only over-the-air network television will not produce pieces that reflect these new realities, and their columns are likely to become less and less relevant to the interests and needs of the cable-ready audience. As business fine-tunes its marketing strategies to more precise demographic and psychographic (life style) targeting, the trend to more specifically tailored programming seems likely to accelerate. The advertiser's concern for cost-per-thousand gratification remains a constant, but in today's segmented world, raw rating and share numbers—and the tonnage mentality they signify—are becoming less and less meaningful to all but the most diversified packaged goods manufacturer. Critics, then, face the unenviable task of sorting through a burgeoning amount of aired product. Indeed, the "sheer volume of American television sets up the critic for a feeling of guilt," observes former *Washington Post* writer Lawrence Laurent. "You keep thinking about all the things you're not able to cover."[14]

Scheduling and Flow Analysis

One critical approach to both greater audience segmentation and the continuing multiplication of radio/television program sources is to examine how and why elements are scheduled as they are. In this way, the critic can examine whole blocks of television programs in much the same manner that a radio format is critiqued as a means of ascertaining the programmer strategies and show components that are designed to hold a listener to a given channel. Sometimes referred to as flow analysis, this procedure makes the assumption that a program in isolation is perceived differently than one experienced as part of a listening or viewing block. Certainly, the values of each program need to be analyzed, but so, too, goes the theory, does the media environment in which the entity is placed. This environment includes not only (1) what comes before and after it on the show's own channel/station but also (2) what has been scheduled against it on opposing services. As Todd Gitlin describes it:

> Producers produce programs, and development executives advocate them, but the top executives as a group compose schedules. Scheduling meetings dwell not only on the demographics expected but on problems of "flow": Would an eight-o'clock audience of a given demographic stay tuned to show X at eight-thirty, given the competition? Many executives have also come to believe in what is called "counterprogramming"—say running a show watched disproportionately by men (*Hill Street Blues*) against a show that appeals more to women (*Fantasy Island*). Such scheduling is no longer an annual affair, but a year-long process of rearrangement, like a frantic, continuous round of interior redecoration.[15]

Whether the goal is tonnage or precise demographic delivery, the business gratifications attributed to successful scheduling strategy are measured by the meteoric rises and catastrophic plunges of the careers of station and network program executives. CBS's former head of programming Michael Dann has frequently stated that the position a program is assigned is much more important than the content of the program itself. In fact, a program can be a rating/share failure but still a business success if its scheduling accomplishes the job it was designed to do in a cost-effective manner. Former NBC News correspondent Lloyd Dobyns illustrated this phenomenon in discussing a scheduling move made by ABC for the 1986/87 prime time season:

> In September ABC News started running *Our World* with Linda Ellerbee and Ray Gandolf in prime time. The new show is up against NBC's *The Cosby Show,* television's monster hit. But *Our World* is cheaper to produce than an entertainment program. If by some miracle *Our World* can succeed against *Cosby,* its return on investment will be enormous. Even it if dies, its failure will cost a lot less than a Hollywood sitcom. Either way, ABC's profit-and-loss sheet will look better.[16]

In a typical week, *Cosby* outdrew *Our World* in audience by a ratio of at least 4 to 1, but the news show remained on the schedule to prove Dobyns's point. It must also be added that the show constituted a business success for certain advertisers in search of the older and up-scale male audience that was *Our World's* primary constituency. Given the program's low tonnage numbers, these advertisers were able to purchase time at bargain-basement rates while ABC still turned a small bottom-line profit because of *Our World's* comparatively low production costs.

The business dynamics of scheduling and flow are not merely complex; they can also be downright bewildering. This is especially true in attempting to blend a network's national line-up with the offerings of its local affiliates. John Sias, Capcities/ABC Television Network group president, provides an example of this in a discussion of the decision making that must go into how his network's *ABC Monday Night Football* is timetabled:

> I'm told by Dennis [Swanson, president of ABC Sports] that the league would like to have the games start at 8 o'clock. Most of the affiliates in the East—well, all of them in the East and Midwest—want them to start at 8 because of the runovers. As the games have gotten longer and longer, and they're now going three-and-a-half hours to three hours and 45 minutes, they're devastating to affiliates' 11 o'clock news, which is a critical part of their weekly offering. So the affiliates are more than aroused on the subject, and very, very distressed with it.
>
> The West Coast has a different problem. If we start at 8 Eastern time, and they're starting at 5 o'clock, which is right in the middle of their drive time and at the start of two-and-a-half hours or three hours of local programming, with the exception of network newscasts.
>
> And our entertainment division points up a very serious problem if we abdicate entertainment programming from 8 to 9, for whatever number of weeks we televise football. That means it's very difficult to get a viewing pattern going, and you kind of give away any kind of female viewing. So we are very concerned about giving up 8 to 9 for 16 to 22 weeks. And when you throw baseball in there, and ex-

pect to woo viewers back with some kind of programming that is not in the ball-park, and the opposition's got a chance to build up viewing patterns and habits. We would not like to create one more night when we're out of business once football is over.[17]

Nor is scheduling only a television quandary. Radio programmers must wrestle with this aspect too and design elaborate "hot clocks" to specify the type of element that will happen at a given time within a given hour during a given daypart. Sometimes, they will turn to an outside program supplier or syndicator who can deliver the entire format ready for local announcer customization. Unfortunately, a format that works very well in audience delivery in one market can be a bust in another even if the competing stations in the two cities are closely comparable. The reason for this inconsistency of performance may have nothing to do with the competence of the format developer or the local air people but instead may be a function of life-style misscheduling. The hot clock that succeeds beautifully in a market in which factory shift changes and/or school starting/dismissal times occur on the hour can be completely out of sync with a town in which such events occur at the quarter or half hour. Similarly, a city in which the average commute is one hour will have significantly divergent format needs from one in which most people can get to or from work in fifteen minutes. The astute radio critic should learn to recognize these variables in music or talk segment design—even if some radio programmers do not.

Ultimately, schedule and flow analysis reduces itself to five fundamental questions to which the programmer must prepare the answers that the critic comprehends and judges:

1. Is the program/element length appropriate to the subject matter?
2. Is the time-of-day appropriate to the available and sought after audience?
3. Is the content choice advantageous in terms of the competition's simultaneous offerings?
4. Does the feature assist audience flow from the event that precedes it to the event that follows it?
5. Is the cost of the program compatible with the likely revenues to be derived from it? (For public broadcasting this entails whether an underwriter can be found to support it and/or whether the program will appeal to citizens most likely to contribute to the station's pledge drives.)

Even though no single critique will discuss all of these points, critics need to be attuned to them in an ongoing manner. Each element becomes part of the critical ascertainment process, and the critics bring the elements to the fore as they appear most relevant to the process of public enlightenment. The following piece by *The Detroit News*'s Marc Gunther, for example, includes elements of questions 2, 3, and 5 in helping readers understand an independent station's program purchase and scheduling mechanisms.

LOOKING AT THE BIG PICTURE
by Marc Gunther

Seen any good movies lately? Paul Prange, program director of Detroit's Channel 50, enjoyed *Stand By Me* ("a great movie"), *This Is Spinal Tap* ("a funny movie") and *Brighton Beach Memoirs* ("very dry").

But Prange, 33, who buys and schedules the movies that run at 8 p.m. and 1:30 a.m. Monday through Saturday on WKBD–TV, is in no hurry to obtain any of those films for his station.

Prange thinks *Stand By Me* would be "an awful TV movie" and *Spinal Tap* and *Brighton Beach Memoirs* "won't work" on Channel 50. "Heaven forbid I should program my tastes on the station," he adds, sounding a bit scandalized by such a notion.

Not that his tastes are highbrow. Prange also liked *Top Gun* and *Star Trek IV,* and says he'd like to buy them for Channel 50. It's just that there's no room for personal preferences when making business decisions with a huge impact on a station's bottom line.

So how does Prange decide, say, to buy *The Fog* for tomorrow, to play *Bachelor Party* on Monday, and to schedule *My Bloody Valentine* for Friday the 13th?

Among other things, he uses sophisticated computer analyses of about 1,800 movies, box-office records from local theaters and the trade publication *Variety,* and a healthy dose of old-fashioned gut instinct about what will attract viewers.

His judgments will be critical to Channel 50 during the next four weeks, a "sweeps" period—when local ratings are measured intensely and used to set advertising rates. Picking movies for the sweeps, which begin today, is an especially tricky business because the commercial networks load their schedules with specials, high-profile TV movies and big impact mini-series.

By now, though, Prange's work for February is done. He bought most of the station's movies months or years ago, typically in packages of 10–30 films assembled by the Hollywood studios. Prices vary widely, but a package of 20 movies can cost from $250,000 to $500,000 depending on the titles. The station can run each movie several times, at different hours.

While independents like Channel 50 formerly got theatrical movies after their network runs, such stations are now getting more and more TV premieres. Theatricals have become less valued by the networks because they have been exposed on videocassette and cable.

That doesn't matter much to the independents, however, Prange notes that fewer than half the viewers in Detroit get pay cable, and even fewer rent videocassettes. Besides, he says, viewers will watch many movies more than once.

As a buyer, Prange favors hard action, broad comedies and horror movies. "We've had success with Charles Bronson and Clint Eastwood types," he says. "*Animal House* and *The Blues Brothers* are movies that have legs for us." A "Shocktober" promotion of fright movies last fall was also a big hit.

In contrast, "something that would not do well on this station would be *The Turning Point,*" Prange says. To show Oscar-winner *Chariots of Fire,* "we'd have to overcome the perception that it's a long drawn-out movie about a bunch of British guys running on the beach."

Prange says he generally regards Channel 50 as "an escape valve. Day-to-day life is a pressure cooker for many people. We're offering some relaxation for people at night."

The networks try the same thing, of course, so Prange's scheduling strategy is to see what the networks are doing and try something different. "We're always looking for the void," he says.

Horror movies, for example, work well because there's nothing like them on the networks. Prange tends to use them on Thursdays, opposite *The Cosby Show,* and will run *The Howling* and *Exorcist II* against ABC's *Amerika* mini-series later this month.

On Mondays, Prange schedules male-oriented comedies. That's because CBS' Monday lineup has a strong appeal to women, while ABC and NBC tend to run movies oriented to women at 9 p.m. This month, Prange will try Tom Hanks in *Bachelor Party* and a repeat of *The Blues Brothers* on Mondays.

Gimmick scheduling has also proven effective for Channel 50. *My Bloody Valentine* will air the night before Valentine's Day, and for the third consecutive year the station will show *The St. Valentine's Day Massacre* on Valentine's Day—when "everyone is showing things like *Love Story,*" Prange says.

A lifelong TV fan, Prange got into the business as a copywriter in St. Louis. He became a promotion manager, then a program manager, then a salesman of syndicated shows. In 1983 he came to Channel 50, where at age 30 he was one of the youngest program directors in the country.

As program director for an independent, Prange is responsible for filling the air nearly 24 hours a day—unlike managers at network affiliates, who don't have to worry about the prime-time and daytime hours.

"I have fun doing this," Prange admits. Still, work can be a pressure cooker for him, too, especially given the financial stakes. Finding an escape valve, alas, is not easy.

Watching television and going to the movies are out, if only because Prange tends to analyze everything he sees. "I go to the movies and instead of saying the acting is great or the directing is great, I say, 'Boy, this is going to play great on TV!'"

(Courtesy of Robert H. Giles, *The Detroit News*)

The importance of the scheduling/flow factor must not be underestimated by the broadcast/cable critic. As to flow, Les Brown avows that "there are really two kinds of television—the kind that comes on cassette and the kind that flows over the air."[18] Though he was referring to home video rental tapes as compared to broadcast programs, Brown's point also relates to the critic's monitoring of broadcaster-supplied preview recordings. With stacks of nonconnected cassettes piled around the VCR, it is easy for the critic to ignore the perceptual progression experienced by the viewer in an afternoon or evening with the tube. As to schedule, Robert Lewis Shayon recognized years ago that, in the electronic media

> the creator's view had to be broadened to include the market-place complex in which the creator is the least important element. Talent, however publicized and misrepresented as the *sine qua non* of the game, is really the pawn, disposable, dispensable, and easily replaceable. The man who can choose the winners in the program race has the talent that is truly treasured by the managers behind the scenes.[19]

Bottom-line return, as facilitated by the creation and scheduling processes that make audience delivery possible, is certainly radio/television's core business gratification. While it is vital that the critic probe the artistic, sociological, and psychological dimensions of broadcast and cable content, the enterprise's motivating economic reality also must be taken into consideration. If it is not, the critic's judgments will be seen as irrelevant by the industry and the critic's suggestions will be dismissed as unworkable. The best media professionals, maintains Bernadette McGuire of the National Association of Public Television Stations, "are those who understand the business side of broadcasting and know how to use it for the benefit of society."[20] The same criteria could be said to apply to the best media critics. "What is called for," in the words of Les Brown, "is knowledgeable criticism and commentary that accepts the reality of the television system which exists, and that seeks to help it raise its aims—criticism that spurs the industry to self-examination rather than to arguments in self-defense."[21]

Notes

1. George Boas, *A Primer for Critics* (New York: Greenwood Press, 1968), 124–25.
2. Carl Grabo, *The Creative Critic* (Chicago: University of Chicago Press, 1948), 123.
3. Richard Wald. Speech presented at the International Radio & Television Society Faculty/Industry Seminar, 22 February 1979, at Glen Cove, N.Y.
4. Ben Stein, *The View from Sunset Boulevard* (New York: Basic Books, 1979), 27.
5. Wolfgang Amadeus Mozart, letter to his father, 20 February 1784, quoted in Sam Morgenstern, ed., *Composers on Music* (New York: Pantheon Books, 1956), 84.
6. Les Brown, quoted in "Bang-up NATPE for Action-Adventure Shows," *Broadcasting* (February 2, 1987): 67.
7. S. Becker, "Critical Studies: A Multidimensional Movement," *Feedback* (Fall 1985): 24.
8. Joseph Russin, "Confessions of a Rookie Owner," *Adweek Radio 1984 Issue* (November 1984): 44.
9. Gene Jankowski, "Media in America: Perception & Practice." Speech presented at the Abe Lincoln Awards, 17 February 1983, at Fort Worth, Tex.
10. David Poltrack, quoted in "Bang-up NATPE for Action-Adventure Shows," *Broadcasting* (February 2, 1987): 69.
11. Les Brown, "Trends in TV Criticism." Speech presented at the Broadcast Education Association, 28 March 1987, at Dallas, Tex.
12. Poltrack, "Bang-up."
13. Charles Warner, "Selling in the New Competitive Era." Speech presented at the Broadcast Education Association, 27 March 1987, at Dallas, Tex.
14. Lawrence Laurent, "Still Wanted: The Complete Television Critic." Speech presented at the Broadcast Education Association, 28 March 1987, at Dallas, Tex.
15. Todd Gitlin, *Inside Prime Time* (New York: Pantheon Books, 1985), 60.
16. Lloyd Dobyns, "Producer to Reporter: 'Think Weird, Think Live, Good Luck'," *TV Guide* (February 14, 1987): 37.
17. John Sias, quoted in "Life on the Downside at Capcities/ABC," *Broadcasting* (December 22, 1986): 64.
18. Les Brown, "Trends" speech.
19. Robert Lewis Shayon, *Open to Criticism* (Boston: Beacon Press, 1971), 120.
20. Bernadette McGuire, "Self Regulation and Government Regulation." Speech presented at the Broadcast Education Association, 27 March 1987, at Dallas, Tex.
21. Les Brown, "Remarks to the Iowa TV Critics Conference," *Critical Studies in Mass Communication* (December 1985): 395.

Audience Gratifications

Audience research, in catering to the business gratification, is producing mounds of data about who is watching and listening and for how long. With diaries, telephone coincidentals, shopping mall intercepts, set-top electronic meters, and now with people meters, which can monitor individual viewing as well as product purchases, industry decision-makers can define and divide electronic media patrons into a number of demographic and psychographic (life-style) categories. Yet, while we are gathering ever more precise data on the *who,* the counterpart explanation of the *why* remains much more illusive. Often referred to as "uses and gratifications" research, this forty-year quest for the *why* attempts to isolate the reasons and satisfaction-seeking that motivate consumer selection of one programmatic entity over another. In addition, it probes why the medium itself is chosen by a consumer for use.

An Audience Uses Overview

Establishing that a hit television program has a rating of 21 and a share of 33, for example, gives broadcasting and advertising executives a reasonably accurate count of audience size but does not, in and of itself, illuminate these viewers' reasons for choosing this show. Lacking such knowledge, the industry decision-makers cannot predictably duplicate that program's success in fashioning another series. In fact, they cannot even guarantee that this same program will continue to perform at its current level! Is it the star or stars that attract the viewers? The show's locale and/or basic premise? The script/plot development? Or merely the fact that it happened to be the only new show of its genre (type) airing at that hour? If we know the viewer satisfactions served by the program, we can come much closer to answering these questions and thereby to strengthening that appeal in this particular vehicle or in future series under development.

In their writings, careless critics are as likely to hinder as to help in solving the uses and gratifications mystery. The critic may take pleasure in a programmatic element that escapes the audience entirely, or the audience may choose to listen or watch in order to enjoy an aspect the reviewer considers trivial. This is one reason critics' pronouncements and audience choices are at times so diametrically opposed, with the reviewer praising a series the public avoids or the public flocking to a program the critic despises. It is not necessarily a matter of critic and consumers having conflicting tastes but rather of possessing different priorities in their search for broadcast/cable-derived servicing. In such instances, what falls to the critic is the difficult task of explaining professional preferences while simultaneously attempting to ascertain and consider audience inclinations.

In the following preview by *New York Times* critic John J. O'Connor, for instance, several possible audience appeals are clearly isolated while at the same time the columnist makes it clear that these are *not* appeals to which he personally would subscribe. The critic's own inventory of "solid assets" is not allowed to obscure an articulation of what other people might consider positive attributes. On the other hand, the critic's point of view is not compromised. If you seek these elements, you will find them here, he reports, and he even cites internal HBO research to evidence the satisfaction level that the program's prototypes have achieved. That this is not a measure of his own preference also comes through clearly to fulfill the critic's ultimate responsibility of making and stating his own carefully considered judgment.

'TRAINING CAMP,' AN HBO SITCOM
By John J. O'Connor

Taking stock of its more obvious exploitation ploys, Home Box Office seems to have put them all together in a series of half-hours called "First and 10" and "Training Camp." Here we have a kind of sitcom exposé of football, a subject likely to appeal to male viewers while, at the same time, the locker-room scenes of beefy jocks in various stages of undress attract the female contingents. Sprinkle liberally with "dirty" words and smutty jokes, the kind of material that is still—although just barely—banned from commercial television, and the gang in audience marketing can almost be heard smacking their lips over the entire "give 'em what they want" exercise.

The show, created by Carl Kleinschmitt and produced for HBO by Kushner-Locke Productions, made its debut in August 1985 as "First and 10," introducing a fictitious team called the California Bulls. The new owner is a gorgeous woman named Diane Barrow, played by Delta Burke (who in the meantime has also become one of the stars on the CBS series "Designing Women"). In its first season, Miss Barrow brought the team from the cellar to the championship playoffs. This year, she and the team returned in six half-hour episodes called "Training Camp: The Bulls are Back." The first three, directed by Bruce Seth Green, will be repeated back to back on HBO tonight at 10; the others can be seen next Tuesday at the same time.

Mixing real football players—among them O. J. Simpson—with actors, the show offers a combination of comic strip and good-old-boy beer commercials, spiked with what the more innocent among us might perceive as gritty realism. While most of the humor seems to have been inspired by the movie "Animal House," complete with characters named Dr. Death and Mad Dog, the scripts take periodic swipes at such serious issues as unscrupulous agents, escalating salaries, widespread drug taking and opposition among players to volunteer urine testing. The latter, as might be expected, inspires endless unprintable jokes.

Produced by Jonathan Debin and Gary L. Miller, who is also one of the writers, "Training Camp" has some solid assets. Mr. Simpson and Marcus Allen, of the Los Angeles Raiders, manage to be appealing while carefully refusing to be buffoons. Playing Yinessa, a noncollege rookie trying to make quarterback, Jason Beghe is a convincing tough guy, Jeff Kaake is sympathetic as his cocaine-addicted roommate. And Cliff Frazier and Prince Hughes are diverting as a couple of oversized roustabouts called Jethro and Bubba.

On its gritty ledger, "Training Camp" offers team owners who, except for the idealistic Ms. Barrow, are vicious, greedy businessmen; a football commissioner who is interested only in protecting the image of his wards; football stars who know they can get away with anything while they're "hot," and agents who will push any deal that will bring them bigger dollars. In the middle of this scheming, we have the players themselves, some of them perhaps unruly or even dangerous, but most of them essentially perpetual adolescents. Beneath the pranks and practical jokes beat the innocent hearts of eternal high-school heroes. They live in a world of pure male-bonding. Women are allowed in as either one-night stands or tolerant mother figures who will put up with their endless shenanigans.

In short, while toying with a few realities, "Training Camp" is glorifying the standard man-boy myths imbedded in the selling of football. Does it work? Consider: HBO research has found that "First and 10" and "Training Camp" have been the most satisfying series ever on the pay-cable service, scoring a TSS (total subscriber satisfaction) score higher than 66 percent of the movies on its schedule. One result is that these "Training Camp" episodes will be followed, beginning Dec. 30, by a four-part series called "First and 10: The Championships." The final episode will be unveiled the week before the actual playing of the National Football League's Super Bowl.

HBO has what one of its top executives hails as "an unqualified hit." Golly, maybe if the service keeps trying, it will be able to come up with another "People's Court" or "Life Styles of the Rich and Famous." The "promise" of cable seems to be taking another kick in the shins.

In the almost five decades of exploring the uses and gratifications goals of media consumers, many researchers have evolved an even larger number of categories and systems for organizing and inventorying these needs. Through distillation of their central findings, we can derive an operational list of seven admittedly overlapping use/gratification factors:

1. Entertainment/time punctuation
2. Information/surveillance

3. Escapism/nostalgia
4. Companionship/conversation-building
5. Problem solving
6. Personal enrichment and development
7. Catharsis/tension release

While probing this subject, it is necessary to keep in mind the twin qualifications that (a) listening/viewing choices may often be motivated by a combination of two or more of these elements; and (b) neither the consumer nor the critic may be able accurately to detect the core gratifications sought in and/or received from a given program or format.

It should also be understood that a uses and gratifications approach begins at an earlier stage than what is typically referred to as media effects research. In critiquing uses and gratifications, we are not primarily focusing on what radio/television does *to* its consumers but rather on what those consumers strive to do *with* radio/TV. Thus, we scrutinize the listener or viewer, in the words of British theorists Fiske and Hartley, "as an individual with certain psychological needs. He takes these needs with him to the television screen [or radio speaker], and the mass communicator attempts to gratify them."[1] For the mass communicator, the trick is in ascertaining which needs are most prevalent in the target audience being sought.

For the critic, the more complex trick is to determine what gratifications have been built into the program vehicle—specifically, how they have been executed and how they are likely to be received by consumers both intended and unintended. (Was the frank, yet informative portrayal of incest on ABC's *Something about Amelia,* for instance, aired so early in the central time zone as unnecessarily to confuse and disturb young children?) Certainly, this propels the critic into effects speculation, but such speculation is now the logical outgrowth of audience use assessment rather than of isolated assertion. As Denis McQuail maintains, "What is central for mass communication is not message-making or sending and not even the messages themselves, but the choice, reception and manner of response of the audience."[2]

Entertainment/Time Punctuation

Entertainment/time punctuation is the most obvious and most common use for which radio and television are recruited by the public, so little need be said of it here. "In American society," wrote George Comstock and colleagues, "the central use and gratification of television is entertainment. Entertainment is not only predominant in content, but the seeking of entertainment is the predominant rationale offered by the public for viewing television."[3]

A similar statement might also be made for radio, which is even more salient than its video cousin in the punctuating of time. Radio's portability and ease of intake (one is not required to sit in front of it) make it a prime vehicle for waking up to the day, marking the commute to and from work or school, and setting the stage for break time, meal time, fun time, and bed time. Radio listening choices thus divide the day into comfortable, bearable units that provide a sense of continuity over time. With its early morning magazine/talk staples, its afternoon soaps, its early and late evening newscasts, and the variety of boredom-inhibiting programs in between, television is also a time bracketer, though on a less unrelenting basis than radio.

Even though some people see this entertainment and routine-lubrication function as frivolous and unworthy of critical mention, many experts disagree. "One function of mass-communicated entertainment," observed Charles Wright, "is to provide respite for the individual which, perhaps, permits him to continue to be exposed to mass-communicated news, interpretation, and prescriptions so necessary for his survival in the modern world."[4] Even in the pre-broadcast era of the late nineteenth century, philosopher George Santayana recognized the importance of entertainment-oriented diversions when he proposed that

> we may measure the degree of happiness and civilization which any race has attained by the proportion of its energy which is devoted to free and generous pursuits, to the adornment of life and the culture of the imagination. For it is in the spontaneous play of his faculties that man finds himself and his happiness. . . . He is a slave when all his energy is spent in avoiding suffering and death, when all his action is imposed from without, and no breath or strength is left him for free enjoyment.[5]

Information/Surveillance

Our second use/gratification factor, information/surveillance, is, in Professor Wright's earlier comment, what entertainment provides a respite from. Indeed, our modern reliance on mass-mediated news has stimulated DeFleur and Ball-Rokeach's "dependency theory," which suggests that "everyone in modern urban industrialized western society is psychologically dependent to a great extent on the mass media for information which enables them to enter into full participation in society."[6] "Individuals require media-delivered information to function in modern society," add Rubin and Windahl. "The more salient the information needs, the stronger is the motivation to seek mediated information to meet these needs, the stronger the dependency on the medium, and the greater is the likelihood for the media to affect cognitions, feelings, and behavior."[7]

That television is the most sought-after medium in meeting this need was suggested by The Roper Organization's 1987 study, *Public Attitudes toward Television.* Commissioned by the broadcast industry's Television Information Office, the Roper report found:

For the first time, a majority of Americans cite *only* television as their main source of news.

For years, television has been the leading source of news, meaning that more people have cited it as a primary source of news than have cited other sources of news. Today, 66% of Americans mention television as a main news source, compared to 36% who mention newspapers, 14% who cite radio, and 4% who say magazines.

But the number of people restricting their response to television *alone* . . . has been steadily increasing—and has hit 50% for the first time. This is double the level of twenty years ago and up from 39% in 1980.[8]

Even if only partially accurate (and there are other studies that undercut these conclusions), the Roper findings, and the earlier ones leading up to them, are the focal point for a great deal of broadcast/cable criticism emanating from a variety of sources. Much of this commentary concerns itself with whether the comparative brevity of television coverage is capable of functioning as a person's prime—let alone only—world surveillance source.

Even though fewer people consider radio as a prime gratifier of the information surveillance need, those who do can turn to the all-news and more serious news/talk stations to service them. According to the 1985 "Radio Wars II" study by Reymer & Gersin Associates on behalf of the National Association of Broadcasters, 7 percent of the radio audience is made up of "Info-Maniacs"— mostly white-collar and over-thirty-five individuals who look to the medium for enlightenment, not relaxation. These loyal, discerning people listen to learn so they especially prize innovative, investigative reporting.[9]

Escapism/Nostalgia

Escapism/nostalgia, our third factor, is in many ways the antithesis of the information/surveillance need. Even though virtually all people some of the time, and a few people (info-maniacs) all of the time, seek to be informed about the events and forces in their world, there is also the contrary pressure to flee reality's troubles and data overload through escape to a divergent environment. In this case, it is not simply a need to be entertained but to withdraw. However, though "entertainment viewing motivations significantly contribute to substantial amounts of television viewing and to a felt affinity with the medium," says Alan Rubin, "escapist viewing—or using the television medium to forget about personal problems and to get away from other people or tasks—results in reduced viewing levels, and does not contribute to a sense of television affinity. . . . In short, other social activities or functional alternatives may be instrumental in gratifying escapist needs or drives."[10] Rubin's findings thus suggest that television encounters more competition in escape purveying than it does in the supplying of entertainment.

Meanwhile, on the radio front, the Reymer & Gersin study that uncovered the Info-maniacs also disclosed "Cheer-Me Escapists"—a heavily female, 25 and older audience segment who listen to a format that makes them "feel good" and, not surprisingly, are the most antinews element in the radio listening populace.[11]

Whether on radio or television, nostalgia has become a prominent escapism corollary that provides this gratification via a return to what is imagined to be a simpler, happier past. In referring to the renewed interest by audiences in the so-called "Golden Age" television programs of the fifties, former NBC and CBS programming executive Michael Dann believes that "most people look back on the Golden Age not as a reflection of TV, but as a reflection of their youth. So it's a psychological viewpoint, not a historical or critical one."[12] That these vintage, perennial, classic, or evergreen tastes are being catered to by programmers is due to a number of business as well as audience gratification reasons: the expanding number of independent television stations and basic (nonpay) cable networks in search of reasonably priced product to air; the absence of production costs for in-the-can series that have been gathering dust on studio shelves; the shrinkage of the number of available series coming off-network as fewer shows stay on the network long enough to accumulate enough episodes for viable local station scheduling; and that fact that, for today's teen viewers, these shows present a "Back-to-the-Future" escapism to a fabled music-heavy era they did not have the opportunity to experience.

On radio, this same psychological affinity for nostalgia has meshed with the market need to derive distinctive formats. What results is a wealth of new program designs ranging from big band 1930s to 1950s music to so-called rock oldies formats that draw their selections from the 1964 to 1972 era. The oldies constructs have become especially appealing to stations foundering on the AM band because their music does not require state-of-the-art stereo fidelity. In fact, for the older nostalgia-seekers who grew up in an AM-dominant world, the use of this medium deepens the escapism experience. "The nostalgia craze runs deep into every part of American life," says radio programming consultant Jeff Pollack. "Traditional values and good times are back."[13] Joe McCoy, program director for WCBS(FM) asserts that a 1960s-centered format provides the twenty-five to forty-four-year-old audience "with a lot of good memories,"[14] and Al Ham, creator of the big band *Music of Your Life* design, points out that his forty-five-plus target audience "is being rapidly discovered by the media. They make up the greater part of the viewing audience for such shows as *Murder, She Wrote, 60 Minutes,* and *The Cosby Show.*"[15]

For the critic, monitoring these escapism/nostalgia trends often goes beyond the appraisal of how well this gratification is served by a given media product to a delineation of the possible meanings and dangers these trends signal. Literary critic Carl Grabo once cautioned that "in some literature the real and the imagined worlds are confused and the reader cannot separate the false and the true . . . escape purports to be, or is mistaken by its readers to be, an honest picture of life."[16] In speaking of an equally romanticized, yet more classic golden age than the one to which Michael Dann earlier alluded, Grabo adds the broadcast-relevant admonition:

> In our nostalgia for a better world, a world of justice and goodness, we grasp at the enchanted picture of life as it never was except in the fabled Golden Age, which is no more than our vision of the future given the fixity and immortality of the past. . . . If the past is made to seem better than it was, we are encouraged to turn our backs to the future and desire what is impossible, a return to some state of the past, whether real or imagined. This is true escapism, the living in the past; whereas, it is our greatest, our imperative duty, to live in the present and the future and, by wrestling with the evils which we know, make the future better than the past. By living in and believing in a false past we retard the evolution of life.[17]

Or, as television football commentator Don Meredith once less elegantly said on the air: "Things ain't like they used to be and never was."

Companionship/Conversation Building

Companionship/conversation building, our fourth gratification factor, is partially linked to escapism/nostalgia. This affinity is most graphically illustrated in what is called retro TV—the updating of ten- or twenty-year-old television series rather than simply reairing the original episodes. The aim here is to serve simultaneously some viewers' wish to escape with the same or other viewers' felt need for companionship. "These shows' characters have become part of our lives; they're old friends," comments NBC Senior Vice-President Steve White. "In some ways these familiar characters have become bigger today than ever before."[18] Professor Christopher Geist further reveals: "We all grew up letting our favorite TV characters into our living rooms every week. There's a real bond that's developed between these shows and viewers. So it's only natural that we want to see them again twenty years later. We want to check in with them and make sure the characters are turning out all right."[19]

Whether it's "The Beaver" who has now come of age (but remains consistently immature) or the newest character in a contemporary prime-time hit, a radio/television-generated companion can serve an important listener or viewer need. As Professor Mark Levy discovered:

> Although the audience cannot communicate directly with the mass media performers, viewers are still said to interact with the personae. Audiences are thought to [in the words of Donald Horton and R. Richard Wohl] "benefit from the persona's wisdom, reflect on his advice, sympathize with him in his difficulties, forgive his mistakes." For most members of the audience, para-social interaction is considered complementary to social communication. However, for people with few or weak social ties, para-social interaction may offer a functional alternative for inadequate interaction opportunities.[20]

Television's simulated (parasocial) companions thus have the potential for doing good or ill depending on whether these companions facilitate or inhibit viewers' real life interactions with people in their homes, neighborhoods, and places of employment.

This is why we link the companionship gratification with that of conversation building since a positive outgrowth of exposure to media acquaintances is that such exposure gives us the material (and perhaps the methodological models) for communicating more easily with those around us. We can discuss Johnny Carson's monologue and even reflect on his mannerisms, for example, as a way of facilitating casual conversation with an acquaintance. Similarly, we can fume about J. R. Ewing's latest *Dallas* double-dealing or console each other on the fifth successive violence to befall our favorite soap opera heroine. All of these activities efficiently lubricate our interpersonal socialization. If, however, we ourselves begin to behave like J. R. or inflict the soap-opera-depicted violence toward the people around us, our media companionship experience becomes counterproductive and a source of concern to PTAs and congressional committees.

"Television is a personality medium," argues NBC programming chief Brandon Tartikoff. "Viewers relate to the performers in their favorite TV shows as surrogate friends."[21] On the other hand, "The danger television presents to the lonely," warns author Louise Bernikow, "is that it can keep them passive, reducing whatever stirring they might have to bring more people into their lives or to deepen the connections they do have."[22]

On radio, it is the talk format that most unequivocally pursues companionship fulfillment. As former ABC Radio president and talk format developer Ben Hoberman describes it:

> Talk listening is foreground listening. You have to really listen and become engaged in the conversation. Talk is also personal. In fact, talk is the most intimate of all formats. People reveal their deepest problems and concerns on the air. In a sense, talk radio has become a communal backyard fence over which we chat with our neighbors, share experiences, ask for advice and express our opinions.[23]

The fact that such a powerful audience gratifier was, as late as 1986, programmed by only about 9 percent of AM and less than .5 percent of FM stations is explained by its negative attributes as a business gratifier. "Talk may be cheap," admits Hoberman, "but talk radio isn't:"

> You need to invest in good talent and programs. It takes years to become a skilled talk radio host, and general managers must be willing to nurture new personalities. In today's volatile market, success or failure is measured by each Arbitron book. Stations are looking for the quick turnaround, the hot format that can give them a surge in the ratings. Talk does not provide a quick fix. . . . In today's "merger media" marketplace, many owners don't have the leeway of years. They must increase earnings in a very short time. Talk as a format does not offer the speedy relief they need.[24]

Fortunately for radio, and the companionship/conversation-building gratification, other formats at least partially cater to this same audience need. The aforementioned Reymer & Gersin "Radio Wars II" study, for example, found that the 14 percent of the radio audience to which they referred as "Friend Seekers" and the 22 percent labeled "Social Followers" turned to several types of stations to meet their companionship requirements. The mostly thirty-five and older white and white-collar "Friend Seekers" find these friends primarily on talk and MOR (middle-of-the-road)/full service stations but can also be satisfied by adult contemporary, easy listening, and country facilities if the music played matches their taste and on-air personalities are allowed to take a significant role in the format's execution. With two-thirds of them between the ages of twelve and thirty-four, the younger "Social Followers" are heavy listeners who think of radio as a way of belonging to the crowd and adding to the fun (conversation building) they have with friends. Album rock and contemporary hit radio thus figure prominently in "Social Followers" preferences along with, in the case of minority group youth, urban contemporary formats.

The quest for substitute companionship and associated social lubrication, through whatever means, has been a human behavior pattern that far predates the electronic media. Radio/television do not have the monopoly on vehicles for satisfying this gratification nor should they be blamed as the instigators of certain individuals' real-life avoidance of other human beings. What DeWitt Parker wrote about prose fiction in 1920 could, in fact, also be said of broadcast/cable in 1990:

> We read because we are lonely or because our fellow men have become trite and fail to stimulate us sufficiently. If our fellows were not so reticent, if they would talk to us and tell us their stories with the freedom and the brightness of a [Robert Louis] Stevenson, or if their lives were so fresh and vivid that we never found them dull, perhaps we should not read at all. But, as it is, we can satisfy our craving for knowledge of life only by extending our social world through fiction. Fiction may teach us, edify us, make us better men—it may serve all these purposes incidently, but its prime purpose as art is to provide us with new objects for social feeling and knowledge.[25]

Because its moving audio-visual image is, at least initially, more lifelike than the static medium of print, television may not need to possess the expansive stimulation that Parker seems to require from static prose. Gilbert Seldes recognized the more informal nature of TV's companionship when he observed:

> For millions of people television has the same quality as a conversation with friends, almost the same quality as the mere presence of members of the family who needn't do anything exciting or unusual, so long as they are in the house, but who would be sorely missed if they departed.[26]

Problem Solving

Problem solving, the fifth gratification for which people turn to broadcasting and cable, is most overtly catered to by commercials, public service announcements (PSAs), and program promotional materials (promos). Commercials typically unveil a difficulty or lack that, they argue, can best be met by the product or service being advertised. PSAs sensitize us to social or personal needs and their suggested solutions, and promos help us resolve the question of what to watch or listen to tonight, tomorrow, or next week. In the following sixty-second television script for Wisconsin Telephone, for instance, the man's continuing failure to communicate without Call Waiting is contrasted with the woman's success through the advocated service's employment.

VIDEO	AUDIO	
ANXIOUS MIDDLE-AGED MAN DIALING AT FREESTANDING PAY PHONE IN AIRPORT. ALL OTHER PHONES OCCUPIED.	ANXIOUS MAN:	I hope it's not still busy.
	VO:	Right now, for only pennies a day, you can end the frustration of calling home and hearing ---
	(SFX:	Buzz. Buzz. Buzz.)
	(SFX:	Hangs up.)
TO WOMAN STANDING BEHIND HIM.	ANXIOUS MAN:	Always busy.
WOMAN PICKS UP PHONE, DIALS SUPER: "Available in most areas."	WOMAN:	Oughta get Call Waiting, you get through even if somebody's on the phone.
CUT TO TEEN ON PHONE.	GIRL:	Sure. Read it all. (SFX: Beep.) Oh. Can you hold on a sec? I've got a call waiting.
PRESSES RECEIVER BUTTON. PRESSES BUTTON AGAIN.		Hello? Mom? I'm on my way. Listen, I gotta go. I'll call you back.
CUT TO WOMAN HANGING UP WITH ANXIOUS MAN PACING. MAN GRABS PHONE. SPEEDED UP CAMERA SHOWS MAN DIALING, HANGING UP OVER AND OVER AGAIN. SUPER 800#. ADD SUPER OF "$2.50 PER MONTH, PLUS SMALL ONE-TIME ORDER CHARGE."	WOMAN:	(SFX: HANG UP.) All yours.
	VO:	Order Call Waiting from Wisconsin Telephone now. Dial tollfree 1 800 242–7211. It's only $2.50 a month and there's no service visit to your home. With Call Waiting, there's no fear of missing calls. You can even switch between callers. It's almost like having a second line.

VIDEO	AUDIO	
ANXIOUS MAN HOLDS BUZZING PHONE AND HAS GLAZED EXPRESSION.	(SFX:	Buzz. Buzz. Buzz.)
	ANXIOUS MAN:	I gotta get Call Waiting.
CAMERA STAYS ON MAN HOLDING BUZZING PHONE. 800# IS SUPERED.	VO:	To get Call Waiting, dial 1 800 242-7211. 1 800 242-7211.

(Courtesy of Alan Fonorow, Cramer-Krasselt/Direct)

In the same manner, this thirty-second radio PSA for the American Red Cross shows one graphic social need already being met while raising a financial support question that only the listener's donation seemingly can answer.

(SFX:	RUBBLE FALLING)
RESCUE WORKER:	Can you hear me?
TRAPPED GIRL:	Yes --- everything fell on me.
WORKER:	Okay, don't worry, we're going to help you.
GIRL:	I'm scared.
ANNCR:	We hear you. We're the American Red Cross. We help train rescue workers. Provide medical attention, food and shelter. And work to get people's lives back to normal. Last year, millions of people needed our help. Desperately. Now we need yours.
GIRL:	Please hurry ---
ANNCR:	The American Red Cross.

(Courtesy of Pam Freeman, The Advertising Council, Inc.)

Only slightly less obviously, radio and television programs also serve as audience problem-solvers. Local newscasts and news magazine features now include tips on nutrition, money managing, cooking, child-rearing, vegetable purchasing, and a host of other consumer-help topics. Entire cable services devote themselves to financial matters, weather information, and health care. Even the seemingly fictionally derived network and syndicated series can provide some assistance. By frequenting a doctor, lawyer, or socially relevant comedy/drama show, "we turn our personal and social problems over to the characters who can solve them magically," remarks Horace Newcomb, "in the space of an enclosed hour. . . . Doubtless, one reason for the popularity of these successful series is the way in which they deal with contemporary problems in a self-conscious manner. . . . Always the problems are solved. In most cases they are solved by the heroic qualities of the central characters."[27]

In a sense, Americans often use radio/television the way the natives of the African nation of Zimbabwe use music: to call up and ask advice of ancestors and other spirits who would never appear without the medium's assistance. The problem-solving art of the electronic media thus functions like art in general in which, according to Melvin Rader and Bertram Jessup, "Our very defeats in 'real life' become our triumphs in the life of art. Esthetically, we become masters of our troubles, our frustrations, our defeats—by becoming interested in them, by making them into works of art instead of merely suffering them."[28]

Personal Enrichment and Development

The sixth gratification construct, personal enrichment and development, comes the closest to the old British Broadcasting Corporation and National Educational Television ideal of using the electronic media to uplift public and personal taste. Unfortunately, not every member of the listening and viewing audience is willing to be enriched or developed—especially via media that are seen as recreational rather than instructional. In this connection, sociologist Herbert Gans has divided American society into five "taste publics" that exhibit varying preference for (or tolerance of) the enrichment process in their mass media content:[29]

1. *High Culture:* the serious and even avant-garde writers, artists, composers, and critics.
2. *Upper-Middle Culture:* the better educated and generally affluent professional and managerial class and their families who are the prime consumers, but not the creators, of art.
3. *Lower-Middle Culture:* the largest taste public, made up of white-collar workers and possessing at least some postsecondary collegiate or technical education.
4. *Low Culture:* blue-collar skilled and semi-skilled workers; a taste public that constituted the most numerous group in the 1950s but is constricting as these families send their children to college and as the number of industrial/manufacturing jobs decreases.
5. *Quasi-Folk Low Culture:* the very poor and undereducated with limited job skills and uncertain economic futures who inhabit depressed rural areas as well as big-city ghettoes.

In terms of the gratifications they seek from the electronic media, the Low and Quasi-Folk Low Cultures search for entertainment and especially for escapism. Unfortunately for them, however, the Quasi-Folk group lacks the financial resources to be appealing to, and the educational level to be reachable by, most mass marketers. Thus, there is a comparative paucity of programming that takes their interests and attitudes into consideration.

The High and Upper-Middle Cultures, in contrast, perceive their media use choices to be motivated by a quest for the personal enrichment and development gratification. Even though the two groups may, in fact, be entertained by the public broadcasting, documentary, and public affairs programs they seek out, they perceive these more as enrichment activities. Specialty cable services, news, and classical/jazz radio formats, and specially marketed VCR cassettes can economically reach them, but tonnage or near-tonnage delivery systems cannot afford to cater to their rarefied tastes. In fact, the high culture group is so small and sophisticated that the radio/television industry can seldom afford to offer anything at all for them and is usually rebuffed when it tries.

Finally, the ever-enlarging Lower-Middle Culture uses broadcast/cable for both entertainment/escape and enrichment/development purposes. Programming that can touch these two bases at once, consequently, offers special incentives to this taste public as well as to the advertisers and programmers attempting to shorten the odds of reaching them. More than any other genre, the so-called event program is designed to fill this niche with the mini-series accorded special viability. This multipart packaging of a best-selling novel (*Roots, The Winds of War, The Thorn Birds*), famous personage (*Napoleon and Josephine: A Love Story, Peter the Great, Mussolini: The Untold Story*), or historical epic (*How the West Was Won, Holocaust, North and South*) already has at least an assumed familiarity going for it and holds out a self-improvement excuse for indulging in several nights of recreative viewing. If the execution is bungled due to a ponderous script, leaden acting, or mishandled scheduling as to nights or starting times, the project may not be a hit. Still, if well promoted, it starts with a greater chance for success than does conventional programming because the mini-series takes on the role of event in breaking its viewers' mundane routine. Unlike regular entertainment offerings, it does not merely punctuate time but promises a more significant—even enriching—use of it.

There is another program genre that can motivate personal enrichment and development across even a wider public spectrum than that targeted by the mini-series or other carefully promoted event. Unfortunately for the business gratification aspirations of electronic media executives, this programming cannot be pre-planned but is the result of the coverage of a sudden natural, political, or technological disaster. As Louise Bernikow reflects:

> Whenever cataclysmic events have befallen us—the Kennedy assassinations or the shuttle disaster—television has brought us together. On such occasions, it matters less what is being said than that we are all participating, sharing the grief and horror of the Nation. Watching serious coverage on television addresses the need to gather at the river; it is the modern version of an ancient ritual.[30]

This gathering is more than just mediated companionship. It has the potential to develop and enrich our communal sensitivities to a degree not usually attainable through the hurried passages of contemporary existence. It is personal development in its keenest electronic refinement.

Catharsis/Tension Release

Catharsis/tension release, our seventh and final audience gratification, is also the most controversial. When many theorists and critics use the term *catharsis,* they are referring to a highly problematic theory about violence on the media; this theory maintains that radio/television violence is beneficial because its simulated media experiencing relieves people of the tension that would otherwise cause them to perpetrate actual violence. By indirect participation in the electronic assault, asserts this vicarious catharsis theory, the impetus toward direct imitation of real-life violence can be blunted. As professors Copeland and Slater focus it, "This perspective suggests that the desire or need to exhibit aggressive or hostile behaviors is reduced by a release of those desires through vicarious participation."[31]

Yet, as these same two researchers point out, the concept of catharsis can and should be seen in a broader context than the emotion-polluted question of whether media-depicted aggression stimulates or sublimates actual violence:

> Catharsis is a paradigm too often rejected because of a prevalent "common sense" opinion that mediated violence must have some negative impact on viewers. A reformulation of the catharsis paradigm to include levels of fantasy ability, the type of mediated message which best triggers fantasies, and the content of the fantasies evoked could provide a resurgence of interest in catharsis as an effect of viewing mediated violence.[32]

A gratifications orientation poses a yet thornier set of questions: Do people (especially those Copeland and Slater label "high fantasizers") actively seek out aggression-depicting programs and do so because they want to behave less aggressively themselves? Or do they methodically choose these programs because they feel the desire to interact more aggressively? Still more troubling: Would listeners or viewers select prosocially designed programs because they wish to show more compassion toward other people or because they want to reduce their felt need to engage in compassionate conduct?

Clearly, even partial receptivity to the principle of media-induced catharsis as a source of gratification brings the critic face-to-face with an unavoidable acceptance of our natural human frailty. "Art," professes DeWitt Parker, "provides a medium through which the more animal side of our nature may receive imaginative satisfaction."[33]

Aristotle, who first broached the subject of catharsis in his *Poetics,* saw it as a dramatic blending of fear and pity. This was not, as Comstock and col-

leagues point out, pity in the altruistic sense. Instead, Aristotle's pity-engender-
ing catharsis "seems to be nothing more than a fear that has been evoked by
a sense of what today might be called 'identification' or 'empathy with an observed victim'; emotionally it involves caring about oneself much more than it
involves caring about the observed victim."[34] In other words, the "better him
than me" reaction that we are likely to feel in response to a real tragedy in a
newscast or a dramatized one in a scripted series is a human tension-reliever
that has been recognized for more than two thousand years.

The more perceptive radio/television critics have recognized that this fundamental attribute of audience psychology is a particularly important component of certain program types even though the producers of these shows are
seldom functionally aware of catharsis's power or presence. Thus, in speaking
of what she labeled the "savior" (cop, detective, doctor, rescue team) shows,
Rose Goldsen argues that

> the watching nation is nightly asked to share vicariously the attitudes toward death
> and suffering characteristic of professionals who deal with them daily. Profession-
> als must learn to distance their own feeling from sympathy and empathy with the
> agonies endured by sufferers. It's a way of insulating themselves from what would
> otherwise be unbearable emotion if they allowed themselves to feel in an "unpro-
> fessional" way. The watching nation, now, is invited to pick up the same [tension-
> relieving] attitudes of distanced uninvolvement.[35]

Ron Powers cites an even more specific example of this dynamic in referring
to *ABC Monday Night Football*'s initiation while the war in Vietnam raged:

> In the chaotic, inverted reckoning of those times, *ABC Monday Night Football* of-
> fered a benevolent vision of the possible; it offered a game played against chaos
> and death, against entropy. It offered a kind of 'reality' without the consequences
> of reality. It intensified the passions of mythic conflict, but it withheld the horror
> and guilt of America's exposure to living-room war: the images of torn bodies, the
> grief over slain, wasted heroes.[36]

A high-minded critic might charge that catering to the catharsis
gratification, in whatever permutation, is unconscionable because it desensi-
tizes us. This critic might further argue that broadcast violence especially
should be excised. That such a prescription is unfeasible given American business and audience gratification patterns was long ago recognized by Robert
Lewis Shayon, when he observed:

> We fear violence and enjoy it with guilt, because it calls to our own deeply latent
> potential for violence in response to a violent world. With such a sure-fire, instant
> crowd-catcher providing the essential energy which runs our industries, our net-
> works, our advertising agencies—in short, our style of life—to call for the voluntary
> or involuntary regulation of violence on TV is to call for instant self-destruction of
> the system. By "system," I mean TV based on advertiser support. Television can

run on a different system, of course. . . . But to choose another system is to opt for another style of life, one where corporate and consumer acquisitions are not the dominant values.[37]

We examine these and other values more closely in the following chapter.

Notes

1. John Fiske and John Hartley, *Reading Television* (London: Methuen & Company, 1978), 71.
2. Denis McQuail, "With the Benefit of Hindsight: Reflections on Uses and Gratifications Research," *Critical Studies in Mass Communication* (June 1984): 183.
3. George Comstock *et al., Television and Human Behavior* (New York: Columbia University Press, 1978), 11.
4. Charles Wright, "Functional Analysis and Mass Communication," in Lewis Dexter and David White, eds. *People, Society, and Mass Communications* (New York: The Free Press, 1964), 108.
5. George Santayana, *The Sense of Beauty* (1896) reprinted in Melvin Rader, ed., *A Modern Book of Esthetics,* 5th ed. (New York: Holt, Rinehart and Winston, 1979), 168.
6. Fiske and Hartley, *Reading Television,* 73.
7. Alan Rubin and Sven Windahl, "The Uses and Dependency Model of Mass Communication," *Critical Studies in Mass Communication* (June 1986): 185.
8. *America's Watching: Public Attitudes toward Television* (New York: Television Information Office, 1987), 4.
9. Mark Kassof, "Radio Wars II: How to Push Listeners' Hot Buttons." Speech presented at the National Association of Broadcasters, 13 April 1985, at Las Vegas, Nev.
10. Alan Rubin, "Television Uses and Gratifications: The Interactions of Viewing Patterns and Motivations," *Journal of Broadcasting* (Winter 1983): 49–50.
11. Mark Kassof, "Radio Wars II."
12. Michael Dann, "The '50s 'Golden Age'? Today's TV Is Better," *TV Guide* (May 19, 1984): 10.
13. "Everything Old Is New Again in Radio," *Broadcasting* (July 28, 1986): 56.
14. Ibid., 56–57.
15. Ibid., 64.
16. Carl Grabo, *The Creative Critic* (Chicago: University of Chicago Press, 1948), 108.
17. Ibid., 109.
18. Noreen O'Leary, "Networks Get into the Retro Act," *Adweek* (March 18, 1986): 20.
19. Ibid.
20. Mark Levy, "Watching TV News as Para-Social Interaction," *Journal of Broadcasting* (Winter 1979): 69–70.
21. Brandon Tartikoff, "Confessions of a Network Programmer," *TV Guide* (September 7, 1985): 4.
22. Louise Bernikow, "Is TV a Pal—or a Danger for Lonely People?", *TV Guide* (October 25, 1986): 5.
23. Ben Hoberman, "Take Another Listen to Talk Radio," *Broadcasting* (February 24, 1986): 20.
24. Ibid.

25. DeWitt Parker, *The Principles of Aesthetics,* 2nd ed. (Westport, Conn.: Greenwood Press, 1976), 189–90.
26. Gilbert Seldes, *The Public Arts* (New York: Simon and Schuster, 1956), 102.
27. Horace Newcomb, *TV: The Most Popular Art* (Garden City, N.Y.: Anchor Books, 1974), 260.
28. Melvin Rader and Bertram Jessup, "Art in an Age of Science and Technology," in Rader, *Esthetics,* 499.
29. Summarized from Herbert Gans, *Popular Culture and High Culture* (New York: Basic Books, 1974), 69–94.
30. Bernikow, "TV a Pal?" 6.
31. Gary Copeland and Dan Slater, "Television, Fantasy and Vicarious Catharsis," *Critical Studies in Mass Communication* (December 1985): 352.
32. Ibid., 359.
33. DeWitt Parker, *The Analysis of Art* (New Haven: Yale University Press, 1926), 108.
34. Comstock *et. al., Television,* 424.
35. Rose Goldsen, *The Show and Tell Machine* (New York: The Dial Press, 1977), 225.
36. Ron Powers, *Supertube* (New York: Coward-McCann, 1984), 185.
37. Robert Lewis Shayon, *Open to Criticism* (Boston: Beacon Press, 1971), 239–40.

Probing Ethics and Values

For any critic and, for that matter, for any broadcaster or cablecaster, the matter of ethics and values is fraught with perils. It is not a question of the critic or mass communicator being spineless, for courage is as randomly distributed among these vocations as it is among most others. Courage or conviction is not enough, however, in a situation in which one must balance professional standards with the multiplicity of real or imagined standards subscribed to by the public that the programmer or reviewer is charged with serving. How far can one go in presenting programs or positions reflective of one's own value system before members of the public feel that these values are being imposed on them? Conversely, how long can one skirt value-laden issues before being accused of being a shameless libertine, spineless coward, or godless communist? Like it or not, electronic communicators and electronic critics have a mandate to, in turn, serve and guide the populace with respect to media instruments that are, like the public schools, felt to be the property of all. And as in the case of those schools, everyone assumes special prescience as to how they should be postured and from what they must be protected.

Ethics and Values Defined

People decide how the world should operate based on their own internalized conceptions of right and wrong, good and bad, or desirable and undesirable. In very dogmatic individuals, these conceptions can be highly systematized, explicit, and unyielding. For most of us, however, they are quite disorganized and implicit, jumbled together in our minds and behavior patterns like the

131

treasured but randomly gathered keepsakes piled lovingly but haphazardly in our bottom bureau drawer. Such standards may owe as much to Disney as they do to the deity, issue as much from incidental life experiences as from formal parental or institutional instruction. Nonetheless, for all their seeming inadvertence, these appraising "goggles" (as Marshall McLuhan labeled them), formulate our vision of life and also our expectations for how other people should view it.

However assembled, ethics constitute the conduct criteria each of us uses to govern action and belief. Values, in turn, are the translation of these criteria into a system for determining and ranking things as worthy or unworthy of esteem and desire. If we embrace honesty as a prime ethical goal, for example, we are likely to value objects possessing homely authenticity over those that emphasize comely contrivance.

Some theorists, like George Santayana, subdivide this value into two constituent parts: moral and aesthetic. "Moral values are generally negative, and always remote," he maintains. "Morality has to do with the avoidance of evil and the pursuit of good: esthetics only with enjoyment."[1] This definition, of course, raises the possibilities that aesthetic value can exist independently of ethical concerns and that the comprehension of beauty is therefore amoral, or outside the scope of ethical consideration.

For the radio/television critic, this viewpoint is more a theoretical curiosity than a practical consideration, however, because the immensely public nature of the electronic media and his or her critiquing of it make it unacceptable to discuss enjoyment while totally ignoring ethical benchmarks. A reviewer could try to argue that the soft porn amateur video shown on a cable access channel possesses real beauty, but in so doing, that reviewer would probably lose essential credibility with the mainstream public whose patronage pays his or her salary. True, a critic writing for a *Hustler*-type magazine may not care about the mainstream, but by ignoring mainstream concerns, that critic forgoes the chance to be broadly influential. As Northrop Frye affirms:

> No discussion of beauty can confine itself to the formal relations of the isolated work of art; it must consider, too, the participation of the work of art in the vision of the goal of social effort; the idea of complete and classless civilization. This idea of complete civilization is also the implicit moral standard to which ethical criticism always refers, something very different from any system of morals. . . . The goal of ethical criticism is transvaluation, the ability to look at contemporary social values with the detachment of one who is able to compare them in some degree with the infinite vision of possibilities presented by culture.[2]

In short, a critic's purview, especially in terms of the highly public media of radio and television, need not embrace any one moral system but should be capable of encompassing all moral systems. A reputable critique cannot, according to Frye, ignore cultural morality any more than it should attempt to dictate any single moral perspective. One can detach oneself from social (moral) values, but one cannot disregard them and still meet the human-relevant requisites of reasonable criticism. This is because, as Eliseo Vivas pointed out:

> Man, among the other things which make him unique, is a culture building animal. And he has never been known to create a culture which did not include a more or less well defined hierarchy of values: dramatic conceptions about himself and about the nature on which he depends to survive, and animistic conceptions of the forces which define and control his destiny.[3]

That this dynamic is an essential ingredient of television (and presumably, of the more narrative elements of radio) was evidenced some twenty years ago in the observations of Sprague Vonier, then manager of WTMJ–TV, Milwaukee. Since Vonier's comments are those of a media businessman rather than an aesthetics scholar, they acquire special significance for the shaping of broadcast/cable criticism:

> In the very act of telling stories, the television industry is conveying a set of values to the audience. In certain instances, the story would not and could not exist except for the cultural values implied in its telling.
>
> Example: a recent episode of "Twilight Zone," now in world wide distribution, is set in some imaginary future society ruled by a benevolent but tyrannical government. The story concerns a young woman who resists being made over into an "ideal person" (pretty as a cover girl, perfectly adjusted, mindlessly happy). When the young woman loses her battle, the audience understands that a crime has been committed, the destruction of one human being's divine individuality by society. Even though the young woman apparently has been made more attractive and happier, the power of society has been wrongly used, the story seems to say. Clearly, a set of values was at work, both in the men who made the program and most of the audience for which it was made. Without those values, the story could not have existed.[4]

It must be recognized, however, that electronic media programmers seldom if ever set out with the prime goal of promoting a general ethic or specific value to the populace. In most cases, as the Chapter 6 business gratification discussion suggests, they are simply trying to construct a story that will deliver audience and, as in Vonier's illustration, the clash of values is a very appealing plot device. Sometimes, producers even seem unaware of the salience of an implicit values orientation until they are met with a raft of objections from a special interest group or a network standards and practices department. As *Chicago Tribune* critic Steve Daley describes in the following commentary, even programs that, in hindsight, are considered as values groundbreakers are usually the products not of media "visionaries," but of "gamblers and risk-takers" who, in search of mere time period competitiveness, coincidentally strike a massively successful response chord.

'ROOTS' ENTRENCHED IN TELEVISION'S SOUL
by Steve Daley

There are a few moments in television when you can see the wave break, when the medium rides a crest and demonstrates its power in a positive way, rather than the usual negative or simply brain-deadening manner.

It is easy to overstate the importance and impact of "Roots," the ABC mini-series that arrived 10 years ago this week and grabbed a nation by its throat.

It is just as easy to dismiss the mini-series out of hand, just as easy to point to the chronic complaints of job-seeking black actors and producers and, more importantly, to the grim racial reality of Howard Beach and Forsyth County, Ga. But the impact of Alex Haley's search for identity, history and dignity endures, in as vivid a way as this vaporous medium is capable.

When "Roots" began, on Jan. 23, 1977, with the sighting of a rather antiseptic Mandinga village in West Africa, the scope of ABC's gamble was evident. Advertising spots had been offered at bargain rates, and the decision to funnel 12 hours of programming into eight nights was a measure of the network's uncertainty.

The feeling at ABC was that if the show aired in a week's time and collapsed, the network would have forfeited just a week, and could move on, its grand experiment behind it.

As often happens in television, no one was more surprised by the success of the project than its architects. The figure most often quoted in discussing the "Roots" phenomenon was 80 million viewers. On its eighth and final night, the show collected what was then the largest TV audience in history.

In Chicago, A. C. Nielsen figures showed that "Roots" was being watched by more than three million viewers. The City Colleges of Chicago offered academic credit for tuning in to the 12 hours of ABC's video epic, a considerable number of babies were named "Kunta" during that week, and in a grocery store on E. 71st Street, a 21-year-old man, outraged by the depiction of slavery in the mini-series, was charged with stabbing two whites.

When the series was rebroadcast in September, 1978, it was again a ratings winner, as it had been in Britain, South Africa and a number of other countries. "Roots" earned 37 Emmy nominations, and the 1979 sequel, "Roots: The Next Generation," reached the top of the Nielsen ladder.

News stories during the last week of January, 1977, recount the groundswell of fascination and emotion in the nation's black communities, and in white America as well. Most of the stories register shock, pride and anger, an acknowledgement that even made-for-TV history could confront us with how little we know.

Start with the title: The term "roots" fell into the American language 10 years ago, and not solely for black people. In one of the strangest twists in reaction to the generational saga of Kunta Kinte, "Roots" inspired a revival of interest in white and Hispanic families, in the tracing of family lineage and genealogies.

"Roots" succeeded in humanizing the victims of American slavery, not only for white people but, it's clear from the public reaction, for millions of black people as well. This curious but compelling mix of fact and fiction set a major theme in American history into a context, into a way of seeing and understanding the past.

Consider the television context of "Roots." Twenty years earlier, in 1957, a considerable number of TV stations in the South refused to air a network variety show with singer Nat "King" Cole as the host. In the late 1960s, a number of public television stations in the South chose not to air "Sesame Street" because of the racially integrated cast.

In 1965, on NBC's "I Spy," Bill Cosby became the first black performer to have a starring, if supportive, role in a regular dramatic TV series. In the fall of 1968, Diahann Carroll became the first black woman to star in her own TV series, "Julia." But, in 1973, a syndicated series featuring black actress Barbara McNair was pulled when Southern markets dried up.

As television, "Roots" persuaded network programmers that there was more to be done with black people than present them as domestics, as Beulah and Rochester, comic adjutants to white favorites.

The persuasion was in no way a bolt of lightning, of course. The story of Bill Cosby's attempt to peddle his black-family sitcom to the networks in the days before it became the biggest hit in prime-time history is part of television's sorry lore.

The creators of "Roots," producers like David Wolper and Fred Silverman, were not visionaries; they were gamblers and risk-takers. That is the most, and the best we can expect.

Certainly it would be naive to argue that "Roots" changed American society, or even changed television. Our attention spans have been truncated by the same medium that gave us "Roots," and that reality makes the fading of any TV phenomenon inevitable. But, as we cannot ignore television, we cannot ignore one week 10 years ago when the medium touched us, and moved us, and altered our perception.

(Courtesy of F. Richard Ciccone, *Chicago Tribune*)

What Critics Value

It is clear from his commentary that Steve Daley values a program that takes a gamble, especially one taking a risk that furthers the cause of human dignity and equality. As we alluded to in Chapter 4, all critics, being human, bring some type of values orientation, structured or unstructured, to the comprehension, ascertainment, and judgment activities of which all legitimate criticism must be comprised. In the interest of keeping the critiquing process candid and open, however, it is vital that (1) critics recognize these ethical and values structures in themselves as well as being aware of their presence in a given piece; and (2) consumers are assisted, through the critic's own clear expression, in detecting that critic's particular set of "goggles" so these can be taken into consideration in determining the worth and relevance of each evaluative pronouncement. Thus, Professor Robert Smith reminds us that

> critics, like other persons, may wear blinders, which may be ideological (Marxism or conservatism), psychological (a preference for certain kinds of concerns), or expedient (a desire to get by-lines and be quoted). These private commitments of critics may give depth to their writing or may limit their vision.[5]

As far back as 1959, in his landmark analysis of broadcast criticism, Ralph Smith found that practicing critics collectively reflected six value clusters in their output.[6] Specifically, critics prized:

1. Honesty/sincerity in terms of the work's purpose and execution
2. Program variety

3. Maintenance of human dignity
4. Excellence (diligence) in writing and production
5. Relaxation and informality
6. Strong sense of responsibility

Additional elements may have joined the list in the intervening decades, but there is little reason to believe that these same half-dozen criteria are not similarly esteemed by today's critics.

In terms of *honesty*, for example, it is not unreasonable to expect a commercial to be packaged as a commercial and not disguised like program content as it is in the so-called integrated approach. It is likewise not unreasonable to demand, as have critics, children's protection groups, and not a few media professionals, that a character in a kid-appeal show refrain from suddenly shifting into the role of product pitchman. (In TV's so-called Golden Age, *Howdy Doody*'s adult foil, Buffalo Bob, did this all the time, but that did not make it right in many people's ethical assessment).

Turning to programs, the docudrama (drama/fiction based on fact) raises special honesty issues. Even though it takes its inspiration from the people and events of history, it is not itself history but a fictional packaging that can distort reality and harm reputations when the audience perceives it as literal truth. Whether the misinterpretation is unanticipated or encouraged by the docudrama's producer is not important. What matters is that a deception has taken place, the same sort of deception that occurs when sloppy newsroom editing makes an interview subject's position seem substantially different from, if not the complete opposite of, what he or she actually stated.

Notice how, in the following docudrama review, *Variety* critic Tony Scott, in the short-hand style typical of that trade publication, takes special care to evaluate the subject program's historical accuracy as well as its dramatic impact.

LBJ: THE EARLY YEARS
by Tony Scott

Writer Ken Trevey, sifting through thousands of pages, facts, opinions and considerations, has come up with a robust, admiring view of the often-lamented, certainly neglected Lyndon B. Johnson. Helped by an extraordinary performance by Randy Quaid, "LBJ: The Early Years" is, if not 100% official history, surefire entertainment.

Scripter Trevey shrewdly dovetails events, telescopes LBJ's life, combines characters, soft-pedals several less-than-admirable traits; on the other hand, Trevey develops his teleplay with admirable attention to his central figure, a driven man whose commitment was formidable, whose faults were gigantic.

Teleplay's construction, purposefully choosing events and people, leaps forward with dramatic impetus. Trevey, insisting there's as much vigor along the Pedernales as in Camelot, builds his case well.

Hiking back to 1934 when LBJ was secretary to Texas congressman Richard Kleberg, telefilm strides purposely toward 1963. Harking back to the rambunctious courting of Lady Bird Taylor and keeping an eye on how much he worked in harness with fellow Texan Sam Rayburn, "LBJ" never forgets it deals with a Texan.

A leap from the late 1930s to 1948, overlooking World War II, Johnson's participation and FDR's death, seems at first glance an uncomfortable oversight. But selective biography has to spotlight the formative events; "LBJ" does that with style.

The painful Kennedy period has its moments of humor—Bobby Kennedy deer-hunting at the LBJ ranch—but the boomerang: Sitting as Vice President outside JFK's office, LBJ suffers humiliation while he struggles with his pride. For once the Johnson p.o.v. of the Kennedy brothers appears in another light.

LBJ here is plain-spoken, resourceful, quick-thinking, crude, ambitious, dictatorial, dedicated, hot-tempered, exuberant and determined—and, above all, a politician.

Quaid not only resembles him—not so much early on, when Johnson was lankier, thinner than Quaid—he inhabits the man. Peripheral characters in the drama, like Henry Wallace, Humphrey and Eastland, don't look or act like the real McCoy; Quaid's Johnson does.

Though visually off-putting, Patti LuPone's Lady Bird has a soft, becoming nature complementing Quaid's burly Johnson. James F. Kelly's Bobby Kennedy is a sharp, illuminating interpretation, and Charles Frank acts a standard model JFK with flashes of the genuine.

The 1960 Democratic convention rivalry has been built up between JFK and LBJ with surprising suspense, and LBJ's total awareness of how much the Kennedy entourage despises him borders on pathos.

Peter Werner's striking direction draws out illuminating moments about a deeply complex man who, on the surface, seems so defineable.

If Johnson's raw power has been tempered, his coarseness toned down, the man's remarkable rise from dirt farmer to the most powerful man on earth has been touched upon with considerable skill; it's high time someone started taking note of the man.

Except for one day of principal photography in Washington, D.C., and a second day for second unit work, "LBJ" was filmed effectively at Southern California sites—the L.A. City Hall, the Ambassador Hotel (the bathroom scene with LBJ and RFK), the Disney Ranch, Newhall, Hidden Valley and downtown L.A.

Several brief portraits—Kevin McCarthy's assured Joe Kennedy, the Johnson housekeeper Zephyr Wright ("Phoebe" played strongly by Royce Wallace), Johnson's mother (Anne Haney) and father (R. G. Armstrong), LBJ's wealthy love interest Alice Glass (Morgan Brittany), and the arrogant Mrs. Kleberg (Frances Conroy)—contribute ably to the tapestry.

Bobby Baker and Walter Jenkins, among others, have been eliminated, though "Billy Bob," composite figure played by Jack Blessing, includes several folk surrounding the architect of the Great Society. Brother Sam Houston Johnson has been eclipsed, but Sam Rayburn (a slick-headed Pat Hingle) is plainly in evidence.

Singular achievement aside from Quaid's remarkable interpretation, is the recognition of Johnson, whose domestic policies on civil rights, health measures, social and economic welfare programs, Federal aid to education, antipoverty programs and housing were monumental—and were blacked out by Vietnam and the Dominican Republic.

"LBJ" shows the boorish, opportunistic, vigorous politician as a human being. A closer inspection through what has become a trash barrel for overripe romantic slush—the miniseries—would have been in order. After all, "Eleanor & Franklin" and its sequel did all right for ABC in 1977–78.

Johnson, strong FDR disciple, would fill the bill. "LBJ" takes Johnson up to his Presidential swearing in; there's Greek drama in the subsequent years about a genuinely tragic hero whose ambitions were realized—and then crashed down on him.

(Courtesy of Syd Silverman, *Variety*)

The quality of honesty can, of course, be probed for, not only in docudramas, but in all types of broadcast/cable content—especially as it relates to character portrayal. If ages, occupations, genders, religions, or racial groups are represented in stereotypical ways, the treatment becomes more dishonest the longer it is allowed to remain on microphone or on camera. All Texans, all blacks, or all Baptists are not the same; and to treat such groups as monolithic is to be functionally insincere to the concept (and value-belief) of individual human worth and dignity. The creation of stereotypes, however explicable within the forced brevity of the typical series episode, tends to be a shortcut that creates its own barriers to the development and extendability of that series.

To a significant degree, human stereotypes also make a negative contribution to *program variety*, the second Ralph Smith-listed critic preference. By their nature, stereotypes are patterns for assumed commonality rather than actual differentiation. Thus, for example, even though television now frequently features women in occupational roles formerly cast only with men, Robert Alley charges that too often, this practice "deteriorates into a picturing of women as men think women should act doing men's jobs. And therein lies the problem. The jobs, from lawyer, to police, to dozens of other previously all-male professions, bear the male image. One is reminded of those ludicrous outfits Joan Crawford used to wear in order to qualify as a business woman."[7]

Businessmen as a class fare no better in many electronic portrayals, arguably due to the bruising experiences that most program creators inevitably have with the executives of their industry. The most unvaried video theme and, in Ben Stein's words, "one of the clearest messages of television is that businessmen are bad, evil people, and that big businessmen are the worst of all. . . . The most succinct summary of the way businessmen are shown in TV comedies came from a producer at a successful comedy production company. A writer approached him with an idea: How about a comedy with businessmen who were good guys? The producer's answer was, 'Impossible.'"[8]

Another lack of variety frequently mentioned by critics occurs in broadcast children's programming in which the "BAM POW ZAP" of animated productions outstrips any other content type aimed exclusively at kids. Even from a strictly business standpoint, this is bad business, writes advertising director Allen Banks, because the broadcast monotony drives the audience elsewhere:

The audience sees a lot of sameness—one robot show looks like another. No variety, everything is predictable even to the young child audience—which can't be taken for granted . . . too may of the new shows ignored half of the audience universe by appealing primarily to boys and virtually ignoring the female segment . . .

total children viewing hours haven't decreased nearly as much as the ratings for individual programs, so if ratings are down on the commercial over-the-air programs, kids must be watching something else on television. Cable ratings for kids programing such as USA and Nickelodean and nonkids programming like CBN are up.[9]

Taking further aim at commercial broadcasting (in contrast to cable and non-commercial services), Children's Television Workshop President Joan Ganz Cooney sees the variety problem assuming a quantitative dimension:

> We live in a society that does not find children important enough as a market to merit more than a few hours of cartoons on Saturday morning. . . . I'd insist that children's programs not be scheduled in competition with one another. Children should have programming and schedule choices just as adults do.
>
> Given the opportunity to provide more programs for children, I'd like to see good contemporary drama on a daily or weekly basis. ABC's *Afterschool Specials* and NBC's *Special Treat* series have proven that quality drama for children *can* be produced and *will* be watched. . . .
>
> Clearly, our children are falling behind others, West Germans, Japanese, Russians, in science and mathematics. *The Voyage of the Mimi* and *3–2–1 Contact* science shows on public television have shown that programs that educate need not be dull. For preschoolers, more programs should be aired that stimulate intellectual growth. *Mr. Rogers' Neighborhood* and *Sesame Street* are examples of popular programming in these categories, and children should have access to others.[10]

Ironically, were public television to increase the amount and variety of its children's programming, it would thereby intensify the charge that the medium does not serve the diverse tastes of the "public" at all but instead is the exclusive servant of children and only the more upscale adults.

The *maintenance of human dignity,* a third value critics admire in radio/television content, seems put under stress most by game shows in which the participants are encouraged to perform all sorts of demeaning and self-embarrassing activities. That the specific activities have changed over the years does not necessarily make them more dignified, as *TV Guide*'s Don Merrill chronicles at the end of his review of *The New Newlywed Game*:

> In the early days of television, contestants in audience participation shows submitted to physical gags, were hit in the face with pies, dunked in water or mud. The audience laughed because seeing someone else lose dignity is a basic kind of fun and source of laughter.
>
> For this viewer, watching the naivete of *New Newlywed Game* contestants being exploited was an excruciatingly embarrassing experience.[11]

Assaults on dignity are also mounted by news reporters who intrude on private grief at a moment of tragedy, by commercials that picture product nonusers as mindless nerds, and by situation comedies in which parental figures are saved from their own incompetence-caused catastrophy only by the quick thinking of the children or family pet. Even documentaries that allegedly are intended to illuminate a human problem may end up impugning the dignity of their subjects if the show's basic thrust is ill-conceived. Such is the conclusion reached by *Variety* critic Tom Bierbaum in the following review of an ABC effort.

AT A LOSS FOR WORDS—ILLITERATE IN AMERICA
by Tom Bierbaum

If it seems like it would be difficult to find an hour's worth of things to say about illiteracy, there's a good reason for it. As this ABC special showed, once you roll out the statistics and talk about how unfortunate it is, there isn't much else to say.

In fact, what the special is really about is the overall quality of education in the U.S. A lot of what was discussed had more to do with the lack of excellence on the high end of the educational spectrum than with the major segment of the population that's illiterate.

For example, much was made of the country's declining position in the international high-tech market, an area where you'd have to be far more than merely literate to contribute.

And the special seemed disapproving of the political campaign mounted by Texas teachers that opposed regular testing of school instructors. But there was no evidence or strong logic presented to demonstrate that quizzing a teacher is going to do anything to reduce the number of students that come out of the system illiterate.

And while expanding the program's focus to include the issues of over-all educational quality made some of these points valid and thought-provoking, one has to wonder why the show was still built around the issue of illiteracy. Perhaps it was thought to be a more attention-grabbing issue than just general education.

But had the special taken a different tack, we could have been spared the long line of interviews of ineffective silhouetted illiterates. Because there was so little to be proven or learned from these interviews, they turned out to be little more than embarrassing.

(Courtesy of Syd Silverman, *Variety*)

Conversely, when a news or reality program conceives of its guest participants as people rather than as mere problem vessels or points of view, the questions asked by program host or journalist will evince a well-prepared civility that does not force a dignity-surrendering response. Similarly, the sensitive dramatic portrayals of mental retardation, homosexuality, the physically handicapped, and the elderly on which television has recently embarked do not just preserve human dignity but, through their creative commitment, powerfully amplify for viewers some of the diverse sources from which that dignity is capable of springing.

It follows, then, that human dignity is most likely maintained in content vehicles whose creators exhibit the most diligent commitment to thorough *writing and production*—the fourth element Smith found critics to value. We have already discussed extensively in Chapter 5 the productional ingredients from which such excellence can be fashioned and continue to recognize writing as the core of the conceptual event to which broadcast/cable critics devote their attention.

The opposite of diligence, which in the electronic media is mechanical indifference, does not escape the competent radio/television critic's ascertainment process any more than a flat orchestral presentation under the baton of an ill-prepared or unmotivated conductor escapes the censure of the music reviewer. Pride of performance is an essential ingredient in any art or craft, and its absence is relatively easy to detect if not always simple to explain. The radio format rife with "dead air" rather than anticipatory pause and the television sitcom in which a fanatical laugh track bumpers incoherent scripting are both manifestations of the same carelessness that prevents the attainment of electronic media excellence.

Even though the fifth of Smith's critically acclaimed elements, *relaxation and informality*, would seem the opposite of script and production diligence, knowledgeable critics are aware of (1) how hard creators have to work to make content realization seem effortless and (2) how important the casual can be to listeners and viewers in seeking respite both from life's pressures and from the stimulating yet stressful experiences that some other listening and viewing choices (newscasts, action/adventure shows, "heavy" dramatic presentations) can cause. Whether it's Garrison Keillor's *A Prairie Home Companion* on radio or Johnny Carson's *Tonight Show* on television, intricately fashioned nonchalance is a soothing audience therapy when crafted by consummate communicators who know how to conceal the intensity of their labors.

A *strong sense of responsibility*, the final criterion the critics whom Smith studied prized, flows from an ethical belief structure that demands that radio/television operate as a first priority in the service of society rather than in the aggrandizement of shareholders. Profit is fine, but only when in consort with and not to the detriment of the public interest. Just what constitutes this public interest is, ultimately, what at least three out of five Federal Communications Commissioners say it is. Still, the generally held valuation of the electronic media as social resource is strongly embedded in our communications law and critical commentary. Broadcasters and cablecasters, for their part, are almost universally aware of this belief, even if they do not universally service it.

Some would define this social responsibility as mandating that broadcasting and cable outlets exclusively feature content that presents the good, the true, and the morally uplifting (though just who is to determine what constitutes goodness, truth, and upliftment remains a mystery). Mature critics reject this simplistic view, of course, because they recognize that electronic communicators in a democratic society must function as artists, not as law-dictating moralizers. Theodore Meyer Greene draws the distinction this way:

> The artist portrays men as they are, with all their virtues and vices; *and* as they ought to be; the moralist is actively concerned to eradicate vice and to foster human virtue. The artist as artist is content to understand human nature with all its potentialities and limitations, and to reveal his insight through his art . . . Further-

more, the artist's specific insights, as these are expressed in his art, are invaluable to the moral agent, while art in general aids morality in strengthening the imagination.[12]

The socially responsible artist/communicator, then, is right to provide depictions of both good and evil as case studies through which society's moralists can instruct people who rely on their opinion. In fact, by raising an ugly or socially embarrassing issue, the broadcaster/cablecaster can facilitate the audience's coming to grips with it in a values clarifying way.

A perceptive critic understands this and recognizes that an electronic media producer's sense of responsibility is shown not by the chosen subject matter but by the totality of the approach taken toward that subject matter. With this realization Jerome Stolnitz cautions:

> If we consider the subject matter alone, we might just as well be talking about the real life "model," for we ignore all that makes the work a distinctive aesthetic object. It is like saying that *Macbeth* is simply a story about a lot of murders.[13]

DeWitt Parker makes a more extensive case for the moral right (and even responsibility) of the artist to portray the perverse as well as the positive when he argues on behalf of any work of art:

> Even when it offers suggestions for unwonted acts, it furnishes the spirit and the knowledge requisite for determining whether they will fit into the scheme of life of the spectator. It is characteristic of the puritanic critics of art, in their eagerness to find motives for condemnation, to overlook this element of reflection. . . . Only by knowing other ways of life can we be certain of the relative worth of our own way. . . . For morality, to be genuine, must be a choice; the good must know its alternative or it is not good.[14]

Freedom of Expression and Media Access

As this discussion suggests, a core value held by most mainstream critics—and most broadcast/cablecasters—is the freedom to express and expose positive and negative, popular and unpopular, subjects and attitudes. Over the years, political candidates' equal-time rights under the Communications Act and the balanced discussion of controversial issues of public importance required by the Fairness Doctrine showed that powerful forces within the federal government (especially within the Congress) felt it further necessary to mandate freedom of electronic expression on key public issues. These governmental requirements, however, dealt less with the expressive rights of radio/television operators than with the access rights to those channels by people outside the media. The historical federal view thus demonstrates not only an endorsement of the value of freedom of expression as a key social responsibility but also a belief that broadcasters must be compelled rather than relied on to provide it. Whether this inhibits the radio/television communicator's own freedom of expression is, of course, a highly values-charged issue.

The question of what is really meant by "freedom of expression" becomes even more murky when theoretically noble beliefs functionally clash. In 1972, for example, Congress made certain changes to the Communications Act that required broadcasters to provide "reasonable access" to all legally qualified candidates for federal elective office. These provisions thus joined the pre-existing "no censorship" provision of the Act's Section 315 to guarantee that any federal elective office-seeker could secure at least some exposure on any station in the land and say whatever he or she wanted without any right of that station to edit the remarks. In a sense, the libertarian view that values the individual's right to speak out thereby was given precedence over a social responsibility orientation, which seeks to protect society from onerous and patently damaging expression.

That same year, avowed white supremacist J. B. Stoner ran in the Georgia Democratic primary for a U.S. Senate seat with a thirty-second television and radio spot that no station wished to air but that none, under pain of license revocation, could reject:

> I am J. B. Stoner. I am the only candidate for United States Senator who is for the white people. I am the only candidate who is against integration. All other candidates are race mixers to one degree or another. I say we must repeal [Georgia Senator] Gambrell's civil rights law. Gambrell's law takes jobs from us whites and gives these jobs to the niggers. The main reason why niggers want integration is because the niggers want our white women. I am for law and order with the knowledge that you cannot have law and order and niggers too. Vote white. This time vote your convictions by voting white racist J. B. Stoner into the run-off election for United States Senator. I thank you.[15]

That Stoner did not win the election goes without saying. But that seven radio and television outlets in Georgia and another in Chattanooga, Tennessee, were forced to transmit this message over their own objections and those of the National Association for the Advancement of Colored People, the Anti-Defamation League, and the mayor of Atlanta shows just how complex the ethics of expression and access can become.

The same fundamental questions arise, of course, in such areas as obscenity and indecency, wanton violence, expressions of religious bigotry, children's commercials, and hard liquor and cigarette advertising. None of these areas is protected speech in the way the federal candidate's speech is protected, but all involve the difficult if not impossible balancing of socially responsible versus free expressive values. Radio/television cigarette advertising, in fact, is banned by congressional law—a virtually unprecedented U.S. example of prior restraint that has been justified on the basis of objective medical data rather than subjective ethical belief. (A San Francisco peace group subsequently tried to have military recruitment commercials banned because military service was also "hazardous to your health," but this attempt was not successful.)

This book is not, of course, a text on media law, so we will not pursue further the statutory histories and legal precedents involved in these or associated areas. Rather, our aim here is to heighten critical sensitivities to the intricate and, at times, mutually contradictory value systems that inject themselves into expression and access questions. Former CBS/Broadcast Group President Richard Jencks once tried to draw for broadcasters a workable position on the subject that stated: "The concept of free speech means that everyone has a right to speak to whatever audience he can command. It does not, however, mean that he has a right to an audience."[16] Legally commanded media access, in Jencks's view, tries to stretch the right of expression into entitlement to the listeners or viewers that an electronic medium has independently assembled.

On the other hand, Howard Symons, then chief counsel of the House telecommunications subcommittee, wrote that the need for broad public access to the electronic media was essential if we value an unmonopolized exchange of views. To Symons's way of thinking:

> Ultimately, citizen access validates the notion of the marketplace of ideas. We do not tolerate economic concentration in the commercial marketplace, and Congress has passed antitrust laws to prevent it. By the same token, competition in the marketplace of ideas requires many spokespersons putting forward many opinions. Concentrated control of the outlets for expression discourages competition. A citizen (or a citizen group) must have the freedom to present his views in whatever forum he chooses.[17]

Here, again, we find reasonable, ethical viewpoints staked out by reasonable, ethical spokespersons that, from a practical standpoint, are often mutually exclusive. Lacking the wisdom of Solomon, the radio/television critic probably will not be able to resolve this dilemma but should at least be in a position to clarify its ramifications for the watching and listening public. To people who would argue that free expression and access questions are more matters for lawyers than critics, Professor Edwin Diamond asserts:

> First Amendment issues can't be settled solely by the tortsmen. For all of us in the television audience, the way these issues are settled will go a long way toward determining the kind of TV we have in this country, from the presentation of news and public affairs to the content of popular entertainment shows. Broadcasting law may well be too important to be left to the lawyers alone.[18]

If there is any area in which ethical agreements outnumber disagreements, it is probably the issue of what should and should not be directed to children via the electronic media and by whom. Radio/television professionals and their harshest detractors alike recognize that broadcasting and cable are not like print due to their ease of access into the home or car and the way in which their content apprehension by children cannot be easily controlled or anticipated. The 1978 so-called "Seven Dirty Words (Pacifica) Case" dealt not so much with indecency as it did with the fact that a parent witnessed offensive radio verbiage assaulting his child's ears without prior warning. As broadcast executive Richard Jencks recognizes:

> Broadcasting is and will remain a very special medium. It cannot narrowcast to the peculiar clientele of "adult" bookstores or theatres: Any small child in a room or car, fiddling with a dial, can come unaware upon whatever is broadcast. What children see or hear in such a way should not shadow or distort the future joyful discovery of physical love which is their natural right to inherit.[19]

Cable television is experimenting with lock-boxes that are meant to prohibit accidental child exposure to adult pay services. But there is no lock-box on an open circuit radio or television station transmission.

In the seventies, the broadcast industry, in response to the well-meaning prodding of an FCC chairman, came up with a temporal lock-box called Family Viewing to which the major television broadcasters gave their voluntary assent. Basically, the scheme set aside 7 to 9 P.M. as a time in which aired television programming would be of a type suitable to be watched by all members of the family unit. That the plan sometimes ignored time zone differences in network transmission schedules and assumed a uniform bedtime for America's children only showed the limits of its feasibility.

What really killed family viewing was the court-upheld assertion by producers whose shows had been moved or cancelled that the plan constituted First Amendment sabotage through FCC coercion. It was not a question of network prime-time programming's having been obscene or indecent. Rather, it was a case of an industry accommodating its regulator, which was itself under pressure from a Congress beseiged by citizen interest groups who wanted television cleaned up. When the particular value structure of the special interests was allowed to permeate the political process, a free expression defense had to be mounted that seemed to pit the First Amendment against the cause of child welfare. It is through just such comparative ethical quandaries that the electronic media and electronic media criticism are constantly challenged to values reassessment.

The Protestant Ethic and Social Darwinism

In a sense, there are as many value systems present in the listening/viewing audience as there are members of that audience. It thus is impossible for a given media outlet—or even a given program—consistently to mirror any one individual's personal code. In fact, due to the group effort required to create and administer even the simplest media product, program producers themselves are largely unable to sculpt shows entirely to their own values. Further, because of the massness required to make all but the most upscale and narrowcast transmission profitable, broadcasting and most cable efforts anchor themselves in what are perceived to be mainstream ethical waters, refusing to be swept away by the radical currents of either producer or consumer deviance from those norms. Thus radio/television, which Fiske and Hartley refer to as the *bardic mediator*,

> tends to articulate the negotiated central concerns of its culture, with only limited and often over-mediated references to the ideologies, beliefs, habits of thought and definitions of the situation which obtain in groups which are for one reason or another peripheral. Since one of the characteristics of western culture is that the societies concerned are class-divided, television responds with a predominance of messages which propagate and re-present the dominant class ideology.[20]

It is impossible within the confines of this discussion to explore the totality of values from which this predominant ideology is woven, but we can, as primary examples, explore two somewhat parallel belief structures deeply embedded in the American attitude and therefore embedded also in the bulk of the broadcast/cable programming that services it. Both largely economic in origin, the Protestant ethic and social Darwinism were values orientations that vibrated in consonance with the aspirations and needs of the populators of the New World. It is natural, then, that the new communications media that grew up in this world came automatically, if only inadvertently, to reflect the tenets of these two philosophies.

The Protestant Ethic

As identified by German sociologist Max Weber in *The Protestant Ethic and the Spirit of Capitalism,* this Pilgrim-imported belief consisted of a three-pronged commitment to (1) hard work, (2) frugality, and (3) self-denial. Through hard work one developed personal character and aided God in the attainment of His plan for the universe. Through frugality, one conserved the fruits of hard work in order to achieve prosperity. This prosperity consisted of much more than the material wealth that signified it, however, for it was a sign from God as to whether the afterlife would be spent in a heavenly or overheated environment. People who prospered in this world were predestined to succeed in the next, so this theory of predestination was a vital motivator in this entire belief structure. Finally, through self-denial, one avoided squandering resources on sinful pursuits since this practice would also undermine prosperity and the assurance of a postdeath ascent rather than descent.

Notice how the Protestant ethic was perfectly attuned to the development of Europe's post-Reformation middle class. What better philosophy than this for a group that lacked the upper-class birthright of the nobility associated with Roman Catholic or Anglican churches? Rather than being born to wealth or privilege, the aspiring tradesmen, craftsmen, and merchants had to rely on their own hard work and financial acumen to acquire the capital that was replacing land as the basis of power. Instead of putting their faith in a fixed and exclusive hierarchy in which counts and cardinals shared the same family names, these middle-class followers of Martin Luther and John Calvin identified much more comfortably with an ideology that prized and identified individual merit rather than royal prerogative.

Especially when transplanted to the New World, the Protestant ethic soon lost its exclusively Protestant character. In this land, virtually everyone had the chance—in fact, the necessity—to start afresh in building a new society. The persecuted Catholics who settled in Lord Baltimore's Maryland, for example, mirrored the tenets of the now secularized Protestant ethic with as much zeal as had the Pilgrims of Plymouth; and so the crucial American middle-class took root. Not surprisingly, this private-enterprise-loving ethic remains almost inevitably healthy in an electronic media system that is itself the creator and creation of private enterprises. What is unfortunate is that the inherently discriminatory nature of the ethic's standards, separating as it does those positively from those negatively predestined, leads to programmatic portrayals that can be warped, harmful, and cruel. Thus, when it comes to the poor, ill, or elderly, charged Robert Lewis Shayon,

> the media generally ignore them; but when they are admitted to the pseudo-mirror-image of national life, they are usually portrayed in negative terms: the poor are lazy; the mentally ill are violent, unpredictable; and the elderly are burdens on the economy. Their conditions, therefore, are also self-inflicted, for if they deserved their proper share of the good life, they would undoubtedly possess it (Calvin, meet television!).[21]

Social Darwinism

Ironically, the exceptional staying power of the Protestant ethic, with both its helpful and harmful residues was, beginning in the late nineteenth century, heightened by the irreligious philosophy of Social Darwinism. Inspired by the studies of English naturalist Charles Darwin, who originated the theory of evolution, social Darwinism applied the scientist's ideas about species' natural selection and survival of the fittest to the workings of human society. As with the Protestant ethic, social Darwinism found fertile ground in the rugged individualism of the American frontier and the cut-throat competition of the country's post–Civil-War industrial revolution. The naturalistic idea of the strong possessing first right of survival so that the species could prosper was not very different, in effect, from the prosperity-defined salvation that the Protestant ethic preached.

Like the Protestant ethic, social Darwinism is not a philosophy that is unequivocally good or bad. Its character must be judged based on the welcomed or regretted impact that its application has in a given situation. Literary critic Carl Grabo, for instance, would argue that "Survival of the fittest means not the survival of the fittest individual or species by any scale of human values but those forms which have found refuge in their very mediocrity and conformity."[22] This, of course, is the argument raised by those who decry the alleged formula sameness of prime-time television in which the clones of past success are said to drive out meritorious innovations. As Professor Gene Youngblood asserts:

> Commercial entertainment works against art, exploits the alienation and boredom of the public, by perpetuating a system of conditioned responses to formulas. Commercial entertainment not only isn't creative, it actually destroys the audience's ability to appreciate and participate in the creative process. . . . Driven by the profit motive, the commercial entertainer dares not risk alienating us by attempting new language even if he were capable of it. He seeks only to gratify preconditioned needs for formula stimulus. He offers nothing we haven't already conceived, nothing we don't already expect.[23]

Media producers, on the other hand, would argue that any formula started as an innovation that succeeded because it *evolved* and *adapted itself* (key Darwinian concepts) to the needs of the listening or viewing audience.

Another testimony to the fact that social Darwinism's standing depends on the orientation of its beholder comes from the workings of Chairman Mark Fowler's FCC in the early and mid-eighties. From the beginning of their tenure, Fowler and his staff spoke of the need to remove all unnecessary regulations so that the marketplace, not the government, would decide which electronic services were to prosper. Initially enthusiastically embraced by broadcasters, this Darwinistic philosophy soon acquired a sour side when it became clear that, by the same token, the Commission no longer felt its role to be the ensuring of any station's survival. By opening up the spectrum to more stations and whole new services, the Fowler FCC closed the book on the protectionist era in which so-called "free" broadcasting was shielded from the direct competition of cable and other forms of "pay" transmission. Broadcasting, in both its individual and aggregate forms, had to adapt to the deregulated marketplace or die. The fact that, a few years later, all three commercial television networks were subsequently sold or drastically reconfigured within the space of a few months was the most obvious aspect of the accelerated evolution that the industry underwent as a consequence of this governmental values shift. Local stations and entire station groups also were voluntarily sold or subjected to highest-bidder takeovers that fundamentally rearranged the medium's priorities.

Because of their central and historic role in the formation of the American psyche, the Protestant ethic and Social Darwinism continue to shape the underlying value structures contained in our programming and in the total system that creates and carries that programming. By probing for these constructs in a given show, we can not only learn to discern their pervasiveness, but also acquire the critical skills necessary to uncover other value assumptions. What must be kept in mind, however, is that commercial creators normally do not set about to teach us a values system but merely reflect the implicit values of their own upbringing and environment.

The detection of critical values is an essential component of the knowledgeable comprehension of radio/television. Values are an inevitable aspect of every program element. People who naively argue that such standards conveyance should not be a part of the entertainment experience are seeking the impossible. As DeWitt Parker first attested almost seventy years ago:

> We cannot demand of the writer that he have no moral purpose or that he leave morality out of his story. For, since the artist is also a man, he cannot rid himself of an ethical interest in human problems or with good conscience fail to use his art to help toward their solution. His observations of moral experience will inevitably result in beliefs about it, and these will reveal themselves in his work. Yet we should demand that his view of what life ought to be shall not falsify his representation of life as it is. Just as soon as the moral of a tale obtrudes, we begin to suspect that the tale is false.[24]

To explore the decoding of a given program's values structure, let us read the following student critique of an episode of *Lou Grant*. With Ed Asner in the title role, the *Lou Grant* series focused on Mary Tyler Moore's former news-director boss who has been transplanted to California as city editor of *The Los Angeles Tribune*. In this episode, the *Trib* was faced with an employee walkout in reaction to a cost-saving workforce reduction plan. This student critic discusses the revealed reactions and attitudes of Lou and his colleagues in terms of their Protestant ethic and social Darwinistic implications:

The *Lou Grant* episode, "Strike," reinforced social Darwinism and the three aspects of the Protestant ethic: hard work, frugality, and self-denial.

First, the show seemed to revolve around the social Darwinism theme. For example, *The Los Angeles Tribune* faced the possible fate of closing down its operation because of financial difficulties. The paper did not utilize modern, automated equipment, and instead was employing over one hundred extra paste-up employees to do the work that a couple of computers could handle much faster. The owner of the paper, Mrs. Pynchon, had a difficult decision to make. She could either let the paper collapse by supporting a large and unnecessary staff, or she could put a large number of employees, some of them who had worked for her for more than 30 years, out of work. Social Darwinism suggests that only the strong survive, and the weak die. Mrs. Pynchon was afraid her paper would die if she did not change the paste-up process to automation.

The employees realized automation was probably the best route to take as well, but because they needed their jobs, they sought to survive by banding together in their union in order to save their jobs. In the end, both sides, but not every individual, won; the employees could either keep their jobs, retire, or be retrained to do other jobs, and Mrs. Pynchon was able to strike a deal with the union to automate, and save the paper from extinction.

The Protestant ethic element of hard work was reinforced several times throughout the program. The paste-up employees realized they had a tough job to do in order to save their positions, and they decided to work hard to reiterate their stance on the issue by picketing for more than three weeks. The paste-up employees had been working hard all their lives at their jobs and didn't want to see them taken away by machines.

The paper's management, Lou Grant and Charlie, and a few others, also helped to reinforce the hard work aspect. They took it upon themselves to continue to put the paper together, almost singlehandedly, because they did not want to let the readers down. The paper's reporters also believed that if they worked hard for the union's cause, they would benefit later by going back to their job sooner if the strike could be resolved. Billie Newman believed her picketing was the right thing to do. She said she felt like she was putting up a good fight through her picketing and was working hard and feeling good because of it.

Self-denial was also reinforced throughout the program. One example of this aspect of the Protestant ethic occurred when the reporters voluntarily went on strike with the truck drivers and paste-up employees. They didn't want to strike, but believed that it was the best thing to do in order to keep their jobs and support their fellow workers. Some reporters, such as Rossi, were working on exciting projects, yet denied themselves possible big bylines by leaving to join in the strike cause. Mrs. Pynchon also displayed a measure of self-denial in her agreement with the union to retain any paste-up employees who wanted to stay with the paper, even though it would cost extra money to retrain them. The union also displayed a measure of self-denial, by agreeing to cut down the wasteful number of its employees per shift.

Mrs. Pynchon displayed the frugality aspect of the Protestant ethic by wanting to convert her operation to the automated method. This would cost five million dollars, but would pay itself off in one year. The purchase of the equipment would be a one-time thing, while keeping the excess employees would cost an unrecoverable six million dollars each year. The union also displayed frugality. Its employees had been without pay for three weeks so an agreement had to be reached to protect the resources of the whole at the expense of a few.

The *Lou Grant* episode seemed to reflect all three aspects of the Protestant ethic as well as social Darwinism in several ways and through several different types of characters. Union or management all had to respond to the same pressures and ultimately mirrored the same fundamental values.

(Courtesy of Lisa K. Farrell)

For another view of the Protestant ethic and social Darwinism in programmatic action, read the "Theo's Holiday" episode of *The Cosby Show*, the script for which is found in Appendix A. Here, the Darwinistic world is not pictured as an evil jungle, but neither is it viewed as unequivocally benevolent. With the help of his parents, older sister Denise, and younger sisters Vanessa and Rudy, fifteen-year-old Theo learns that (as father Cliff says): "Once you're out in the real world . . . you have to make it on your own." "I can't feed my family on a promise," Cliff later states, and Theo, by the end of the show, has found that the real world's "a lot tougher than I thought. But you know what? So am I." Theo, due to the caring and prudent nurturing of his parents, will be a survivor, even if he still has a lot of adapting to do.

The Protestant ethic's deferred gratifications also underpin this script as college's laying of "a foundation for the rest of your life" is contrasted with the short-term lure of "five hundred dollars a day." A variety of hard-working occupational roles are characterized, as is the frugal reality that you can't squander "this much [money] on one meal . . . I am on a budget." When self-denial breaks down, one ends up with a stereo and no electricity to power it. Still, with the hard work and frugality that create a good credit rating will come financial "approval" so that, as mother Clair puts it in her role-playing, "we can start planning for our future."

Though perhaps not as pervasive as the Protestant ethic and social Darwinism, many other values and value structures inevitably underpin the electronic content to which we watch and listen. The perceptive critic will have, as one goal, the revealing of these values to the public so they can more easily stack them up against their own ethical systems in assessing the programming's appropriateness for themselves and/or their children. In meeting this goal, the critic's own values will, of course, come through in both the selection of the subjects to be probed and his or her personal orientation toward them.

Again, this does not mean that critics have the right to demand public adherence to their own values standards. It does mean that a critique has the responsibility to reveal the values questions that a given content encompasses in as clear and honest a manner as is humanly possible. As Theodore Meyer Greene maintains:

> The critic is ill-advised to insist on the correctness of his own individual philosophy of life, or to appraise the greatness of art solely by reference to any specific moralistic criterion. . . . All that the critic has the right to demand of an artist is that he deal with *some* significant subject in *some* significant way, that is, that he exhibit in his art a genuine breadth of outlook and, simultaneously, a genuine depth of understanding which will reveal specific characteristics and values which had previously passed unnoticed. . . . A critic with limited powers of observation, a weak imagination, and a restricted scale of values, must remain blind to artistic greatness and incapable of distinguishing artistic profundity from artistic triviality.[25]

"If the world were agreed on the most desirable system of ethics," adds George Boas, "there would be no disagreement upon the most desirable works of art."[26] Since this is not the case, the necessity for the broadcast/cable critic to come to grips with values is inescapable—especially given the breadth of the audience, and, therefore, the diversity of audience values, impacted by the electronic media.

To conclude this chapter, we can examine the multiplicity of ethical and value-charged concerns that *The Dallas Morning News*'s Scott Bennett was able to raise in this single, broad-focus commentary that thoroughly probes but avoids dictatorial preachment:

STATIC IN TV'S PREACHERLAND TELLS OF FLAWS IN OUR SOCIETY
by Scott Bennett

Thanks to a last-minute contribution of tainted money from a dog-racing magnate, Brother Oral Roberts will live to pray another day. Oh well, the Lord works in mysterious ways.

There is, however, still plenty of static in TV's preacherland. Brother Jim Bakker, following recent political fashion, has confessed some past sins. One seems to have been a sexual encounter with someone years back when Brother Bakker's marriage to wife, Tammy Faye, who is now undergoing treatment for drug dependency, was on the skids. Another seems to be that he paid "hush money"—to someone he believes set him up—to keep the event quiet.

Brother Bakker was apparently moved to this testimony because a fellow TV preacher, following current capitalist fashion, hatched a "diabolical plot" to launch a hostile "takeover" of the PTL (Praise The Lord or People That Love, take your pick) evangelical network.

The instigator of this plot apparently was that most electrifying of electrified preachers, Brother Jimmy Swaggart, cousin of well-known country and rock singers Jerry Lee Lewis and Mickey Gilley. Brother Bakker's attorney has suggested that Brother Swaggart should spend more time worrying about his own sins, which Brother Bakker's lawyer says are considerable.

To thwart the "devil's work" being done by Brother Swaggart, Brother Bakker asked Brother Jerry Falwell, of Moral Majority fame, to act as celestial whiteknight and save PTL for God's work. To all of this, GOP presidential contender Brother Pat Robertson, for whom Brother Bakker once worked and who has his own, more genteel evangelical network, says, "God is just doing a little housecleaning." Hallelujah!

At first blush, it might appear all this bad press, all this airing of soiled heavenly linen, would be devastating to these prophets' profits. Actually this soap opera saga may prove to be a, forgive the phrase, godsend. Martyrdom has sold well for centuries, and with the devil on the loose and charges of false propheteering being hurled about, it is a good bet that that flock out there in TV land will dig ever deeper into depleted pocketbooks to help their chosen ones stay on the air.

Indeed, one is moved to wonder if Brothers Bakker, Swaggart, and Falwell may not have cooked the whole thing up out of jealousy over brother Oral's magnificent fund-raising scheme. If Brother Roberts can claim the Almighty wants greenmail to spare his life, then maybe a good feud with the devil could spur even greater sums. The mind boggles at the possibilities.

Imagine how much Brother and Sister Bakker will raise when, after an appropriate passage of time, they make their first appearance on PTL. And imagine how much the sudden acquisition of his very own TV network and theme park will mean to Brother Falwell, whose own fortunes had fallen on lean times. And Brother Swaggart can shake the swamps of his native Louisiana clean in his no-compromise fight for purity in the pulpit.

It is certainly tempting to write "Pearlygate" off as a falling out among charlatans; most Americans have long assumed the worst of their charges about each other to be true. But there are multiple tragedies here. If the Bakkers' sex and blackmail saga is indeed true, then there is a human tragedy and object lesson: Even those who heed God's call can become so driven, so obsessed that they lose all sense of balance and perspective. Ego and jealousy are at work even among the pious, and can bring down even those who consider themselves godly.

Another tragedy is the failure of mainstream American Christianity to fulfill the needs of so many who are seeking a spiritual dimension to their lives. Many of those who sit for hours before the TV's light and watch these passionate prophets rave on have tried the mainstream and found it wanting. What they often find is a religious country club dominated by standoffish social cliques, and pastors hired for social skills and administrative abilities, not their ability to minister to individual human beings struggling to stay afloat in the high-tech world.

Perhaps the greatest failure is that of a modern American society that has done so well at supplying the material needs and wants of life and so poorly at nurturing the spirit. There is no inherent sin in expensive cars, or fine food or trips to Europe. But there is more. There is family, and friends and community. In too many rushed American lives there is no time for fulfilling spiritual needs. Too many feel alienated in a world of circuit boards, alloys and VCR's.

The physicist Max Pagel has suggested the religious drive is biological, and as such is as irresistible as the sex drive. If so, we may better understand why Brother Bakker succumbed to temptations of the flesh. But one task of religion is to provide humans a spiritual anchor in seas made increasingly rough by the discovery of God's physical laws.

Inventions like TV, which arise from the manipulation of these physical laws, are morally neutral; they are what we choose to make of them. Right now, Brother Oral, Brother Bakker, Brother Swaggart and their ilk seem to have hoisted anchor in the boiling TV seas. Let us hope they don't take their flocks down with their ships.

(Reprinted with permission of *The Dallas Morning News*)

Notes

1. George Santayana, "The Nature of Beauty," in Melvin Rader, ed., *A Modern Book of Esthetics,* 5th ed. (New York: Holt, Rinehart and Winston, 1979), 172.
2. Northrop Frye, *Anatomy of Criticism* (Princeton: Princeton University Press, 1957), 348.
3. Eliseo Vivas, *Essays in Criticism and Aesthetics* (New York: The Noonday Press, 1955), 126–27.
4. Sprague Vonier, "Television: Purveyor of Parables," *Journal of Broadcasting* (Winter 1965–1966): 4–5.
5. Robert Smith, *Beyond the Wasteland: The Criticism of Broadcasting,* rev. ed. (Annandale, Va.: Speech Communication Association, 1980), 5.
6. Ralph Smith, *A Study of the Professional Criticism of Broadcasting in the United States 1920–1955* (New York: Arno Press, 1979), 483–90.
7. Robert Alley, "Values on View: A Moral Myopia?" *Critical Studies in Mass Communication* (December 1985): 405.
8. Ben Stein, *The View from Sunset Boulevard* (New York: Basic Books, 1979), 15–17.
9. Allen Banks, "The Problem with Kids These Days is Programmers," *Broadcasting* (March 9, 1987): 22
10. Joan Ganz Cooney, "A Long Way to Go in Children's Television," *Broadcasting* (October 13, 1986): 26.
11. Don Merrill, "The New Newlywed Game," *TV Guide* (February 28, 1987): 40.
12. Theodore Meyer Greene, *The Arts and the Art of Criticism* (Princeton: Princeton University Press, 1940): 266.
13. Jerome Stolnitz, *Aesthetics and Philosophy of Art Criticism* (Boston: Houghton Mifflin, 1960), 356.
14. DeWitt Parker, *The Principles of Aesthetics,* 2nd. ed. (Westport, Conn.: Greenwood Press, 1976), 273–75.
15. "Broadcasters' Hands Tied as Racist Buys Time to Air His Message," *Broadcasting* (August 7, 1972): 14.
16. Richard Jencks, "Is Taste Obsolete?" Speech presented at Conference of CBS Television Network Affiliates, 20 May 1969, at New York.

17. Howard Symons. "Making Yourself Heard (and Seen): The Citizen's Role in Communications," in Robert Atwan, Barry Orton, and William Vesterman, eds. *American Mass Media: Industries and Issues,* 2nd ed. (New York: Random House, 1982), 35.
18. Edwin Diamond, "The First Amendment Dilemma," *TV Guide* (October 29, 1977): 6.
19. Richard Jencks, "Manning the Barricade against Permissive Speech," *Broadcasting* (March 16, 1987): 22.
20. John Fiske and John Hartley, *Reading Television* (London: Methuen & Company, 1978), 89.
21. Robert Lewis Shayon, *Open to Criticism* (Boston: Beacon Press, 1971), 227.
22. Carl Grabo, *The Creative Critic* (Chicago: The University of Chicago Press, 1948), 30.
23. Gene Youngblood, "Art, Entertainment, Entropy," in John Hanhardt, ed., *Video Culture: A Critical Investigation* (Rochester, N.Y.: Visual Studies Workshop Press, 1986), 225–26.
24. Parker, *Aesthetics*, 200.
25. Greene, *Criticism*, 471.
26. George Boas, *A Primer for Critics* (New York: Greenwood Press, 1968), 123.

Aesthetics and Art

Throughout our discussion, we have considered radio/television content to have aesthetic potential—to possess the capability, in other words, to offer us art. In this chapter, our assumption is explored in detail, and in Chapter 10, a comprehensive schema for aesthetic analysis of broadcast/cable product is presented. For now, as in the previous chapter on ethics and values, it is important, at the outset, to delineate our terms.

Interpreting Aesthetics

The word aesthetic derives from the Greek *aesthesis,* meaning sensuous. Its contemporary spelling is often shortened by dropping the phonetically irrelevant initial *a*. The fundamental definition of *aesthetics* or *esthetics* remains the same, however, and concerns itself with the sensuous apprehension of beauty. At the beginning of this century, literary critic F. V. N. Painter identified aesthetics as "the science of beauty in general . . . to which we have to look for some of the principles that are our guide to critical judgment."[1] To Painter's more famous contemporary, poet and philosopher George Santayana, this beauty

> is an ultimate good, something that gives satisfaction to a natural function, to some fundamental need or capacity of our minds. Beauty is therefore a positive value that is intrinsic; it is pleasure. . . . Morality has to do with the avoidance of evil and the pursuit of good; esthetics only with enjoyment.[2]

It follows, then, according to Jerome Stolnitz, that aesthetic activity is "perception of an object just for the sake of perceiving it. . . . When we approach the work as a sociologist or moralist, we do not grasp its intrinsic value. To do so we must look at the work without any preoccupation with its origins and consequences."[3]

Clearly, the process of aesthetic analysis will involve the critic with a much different (though complementary) procedure than the ethics and values approach probed in the previous chapter. The study of beauty, of what might give us sensual pleasure, has its roots in emotion and not in ethics. As critic Clive Bell affirms, "The starting point for all systems of esthetics must be the personal experience of a peculiar emotion. The objects that provoke this emotion we call works of art."[4]

There are many different theories as to how one can detect and appraise these emotive provocations and an explication of them all would fill this book. For our purposes, it is more efficient to summarize the five orientations that critical theorists bring to the question of beauty's (aesthetic) determination. Even though they are assigned various designations by various authorities, we refer to these five schools of thought as follows, in approximate reverse order of their utility for radio/television criticism:

1. Absolutism
2. Individualism
3. Objectivism
4. Cultural relativism
5. Biopsychological relativism

Absolutism

Absolutism decrees that beauty/pleasure is vested in an object independent of humanity's response to it. In a sense, this is the aesthetic equivalent of the tired conundrum about whether a tree falling in the woods makes a sound if no one is there to hear it. The Absolutist, of course, would say that it would, because no human response is necessary for a natural phenomenon to exist. Whether the sound of that tumbling trunk is aesthetic is another matter, however. The Absolutist would claim ignorance because of this school's view that humanity is not really capable of understanding beauty's ethereal essence any more than mortals are needed to attribute beauty to an independently beautiful object.

One can imagine the excitement with which an absolutist radio/television critic would be greeted by consumers and editors. In essence, the commentary could conclude nothing more than: "Here is a show I may or may not enjoy and you may or may not enjoy but if it is legitimately enjoyable there is no assurance that you or I would experience this pleasure anyway." (Something akin to this does occur when some writer laments a long-dead program from radio or television's past by making us feel guilty for being too aesthetically insensitive back then to appreciate it.)

Individualism

Individualism, in contrast, believes that human beings are eminently capable of understanding and ascribing pleasure—so capable, in fact, that one person's determination of beauty is as good as another's. From this viewpoint, no evaluation outside what individuals make for themselves is appropriate, with disagreements being inevitable and unresolvable. When actor George C. Scott, as General George Patton, overlooks the human carnage littering a battlefield, for example, he confides to his aide that, "God help me, but I love it." To the Individualist, Patton's affirmative aesthetic evaluation would be entirely appropriate with no need to apologize. That the general does apologize to the deity is a moral rather than aesthetic judgment in any case.

If applied to broadcast/cable criticism, this school of thought would largely reduce the critic to the role of inventory taker. "Here are all the things you might like about this program," the alleged critique would say, "but whether you will enjoy any of them or not is entirely up to you and fine with me since your guess is as good as mine." As C. J. Ducasse would have it:

> That a given railroad bridge is a good bridge can be proved or disproved by running over it such trains as we wish it to carry, and observing whether or not it does carry them. But there is no similar test by which the beauty of a landscape would be proved or disproved. Judgments of beauty . . . have to do with the relation of the object judged to the individual's own pleasure experience, of which he himself is the sole possible observer and judge.[5]

By this standard, even a TV test pattern could constitute authentically beautiful programming if, for instance, it reminds you of the past pleasure of making love while a similar graphic was on your screen.

Objectivism

Objectivism, our third school of thought, takes evaluative primacy away from each individual and bestows it on a stable set of standards through which the experts can advise us as to what constitutes beauty and what does not. Thus, Objectivism in Stolnitz's nonendorsing explanation,

> makes no reference to the spectator or, indeed, to anything else except the work. It ascribes value to the work as though beauty were something "out there," in some things and not in others. . . . Therefore, when two people disagree about the value of a specific work, only one of them can be right. . . . "Good taste" is the capacity to apprehend the property of aesthetic value, when it occurs in an object. A man has "bad taste" when he lacks this capacity. . . . Therefore, some aesthetic judgments are authoritative, others are not.[6]

Critics, as defined by this doctrine, would be expected to comprise this body of authorities and would exercise their own good taste in the guidance of other people. There is no tolerance, however, of the notion that consumers' individual backgrounds might modify what, for certain audiences, would constitute a pleasurable experience. Instead, Beethoven is Beethoven, Picasso is Picasso, and even if you do not know their works, you had better learn to like them because cultured people do.

This sort of dogmaticism on the part of a few radio/television critics has rendered their work largely ineffectual. For the public to be told over and over that they should like a given program or format will not cause them to like it if, through premise, content, or scheduling, it fails to tap into the reservoir of the listener/viewer's own experience or expectation. *Beacon Hill,* the much-acclaimed CBS series of 1975, met its demise after thirteen weeks because it attempted to be an upscaled prime-time soap opera by downscaling a classier British series (*Upstairs, Downstairs*). The result was something with which few could really take pleasure even though all the critically specified taste elements were industriously engaged.

Cultural Relativism

In the case of Cultural Relativism, it is not the gods, the individual consumers, or the experts who are thought to play the major role in determining aesthetic standards but rather the cultural institutions of the society. We are all members, willingly or unwillingly, of a culture and one or more subcultures. Therefore, says the Cultural Relativist, we cannot be immune to the way schools, churches, neighborhoods, occupational settings, and political structures form and shape our concept of the preferable and the pleasurable. Neither individual citizen nor critic can escape these influences, goes this school of thought, so the aesthetic standards that the culture implicitly or explicitly sets should be recognized and respected for their beauty-defining power.

At its most extreme and most damaging, this orientation results in the enslavement of art such as happened in Nazi Germany and Stalinist Russia, where the beauty of work was measured in direct proportion to how much it mirrored the ideology and goals of the State. This was much more than the voluntary reflection by the artists of the indigenous concerns of their culture. Instead, it was the impressment of art to the servicing of the State's rather than the citizens' pleasure.

In a conversely principled and productive application of cultural aesthetics, the Canadian government sought to nurture authentic Canadian pleasure by requiring the country's broadcast licensees to feature gradually escalating percentages of Canadian-origin programming on their schedules. With some 80 percent of their people living within 100 miles of the U. S. border, such action was felt to be necessary—not to dominate the broadcasting institution, but to assist it in achieving cultural independence from the much more massive electronic media presences to the south. This Canadianization policy represented Cultural Relativism in action and undertook not only to sustain the growth of uniquely Canadian constructs of beauty but also to strengthen the vehicles that carry them. The problem, however, is that, even though an undeniably distinct French Canadian culture exists and is well-served by its own language radio/television services, some scholars within the Dominion argue that English Canadian culture, if ever there was such a thing, has long ago melted into an aesthetic outlook that is genuinely and nonnationalistically North American.

That a retreat from Canadianization has taken place is the central point of the following critique, which appeared in *The Toronto Star.* Even though the subject of aesthetics is never specifically raised, the foundation for Gerald Caplan's article is clearly a belief in the institutional role that broadcasting should play in "safeguarding, enriching and strengthening" a distinct "fabric" that has the latitude to display its own designs for cultural beauty.

CRTC ALLOWS U.S. TO RULE OUR AIRWAVES, CAPLAN SAYS
by Gerald Caplan

André Bureau, the chairman of the Canadian Radio-television and Telecommunications Commission (CRTC), is unhappy with my recent remarks in this newspaper.

His regulatory agency, I argued, seems to be operating in a vacuum, with no sense of direction that is apparent to the naked eye. The rules of the broadcasting game, which are in the hands of the CRTC to set, have rarely been murkier.

In a Montreal speech March 19, Bureau responded to my "lack of perception" by outlining the CRTC's objectives as they have been pursued since he took over.

The commission "wanted to lift the yoke that limited the choice Canadians had . . . of television and radio services." Then it has sought to replace regulation with supervision combined with self-regulation wherever possible. "We are counting on the broadcasters and advertisers to act responsibly."

After all, the CRTC, its chairman informs us, cannot ensure that "services are varied, appealing and innovative. It is the people who make their living in the broadcasting industry who know what our system needs, and how, when and under what conditions to provide what is lacking."

Well, perhaps André Bureau is right and I should apologize to him. This does add up to a pretty coherent package, and one even more frightening for our broadcasting future than I had understood. For the trouble with the objectives he so proudly outlines is that they contradict the statutory mandate of the CRTC as set down by the Broadcasting Act of 1968.

The CRTC was given the powerful responsibility to regulate and supervise all aspects of Canadian broadcasting according to principles and objectives set down in Section 3 of that act. Their intent is not easy to misinterpret. They were to ensure that Canadian private broadcasters do something more than merely make unlimited profits by showing little more than American programs.

On the contrary. They call for the maintenance of a predominantly Canadian broadcasting system whose lofty goal it is to "safeguard, enrich and strengthen the cultural, political, social and economic fabric of Canada." I'm afraid I cannot find any of these high-minded objectives in Bureau's list.

In fact, while the act itself speaks for the interests of citizens in the broadcasting system, under Bureau, the CRTC seems to speak for the interests of the private broadcasters who can maximize their profits by showing as many popular American shows as they can get away with; these they buy from Hollywood at less than one-tenth the cost of making a Canadian show of roughly equivalent quality.

That is why it's up to the regulator to ensure that private broadcasters make a significant contribution to Canadian programming in return for the privilege of holding their precious—and very profitable—licenses.

For the past quarter century, the CRTC has struggled with private broadcasters to achieve such a contribution. It has failed.

In the last year for which our Task Force had data, 1984–85, private English-language TV stations in Canada spent 33.7 per cent of their program expenditures on "foreign" entertainment and only 10.3 per cent on Canadian entertainment.

In 1985–86, CTV's prime time Canadian entertainment programming consisted of exactly 1 1/2 hours a week. When the Global TV network sought its renewed licence from the CRTC last year, it actually had the chutzpah to want to reduce its already derisory amount of Canadian programming.

In the face of endless evidence of private broadcasters doing exactly what one would expect them to do—make as much money for their shareholders as possible—Bureau speaks of counting on them to regulate themselves in a responsible way, and leaving it to them, "who know what our system needs . . . to provide what is lacking."

He even lists as one of his achievements—under "lifting the yoke that limited the choices Canadians had"—the granting of licences for new independent TV stations across the country, even though our report documented the unassailable evidence that such stations have the poorest record when it comes to providing quality Canadian programming. And in renewing the licences of Global and CTV, the commission made only modest new demands.

The difference between Bureau and his predecessors at the CRTC is this: They, at least, were embarrassed by their failure to ensure a predominantly Canadian broadcasting system. He seems positively to rejoice as, more and more, he allows America to rule the Canadian airwaves.

(Gerald Caplan was co-chairman with Florian Sauvageau of the federal task force on broadcasting.)

(Courtesy of Gerald Caplan)

Biopsychological Relativism

Biopsychological Relativism, the last of our five theories of how pleasure is determined, is the most modern approach and owes the greatest debt to the life sciences. In essence, this orientation takes the position that there is a basic pattern of likes and dislikes native to the organism. The organism thus is not as dependent on cultural/institutional forces, as the Cultural Relativist would suppose. These basic pleasure preferences are found in all men and women, it is argued, because we all share the same biological characteristics—particularly as relates to our sensory apparatus. Therefore, says the Biopsychological Relativist, there are grounds for asserting that one work is better than another based on common psychological laws that grow out of our sensory system similarities.

We seek most of all equilibrium; thus, works that radiate this quality give us pleasure and are a source of beauty. A room with a black ceiling is, for example, psychologically perceived as the antithesis of equilibrium because it seems to press down on us and throw our sense of environmental balance out of kilter. Similarly, random shrieks and whistles repel us because their unstable aural dissonances and unpredictable beats do not provide us with a sense of symmetry in either pitch or rhythmical progression.

The Biopsychological Relativist would concede that cultural institutions shape our initial preferences but that these can be broadened and shifted through formal or experiential education about additional psychologically acceptable stimuli. Thus, Westerners can learn to appreciate the quarter-tone music of the East, and Easterners can learn to prize the diatonic (half and whole tone) scale of Bach and Beethoven because both tonal systems have an internal equilibrium that one can be taught to detect. This does not mean that tambura or koto music could suddenly supplant the rock group's guitars or the jazz band's saxophones in American media music; the cultural ratification of these instruments and their stylings are too widely established (and broadcast) for such a radical shift to take place. What the Biopsychological Relativist would maintain, however, is that there is no long-term psychological barrier to the acceptance of even radically different systems for pleasure production so long as they do not break fundamental perceptual laws. That Orientals have imported more Occidental music than Westerners have adopted the tunes of the East has much more to do with politics and economics than with any inherent aesthetic hierarchy.

The following Mike Harris review for *Variety* evidences several applications of a Biopsychological yardstick for aesthetic evaluation. In Harris's mind, this awards telecast failed because of its multifaceted disdain for the sensory needs of its audience. With a "bitchy" and "mispronounced" script that made one psychologically "cringe," "shoddy and uncoordinated" visual clips that left the audience disoriented, shortage of auditorium and "reaction shots that give awards shows moments of emotion and a chance for audience empathy," and an awards structure that honored the capital 'A' Art of "industry fringe dwellers and buffs" rather than art attuned to the perceptions of the film industry's main audience, the telecast manifested a disequilibrium that would make any public uneasy, regardless of the culture in which they had been raised.

THE 1986 AUSTRALIAN FILM INSTITUTE AWARDS
by Mike Harris

The Australian Film Institute Awards ceremony was late this year because the institute couldn't convince a network it provided the kind of fare that would attract viewers.

Eventually, it was accepted by the government-funded Australian Broadcasting Corp. as a total package, put together by freelance producer Richard Sattler for the AFI and provided at a nominal fee in exchange for air time.

The commercial networks' sense of the show's allure to the public was vindicated since what aired was marred by continual technical glitches and frequently poor directorial judgment.

Host Pamela Stephenson was given a painfully unfunny and astonishingly bitchy script, her oft-mispronounced delivery of which bespoke insufficient attention, lack of rehearsal or both. The whole must have set an Australian record for reasons to cringe.

In an attempt to give the show pace, the producers opted for a compilation of clips linked occasionally by Stephenson and others live from the ballroom of Sydney's Regent Hotel. This was a serious misjudgment because the result came over as not so much swift-moving, glamorous and glitzy as sophomoric, shoddy and uncoordinated. The show simply lacked the professional polish these proceedings require to maintain the remotest vestige of prestige.

The feeling of lack of occasion was exacerbated for those at home by a shortage of auditorium shots, and this non-coverage did nothing to allay the suspicion that there were probably few among the famous in local filmdom who had bothered to attend. Also missing therefore were the reaction shots that give award shows moments of emotion and a chance of audience empathy.

Those watching the box were constantly kept in the dark as clips, pre-recorded by those involved in the various films, were screened sans subtitles that would have revealed the individuals' names and any association with whatever production. Sattler, Molloy and their AFI colleagues obviously knew who the people were and what they did to be included, but for some reason they deigned not to pass on the information to the uninitiated. Thus the prime criticism of the awards as an insular event was reinforced systematically.

As in previous years, the non-cognoscenti were ill served because many of the films nominated have yet to be seen by the general public since unlike the rules for the Oscars, some nominated films have still not managed to secure commercial distribution.

The AFI's system is to allow their nomination, but require those of its mere 2,000 members choosing to vote to have seen all the films or be disenfranchised.

Ergo, critics postulate the awards are more than likely decided by some 600 people, many only industry fringe dwellers and buffs. It is often pointed out that the AFI Awards are orientated towards Art—not so much art with a simple capital, but with an initial letter as elaborately illuminated as any in a medieval tome.

This year's AFI nomination procedure was shunned by the producers of such manifest commercial successes as "Crocodile Dundee" and "Mad Max—Beyond Thunderdome," among others. In what might have been intended as a tongue-in-cheek move that turned out only to be ungraciously heavy-handed and self-conscious, the AFI presented "Dundee" with a special award for the "Best Film That Was Not Nominated." What might have been faintly amusing thus was rendered tawdry.

The evening was one of those where few if any emerge with honor intact, and on this effort there seems evidence enough that it is high time to halt or restructure the AFI Awards, if not the entire backing organization.

(Courtesy of Syd Silverman, *Variety*)

A Schools-of-Thought Conclusion

Whichever the school or schools of aesthetic determination to which one subscribes, the critic and the creator must never forget that it is pleasure, however defined, that brings perceivers to a work and pleasure that keeps them there before it. Though the listeners or viewers may not be able to articulate the sense of beauty they are deriving from a program's characteristics, description is not essential to enjoyment. It remains for the radio/television critic to discern and delineate the elements of a given aesthetic expression in such terms as to construct options assistance rather than taste mandates for the public.

If *aesthetics* refers to pleasure-igniting beauty experiences, then *art* is that collection of articles in which the potential for achieving such experience resides.
In the words of Theodore Meyer Greene, any piece of art is "an object of delight, a vehicle of communication, and, at least potentially, a record of
significant insight."[7] The importance of this communication function is also
stressed by DeWitt Parker, who considers art to be "man's considered dream;
experience remodeled into an image of desire and prepared for communication."[8] Thus, to Parker, art is "the putting forth of purpose, feeling, or thought
into a sensuous medium, where they can be experienced again by the one
who expresses himself and communicated to others."[9]

It could be argued that because radio and television are the quickest and
most efficient vehicles for widespread communication, the electronic media
constitute the richest of all art forms. Such a contention, of course, ignores all
the evaluative questions as to the depth of delight, insight, desire, feeling, or
thought found in a given artistic product. Our point here is that radio and television possess at least as much potential to formulate and communicate aesthetic experiences (and therefore to constitute art) as do older and less amalgamated artistic media. Broadcast/cable critics must estimate to what degree
this potential was realized in the same way as their colleagues in music,
drama, literature, dance, and the visual arts must assess the sensuous effectiveness of specific expressions in those formats.

A more specific and functional way of defining art is to examine the tasks
for which art is recruited. By distilling the insights of a number of aesthetics
scholars and critics, we arrive at a list of six artistic missions, of which three
can be said to be outer-directed toward one's environment and three labeled
as inner-directed toward one's self:

Outer-Directed Tasks of Art

1. Refine society and culture by offering the ideal.
2. See into the present to reveal our world.
3. Cope with the labors of life.

Inner-Directed Tasks of Art

4. Liberate the imagination and put oneself in the place of others.
5. Lessen tension and internal conflict as an aid to mental health.
6. Inspire fear, disgust, and indignation.

Outer-Directed Tasks of Art

Art's first mission, to refine society and culture by offering the ideal, is the
most noble of the six purposes and the one most often thought of in traditional conceptions of artistic merit. "What does improve in the arts is the comprehension of them, and the refining of society which results from it," writes

Northrop Frye.[10] "Art *creates* culture: it creates the values and meanings by which a society fulfills its destiny," adds Eliseo Vivas,[11] and Monroe Beardsley observes that "aesthetic experience offers an ideal for human life."[12]

This task is thus tailor-made to the more lofty goals of public and state-sponsored broadcasting and is the frequently articulated and just as frequently unfulfilled promise that accompanied the initiation first of radio and then television service. Commercial broadcasters also have embraced this objective in their codes, corporate policies, and public pronouncements. Thus, it was that on the introduction of RCA's consumer-aimed telecasting at the 1939 New York World's Fair company Chairman David Sarnoff entoned:

> It is with a feeling of humbleness that I come to the moment of announcing the birth in this country of a new art so important in its implications that it is bound to affect all society. It is an art which shines like a torch of hope in a troubled world. It is a creative force which we must learn to utilize for the benefit of all mankind.[13]

Broad-based agreement as to just what constitutes the "ideal" or universally beneficial program is, of course, difficult to reach and perhaps even more difficult to execute within the time and fiscal pressures of the broadcast/cable industry. Still, as poet Robert Browning knew, "Ah, but a man's reach should exceed his grasp, Or what's a heaven for?"

Art's second task, the idea of seeing into the present to reveal our world would seem, in the electronic arts, to refer mainly to news programs. In fact, it has much broader applications when construed in terms of Greene's explication of this artistic role:

> A work of art is expressive in proportion as the artist succeeds in "telling us something," in *revealing* something about human experience and the reality of which we are a part. . . . Sheer prosaic statement of fact in its unrelieved particularity is, in every universe of discourse, wholly unilluminating and uninteresting. What we crave as intelligent beings is a commentary on our human experience and on the world around us. We want to escape the boredom of sheer particularity by discovering the inner nature of things, their relation to one another, and their larger meaning and significance.[14]

When seen in this light, a sensitive drama, sitcom, or soap opera may have just as much if not more chance than the "unrelieved particularity" of a ponderously structured newscast to accomplish our world revelation task and thus to constitute art.

Further, this concept of seeing into the present is more profound than might be seen at first glance. In the opinion of media theorist Marshall McLuhan, only the artist "has the courage or the sensory training to look directly into the present. [Painter and writer] Wyndham Lewis said years ago, 'The artist is engaged in writing a detailed history of the future because he alone is capable of seeing the present.'"[15] This may be why many people over age thirty value decades-old entertainment programs—and value them much more than documentaries made from decades-old news. The fictional shows seem to reveal to them what living in the fifties or sixties was like with a selective clarity that was missing from the actual experiencing of those times. Certainly, these old series are not scrupulously true to life—but neither are they as untrue as they might have seemed at the time of their first runs.

Showing us our present is just one way art helps us cope with the labors of life, the third and final outer-directed artistic task. At its most functional, art can show us what to do, how to do it, and most important, the way we can feel about this doing. According to perceptual psychologist Rudolf Arnheim, "Art is not the hobby of making reproductions, a game quite independent of other aims and needs, but is rather the expression of an attitude toward life and an indispensable tool in dealing with the tasks of life."[16]

In this regard, the most successful commercials are often not those that merely promote a product as a precise solution to a problem but that move beyond to convey the agreeable feeling that such solution-attainment bestows. The Sealtest TV spot in Figure 9–1, for instance, concentrates on the homey glow that results from experiencing the all-natural product rather than on the mere consumption of the ice cream as food. Even in today's fast-paced, glitzy world (as epitomized by the sports car in Frame 1), one can still "go home" to simpler, nonartificial endeavors by prying open a carton of this product.

Inner-Directed Tasks of Art

The inner-directed counterpoint to coping with life's external tasks is one's need to liberate the imagination and put oneself in the place of others. Art can and should set free our imagination whether or not the art object has an externally pragmatic or mechanical purpose. To DeWitt Parker's way of thinking:

> It must be insisted that the beauty even of useful things exists for the imagination and for it alone. This is true not only of whatever free beauty we may suppose them to possess, but of their functional beauty as well. . . . In either case the work of art becomes the focus of an activity of the imagination, and the values generated by it are realized there. The beauty of utility, therefore, like the beauty of poetry or song, is a beauty for the imagination. And, I would add, it offers the best possible illustration of our definition of beauty, as a value for the imagination taken sensuous shape.[17]

That radio listening or television viewing does not always lead to the accomplishment of some overtly validated chore, then, does not automatically render these activities artistically unproductive. To the extent that the media experience furthers the sensuous shaping of our active imagining, Parker would argue that beauty has been savored.

Often, the liberation of imagination is most easily accomplished through sympathetic (feeling for) or empathetic (feeling as) reactions to depicted characters. As Beardsley sees it, the experiencing of an art object inherently "develops the imagination, and along with it the ability to put oneself in the

Sealtest

CLIENT: Ault Dairies
PRODUCT: Sealtest All Natural Ice Cream
TITLE: 'All Natural Man/Woman'
LENGTH: 30 second TV - English

(MUSIC & SINGERS)
HE: You're a natural woman

SHE: And you're

a natural man

HE: We've found a fabulous ice cream

Full of good things from the land

SPOKEN: People are going natural, discovering

the taste of Sealtest All Natural Ice Cream.

No artificial flavours...

just all natural ingredients.

HE: All natural woman

SHE: All natural man

HE: Yeah...All Natural.....

Figure 9–1 Sealtest "All Natural Man/Woman" Photoboard (Courtesy of Barry R. Base, Base Brown & Partners Limited)

place of others."[18] The apparently widespread acceptance of this dynamic is what motivates public interest group insistence that radio/television portrayals, particularly in programs to which children are frequently exposed, offer characterizations that feature positive role models. "Putting oneself in the place of others" can also entail a heightening of understanding for the needs and problems experienced by society's less fortunate. TV programs and radio songs (*We Are the World; That's What Friends Are For*) that facilitate such understanding are singled out for special praise, even though such praise is often more from a sociological than an artistic perspective.

The lessening of tension and internal conflict as an aid to mental health, our fifth task of art, was recognized by Beardsley as an artistic mechanism that works "perhaps more as a preventative measure than as cure."[19] Art, in other words, cannot solve mental anguish, but it can provide recreative respite from stress and anguish-building situations. Even though, in terms of our Chapter 7 discussion, this may be viewed as escapist, it is also a therapeutic aspect of art that has been recognized for centuries. Thus, as Arnold Hauser observes of the role of literary art in the outwardly prudish chivalric court:

> There is hardly an epoch of Western history whose literature so revels in descriptions of the beauty of the naked body, of dressing and undressing, bathing and washing of the heroes by girls and women, of wedding nights and copulation, of visits to and invitations into bed, as does the chivalric poetry of the rigidly moral Middle Ages. . . . The whole age lives in a state of constant erotic tension[20]

a tension that only art was in a position to relieve without personal risk.

Note, in the following *Adweek* critique by Barbara Lippert, that a similar orientation can be observed in the commercial art of our own sexually tense era:

FEMALE FITNESS COMMERCIAL DROPS THE WEIGHTS ON MEN
by Barbara Lippert

Way back when, we could count on detergent commercials to offend women. They showed homemakers so bug-eyed at the prospect of a brighter-whiter peak experience that with a few more interests they'd measure up to Stepford status. Boy, did those gals have a great time with the measuring cups and those front-loaders. But the detergent people have wised up. Lately, those kinds of soap commercials are becoming a regular feminist oasis. The best of the bunch, I think, is for Bounce: It shows people, not just women, enjoying clean clothes.

These days, strangely enough, the gender offenders in advertising are in the health and fitness area. Because of this new boom, advertisers think they have permission to show a lot more women in bathing suits. While ostensibly showing off strong, lean bodies, they also somehow manage to get in the new cleavage (the sides of breasts) and the new, super-duper, ever revealing, triangulated groin area.

This is a commercial for Marcy Fitness Products' "serious" home-fitness equipment, one of the first in the category aimed at women. In a previous spot, the company set trends in the relationships department by showing a cute, muscular young guy getting up around dawn to use his living-room weight-training machinery, pumping and making Sly Stallone-like monogrunts. The young woman in his bed comes out to squint at him and ask, "Do you do this every morning?"

The tag line, also used in the new spot, is "Marcy. When you finally get serious."

This one shows a woman going through your average day in a rough, male-dominated urban jungle. A man almost runs her over with his cab, some toughs shove her around in the subway, a manly arm dumps a new pile of work on her office desk, and when she gets home, the elevator isn't working (another male screw-up, no doubt). She climbs the stairs to her apartment, gets in the door, leans back and sighs with relief. Then, in the general direction of the living room, she says in a sultry voice, "Boy, do I need you tonight."

She's speaking, of course, to her Marcy home gym, an imposing piece of gleaming steel and black vinyl.

At earlier points in the spot, we get some foreshadowing of the nature of her relationship: After each bad experience with males, we see cuts of this woman working out with her machine, showing the butterfly station, leg extension and the weights slamming down on the stack. This probably satisfied the manufacturer, as it gets in more shots of the product. But it dulls the impact of the shocker, "I need you tonight." And the cuts are too quick.

More power to Marcy for acknowledging the economic strength of women. The resulting spot is intelligent and says a lot in 30 seconds. And doubtless there are many women who use working out as therapy for a bad day (it's one way to gain personal control) and even as sexual sublimation. But there are plenty of men doing that, too. Does a commercial have to play on anti-male feelings in order to show a strong woman?

(Reprinted with permission of *Adweek*)

The tension-release feature of art need not, of course, be limited to the offering of a psychosexual catharsis. In radio/television it can be found in such diverse material as "easy listening" radio that mitigates the staccato stresses of a business day, the sports broadcast that "provides an acceptable outlet for exhibiting emotions and feelings,"[21] and the soap opera that allows one vicariously to settle domestic conflict in even the most autocratic manner without alienating one's own family members. In the words of the painter Pablo Picasso, "Art washes away from the soul the dust of everyday life," and amidst that dusty runoff can be a significant discharge of now neutralized tension.

Our last use of art, to inspire fear, disgust, and indignation, seems, when compared to the other five tasks, both counterproductive and antisocial. Yet, it is this artistic purpose more than any other that distances art's vibrancy from the frail and fragile nature ascribed to it by the prissy. It is this inclination that most clearly epitomizes art's labors in the service of individual humanity. For, as DeWitt Parker asserts:

Despite their painfulness, man has a need for anger, fear, horror, hate and pity— for all the emotions that are his natural reactions to the evil in the world. Man is an organism predestined to life in a difficult, hazardous, and largely hostile environment; he possesses therefore, partly by inborn constitution, and partly as a result of habit and tradition, tendencies to reaction appropriate to such a world. Like all others, these tendencies demand stimulation and expression, and provide their modicum of pleasure when not too strong. Man has a need to hate as well as to love, to fear as well as to feel safe, to be angry as well as to be friendly, to destroy as well as to construct, even to experience pain itself . . . to give vent to hot anger and indignation and, in the imagination at least, to destroy things that one hates and loathes.[22]

Anyone who has cheered as evil is gunned down by the marshal from Abilene or the cops of Hill Street precinct has a referent for what Parker is saying. The same dynamic is present when the pompous boss or conniving seducer gets his come-uppance in a sitcom (or song lyric).

When carefully contemplated and well crafted by the artist/producer, these expressions can further a very positive objective because, states Parker, "there is the intention to inspire fear or disgust for the evils portrayed, in the hope that men may be persuaded to relinquish them. Such works of art are like the 'scare' advertisements that have begun to compete with the older type that appealed through attraction."[23] For the electronic media critic, a 'scare' commercial itself can be considered art—at least, until critical analysis determines it to be too aesthetically deficient to merit that label. In the following television spot, fear, disgust, and indignation are all artfully blended to persuade viewers that the evil of cocaine must, to use Parker's word, be "relinquished."

VIDEO	AUDIO	
OPEN ON LONG SHOT OF LINE OF PEOPLE.	ANNCR VO (WOMAN):	(SEDUCTIVE, ALLURING): Will you lie, cheat and steal for me?
DISSOLVE TO CU OF TEEN BOY.	BOY:	Sure.
CLOSE UP OF BLACK MAN.	ANNCR VO:	Will you give up your job?
	MAN:	Okay.
CLOSE UP OF CAREER WOMAN.	ANNCR VO:	Will you risk prison?
	WOMAN:	Yes.
CLOSE UP OF FAMILY MAN.	ANNCR VO:	Will you abandon your family?
MAN NODS HIS HEAD YES.		(MAN NODS HIS HEAD)
CLOSE UP OF YOUNG MAN.	ANNCR VO:	Will you die for me, if I ask?
	MAN:	I'll die.
	ANNCR VO:	I knew you would.

<u>VIDEO</u>	<u>AUDIO</u>

DISSOLVE TO TITLE CARD.

SUPER: CAREUNIT   ANNCR VO:
        NOBODY CARES THE WAY WE   (MALE):   If you or someone you love
        DO.   loves cocaine, call CareUnit.
                                                We can help.

(Courtesy of Mark Frazier, DDB Needham Worldwide)

Any piece of radio/television content can be analyzed as to how many of art's six purposes it covers and judged as to the pleasurable expressiveness of this coverage. Even though a given program, format, or commercial message will seldom focus on more than one or two of these artistic tasks, the beauty of treatment depends not on task spread but on task depth.

Still, there are those rare creations that manage to treat most if not all of these six artistic employments without causing our perception of the piece's beauty to fragment. Such is the case with *The Cosby Show*'s "Theo's Holiday" episode to which we referred in the previous chapter. By turning to Appendix A and rereading this script, you will find that the show touches on each task of art we have been exploring:

1. We are offered the ideal of a family that goes out of its way to help each other and of parents who work to refine society by the living instruction they provide to make of their children responsible citizens.

2. The present world of high rents, financial rebuffs, and job search complexities is also revealed to be the future world which *The Cosby Show* kids, and the viewing kids, must learn to face.

3. It is through #1 and #2 endeavors that the coping with life's labors is skillfully revealed to constitute the central focus of the entire episode.

4. Theo was given the opportunity to put his present self in the place of his future self and, along with the younger members of the audience, imagine what it will be like to have to function as an independent adult. Through the same parent-directed game, Theo's younger sisters, Vanessa and Rudy, were also able to imagine themselves as other people in a similarly instructive yet pleasurable way—a pleasure in which the viewer could easily share.

5. *The Cosby Show* is generically a sitcom and therefore can explore the tensions of growing up and of parenting in a comedic, stress-lessening manner. The same premise artfully could be treated in the drama of a teenage runaway but with much more anxiety build than tension release.

6. As a "family" program as well as a sitcom, fear, disgust, and indignation are inherently soft-pedaled. Still, the fear of being destitute, of not being able to make it on one's own, is a constant prod to Theo to succeed and to his caring parents as they nudge him toward success.

"The activity of art," maintains Stolnitz, is "the skilled, deliberate manipulation of a medium for the achievement of some purpose."[24] As we have demonstrated in this section, that purpose can be both multifaceted and achievable by the artists serving the radio/television industry. It is the critics' job, like that of Cliff and Clair Huxtable, to nudge those people for whom they are responsible into more mature and personally pleasurable choices.

The Three Sources of Art

We cannot conclude our attempt at art definition without a brief examination of the three categories into which many theorists subdivide the artistic phenomenon. It must be said at the outset that, for the broadcast/cable critic, these categories may be more fancy than function because they focus, to a great extent, on a work's heritage instead of on the more relevant question of the pleasure the work could engender for the listening or viewing audience.

Fine Art

Sometimes also referred to as elite, fine art is described by D. W. Gotshalk as "the production by man of objects intrinsically interesting to perceive; and any object so skillfully produced by man that it has intrinsic perceptual interest has fineness of art."[25] According to this expression, the art of the electronic media has as much chance as any painting, sculpture, poem, or symphony to be designated as "fine" since skillful production and intrinsic interest are certainly to be found in the more competent radio/television creations. In a much more narrow sense, however, fine art is thought of as the art of high culture, which, in its technical and thematic complexity, can only be produced by the most rigorously trained and aesthetically sensitive individuals. With an appeal primarily to the highly educated intelligentsia, fine art impacts a small but international public that accords the artist immense recognition. In short, this is art for art's sake, which, at best, is treated with a pleasure-filled awe and dignity and, at worst, is the plaything of the snobbish and pretentious.

Folk Art

Folk art, meanwhile, is the indigenous art of a culture that grows up spontaneously among and in the service of the commoners. Unlike fine art, it is inherently functional, like the shepherd songs to quiet the sheep and the patterned wall hanging to keep out the draft. Folk art is often produced by anonymous consumers for their own use with no formalized education required for either the art's conception or consumption. It is even the cable public-access channel and the community-licensed volunteer radio station on which everyone is equally free to attempt their untutored aesthetic best. Because it has its genesis in the traditions of a single people, folk art is usually unknown or uncomprehended outside the boundaries of its own region unless, like the Cabbage Patch Doll, it becomes exploitable on the mass market.

The following chart isolates fine/folk distinctions based on the five key elements we have just touched upon:

Characteristic	Fine Art	Folk Art
1. Artist identity	usually famous	usually anonymous
2. Artist/consumer connection	separate people	often the same person
3. Artist training	highly formalized	informal/self-taught
4. Transferability	international; crosses cultures	region-bound
5. Utility	art for art's sake	functional/practical

Pop Art

Pop (popular) art is a much more controversial category because many theorists charge it with doing violence to the two previously discussed art types. Particularly when referred to as *kitsch* (the German term for mass culture), this mass media-created art is viewed as a parasite that feeds off and could ultimately destroy both fine and folk art. More than thirty years ago, for instance, Dwight Macdonald charged:

> Mass Culture is imposed from above. It is fabricated by technicians hired by businessmen; its audiences are passive consumers, their participation limited to buying and not buying. The Lords of *kitsch,* in short, exploit the cultural needs of the masses in order to make a profit and/or to maintain their class rule. . . . Folk Art was the people's own institution, their private little garden walled off from the great formal park of their master's High Culture. But Mass Culture breaks down the wall, integrating the masses into a debased form of High Culture and thus becoming an instrument of political domination.[26]

The "wall" between the fine and the folk was not always as rigid as Macdonald suggests. Beethoven, for instance, freely borrowed from German peasant dances to create the third movement of his Pastoral Symphony. This taking did not debase the peasant dance but refined and preserved it. When *kitsch* reduces that same movement to a ninety-second "hooked-on classic" with a disco beat, however, "fabrication" rather than enrichment has clearly come to pass and the pleasure potential of the work has been pulverized, just as Macdonald predicted.

In contrast, even though rock-and-roll has been similarly castigated as *kitsch,* musicologists point out that it was, in fact, a blending of the rich folk traditions of primarily black rhythm-and-blues with primarily white country music into a new pop authenticity that radio carried but did not contrive. True, some debased versions of rock-and-roll did later emerge, but they are as far from the original as disco is from Beethoven's Pastoral.

That radio and television are referred to solely as "popular arts" conveyors suggests a somewhat invidious comparison. From what can "popular" arts be distinguished except unpopular arts? Can there really be such a thing? Of what possible value is this implied dichotomy except to demean equally the well-crafted sitcom, the intricately poetic ballet, and the brilliantly woven Native American blanket? Russel Nye persuasively argues that an art can be "popular" without being *kitsch* and without raping the other art forms when he writes in *The Unembarrassed Muse:*

> The fact that the mass audience exists, and that the popular artist must create for it, are simply the primary facts of life for the popular arts. Popular art can depend on no subsidy, state or patron; it has to pay its way by giving the public what it wants, which may not always agree with what the artist may feel to be the most aesthetically apt. Satisfying a large audience involves no less skill than pleasing a smaller or more sophisticated one; popular artists can and do develop tremendous expertise and real talent. A best-selling paperback is not *ipso facto* bad; a song is not necessarily worthless because people hum it; a painting is neither bad because many look at it with pleasure nor good because few do.[27]

And Northrop Frye makes an historical case for the legitimacy of sturdily constructed popular art as he observes:

> Popular art is normally decried as vulgar by the cultivated people of its time; then it loses favor with its original audience as a new generation grows up; then it begins to merge into the softer lighting of "quaint," and cultivated people become interested in it, and finally it begins to take on the archaic dignity of the primitive.[28]

Television's *The Honeymooners* and *Leave It to Beaver,* together with radio's renewed attention to everything from big band to classical soul recordings, are thus figments of an artistic imagination that seems only to grow stronger as the so-called popular arts evolve.

Nonetheless, radio/television's alleged preoccupation with only the popular arts hobbled critical appreciation both of these media and of these arts until Gilbert Seldes blazed a new trail. Indeed, more than any other critic, Seldes dismantled the contention of art segmentation by championing broadcasting as the carrier of not just pop art but of the *public* arts. As Seldes delineated the artistic spectrum, his central premise was this:

> The fine arts, it can be said, express the soul of a people (the eternal), and the folk arts reflect earthly experience over the centuries (the past). The popular arts express the present moment, the instant mood. . . . I am now trying not to isolate, but to connect them, and the essential connection is this: they [the public arts] are

a cross-section of the classic, the folk, and the fine arts, and you may think of this cross-section as fanning out from a narrow base in the classics, widening in the folk arts, and almost as broad in the field of the popular arts as the field itself. . . . Whenever any art, because of specific circumstances, takes on the quality of a public art, it has an effect on us and, in principle, invites or requires an action on our part—acceptance, criticism, rejection.[29]

Most made possible by the scope and reach-efficiency of the broadcast/ cablecast, the "cross-sectional" public arts thus constitute unparalleled opportunities to experience pleasure—and unparalleled work for the critic in aiding audiences in the quantitatively massive acceptance/rejection process. The number of available radio and television choices has multiplied three or four fold since Seldes wrote his observation. Our "invited or required actions" to the public arts are therefore now all the more perplexing because they are all the more numerous.

The core definitions for *aesthetics* and *art* have not changed—but the number of works that potentially relate to these definitions, and the opportunities to exhibit and experience such works, have increased exponentially in the electronic age. Radio/television criticism has yet to catch up with these burgeoning and cross-pollinating public arts; and it must. As Moses Hadas believes, "The larger and more indiscriminate the audience, the greater the need to safeguard and purify standards of quality and taste."[30] The critic should not attempt to make decisions for audience members but must be available and able to provide the benchmarks by which they can derive aesthetic (pleasurable) determinations for themselves.

Notes

1. F. V. N. Painter, *Elementary Guide to Literary Criticism* (Boston: Ginn and Company, 1903), 34.
2. George Santayana, "The Nature of Beauty," in Melvin Rader (ed.), *A Modern Book of Esthetics,* 5th ed. (New York: Holt, Rinehart and Winston, 1979), 172.
3. Jerome Stolnitz, *Aesthetics and Philosophy of Art Criticism* (Boston: Houghton Mifflin, 1960), 30–31.
4. Clive Bell, "Significant Form," in Rader, *Esthetics*, 287.
5. C. J. Ducasse, *The Philosophy of Art* (New York: The Dial Press, 1929), 286.
6. Stolnitz, *Art Criticism*, 390–92.
7. Theodore Meyer Greene, *The Arts and the Art of Criticism* (Princeton: Princeton University Press, 1952), vii.
8. DeWitt Parker, *The Analysis of Art* (New Haven: Yale University Press, 1926), 180–81.
9. DeWitt Parker, *The Principles of Aesthetics* (Westport, Conn: Greenwood Press, 1976), 13.
10. Northrop Frye, *Anatomy of Criticism* (Princeton: Princeton University Press, 1957), 344.
11. Eliseo Vivas, *Creation and Discovery* (New York: The Noonday Press, 1955), x.
12. Monroe Beardsley, *Aesthetics: Problems in Philosophy of Criticism* (New York: Harcourt, Brace and World, 1958), 574.

13. Allison Simmons, "Television and Art: A Historical Primer for an Improbable Alliance," in Douglas Davis and Allison Simmons, eds., *The New Television: A Public/Private Art* (Cambridge, Mass.: M.I.T. Press, 1977), 3.
14. Greene, *Criticism*, 43.
15. Marshall McLuhan, "Great Change-overs for You," in Harry Skornia and Jack Kitson, eds., *Problems and Controversies in Television and Radio* (Palo Alto, Calif.: Pacific Books, 1968), 26.
16. Rudolf Arnheim, *Toward a Psychology of Art* (Berkeley: University of California Press, 1966), 41.
17. Parker, *Analysis,* 131–32.
18. Beardsley, *Aesthetics,* 574.
19. Ibid.
20. Arnold Hauser, *The Social History of Art,* Vol. 1 (New York: Vintage Books, 1951), 219.
21. Walter Gantz, "An Exploration of Viewing Motives and Behaviors Associated with Television Sports," *Journal of Broadcasting* (Summer 1981): 264.
22. Parker, *Analysis,* 118–19.
23. Ibid., 114.
24. Stolnitz, *Art Criticism,* 93.
25. D. W. Gotshalk, *Art and the Social Order* (Chicago: The University of Chicago Press, 1947), 29.
26. Dwight Macdonald, "A Theory of Mass Culture," in Bernard Rosenberg and David White, eds., *Mass Culture* (New York: The Free Press, 1957), 60.
27. Russel Nye, *The Unembarrassed Muse* (New York: The Dial Press, 1970), 6–7.
28. Frye, *Anatomy,* 108.
29. Gilbert Seldes, *The Public Arts* (New York: Simon and Schuster, 1956), 286–87.
30. Moses Hadas, "Climate of Criticism," in Robert Lewis Shayon, ed., *The Eighth Art* (New York: Holt, Rinehart and Winston, 1962), 16.

10

The Logic
of Aesthetic Form

As we discussed in Chapter 9, broadcast/cable content possesses the potential to serve as art and thus to satisfy us aesthetically. As part of that discussion, it was necessary to explore how radio and television material is capable of performing each of the six definitional tasks of art. We now present a system by which we can estimate and evaluate this artistic potential.

Of the myriad standards that attempt to judge art, many can be applied only to a single art form or were developed to serve the appraisal needs of fine (elite) art exclusively. Fortunately, other benchmarks exist. One of the most eclectic and thus most adaptable to the multiple components from which radio/television content is derived is DeWitt Parker's logic of aesthetic form. Consisting of six elements, this logic coalesces the insights of philosophers and aestheticians dating back to the ancient Greeks and fashions these in such a way that they do no art a disservice. With such a heritage and utility, Parker's logic can be supremely useful in the aesthetic critiquing of the variegated electronic arts. As delineated in his 1926 book, *The Analysis of Art*, Parker's logic derives from:

1. Organic unity
2. Theme
3. Thematic variation
4. Balance
5. Evolution
6. Hierarchy

The following sections examine each element in turn by defining its scope and illuminating its possible manifestations in broadcast/cable material.

Organic Unity

This concept, at least as old as Aristotle, means that in the construction of an art object, the whole must be greater than the sum of its parts. Further, as Theodore Meyer Greene instructs, "No whole can exist without its parts, and the more organized the whole, the more essential the contribution of each constituent."[1] Thus, whole and parts are mutually interdependent, resulting in what Greene would characterize as a work of art that

> has an artistic vitality of its own. Its parts derive their artistic significance from the larger whole of which they are the constituent members, and its artistic unity, in turn, depends upon the contributions of its several parts and aspects.[2]

Professor Gerald Herbener provides a specific example of this phenomenon when he observes that "for instance, we may think of the point in the creation of a painting in which the final dot of paint has been applied. Before that moment the picture was not yet 'complete.' A speck more, however, will be too much."[3]

Organic unity is what is sought in a solid debate case or a brilliant legal brief. In each, every part of the argument presented is relevant and necessary to winning the issue. Part also dovetails with part in such a way that one cannot attack any link in the chain of reasoning and therefore must surrender to the unassailability of the interlocked whole. So it is in a work of art, where, as philosopher/educator John Dewey realized:

> Different acts, episodes, occurrences melt and fuse into unity, and yet do not disappear and lose their own character as they do so—just as in a genial conversation there is a continuous interchange and blending, and yet each speaker not only retains his own character but manifests it more clearly than is his wont. . . . The existence of this unity is constituted by a single *quality* that pervades the entire experience in spite of the variation of its constituent parts.[4]

Organic unity is a characterizable whole but one that, in the words of Professor Thomas Olson, "avoids monotony (too few materials) with variety through design and avoids confusion (too many materials) with unity through pattern."[5] The result, according to Greene, is "the product of a happy resolution of the dynamic tension between the extremes of empty simplicity and unorganized complexity."[6]

In television, a frequently cited example of monotony or "empty simplicity" is the so-called talking head, in which an on-camera speaker addresses the viewer for an extended period without benefit of shot changes or interest-enhancing visual embellishments. There are too few materials here to retain audience interest, because unlike a real-life conversation situation, the viewer cannot break the monotony by talking back. At the other extreme is the video kaleidoscope that shows the speaker from so many rapidly shifting perspectives that the meaning of his or her words is lost. For the audience, this is like trying to comprehend what is being said by a person in the back seat of a rollercoaster car when you are seated in the front. There is, of course, a middle ground between these two approaches, and it is precisely at the center of this middle ground that a productional organic unity can be found by the director who functions as artist rather than as mere technician.

On radio, the organic unity of the format is of preeminent importance. Too few elements, and listener attention will wane; too many elements, and an unsettling fragmentation sets in. The artistic trick is to feature format events that can be individually enjoyed and yet collectively clustered so our enjoyment of the first element to which we tune sets up an anticipation that is cumulatively fulfilled by the linkage of other events to follow. For a specific example of radio organic unity realized, turn back to the Alan Bunce review of *Performance Today* in Chapter 2. When Bunce alludes to a "skillfully integrated diet of classical music and arts features," "a timely mix," and the "seamless" merging of national and local identities and contributions, he is, of course, detecting the presence of organic unity.

"Unity and multiplicity—these are not disparate but complementary aims," Carl Grabo affirms.[7] That such a complement is difficult to assemble only attests to the fact that the creation of art is not an effortless task. This is as true for radio/television programming as it is for any other artistic endeavor, and in every case, the artistic effect is diminished when the audience perceives the creator's struggles. The intricate jazz textures of the great Duke Ellington Band, for instance, are so pleasing because they seem so facile. But as the Duke himself once revealed, "Simplicity is, you understand, really complicated." There can be no better encapsulation of the essence of organic unity.

Theme

At its most fundamental, theme is the single or main course that a work of art charts. It is the core of the piece that the audience should be able to examine or ignore as it prefers. Theme undergirds the work, but it must not be so apparent that the perceiver is forever stumbling on its unrecessed beams. As George Boas cautions, "one of the things of which no one approves—except a professor—is to see the bare bones of structure and formula protruding through the substance and flesh."[8]

Theme arises from conflicting elements, whether these elements are of color, shape, tone, value, attitude, or design. This conflict tests and judges the theme, but it should never be mistaken for the theme itself. Thus, theme is a statement, never a question, and the affirmation or negation of this statement constitutes the motive force for the entire work. More than any other element, theme is the work's value-carrrier, even though this value may just as likely express tonal, emotive, or design significance as it does a moral or ethical stand.

Finally, a valid theme endures because it contains within itself a declaration not limited to a certain time or culture. Other ages or peoples may interpret this theme differently, but it remains impressive in the sense that it strikes a chord of expressive recognition (if not agreement) and strikes it in a distinctive manner. "Basic human situations like love, death, celebration, and illness constantly recur as the themes of art," writes Edmund Feldman, "but they can be saved from banality by the uniquely personal comment the artist seems to make about them."[9]

Obviously, any broadcast drama, sitcom, action/adventure, or soap opera encases a theme, and it is up to the critic to determine whether that theme in each case is banal, profound, or somewhere in between. Newscasts, game shows, and sports broadcasts can be said to possess themes, too: the recurring theme of the news anchor as your omniscient sentry; the game show's insistence on the intellectual supremacy of cute and perky; the sportscast-asserted triumph of the outclassed cellar-dweller's spirit. Such themes structure these programs to our expectations as, week after week, they fulfill their own prophecies.

Commercials brandish their own themes, of course, and these tend to be much more pointed because they fundamentally exist to sell a thematic concept within a bare minimum of time. Unlike other radio/television content, the commercial's theme cannot usually afford to be subtle underpinning but instead must function as overt message and audience motivator. This is especially true in the increasingly cluttered environment of the North American broadcast media. Thus, in the Canadian Sealtest spot in Chapter 9, the theme of the product as purveyor of traditional, "all natural" goodness to modern people comes through in every frame. That same theme is the basis for the Figure 10–1 spot on behalf of a Minneapolis dairy. In this instance, however, thematic execution relies on humor rather than human interest. As in the case of programs, any given theme, in the hands of skillful creators, can be propelled in several ways to service the needs of different shows or products.

In less congested commercial environments, spot themes can afford to be more subtle, and perhaps even ironic, like the British advertisement in Figure 10–2. Though our man Arkwright's memories of past anniversaries seem limited to what part of the pub he occupied, they apparently are anchored by his continuous consumption of John Smith's Yorkshire Bitter. The tongue-in-cheek expression of commercial theme is withheld until the last frame, in which the viewer is invited to chuckle at its sardonic expression and thereby inadvertently to accept it.

Thematic Variation

This third element in DeWitt Parker's logic serves to showcase or illuminate the theme from several different angles. To aesthetician Eliseo Vivas, "The

Kemps Ice Cream
"Peppermint Bon Bon Cow"
:30 Television Spot

"Now you probably know that Kemps Ice Cream comes in over 30 delicious flavors. But did you ever stop to think of where we get 'em all?

Well, Kemps Vanilla ice cream comes from one of these — a Vanilla cow.

Chocolate ice cream...

...a Chocolate cow.

And Kemps Chocolate Chip ice cream...

...from one of these.

OK you ask, where does Kemps Peppermint Bon Bon ice cream come from?

Where do you think?"

ANNCR: Kemps Ice Cream. It's The Cows.

Produced by Martin/Williams Advertising

Figure 10–1 Kemp's Ice Cream "Peppermint Bon Bon Cow" Photoboard (Courtesy of John G. Jarvis and Mark Haumersen, Martin/Williams Advertising Incorporated)

181

WIFE: A fine way to spend our 30th wedding anniversary. (PAUSE).

WIFE: We came here for our 20th anniversary.

ARKWRIGHT: No we didn't. We stood at the bar.

ANNCR (VO): John Smith's Yorkshire Bitter. It's what memories are made of.

Figure 10–2 John Smith's Yorkshire Bitter "Anniversary" Photoboard (Courtesy of Bill Galacher, Boase Missimi Pollitt)

variation of the theme aids it in providing the striking quality required to shock attention, to surprise it, and to present it with some degree of difficulty, without which it would become lax through boredom."[10] Parker himself would add:

> It is not sufficient to state the theme of a work of art; it must be elaborated and embroidered. One of the prominent ways of doing this is to make it echo and ree-cho in our minds. . . . Yet to find the same thing barely repeated is monotonous; hence what we want is the same, to be sure, but the same with a difference; thematic variance.[11]

Parker then proceeds to list the four main techniques by which the variation can be accomplished: recurrence, transposition, alternation, and inversion.

Recurrence

Recurrence is the simplest of these devices; it involves the mere repetition of the theme, such as the wallpaper pattern that uniformly reproduces itself from one corner of the room to the other or the musical round in which we *Row, Row, Row Your Boat* to a musical theme varied only in terms of the moment at which each of its expressions begins.

In radio, we most clearly find recurrence in the short-playlist CHR (Contemporary Hit Radio) or Top-40 format in which the same few tunes are constantly recycled throughout the day. *CNN Headline News,* meanwhile, is recurrence in video as we encounter like modules, in like order, every thirty minutes. The presence of this phenomenon is also readily apparent in the construction of every episode of a game show or action/adventure series in which the same type of activities (be they a wheel spin, the move into double jeopardy, or car/plane/boat chase) push along the program's premise at a consistent time in each episode.

Transposition

Transposition, in contrast, takes the same thematic element and shifts it into another key, tonality, color, design, shape, brightness, or character articulation. We experience the thematic idea higher or lower, darker or lighter, more straight or more curved, or more happy or sad. It is the same theme, but in a new dressing.

Thus, a radio music format will typically feature more "down" than "up" tempo tunes in afternoon as compared to morning drive time, but the thematic type of music conveyed (country, urban contemporary, easy listening, etc.) remains consistent. Similarly, a noon TV newscast may feature a softer and more hints/helps packaging than that station's late evening effort, but the central concept of "Eyewitness News," "Looking Out for You," "Move Closer to Your World," or "News When You Need It" is maintained across all dayparts.

Alternation

Alternation, the third category of thematic variation, is more complex; in order to function properly, it requires the presence of two themes or at least of two transpositions of the same theme. Because of this, alternation is more difficult to find in the more basic and formulary radio/television endeavors, in which a single thematic presence is relied on to avoid complications that can confuse an audience.

The block-programmed radio station, which features fundamentally different kinds of content during different dayparts, faces this problem. Thus, though it may try to project itself as "the spot for discriminating moderns," a facility that, for example, splits itself into classical and jazz or, 'lite' music and talk blocks, lacks a functional thematic consistency in addressing listener needs. In local television, a like difficulty is faced by the prime-time access (early evening) checkerboard as opposed to the stripped program schedule. In the former, a different program appears in a given time slot each day of the week; in the latter, five installments of the same series fill the time period. Even if the five checkerboarded programs are all game shows or sitcoms, this alternation still forces viewers to be more thematically flexible in their expectations than the program strip requires. Unfortunately, many viewers do not want the complications of prime time's night-to-night variation in a preprime time period.

Inversion

Inversion, finally, is thematic reversal in which we view the theme from the completely opposite perspective. Black is now white, good is now bad, light is now dark, and high is now low. Such radical shifts of perspective can be accommodated in the fine and folk arts, in which an attentive clientele accustomed to the subject's nuances exists. But inversion for the more heterogeneous pop arts audience can be more distortive than delineating. A personality-heavy radio format cannot, at the same time, express itself with "more platters, less chatter;" a lovable sitcom or soap opera character cannot be permitted to simultaneously project evil lest we lose mass audience identification and involvement. True, longer forms such as the made-for-TV movie and the mini-series could cope with inversion but only at the risk of losing by confusing a less perceptive or often distracted viewership.

Still, when one thematic statement has been relentlessly established in other media messages, thematic variation by inversion can be used to provide the "attention shock" of which Vivas spoke. As described by Barbara Lippert in her weekly *Adweek* critique column, such is the case in a recent New Fab commercial in which the twin inversion of using a male rather than a female and of robing rather then disrobing embroider the premise (the theme) that this detergent makes clothing "so sinfully soft your family will love to put it on."

NEW FAB'S BUMP AND GRIND AWASH IN GOOD, CLEAN FUN
by Barbara Lippert

It only took about 20 years of showing women nosing around laundry baskets, comparing whiteness and freshness, for advertisers to realize that being good washerwomen wasn't all women wanted to be. Not unless they already had a few lobes removed. These days, it seems, detergent makers have gone contempo and come clean. So inoffensive, so grown up are these commericals that everyone appears to like clean clothing, not just Mom.

Into this enlightened world pop two new spots for New Fab with the "unique advanced softening system." That system may not sound very sexy, but that's what it seemingly suggested to the agency. In these spots, clothing becomes "so sinfully soft your family will love to put it on." In turn, the commercials feature a "reverse strip," showing a naked man dressing, even going in for a little hip bump as he puts it on, puts it on, puts it *all* on. He's accompanied, of course, by stripteasy music.

This spot may not offer the most original way to propel us into the 21st-century wash cycle. But it's not without humor. It takes the curse off the whole whose-wash-is-it-anyway issue. Showing sex objects doesn't particularly help anybody, but if you're going to do it, it's safer to stick with male skin. That way, advertisers don't set off the Emergency Feminist Broadcast System.

In the spot for Fab powder, the male model is shown putting on a pair of jeans. The tight jeans, the rear-end watching, the male-strip joke all struck me as rather 1970ish, but that was before I consulted one of my impeccable sources, *Weekly World News*. Under the headline "500 Fire-Breathing Females Demolish Disco," and subhead, "Women Riot When Male Strip Show is Canceled," comes this: "Wild-eyed women threw bottles, slugged it out with fists and pocketbooks, broke glasses and smashed lights at the Howard Johnson's Ritz disco in Monroeville, Pa., after an announcement that the male strippers were not going to strut their stuff."

In the face of that account of 500 fire-breathing women, it would be difficult to suggest that male striptease has gone the way of casual sex.

The spot for Fab liquid shows the same guy, hitting the ground running in the morning (his bare legs touching the wide-planked wood floor) and then donning a pair of yellow sweat pants—and tightly pulling the drawstring. He looks particularly pleased after that pull, the kind of pleasure usually seen in commercials as a way of conveying the delicious taste of pancake syrup.

Curiously, there's another spot around that has to do with washing machines and near-naked men: the British-made Levi's commercial now being seen in the U.S. Set in the '50's, it shows a guy going into a laundromat and stripping down to his shorts, in public, to throw stones and his jeans in the washer.

He's doing his own stone-washing, of course, and there's some romance to it. The Fab guy, of course, has a more limited script. But if nothing else, he'll clean up in Monroeville.

(Reprinted with permission of *Adweek*)

Balance

The fourth of Parker's logic components, balance is defined by Feldman as "the resolution of all forces in a structure leading to equilibrium or equipoise. It is evident in nature, in man, and in the man-made world."[12] "Balance not only adds clarity and vividness to a work," submits Olson, "it is intrinsically satisfying."[13] For his part, Parker asserts that balance "is equality of opposing or contrasting elements."[14] Such equality or stability comprises this artistic ingredient's essence, an essence construed, as Parker inferred above, by employing the mechanism of contrast.

To Jerome Stolnitz, contrast entails "setting against each other *unlike* elements which nonetheless harmonize with each other. The distinctive character of each element calls attention to that of its opposite, e.g., a 'warm' and a 'cold' color. Yet together their dissimilarities become unified; so the juxtaposition of 'warm' and 'cold' colors constitute a sensuously pleasing pattern."[15] We cannot, then, have balance without contrast, and we cannot derive contrast without the dynamic workings of a pair of equally matched opposites. In a very rudimentary sense, this can be observed in a dialogue commercial like the following, in which both the seller voice (NORM) and the buyer voice (EDDIE) must be evenly paired if we are to believe in the truth of the persuasive progression. A reticent buyer who succumbs almost immediately to the loquacious sales pitch is a feeble opponent, a straw man incapable of properly exemplifying the listener's ingrained reluctance to purchase. In this spot from the Dick Orkin Radio Ranch,[16] however, both the salesman and the prospect make a balanced contribution that thus maintains a pleasing equilibrium in point of view as well as in the number of words apportioned to the uniformly brief speeches of each.

(SFX: COCKTAIL PIANO, CLINKING GLASSES IN BACKGROUND)

NORM: Eddie, this is some grand opening.

EDDIE: Uncle Normy, I owe it all to you.

NORM: Aunt Verna said I was a nincompoop to invest in your business.

EDDIE: A nincompoop! (laughs)

NORM: But seeing all this --- the champagne, the plush carpeting --- I did the right thing.

EDDIE: Sure made my day.

NORM: Listen, I need to use your phone.

EDDIE: There's a pay phone in the gas station across the street.

NORM: Eddie, this is the man who sunk his life savings into your new business.

EDDIE: I don't have an office phone.

NORM: How can you run a business without a phone system?

EDDIE: It was so complicated: who to call, what to get. So I put in a hot tub instead.

NORM: Why didn't you call AT&T Small Business Connection?

EDDIE: I dunno.

NORM: With AT&T you can buy your phone --- traditional or state-of-the-art equipment.

EDDIE: Track lighting took a big hunk.

NORM: There's other options, Eddie. Financing arrangements and service contracts.

EDDIE: I dunno.

NORM: What if you have to make a conference call?

EDDIE: That phone booth is pretty darn big.

NORM: Verna was right. I'm a nincompoop.

EDDIE: Okay, I'll call AT&T.

NORM: Thank you. Now I've got to splash some cold water on my face. Where's your washroom?

EDDIE: Across the street at the gas station.

NORM: What?

EDDIE: It was either that or a big-screen TV.

NORM: Oh, for crying out ---

ANNCR: Call 1-800-247-7000. AT&T Information Systems. When you've got to be right.

(Reprinted with permission of *Adweek*)

Balance, in an even more literal sense, is a dominant concern of electronic news. For not only must the newscast balance the coverage of controversial issues to stay on the good side of journalistic ethics and fairness, but it must also provide an equilibrium between heavy and light (or hard or soft) stories, between sports and weather, and even between one anchorperson and another. Twin anchors are seen as necessary not just to even out the workload and provide a stable and contrasting pictorial/verbal environment, but also to represent an equal opportunity equipoise among the population groups who make up the outlet's viewership.

The complexities of this managerial, sociological, and aesthetic balancing act are sketched in the following column by *The Chicago Tribune*'s Steve Daley. Clearly, what germinated with Huntley and Brinkley in 1956 as an accidentally discovered method for perceptually stabilizing a newscast has sprouted into a tangled thicket of considerations that nurtures as well as obscures the concerns of artistic equilibrium.

CHANGES AT CHANNEL 5 MAY BE JUST TEMPORARY
by Steve Daley

There may be as many ways to interpret the latest anchor shuffle at WMAQ–TV–Ch. 5 as there have been game plans over the years at the NBC-owned station. Editorial director Mary Laney and reporter Art Norman have been handed the station's 6 P.M. newscast, and Carol Marin moves to join her 10 P.M. partner, Ron Magers, at 4:30. The new arrangement begins Monday.

You can accept vice president and general manager Richard Lobo's notion that he wishes to solidify the pairing of Magers and Marin, moving Marin into the chair left vacant by Deborah Norville.

You can note the continuing ratings difficulties endured by the 6 P.M. show and consider that despite Marin's estimable reputation, television news is a ratings-driven endeavor.

Or, you can listen to some voices in the Channel 5 newsroom and at rival stations, voices that insist the professional marriage of Laney and Norman is a shotgun affair that, once the public-relations bloom has faded, will lead to an abandonment of the station's 6 o'clock newscast.

"I see our real strengths at 4:30 and 10, and we think asking Carol to team up with Ron on both shows will do that. At 6, I believe we can take a flier with Mary and Art, two people we think have great potential in this market."

Lobo denied he was interested in getting out of the news business at 6. "I know this isn't being seen as a traditional kind of move," he said, "but I can afford to take some chances at 6. We're not exactly in a lead position there. And it's a luxury to be able to promote people from inside rather than import them."

Despite a tidal wave of leaks reaching back to November, Channel 5 kept bailing on an announcement about Norman and Laney, waiting until Marin returned from a reporting assignment in Honduras Jan. 29.

New financial deals were cut with Laney and Norman, deals that reportedly would bring a smile to the face of any budget-minded station manager. "They've now got the cheapest anchor team in the free world," said one executive at a rival station. "The whole thing was done so Dick Lobo could get on the air doing editorials."

That's a harsh and unrealistic assessment but, inside Channel 5, the switch at 6 o'clock has engendered a wild-eyed search for motive.

Is the crux of the move a corporate nod in the direction of Operation PUSH, which, during its 1985–86 boycott of Channel 2, expressed a preference for black male anchors over black female anchors?

The rise of Norman [who is represented by former PUSH president Tom Todd], and Channel 2's Lester Holt, as well as the recent departure of Channel 5's Marlene McClinton and the weekend placement of Channel 2's Robin Brantley in that station's anchor line-up make the question inevitable.

The elevation of Mary Laney is part of a continuing saga, one that reaches back to the reign of former Channel 5 general manager Monte Newman.

"There's nothing new about this, really," said one newsroom source who requested anonymity. "Mary would sit in those editorial board meetings with Monte and tell him she was the only person in the building who really knew Chicago. For some reason, Monte was never able to get her back in the newsroom, but Dick Lobo has."

Marin welcomes the chance to work twice a day with Magers. Other matters, she says, have been straightened out to her liking.

"I wouldn't have done it if the station hadn't addressed my primary concern," said Marin, who won an Alfred duPont–Columbia University award for broadcast journalism Wednesday. "That's the reporting. The station has allayed those concerns, to the point of not making me be here everyday [at 4:30] when I'm out doing the reporting."

Both Lobo and Marin insist that the nature of the early newscast will not change, that the show will not wander in the interview-based direction of WBBM–Channel 2's "First Edition." For Marin, that call was easy: "It's simple. I'm not going to interview Carol Channing."

Station insiders, imbued in recent months with a sense that circumstances were improving at Channel 5, worry about the Laney–Norman gamble and about the "negative feelings" that must come with taking Marin off the 6 o'clock newscast.

Dick Lobo thinks his new pairing may be underestimated. The February ratings "sweeps" are upon local TV, and the May ratings book rushes in right behind it. A verdict on this latest change may not be long in coming.

(Courtesy of F. Richard Ciccone, *Chicago Tribune*)

In anchor selection or any other programmatic endeavor, one cannot lose sight of the fact that balance comes not just from the pairing of two entities, but from the pairing of two equivalent entities. As Parker asserts:

> Hence, just as only equal weights will balance in a scale pan, so only elements that are somehow equal in value, despite their opposition, will balance aesthetically. . . . The essential thing about balance is equality of opposed values, however unlike be the things that embody or carry the values.[17]

Balance is so important to our valuation of an object because more than any other element of the logic of aesthetic form, it serves a deep-seated human need that the Biopsychological Relativist would especially appreciate. Parker himself best articulates this need when he recounts that:

> our entire emotional life is constructed on the principle of polarity: stimulation, repose; joy, sadness; love, hate; tension, relaxation. Not only is the organism bilaterally symmetrical, and the muscles built in pairs of balancing antagonists; the inner life has a similar plan. Furthermore, each polar element *demands* its antagonist; it contains within itself already a desire and a premonition of its opposite. Joy contains an impulse to sorrow, and vice versa; hate to love; love to hate. . . . This principle is of the greatest value in explaining the presence of evil and pain in art; for in the long run man prefers a world in which there is the night side as well as the daylight side of life.[18]

Evolution

For art, the term *evolution* is not used in the Darwinian sense to chart species adaptation but rather decrees that the parts we perceive first in examining an art object should pleasingly determine those we encounter later. In contrast to the frozen quality of balance, evolution is fluid. As Parker puts it, "The static character of balance is opposed to the dynamic character of evolution; indeed, all movement depends upon the upsetting of an established equilibrium."[19] Were we to have nothing but balance, nothing but equilibrium, we could have no such thing as plot progression since conflict would always be frozen at arm's length, like pieces on an unplayed chess board. Instead, in our dramatic experiences (whether they come from soap opera, sitcom, news story, or commercial), we seek a further kind of balance—what Herbert Langfeld called a balance between the strain of complication and the relief of unraveling.[20] Balance in this sense is evolution's province.

Some people would mistake evolution to be the rhythm or pulse of a piece, but rhythm lacks evolution's progressive expressiveness. "Rhythm never really gets anywhere," maintains Olson, "unless joined with evolution as for example when time rhythm is joined with harmonic evolution in music. On the other hand, evolution as accumulation of meaning need not be rhythmic."[21] Rhythm, in fact, has a different genesis altogether, Olson continues, since "a combination of balance and thematic variation creates rhythm which is a pattern of repeated [not evolving] emphasis and pause."[22]

With evolution, then, we are talking about a cause-and-effect or means-and-consequences phenomenon, just as a line has a beginning, middle, and end and a well-wrought painting a visual flow. In the case of radio formatting, we can examine the flow of one element to the next in the actualizing of the hot-clock schematic that is supposed to govern and motivate each programming hour. We can also look at succeeding hours and whole dayparts to determine whether these build one on the other or diverge at certain points to pursue a different audience. (The evolution of WGMS's program day, as one example, is presented in Lon Tuck's piece in Chapter 5.)

The virtual demise of network radio in the 1960s and its gradual rebirth in the 1980s were, to a significant degree, evolution-driven phenomena. When the networks' offerings broke the flow of increasingly tightly formatted local radio, they were abandoned; when they learned how to enhance this flow through their own format specialization, they were embraced. Thus, ABC Radio divided itself into four separate services in the late 1960s to provide subject-and-flow-matched product for different types of stations. Other networks subsequently have engaged in similar segmentation in order to make possible services that contribute to a deeper listener involvement with affiliate stations as the network-assisted (not network dominated) program day progresses. Meanwhile, new radio syndicators have arisen whose satellite-delivered products provide flow-complete programming packages to like-formatted stations around the country.

Turning to television, we again see evolution as governing not only the construction of individual program units, but also how those units are linked together to build the daily schedule. The segue from one news story to another or the involvement-heightening interlock of one sitcom scene to the next are just as much evolutionary concerns as is the creation of whole program blocks calculated to attract and nurture a 6 to 11 P.M. viewership. Even the scheduling of commercial pods (clusters) can further, rather than retard, evolutionary goals. As aesthetics professor Stanley Cavell muses:

> The aesthetic position of commercials, what you might call their possibility—what makes them aesthetically possible rather than merely intolerable—is not their inherent aesthetic interest . . . but the fact that they are readable, not as interruptions, but as interludes.[23]

Like many evolutionary devices, commercials can increase our sense of suspense by momentarily interrupting programmatic revelation. This will only work, however, if the commercial pod is not too lengthy. Cognizant of evolution's needs, the networks will usually begin a multihour movie telecast with a bare minimum of advertisements but will expand commercial pods at the film's later stages. Once the viewer has been hooked on the storyline, longer and longer interludes are tolerable. Schedule multiple spot clusters before the viewer has become absorbed, however, and these are more likely to be perceived as interruptions that cue an excuse for channel-switching. (If the movie itself exhibits faulty evolution such as senseless or random transitions, however, even the most astute commercial traffic plan won't help.)

Ultimately, then, evolution is concerned with how segment follows segment, with each part determined by, and in consonance with, what has come before. Organic unity, in contrast, focuses on the relevance of all of these parts to the whole. Thus, while the commercial pods in a program arguably may enhance evolution, they could not easily be considered as contributing to organic unity. In the past, this difficulty was solved by placing the advertisements themselves within the plot development of the program—Little Orphan Annie drank her Ovaltine and Jack Benny shared his Jell-O with announcer Don Wilson. Even though such a practice both created unity and enhanced evolution, it also led to charges that broadcast advertisers were furtively, even subliminally, ambushing attention. Especially for children's programs (radio as well as television), the aesthetic theory was correct—but the ethical practice was not.

Hierarchy

This final logic of aesthetic form component relates to the positioning and selection of a work's aspects in terms of their predominance. In a sense, the previous discussion of commercials as interludes is a hierarchical as well as an evolutionary phenomenon because the spots momentarily postpone plot causal linkage (evolution) due to their presumably lesser perceptual importance (hierarchy). Unfortunately, however, in some poorly structured shows, commercial placement may occur in such a way that the spots, rather than the turning points of story action, occupy the ground of highest attention. The hierarchy of the programmatic event is thus upset, even if the commercials stay brief enough to avoid derailing evolutionary progression.

One reason the made-for-TV movie is more effective on commercial television than the theatrical feature film is that the former has been hierarchically constructed with commercial breaks in mind. Plot action thereby occurs in a way that will not be harmed (and may even be helped) by the interposition of spot clusters. Created initially for uninterrupted movie house or pay cable exhibition, the feature film, on the other hand, has not been written to breaks. When a commercial network injects advertisements, these often come at inopportune moments and sever the stair-step pattern of rising tension. As perceptual psychologist Rudolf Arnheim tells us:

> In order to hold our attention, the dominant masses, which determine the basic "plot" of the work at the top level of structure, are made up of secondary units, whose interrelations represent an enriching refinement of, or counterpoint to, the top structure.[24]

However, if a secondary unit of the show is followed, not by a primary unit but by a commercial break (at best, another secondary unit), we have the potential for audience boredom or malaise to set in.

It must be understood that hierarchy springs from the alternation of the more and less important components within a work—not the more or less *relevant*. To the extent that their entrance and subject matter are so extraneous as to disrupt our experiencing of artful build, commercial pods are not just weakly hierarchical but antihierarchical and thus anti-aesthetic.

Another name for hierarchy is *dominance*; but this term can be misleading. Hierarchy is the intermixing of both dominant and subordinant elements. Dominance alone will not create hierarchy—only fatigue. As an example of this distinction, let us examine schematically the build of a well-structured story. Be it sitcom, action/adventure, drama, or documentary, a tale of any appreciable length should possess a gradual but perceptible rising of tension/in-

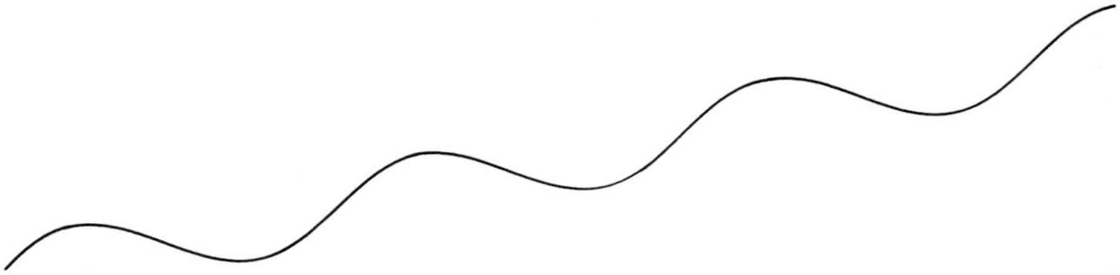

Figure 10–3   True Hierarchy

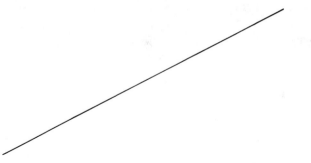

Figure 10–4   The Absence of Hierarchy

volvement in which momentary relaxants help set up the next climb, as demonstrated in Figure 10–3.

   Without subordinate elements, without those momentary lulls, the rising points of interest would not seem so interesting because there is nothing to set them off, one from the other. Such a structure, shown in Figure 10–4, not only blurs the highs into undistinguished togetherness, but also tires and even exhausts us because there is no place to pause and catch our breath. A small hill whose side goes straight up is more fatiguing to climb than a mountain-side interspersed with tiered plateaus. Similarly, a dramatic plot-action that gives us no moment of reprieve or a frantic sitcom in which every succeeding event is verbal gag or visual slapstick invites the audience to tune away to avoid exhaustion.

   This is not to say that hierarchy does not require an overall build of inten-sity, only that this build should be gradual, with brief resting places to mark our progressive advancement. If those rest stops are too extended or too uni-formly low key, we experience an emotional roller coaster that is progressively unsatisfying because of its repetitiveness, as Figure 10–5 graphically suggests. This is the pattern of the chainsaw murder movie or the porno flick in which succession of interchangeably gory or perverted acts are strung out in time with uniformly dulling drivel between them. It is about as dramatic as clipping your nails.

   True hierarchy, only slightly less than balance, taps into our psychological mainframe because it conforms to the passage of our existence. Balance pairs up our experiential opposites; hierarchy intersperses these pairs so that all the major and all the minor elements of existence are not grouped together. As Parker observes:

Figure 10–5   False Hierarchy

The concerns of life fall naturally into focus and fringe, vocation and avocation, important and less important [not less relevant]. Matters of high interest are salient against a background of things of less moment. There is never a dead level of value in life. No life is satisfactory without its hours of intense significance, which give it luster, yet man cannot always 'burn with a gemlike flame'; he must fall back, for rest and refreshment, on the little things. These latter are just as important in their way as the great moments. Some of them function as recreation, others as stage or preparation for the high moments. Yet when life is most satisfactory, these moments of preparation or repose are never merely means to ends; they possess charm of their own as well. When life is so lived it becomes an art, and when a work of art is so constructed, it is an image of life at its best.[25]

The Complete Logic Applied

To demonstrate how all six of the Parker-specified elements can coalesce as a critique methodology, let us first examine a student-prepared paper that uses the logic of aesthetic form to ascertain the artistic worth of an episode of the funny but by no means frivolous sitcom, *WKRP in Cincinnati*. In this two-part story, aging rock-and-roll disc jockey Dr. Johnny Fever is offered the opportunity to transform what a colleague calls his "miserable excuse for a career" by hosting a television dance show. The dance show is disco, however, the *kitsch* antithesis of Fever's lifelong commitment to the folk purity of rock-and-roll. In an attempt to bridge this gap, Fever creates a sequin-clad persona called Rip Tide for his television endeavors, but the schizophrenia that gradually overtakes him as he tries to be a radio rocker in the morning and a TV disco dynamo at night ultimately pushes him to the breaking point. This, of course, is all plot summary. Here, in one student's view, is how the show's creators transformed this plot into aesthetic experience:

This particular episode of *WKRP in Cincinnati* is a solid example of Parker's Logic of Aesthetic Form. The episode allows for an interesting intrinsic analysis in relation to Parker's six components.

In discussing organic unity, it is clear that everything in the show revolved around, or was geared toward, Johnny Fever and his problems with schizophrenia. The writer could have easily let the other characters play more passive or irrelevant roles but instead, they contribute to the show's premise in a very strong way, so that all are interdependent in the helping/hurting of Johnny through their own theme-focusing attitudes.

The theme of this episode was an attempt at a universal statement of moral values. It basically tells us that superficial wealth and fame are unimportant, when compared to personal peace-of-mind and friendship. *One must, ultimately, be true to oneself.* In the beginning of the episode, Johnny decides to take what looks good, and despite his initial reluctance, is swept into a fantasy world that causes his own personality and values to progressively deteriorate. It is true that the theme revolves around only one character, but the manner in which the other characters react to Johnny's problem accomplishes a good sense of thematic variation. TV producer Avis and radio colleagues Herb and Les all encouraged Johnny's changes for various reasons, and function as anti-theme. True radio friends, Venus, Bailey and Jennifer, on the other hand, affirm the theme by denouncing Johnny's contrived personality, Rip Tide. Radio program director Andy and manager Mr. Carlson remain oblivious to Johnny's problem, until the business issue of using Rip Tide on WKRP forces them to face up to his mental anguish. Thematic variation is well-accomplished by these various character perspectives that challenge and probe the theme's authenticity.

The episode included many good examples of balance. One way the show provided balance was, again, through the characters. Carrying over from the discussion of thematic variation, balance was attained by having different characters relate to Johnny differently, either seriously or with humor. On one side we have radio sales manager Herb, news director Les, and the inept Mr. Carlson all encouraging Johnny to "go for it" in a humorous way. Conversely, radio producer Bailey and fellow d.j. Venus give Johnny continuous opposition in a primarily serious fashion. Finally, radio receptionist Jennifer gives Johnny a harsh, honest awakening to balance the manipulation of TV producer Avis' sexual come-ons. Overall, the contrast between humor and drama is well accomplished as is the pairing of the real and the phoney. Another way the show adds balance is through setting. The changes of scene, from darkened, evil TV studio to bright, upright radio station keep the show stabilized. One minor element of balance is how Johnny's loyal friends, Bailey and Venus (a white woman and a black man), are teamed up throughout the show against the motives of a pair of connivers—one skilled (Avis), the other bungling (Herb).

In relating the concept of evolution to this production, it is easy to see that the progression of events is quite logical, as it follows Johnny's developing plight. An interesting note is that, as Johnny goes deeper and deeper into his schizoid Rip Tide, the other characters' reactions to him become stronger. Bailey and Venus become more and more disgruntled with Johnny, until they no longer speak to him. Les and Herb become more and more enthralled by his superficial success as the show progresses, so that the thematic variation parallels the plot's evolution.

In terms of hierarchy, the most important moments of the show are easily seen. Basically, the less important moments were those lightened by humor, and the most important were the more serious, dramatic occasions. The less and more important elements of the show are strung together very nicely by interjecting the comedic bits at times when it was necessary to lighten the mood (such as Herb clumsily burning himself with the coffee before Johnny's explosion in Carlson's office); and by being very serious when it was time for Johnny's problem to be dramatically exposed (such as Jennifer's outer office 'sermon' to Johnny that finally breaks through his delusion).

In summary, it is evident that this episode of WKRP was done very effectively because it made skilled use of all six of the Logic's components.

(Courtesy of Mark Wesley Fassett)

For another experience with applying Parker's schema, we turn to "The Income Tax" episode of *Ethel and Albert*—the script for which is found in Appendix B. To put this show in perspective (and to make it clear that the logic's applications are not limited to contemporary properties), it is necessary to sketch a brief background of this series.

Ethel and Albert was a fifteen-minute radio comedy that moved to television as a featured sketch on *The Kate Smith Hour.* (Ms. Smith had earlier given the property its first exposure on radio as well.) *Ethel and Albert* then acquired its own half-hour and successively ran on all three TV networks between 1953 and 1956. The show was created and written by Peg Lynch, who also starred as Ethel, and Alan Bunce (father of the *Christian Science Monitor* radio/television critic of the same name) played Albert. Since video tape was not yet in commercial use and recordings filmed off of monitors (kinescopes) were too visually crude for prime network employment, *Ethel and Albert,* together with accompanying commercials, was done live. This factor helped reinforce the program's natural sense of simplicity and the down-to-earth aura that surrounded it.

In examining "The Income Tax," we find that all elements of the episode relate to that title's referent. Even the seemingly extraneous matters of devil's food cake, a boy scout hat, and a Woman's Club minutes book are interwoven within the concept of the government audit to comprise an organically unified program. Nothing here is irrelevant, although one beauty of the show is that these elements appear irrelevant when first introduced. That these are all ultimately tied in provides a sense of satisfaction and wholeness.

The theme that undergirds this comedy seems to be that honesty and frugality are respected and ultimately rewarded virtues. The viewer is not compelled to salute this theme overtly, and it is never boorishly mouthed by any of the characters. Still, the cumulative effects of the portrayed incidents are a consistent endorsement of this thematic premise and a testimony to its operation. Even though they make "honest mistakes," "most people seem to be fundamentally honest," states tax examiner Gilbert; this is the essence of the show's point of view.

Variations on this theme are numerous. We see, for example, Grace's and Bunderson's gentle but still reproachful reactions to what they perceive as Albert's attempts to con the tax man by "wearing a boy scout hat" and deducting "a little too much for entertainment, huh?" Ethel's prudence and industry in putting aside money "in case he loses his job or something" seems ultimately to be rewarded despite the trauma this caused Albert. Her variant dependence on hidden or buried cookie jars may be less businesslike than his investment ideas, but they are no less endorsing of the episode's theme. Finally, Ethel's off-stage suggestion that "you can always tell the tax man that it was an OUT OF POCKET contribution . . . there isn't any way he can check on you," though unwittingly made in the examiner's presence, merely illuminates thematic function from a more pragmatic perspective.

A number of balancing forces create a sense of stability within the episode. The fundamental and continuing balance, of course, is between the contrary yet complementary world views of the two principals. Albert's exasperated search for order is forever impeded by Ethel's masterful disorder; but the synthesis of these two extremes is that, in Gilbert Seldes's observation, "you become aware of the substantial element: that Ethel and Albert have made a life together."[26] Balance is also achieved by the two male strangers who enter the Arbuckle home—each of whom brings his own complication. A unifying contrast between the two accrues from the fact that, while Bunderson left the house with what he came for (the Woman's Club minutes), Gilbert leaves with the tax audit unconcluded and a new Ethel-planted worry that his own home finances are in disarray. In this sense, both Gilbert and Albert become twin victims of Ethel's fiscal inventiveness and thus nicely bookend its display.

The evolutionary pattern of "The Income Tax" is cleanly wrought and can be causally expressed as follows: Deepening Worry—Worry Reprieve—Worry Revitalized—Reprieve Repeated. Within the show's first ten seconds, Albert encounters his tax audit problem, which intensifies (Deepening Worry) until Gilbert initially concludes that "everything seems to be in fine order" (Worry Reprieve). Then, when Ethel reveals her "little nest egg that I've hidden away" the problem reappears with new magnitude as several of poor Albert's tax returns are now brought into question (Worry Revitalized). At last, when Gilbert estimates that "the government may wind up owing you a refund," it appears we have the stock happy ending (Reprieve Repeated)—that is, until the future-projecting twist on the end as Ethel heads for the yard with her flashlight and spade. Each of these happenings is linked to what precedes and follows it through a cause-and-effect affinity that any rearrangement of parts would only have shattered. Evolution's requirements are therefore fulfilled.

The tension that emanates from this means/consequences chain is kept in check by the episode's hierarchical pattern. This is, after all, a light comedy, not a dark drama. Too much anxiety as to Albert's dilemma will tip the scales toward the tragic. On the other hand, unrelieved farce would destroy the show's cozy realism. Flashes of funny happenings are thus interspersed with pinches of panic to engender in the viewer rising interest but not rising fright. Specifically, the program's successive components deftly form the following stair step of tension escalation and tension recess:

Recess	*Escalation*
	Albert discovers the letter and tries to cope with his uncovered tax problem.
In the attic, Ethel complains about leaving her in-progress cake and Albert puts on his old boy scout hat.	
	Grace adds the further concerns of the Woman's Club minutes delivery and Albert's susceptibility to Alcratraz.
Albert leaves for work still wearing his scout hat.	

Recess	*Escalation*
	Bunderson arrives and, after nervous small talk, seems to want to remove Albert's records.
Albert finds Bunderson just wants the Woman's Club book.	
	The search resumes for the missing check as Gilbert arrives and hears Ethel's offstage suggestions for creative excuses.
Gilbert finds the tax return to be in apparent order.	
	Ethel reveals her nest egg and the expanded audit reopens.
Gilbert determines Albert may get a refund and that he needs to check on his own wife's finances.	

The program then concludes with Ethel's departure to bury her wealth in order to project a creative tension into future episodes. This is because we want the couple's lives to remain open and unsettled so there is something to come back for next week. Too great a sense of episode finality would destroy our sense of series continuity and of the cause-and-effect progression (evolution) that will maintain our involvement with *Ethel and Albert*'s existence.

Notice how each succeeding escalation makes the situation more taut and how each succeeding recess—until the final one—provides less and less slack. Thus, the show's sense of build is enhanced through hierarchy's keen exploitation while the seeds for a new building process are planted at the program's conclusion.

In terms of Parker's standard, then, "The Income Tax" is an aesthetic success. Looking at the program through the mists of thirty years, we can perhaps perceive content that no longer rings true. The portrayal of wives as bustling stay-at-homes who assert independence in cake sales and cookie jars is as foreign to today as is a $30-a-month apartment. Yet, these situational specifics do not compromise the aesthetic integrity of *Ethel and Albert* any more than a painting by Rembrandt is outmoded because the subjects in it wear archaic clothing. In both cases, it is the universality of the human perspective that art can bring to the fore. Social conventions, like price tags and costumes, only serve to place the work in time so we can apprehend it.

To be fully appreciated, any art object seems to project a past and future, between which the aesthetically structured present lives and from which it seems to draw life. It is as Gilbert Seldes observed in discussing Ethel and Albert's perpetual wrangling:

> The sense that they could not be happy without their little quarrels is always there. It is part of our feeling that they have had a past and did not come suddenly to life

at 7:30 and disappear at 8:00. When Albert is grouchy and does not respond to a pun, Ethel taps him with a ladle she happens to have in her hand and says, "That's a joke"—and, after a moment, "I always laugh at your jokes"—without rancor, just stating a fact. And the fact, so flat in itself, creates a third dimension, a hundred episodes in the past of Ethel and Albert which we have never seen, which were never written, but which exist in the background for the writer and the actors, and so for us.[27]

As Monroe Beardsley observes of the logic-measured aesthetic experience, and of art and life in general:

What is the good of life itself, except to be as fully alive as we can become—to burn with a hard gemlike flame, to choose one crowded hour of glorious life, to seize experience at its greatest magnitude? And this is precisely our experience of art; it is living the best way we know how. Far from being a handmaiden to other goals, art gives us immediately, and richly, the best there is in life, intense aware-ness—it gives us what life itself aims at becoming, but seldom achieves outside of art.[28]

Notes

1. Theodore Meyer Greene, *The Arts and the Art of Criticism* (Princeton: Princeton University Press, 1952), 137.
2. Ibid., 29.
3. Gerald Herbener, "The Idea of Aesthetics." Speech presented at the Broadcast Education Association, 7 April 1978, at Las Vegas, Nev.
4. John Dewey, "Having an Experience," in Melvin Rader, ed., *A Modern Book of Esthetics,* 5th ed. (New York: Holt, Rinehart and Winston, 1979), 138.
5. Thomas Olson, "Lectures on Aesthetic Form." Lectures presented at Wayne State University, February 1964, at Detroit.
6. Greene, *Art of Criticism,* 403.
7. Carl Grabo, *The Creative Critic* (Chicago: University of Chicago Press, 1948), 18.
8. George Boas, *A Primer for Critics* (New York: Greenwood Press, 1968), 58.
9. Edmund Feldman, *Art as an Image and Idea* (Englewood Cliffs, N.J.: Prentice-Hall, 1967), 4.
10. Eliseo Vivas, *Creation and Discovery* (New York: The Noonday Press, 1955), 98.
11. DeWitt Parker, *The Analysis of Art* (New Haven: Yale University Press, 1926), 37.
12. Feldman, *Art as Image,* 263.
13. Thomas Olson, "A Basis for Criticism of the Visual Esthetic Elements of Television," Ph.D diss., Wayne State University, 1966.
14. Parker, *Analysis,* 38.
15. Jerome Stolnitz, *Aesthetics and Philosophy of Art Criticism* (Boston: Houghton Mifflin Company, 1960), 235.
16. Larry Dobrow, "The Best Ads," *Adweek Radio 1985 Issue* (July 1985): 25.
17. Parker, *Analysis,* 38–39.
18. Ibid., 57–58.
19. Ibid., 45.
20. Herbert Langfeld, *The Aesthetic Attitude* (New York: Harcourt, Brace, 1920), 241.
21. Olson, "Basis for Criticism," 132.
22. Ibid., 130.

23. Stanley Cavell, "The Fact of Television," in John Hanhardt, ed., *Video Culture* (Rochester, N.Y.: Visual Studies Workshop Press, 1986), 206–207.
24. Rudolf Arnheim, *Toward a Psychology of Art* (Berkeley: University of California Press, 1967), 174.
25. Parker, *Analysis,* 61–62.
26. Gilbert Seldes, *The Public Arts* (New York: Simon and Schuster, 1956), 111.
27. Ibid., 111–112.
28. Monroe Beardsley, *Aesthetics: Problems in Philosophy of Criticism* (New York: Harcourt, Brace & World, 1958), 563.

Depiction Analysis

In the past several chapters, we have looked at broadcast/cable critiquing from a number of different perspectives, including the perceptual, productional, gratification-based, ethical, and aesthetic orientations. In this chapter, we adopt a somewhat wider focus and examine radio/television content from the standpoint of what we ultimately learn from it. This does not mean that this chapter is devoted to in-school broadcasting (ITV). Instead, we look at the lessons that any and every piece of electronic media content inherently and unavoidably teaches. Then, in Chapter 12, we examine the systems, the instructive pedagogies that give these lessons their structure. Often, as mentioned in Chapter 8, program creators no less than consumers are unaware that such teachings are present. But producers, just like critics, are the products of their own upbringing and environment and thus inevitably reflect their personal background in their public messages. That media creators often convey their courses of study unintentionally does not diminish these lessons' pervasive, if subtle, impact.

The most straightforward method for decoding radio/television lessons is to apply a depiction matrix to the media content we wish to examine. This involves determining that content's answer to the five questions depiction encompasses. A given program may emphasize only one or two of these queries, but the seeds of all five are implanted in every broadcast/cable work that we hear or see. The five specific questions from which depiction-deriving lessons spring are:

1. How is our physical environment constituted?
2. What is society like?

3. What consequences flow from our actions?
4. What are our responsibilities?
5. What are the standards by which we should evaluate ourselves?

Let's look at each question and at some ways in which they are answered, in order.

How Is Our Physical Environment Constituted?

Radio and television bring us instantaneous and even interplanetary pictures of the habitat that surrounds us. Even though this may not be the precise locale in which we ourselves live, we can compare our conditions with those of other people to assess our own situation. Thus, we are grateful that we do not live in the existence-threatening dust of drought-stricken Ethiopia, the war-ravaged streets of Beirut or, for that matter, the *Hill Street* precinct's urban squalor. On the other hand, we may envy the posh surroundings in which our favorite daytime or prime-time soap opera characters cavort. If, through our programming selections, we choose to experience more of the former, we will probably be more self-satisfied than if we select a preponderance of the latter. As Marshall McLuhan once commented, a refrigerator can be a revolutionary symbol of deprivation to people who have no refrigerators, and the more the media suggest we are living outside the physical comfort of the "good life mainstream," the greater the possibility of anger or self-pity.

Audience perception of physical setting cannot always be predicted, however. Several years ago, a minor Soviet bureaucrat thought citizen morale would be substantially boosted if Soviet citizens perceived how much better were Russian working-class conditions than those of the proletariat in the United States. So the American movie version of John Steinbeck's classic *The Grapes of Wrath* was secured and screened. The bureaucrat expected his rank-and-file countrymen to be repelled by the poverty and homelessness of Steinbeck's dust-bowl-fleeing Okies and therefore to be grateful for their spartan, state-owned dwellings. What the workers focused on, however, was not the migratory landlessness of the Okies but the jealousy-producing fact that even these poorest of Americans owned their own automobiles! Clearly, *The Grapes of Wrath* answered a physical condition question for Soviet citizens— but not in the way the bureaucrat had hoped!

This overt and unsuccessful attempt at attitudinal manipulation is a far cry from the commercial (broadcast or cable) producer's selection of setting as a mere formulary backdrop for character interaction. Still, that backdrop is a factor nonetheless, and the lessons flowing from it are not always ignored. Indeed, the view of the perfect yet frustratingly unattainable California life-style that taunts so many viewers is not a plot by the Los Angeles Chamber of Commerce but the by-product of the fact that most television writers live there and directors still find it easier to shoot there. During a stay in Los Angeles, East Coast lawyer-turned-critic Ben Stein noticed that the lives of men and women and children on TV shows, so different from any life I had ever seen or participated in, was really the life of Los Angeles—the clean streets; the polite, handsome police; the shiny new cars issued to everyone over sixteen; the strong-jawed men and the lean, unthreatening women; the tinkling of glasses around a swimming pool; the pastel hues of storefronts; the dark, richly upholstered restaurant interiors; the squealing of tires along canyon roads; and much more.[1]

To a significant degree, TV-land remains L.A.-land or, at the least, urban, coastal American. The thousands of miles and municipalities large and small that separate Los Angeles (and San Francisco) from New York (or Miami or Boston) are something of which most network-serving television and radio producers are aware—but do not really comprehend.

For some reason (perhaps because of the weather or the fact that they grew up on the East Coast and moved to the West) writers portray New York, Boston, and (as a generic if geographically mismatched convenience) Chicago as much more dirty and dangerous environments than the other ocean's California cleanliness. The cities of both coasts are depicted as exciting, crime-ripe, and trend-setting, but the East seems more gloomily violent. Obviously speaking of *Vice*'s Miami, a small-town New Mexico girl recently told a visiting critic: "How could you want to go to a place where people get caught in gun battles between pushers on their vacation?" and a fellow student added, "I've never gone to New York. But you watch *Cagney & Lacey* and its all subways and real dark. Somebody is getting murdered all the time, and it's like you have to get used to it if you want to live there. I don't ever want to go to New York."[2]

Certainly, residents of Miami and New York may, through their direct experience, see things much differently—and might harbor their own fears of small-town New Mexico. But because most people do not live in these two metropolises, the media depictions of their environments can have a significant impact. Similarly, to the city dweller in Detroit, Flint, or Saginaw, the Michigan conveyed in the Figure 11–1 spot may or may not be the State with which they are familiar. Obviously, the commercial seeks summer tourists and so evokes only locales thought most pleasing to them. This is a skillfully positive sampling of physical reality in the same way that *Miami Vice* and *Cagney & Lacey* made their negative selection.

Although neither the advertisement in Figure 11–1 nor the two programs reflected the entire environment (and television's one-eyed view never can), each has taught us, in respectively purposeful or incidental ways, a lesson of physical habitat. This lesson will be construed as accurate to the extent that it does not conflict with any past belief or experience that the viewer—or the critic—possesses. It is mainly from the total absence of other experience that distortion can arise. As Michael Leahy cautions:

> Perhaps the gritty, urban dramas would pose no hazards at all if there were other dramas that shed a less sensational light on everyday life in cities at once vibrant, troubled, intimidating, exhilarating—a challenge.[3]

"I AM MICHIGAN (GULL & PEOPLE)"

SINGERS: I AM MICHIGAN.

V/O: I am vast waters along endless coastlines.

I am deep forests sheltering majestic life.

I am towering cliffs that guard the immensity of the Great Lakes.

And miles of sand gathered by the wind.
SINGERS: THIS IS WHAT I AM.

V/O: I am exuberance.

I am tranquility.

I am moments.

I am memories.

I am rivers that roll and bend and sometimes fall.

I am rich, green meadows.

...and elegant places.

SINGERS: YES, MICHIGAN.
THE FEELING IS FOREVER.
YES, MICHIGAN,
THE FEELING IS FOREVER.

Figure 11–1 "I Am Michigan" Photoboard (Courtesy of Sheila I. ODonnell, Ross Roy, Inc., Advertising)

What Is Society Like?

As we have mentioned, people can come to fear small towns as well as big cities if they lack first-hand experience and encounter unchallenged and negative media depictions. In fact, Ben Stein found just such a Hicksville phobia to be present in prime-time television and in the minds of the producers whose work is displayed there. This, however, is more a social than a physical environment fear, and it is attributed by Stein to the simple fact that:

> most of the writers and producers originally come from large eastern cities or from Los Angeles, and they are uncomfortable with the whole concept of small towns. . . . It is largely *terra incognita,* and like everyone else in the world, TV writers and producers are frightened by what they do not know.
>
>   There is also an ethnic difference that frightens some. The Hollywood TV writer tends generally, although not always, to be Jewish or Italian or Irish and he sees people in the small towns as not being ethnic at all. He sees them, moreover, as not being friendly toward ethnics, especially Jews. . . . And, of course, it could hardly be more natural for people who fear they might be 'beat up' in small towns because of their race to feel some anger toward them.[4]

Thus, it did not surprise Stein that in much of the television programming he watched, "Small towns were superficially lovely, but under a thin veneer of compone there was lurking, terrifying evil, waiting to ensnare the innocent Natty Bumpo [James Fenimore Cooper's woodsman hero] of the big city.[5]

  Our society's government, particularly that which sprawls on the shores of the Potomac, is also the frequent subject for portrayals that range from fawning adoration (seldom encountered since Vietnam and Watergate) to scathing indictment. Senators William Cohen and (ironically) Gary Hart found television's prime-time picture of the society of public servants to be so deplorable that, in 1985, they penned an insiders' bipartisan rejoinder for *TV Guide.* While conceding that some public officials lack competency, the two legislators found negative politician stereotypes to be the prime-time rule rather than the exception:

> They are flat, one dimensional, mildly corrupt, always conniving and driven by a lust for power and personal aggrandizement. In a phrase, television has tended to see Washington's political figures as people made up in equal parts of stupidity and cupidity.[6]

  Electronic journalism, the lawmakers felt, presented a much more balanced picture, but its brief snippets of coverage do not have the bulk or single-mindedness of theme of a fictional series or movie. Reality, after all, is not as neat as the scripted determinism of a prime-time melodrama. The examples of individual ignominy and contravening integrity that were Watergate took years to uncover; the foibles of characters in the made-for-TV "Washington Mistress" could be exposed in a single night. Such distortive entertainment images and journalistic intolerance for even the smallest official miscue may undermine faith in what our political society is like. This worries veteran public servant Brent Snowcroft, who, not long ago, told a Georgetown University audience:

> Disdain for Government leads the best people to shun service in that Government; less talented people are even more prone to provide a grist for investigative reporting, which further tarnishes the image of Government and so on.[7]

This, of course, is not to imply that electronic images of our government must be uncritically deferential—only that they be willing to accept the possibility of the good as well as the bad. (For a critique of a TV movie that showed just such acceptance, review Tony Scott's assessment of *LBJ: The Early Years,* in Chapter 8.)

Even though many people feel that the negative stereotyping of governmental occupations has gotten worse on radio and television, distortive ethnic depictions, conversely, have markedly declined from the days of *Amos and Andy* and the Indian-bashing cowboy show. The recognition that the electronic media have a substantial influence in shaping our perceptions of others' ethnicity has caused broadcast standards and practices departments (less charitably referred to as network censors) to be especially vigilant as to nationality-based generalizations. Asserted examples of the progress made, and still to be made in these broadcast/cable sociology lessons, are set forth in the following observation by Fulbright scholar and communications professor Jack Shaheen:

> Most minorities have come into their own on the television screen. Blacks have graduated from their janitorial and servant jobs to become doctors, lawyers and scientists. Latins are no longer seen as Frito Bandito or Chiquita Banana types. The American Indian does not massacre helpless whites. The Oriental no longer acts like the shuffling coolie or barbaric villain. Television, for the most part, has discontinued pejorative characterizations of women and other minorities. Only the Arab has been excluded from television cultural reorientation. . . . At a time when news presentations of Middle East affairs are becoming more balanced, entertainment programs provide an unjustifiable and erroneous portrayal of the Arab. Comedies and dramas contend that Arabs are innately cruel and decadent, that their leaders are either blood-feuding Bedouin or oil-blackmailers and that they spend their free time abducting young virgins from California to sell in "Arabia." . . . For two million Americans of Arab descent, the belligerent anti-Arab bias is an inescapable fact of life.[8]

Depictions of what society is like are not, of course, limited to the family of races but also concern what nuclear families are like. In its 1985 study, "Prime Time Kids: An Analysis of Children and Families on Television," the National Commission on Working Women found, for instance, that in very few sitcoms (*The Cosby Show* being a notable exception) are the parents in charge; they seem to have relinquished this role to precocious or devious children. Further, even though most single mothers in the entertainment programming analyzed were middle class or wealthier, in reality, 69 percent of all households headed by women were found by the study to be poor. The social inferences that child viewers in particular draw from such electronic portraits may or may not cause them to become more obnoxious, or feel more deprived; but such portraits certainly fail to provide meaningful coping suggestions.

What Consequences Flow from Our Actions?

Coping, of course, is the adoption of a plan of action that has the anticipated effect of controlling if not reducing our personal stress level. Like any consequence, we would like the results of coping activities to be forecastable, and radio/television depictions oblige by teaching a curriculum of prediction. The many media-provided answers to the "What would happen if I . . . ?" question range from the scrupulously scientific to the most fantastically improbable.

Clearly, commercials are the most streamlined consequence teachers, and they can project us into a future that is bright with the product or dismal without it. The more extreme the claim—particularly in terms of assertions that move beyond the product category—the more likely is this lesson to be a con job. Thus, the toothpaste spot that claims to convert your mouth into a beacon of sexuality is a charlatan tutor because it moves outside of its area of competence.

In contrast, this radio advertisement for Kempner's Clothing Store restricts itself to feasible assertions that the shop's great selection features items that match your size, style, and budget needs. The positive consequences of shopping at Kempner's thus seem more believable because they realistically relate to clothing stores. Kempner's Clothes may not make you a fashion trend setter and idol of the Western world, but you will feel comfortable in public and not waste your money.

MAN: Susan, this is Mr. Rudolpho. You're my star model, now please come out of there.

WOMAN: I'm not leaving this dressing room!

MAN: But the fashion show's about to begin!

WOMAN: Not until you take me to Kempner's Clothing Store!

MAN: What have they got that my designs don't have?

WOMAN: Wonderful fit, low prices, great selection ---

MAN: Just put this dress on.

WOMAN: How can I! There's only room for one leg!

MAN: It's so avant garde! It's part of my 'Hop Into Spring' collection.

WOMAN: And this sweater top --- it's ugly! And there's no opening for my head to go through!

MAN: It's my sweater they want to see, not your head.

WOMAN: When I go to Kempner's Clothing Store I know I'll find something that's --- just right for me, that fits --- and at the right price.

MAN: If I take you there, will you take one quick hop down the runway here?

WOMAN: On one condition. First, you go to Kempner's too. They have great men's clothing.

MAN: What's wrong with my clothes?

WOMAN: Paisley tights and a Nehru jacket?

MAN: Okay, I'll go there. What else?

WOMAN: Let me take off this stupid belt.

MAN: But it's a fashion statement.

WOMAN: It's a live boa constrictor!

MAN: Shhh! He thinks he's a belt. Easy Binky, you're a belt, you're a belt ---

WOMAN: I don't believe this --- get this thing off me.

ANNCR: Good fit. Good selection. Great prices. If Kempner's Clothing Store has something you haven't had lately, perhaps you'd better drop by --- before your next public appearance! Kempner's Clothing Store, 370 15th Street, at Yale Boulevard.

(Courtesy of Fran Sax, FirstCom)

In a more serious vein, social psychologists and radio/television critics have been particularly concerned with the programming-displayed consequences (or lack of them) associated with sexual or violent portrayals. In 1985, for example, a task force of the American Academy of Pediatrics charged that television's treatment of sex roles and human sexuality was "unrealistic and misleading." Adolescence is painted as a period of constant sexual crisis, sexual relationships are shown to develop rapidly, and the risk of pregnancy is rarely explicated, stated the task force's report.

Erroneous teachings on the consequences of sex and love experiences, made all the worse because of the failure to differentiate between these two interactions, have long been attributed to television and radio programming, with audio song lyrics seen as no less guilty than television melodramas. Sex and love are blurred together into a commodity, say the electronic media's accusers, and the results of both are thereby cheapened. Thus, as Cathy Schwichtenberg asserted of one long-running series:

> In *The Love Boat,* to purchase a ticket is to purchase the experience of love. *The Love Boat* is similar to a before-and-after advertisement which has been animated. Before the characters begin their "love boat" journey they are beset by problems such as lack of love, wrong love-partner, or love based on mistaken identities. But by the end of the cruise, characters are coupled with their proper mates. The show, which illustrates this shift from lack to gain, from sad to happy, teaches viewers that they can buy happiness and love for the price of a ticket on a luxury cruise. . . . Indeed, love as advertised by *The Love Boat,* can be bought like any other product.[9]

In the case of violence, some of the most perceptive concern has come, not from people who wish unrealistically to sanitize its broadcast/cable treatment, but from critics who are concerned with the dangerous precept such sanitization conveys. Physician Mike Oppenheim frames the issue this way:

> Critics of TV violence claim it teaches children sadism and cruelty. I honestly don't know whether or not TV violence is harmful, but if so the critics have it backward. Children can't learn to enjoy cruelty from the neat, sanitized mayhem on the average series. There isn't any! What they learn is far more malignant: that guns or fists are clean, efficient, exciting ways to deal with a difficult situation. Bang!—you're dead! Bop!—you're unconscious (temporarily) . . .
>
> Seriously, real-life violence is dirty, painful, bloody, disgusting. It causes mutilation and misery, and it doesn't solve problems. It makes them worse. If we're genuinely interested in protecting our children, we should stop campaigning to "clean up" TV violence. It's already too antiseptic. Ironically, the problem with TV violence is: it's not violent enough.[10]

Conversely, for a review of a program that, to one critic's mind, seems to teach consequences in a realistic, though often oblique way, read the following critique by *TV Guide*'s Don Merrill. In *227,* Merrill asserts, we encounter a series that can deliver messages about social results arising from such topics as urban burglary prevention or helping the homeless, "in a subtle but effective manner."

227
By Don Merrill

NBC's *227* is not a great situation comedy. But it is a good one. It has humor and warmth and it leaves you with a good feeling. And that's as good a test as any. At first, in its Saturday night spot following the hit *Golden Girls, 227* seemed to suffer by comparison. But gradually it found its direction and now, like *Family Ties* after *The Cosby Show,* no longer needs the help of a strong lead-in. (That's show-biz talk, folks, to show how hep we are.)

The star and spark plug is Marla Gibbs, an accomplished singer and comedienne who can do more with her eyes than most actresses can do with their entire bodies. As Mary in the show, she has a loving, believable relationship with her husband, Lester (Hal Williams), and their daughter. Their neighbors are Rose (Alaina Reed), the woman who inherited but does not manage very well the Washington, D.C., apartment house they live in; Pearl (Helen Martin), an elderly busybody who observes—and gossips about—everything that happens; and Sandra, a man-chasing lady of rather easy virtue who has to be one of the funniest characters on television. Jackee Harry plays Sandra broadly, sexily and brilliantly. She walks funny, talks funny, makes funny noises and is a complete delight. Sandra is big on innuendo, and while what she says is merely blue, some of her glances and stares are worthy of an "R" rating.

While the goings on in a lower-middle-class apartment house inhabited by comic characters can't be expected to be memorable, this show delivers a few social messages in a subtle but effective manner. Thus, while an episode is chiefly about deciding whether the family should spend money buying Lester a sports car or buying Mary some new furniture, viewers learn that participating in a Neighborhood Watch to thwart burglars is a good thing. They learn this while laughing about Mary and Lester's apartment being burgled while the apartment dwellers are attending a Neighborhood Watch meeting.

Still another episode had to do with helping the homeless and in this case the message wasn't in the least bit subtle. In the midst of a funny, and touching, scene, the teen-age daughter played by Regina King says: "My teacher says that in a country as rich as American nobody should be hungry or cold."

Messages in situation comedies, of course, are nothing new. Norman Lear perfected the technique in *All in the Family* and *Maude,* and sure enough, *227* is produced by Lear's old company, Embassy, although Lear has long since sold out his interest. We hasten to point out that while there are messages in this show, they are normally so well disguised as to be just about subliminal.

A word about the laugh track. Most producers believe that because laughter is contagious, some "sweetening" of the studio audience's laughter is desirable. But whoever sweetens the laughs for this has a heavy hand on the laugh machine's chuckle button. Whenever a viewer at home has to say, "Why are they laughing? Did I miss something?" it is time to tone down the machine-made hilarity. A little is enough. Trust us. This show doesn't need that kind of help.

(Reprinted with permission from *TV Guide*® *Magazine.* Copyright© 1986 by Triangle Publications, Inc., Radnor, Pennsylvania.)

What Are Our Responsibilities?

In a related way, *227*'s consequence lessons also have something to say about our obligations in terms of these consequences. That we should organize that neighborhood watch group or do something to help the homeless is contextually implied but not, apparently, overtly stated. Such a blatant message, of course, is seldom readily accepted from an entertainment medium.

Instead, the responsibility lessons of radio/television tend to be derived more from what characters do than what they say, and this includes the notion that certain role-model occupations are expected to fulfill certain duties. The responsibilities of mother, father, lawyer, law enforcement officer, physician, teacher, clergyman, and journalist historically have been treated with profound and pervasive respect by the electronic media; and depicted characters who fail to live up to these responsibilities tend to be painted with special scorn. On the other hand, the meeting of virtuous obligations by such groups as politicians and business executives has been shown much more infrequently.

Sometimes, the accretion of these media-assigned responsibilities makes it very difficult for people in real life to live up to the positive ones or counteract or live down the negative ones. Many police, for instance were happy to see *Kojak* and *Adam-12* type depictions gradually make room for *The Blue Knight* and *Hill Street*'s denizens, who were attainably human, not heroically sanctified. In discussing their study of how officers in a selected police department reference television dramatizations of law enforcement, Professors Michael Pacanowsky and James Anderson reported that their subjects felt that one major media unreality

is the portrayal of policemen as too good and criminals as too bad. One cop complained about the extent to which the media goes "overboard" to "really build up the bad guy" as bad. And *Adam-12,* for him, was an example of where the media went "overboard on the good cop thing." There is a certain suspicion among some social commentators and social scientists as well that many cops have an "authoritarian personality" and prefer to see the world in simple good and bad terms. Certainly this cop, and many on the Valley View (ficticious name) force, perceived media representation of cops and robbers in good and bad terms to be askew. In fact, the cops seemed to prefer that researchers/ride-alongs not perceive them as "good guys," but just as guys like anybody else doing a job.[11]

Idealized parental figures on the media can present the same problems for mothers and fathers that "too good TV cops" cause police. *Leave It To Beaver*'s Ward Cleaver and the Jim Anderson (Robert Young) of *Father Knows Best* set perfect paternal standards in an unfortunately imperfect world. As in the case of crime drama, the pedestals have since been lowered as much by *Family Ties* as by *All in the Family.* Thus, even though depicted parental responsibilities remain fundamentally the same, the emphasis has shifted to the portraying of parental attempts rather than triumphs.

However, if there is one role arena for which flawless performance is still demanded, it is the image of the broadcast/cable journalist—particularly the correspondent—who is expected to put the story above any other personal or institutional priority. As electronic news has become more competitive, both with the print media and with itself, this heroic presumption becomes as much a promotable necessity as an operational procedure. The kamikaze field reporter, as a result, may too often be sent in pursuit of dynamic danger instead of nonvisual significance; this practice can endanger both the reporter's safety and understanding. As the following review by *Toronto Star* critic Jim Bawden suggests, "Why reporters do it is never adequately explained." Audiences are led to expect reporter heroism but are never given the rationale for it.

VIVID CBC DOCUMENTARY FOLLOWS REPORTERS TO WAR
By Jim Bawden

Why do war reporters feel compelled to seek out hot spots and cover wars no one else dares go near? They call the syndrome "bang-bang." Because of the shifting loyalties of most modern conflicts, it's often a case of "bang-bang, you're dead." And that's how some of them end up.

A Toronto produced documentary, *The War Reporters* (tonight on Channel 5 at 8), captures some of the exhilarating feelings of reporters who venture into war zones. The action sequences are among the most exciting seen on TV this season.

But this is no artful piece of fiction. The bodies lying crumpled everywhere are real. The blood gushing from reporters' wounds is real, too.

The program, made by Lauron Productions, looks at the agonizingly slow death of CTV reporter Clark Todd, who was mortally wounded in 1983 while covering the war in Lebanon.

His cameraman recounts how Todd was hit by Christian militia in an obscure town where two factions were bent on massacring each other. "There was a small, neat hole next to his heart," says Brian Kelly.

"Is there an exit wound?" Todd asked. "It's not death that scares me, it's the embarrassment."

Todd urged his cameraman and soundman to get out before they were hit. They could come back for him later. He scrawled a last message to his wife, Anne, using his blood, and died alone during the next week.

Anne Todd does not say she disagrees with his decision to go there. "They must be sent in," she tells director Brian McKenna.

Should Todd have been left to die on his own? She sighs and says, "It's difficult."

Scenes like that are recounted by newsmen covering the increasingly dangerous business of being a foreign correspondent. Besides Todd, the documentary looks at the experiences of CBC's Brian Stewart, who covered both Lebanon and the Falkland crisis.

The program could have been expanded to include print reporters who have been kidnapped or held for ransom. Some of the experiences of American reporters under fire get short shrift, although we witness once again the squalid murder of ABC reporter Bill Stewart in Nicaragua. He was shot by a government soldier in full view of the TV cameras.

Why reporters do it is never adequately explained. Some are drawn to danger because they think it is somehow glamorous.

The scenes that sting are the real stuff: a camera keeps rolling as it records agonizing last moments of its cameraman as he tries to crawl for cover after being hit.

Clark Todd is seen in a clip talking almost nonchalantly about getting hit in the leg in Northern Ireland. Part of the print I watched in preview notes how little compensation his widow received: Anne Todd got the equivalent of 15 months's pay from CTV and the money has almost run out. CBC cut this sequence from tonight's program, feeling it detracted from the main theme.

(Reprinted with permission—The Toronto Star Syndicate)

The priorities that *The War Reporters* revealed are wrong, news analyst David Schoenbrun argues: "Reporters must be given the opportunity to demonstrate their expertise and become identifiable with their beats, instead of being 'parachutists' dropped in on a war or revolution."[12] Their responsibilities to themselves, no less than to their public, demand it.

What Are the Standards by Which We Should Evaluate Ourselves?

According to the previous discussion, field correspondents are expected to evaluate themselves based on displayed personal courage rather than on intellectual rigor or long-term labor on a single beat. But the electronic media do not just teach standards to their practitioners. In a much more comprehensive way, they also teach self-evaluative measures to listeners and viewers.

Once again, commercials are the most pointed examples of these lessons; they convey a standard based on the consumption or acceptance of the advocated concept. Thus, in Figure 11–2, the "Who You Are" spot for Oldsmobile Calais, we are encouraged to equate our self-realization with how well we project our personal image—as reflected most effectively by this car, which is "more than a car."

The proud Calais drivers shown in this stylish commercial are obviously happy, and many radio/television critics have come to believe that happiness itself is by far the most frequent and overarching evaluative standard that the electronic media purvey. After all, the American Declaration of Independence is unique in asserting that not just life and liberty, but "the pursuit of happiness" are God-given "inalienable rights." What is more natural, then, than the penetration of "the happiness ethic" (less charitably referred to as hedonism) into the very fibre of America's most popular leisure enterprise? "What gets my goat about TV," laments noted actor Jason Robards, "is that everybody has to be *happy* all the time. Rich and happy and thin. If you're not, there's something wrong with you. You need fast-fast-fast relief. It can come from Bufferin, Binaca or booze, but it's got to be fast. There's no problem that can't be solved in a 30-minute sitcom. Sex is the shortcut to love."[13]

The securing of 'fast happiness,' in other words, is not just an immediate gratification but a long-term benchmark for how well each of us is succeeding as an individual. Hence, Robards's comment on sex as a shortcut to love has a special poignancy because of its personal evaluative implications. As J. L. McCary postulates:

> Sex appeal is extolled by the various mass communications media as a means to instant popularity, success, admiration, and security. Young men, whose heightened sex drives are equaled only by their feelings of adolescent insecurity, are particularly susceptible to the idea that their masculinity is measured by the number of women they have seduced. . . . Young women, on the other hand, become indoctrinated by the communications media with the importance of being 'sexy.'[14]

1. (MUSIC UP)   2. SINGERS: IS THAT YOU...   3. WOW!

4. IS THAT YOU...   5. AND THERE YOU ARE. THAT'S   6. LOOKIN' SO GOOD...
                                YOU!

7. IN THE NEIGHBORHOOD.   8. THAT'S YOU!   9. THAT OLDS CALAIS...

10. IS MORE THAN A CAR.   11. THAT OLDS CALAIS IS WHO   12. THAT OLDS CALAIS IS WHO
                                 YOU ARE...THAT'S YOU.   YOU ARE...

13. OLDSMOBILE.   14. (Anncr VO): Oldsmobile Quality.   15. SINGERS: FEEL IT!

Figure 11–2 Oldsmobile "Who You Are" Photoboard (Courtesy of Roger W. Bodo,
214 Leo Burnett Company of Michigan, Inc.)

Sexiness, however, is not the only standard for self-assessment taught by the electronic curriculum. Indeed, for adolescents no less than for their parents, the wealth and glitter that often accompany sexual depictions present as much a comparative measurement of "how I'm doing" as does one's perceived success with members of the opposite gender. In studying the teenagers growing up in blue-collar Cicero, Illinois, for instance, critic Michael Leahy found:

> *Dallas* and *Dynasty* offer titillation and glamour for them too, but always, at some point, the moment comes for kids when the wealth and social prowess of the characters remind them of what they aren't, bring them crashing back to these row houses and factories, leaving them feeling trapped.[15]

It may do little good to observe that *Dallas, Dynasty,* and the like portray happenings and gratifications that not even the well-off typically experience—even in an entire lifetime. The fantasized standards of self-attainment that these programs erect are convincing to viewers because, as Carl Grabo observes of the analogous interaction of readers with print, "in some literature the real and imagined worlds are confused and the reader cannot separate the false and the true. Thus, the literature of entertainment and escape purports to be, or is mistaken by its readers to be, an honest picture of life."[16]

To the extent that the preached standards of broadcasting and cable do not discernibly clash with our internalized measures of self-worth, they are likely, at least, to be passively tolerated. When media-suggested standards collide with the personal assessment mechanisms used by ourselves and our peers, however, they will be preemptorily dismissed. And when we ourselves lack the standard because of a deficiency or omission in our own values formation, the radio/television benchmark, for better or worse, just might be adopted.

It is this last situation that most concerns social and media critics, and is at the core of the debate about children and programming. Child psychiatrist Robert Coles has concluded:

> A child who is having a rough time of it personally—whose parents, for instance, are mostly absent, or indifferent to him or her, or unstable—will be much more vulnerable to the emotional and moral power of television. . . . No question, such children can be badly hurt by television, can be persuaded by it to act cruelly, wantonly, irrationally. A stable family, with a vigorous moral life, well and constantly enunciated by parents, will likely provide a persisting immunity to the influence of various shows—whereas a weak and vulnerable family is more likely to fall under the spell of those same programs.[17]

Depiction Critiquing in Action

Dr. Coles's comment should not be accepted as a generalized indictment of all electronic media content. Many programs, and not a few commercials, are frequently lauded by critics for the positive lessons they teach. To bolster this point, and to provide a specific example of how the five depiction-constituting questions can comprise a single, integrated critique, another student-composed review, this time of the one-hour series *Fame,* is printed below.

Appropriately entitled "Teachers," the *Fame* episode under scrutiny involves two parallel agitations. In the first, aspiring student composer Bruno Martelli has to choose between pursuing a piano scholarship to ease his father's financial burdens or holding fast to his dream of becoming a composer. In the second, both an overweight woman named René and Lydia, the moonlighting dance instructor, learn from personal fitness guru Richard Simmons that doing things for others begins with an understanding of yourself.

In the following student analysis, parenthetical numbers have been added to reference the discussion of each of depiction's five questions.

In the *Fame* episode "Teachers," (2) society was shown to be extremely competitive. The setting was the New York City High School for the Arts, a place set up to foster artistic struggle. In fact, the show's society as a whole seemed to force people to struggle. Bruno had to strain to break out of his father's well-meaning but misinformed hold. Bruno's cab-driving father labored to hold on to Bruno and thereby to see his own and his deceased wife's dreams realized. Composition teacher Shirovsky has to struggle to decide whether or not to let Bruno abandon composition for the financial crutch of a piano scholarship. And Lydia literally had to sweat to modify her professionalist attitude toward dance in order to help raise the self-confidence of her non-dancer exercise students at Simmons' studio.

"Teachers" showed us the consequences of actions (3) in various situations. For Bruno, the consequence of waiting so long to stand up to his father made it even harder to do so. Bruno tells his dad he doesn't need his help on everything and this inevitably made his father feel unneeded until Bruno found a way to tell his parent that love and dependence were not the same thing. Until this stand, Bruno had allowed his father and Mr. Shirovsky to pull him in opposite directions and the consequence was that he never stopped to think what was right for him. For Lydia, the consequence of her condescending attitude toward exercise dancing was that she almost got herself fired. One cannot demean one's job—even if it is only moonlighting. In a further effects [consequences] teaching, Simmons shows Lydia that if you care for people as individuals with unique emotional needs, they will respond to you positively.

This point was also made in the lyrics of Bruno's song which, in addition, set forth a responsibility (4) that we have toward others. The song said: "Wish me well, love me as I am;" "Dream but understand;" "I'll do the best I can." In other words, we have the responsibility to avoid imposing our will on others but the counterpart duty to help them be what they have the capacity to be.

At times, we are assigned appropriate responsibilities, at other times we're afflicted with inappropriate ones. This *Fame* episode provides examples of both situations. A reasonable expectation was that of Richard Simmons when he presumed Lydia to take her work as an exercise instructor seriously even though the members of her fitness class would never be dancers. Lydia had told Richard that, as a professional dancer, his class was not a life or death situation for her. But Simmons taught her that it was *just that* to the self concepts of their overweight students and she then took the revealed responsibility seriously. An unreasonable expectation was that of Bruno's father who felt he had the parental responsibility to make all decisions for his 17-year-old son. Bruno, with Shirovsky's help, demonstrated that part of a father's duty is to help his son assume more of his own responsibilities by letting him chart his own course.

Bruno needed to evaluate himself (5) against himself and no one else. He had spent most of his life doing things for his widowed father. He was even going to try out for a Julliard piano scholarship and abandon composition to please his father. Bruno finally stood up for himself by taking control of his own life. He and we learned the difference between listening to advice and following orders with the former taught as the more mature standard. We should evaluate ourselves based on our ability to make independent decisions. In the case of Lydia, she had to evaluate herself on her ability to give emotional guidance to others through a positive personal attitude. Simmons said that the obese René might not lose her weight because she was losing it for her son and not herself. Lydia and René both learned that internal standards are more motivating than externally imposed ones.

This show featured some complex problems. And though its environment (1) of crowded, urban and multi-racial America came through in every scene, these problems were not caused by the city but by people. The program taught that, in today's struggle-filled, competitive society, we should live for ourselves while at the same time accepting others for what they are. The show tells us that with a positive internal attitude, we can 'teach' others to feel good about themselves. Everything worked out in the end and, though such a complete resolution is unrealistic, it does not seem to contradict the depicted truth of "Teachers'" teachings.

(Courtesy of Chris Cooley)

For another application of depiction analysis, we can again turn to the *Ethel and Albert* episode in Appendix B. If some time has elapsed since you read this script in relation to its dissection in the previous chapter, you may wish to reread it before proceeding. Unlike the *Fame* review, depiction's questions are now addressed in order, but without including query reference numbers.

Ethel and Albert's Sandy Harbor is the white, orderly, middle-class suburbia so popular in 1950s television. Even though it did not typify most of real America, it probably represented the archetype of what most of middle America was striving for. The Arbuckles' home is comfortably functional but by no means lavish or ostentatious. Selecting new drapes is still a major decision that requires a friend's counsel, and losing one's job is an imagined calamity of fearful proportions. For whatever reason, no children clutter the landscape, so we are free to focus exclusively on adult furnishings and the concerns these materials sometimes cause. Basements and attics are structural necessities for storing away our yesterdays (tax records and scout hats) and tomorrows (watermelon pickles, stewed tomatoes, and ready cash). Unpredictabilities in this environment chiefly relate to plumbing and roofs that need fixing and undependable weather—although the latter might be due to "the atom bomb experiments" which seem passively accepted, like the tax laws, as the inevitable prerogative of government.

Sandy Harbor society is a solid white-collar constituency in which men go to offices around nine in the morning and, like Bunderson, find it remarkable when it gets to be 8:30 at night and they "haven't even had dinner." Women do not seem to join this external working world but stay home to bake, knit socks, braid rugs, do a lot of cleaning (so that letters become lost) and ponder the Woman's Club minutes. When wives do engage in the world of commerce, it is of the ten-cent-vinegar and two-cent-stamp variety that has little effect except to disorganize their husbands' record-keeping. Everyone treats everyone else with respect, and matrimonial disagreements are marked only by mild expressions of exasperation. Contributing to charity and going to church are facts of life even if "Reverand Sheridan" would be surprised to "see what you put down for contributions to the collection plate." What crime exists comes from another place and/or another time, with the distant spectre of Al Capone looming as the epitome of wrong-doing.

"Most people seem to be fundamentally honest," as Gilbert has found and, although the consequences of "honest mistakes" may be nerve-wracking, that honesty is ultimately "refunded." Even tiny attempts at deceit usually result in embarrassment and so should not be attempted. One can never fool the government, it is strongly implied, and the fruits of untidiness are unnecessary stress. Tax preparation is "kind of a headache to everybody," but the alternative is "Alcatraz" or, at the very least, "accumulated interest dating from the day on which you should have reported this income." Most fundamentally, complete disclosure between husband and wife is an essential for which there can be no substitute. Sharing instead with an outsider (even if he is a government employee) will only lead to trouble.

As taxpayers, we have a responsibility, not only to report income accurately, but also to "keep nice neat accounts." As public servants, we must be politely thorough and, where appropriate, take the time to reassure. As neighbors, like Grace, we have a duty to give an "honest opinion" in order to save friends from making a mistake; and, as relatives, we need to offer freely and not "begrudge" financial assistance.

More basic to the whole concept of *Ethel and Albert*, spouses have an immutable obligation to care for each other. Albert works hard to make a good home for Ethel and manfully, if somewhat nervously, takes full responsibility for dealing with outside problems, including those flowing from the government. Even though Ethel encourages him to "put the blame on me" for misplacing the audit letter, Albert never considers such a thing and prepares to face the "tax office" dragon himself. He also sees it to be his duty to help Ethel learn "about money" even though his efforts in this regard seem destined to be buried in the backyard. For her part, Ethel believes that she and every other woman have a responsibility to nurture a little "nest egg somewhere—even if it's a small one" in order to provide her husband with "birthday and Christmas presents—so I don't spend YOUR money" and to create a safety net should the main breadwinner's job be terminated. The means by which such caring is expressed may, at times, be faulty, but this does not make the caring any less vital.

As viewers, in summary, we learn from "The Income Tax" to be caring, to be honest, to be tidy (but not too tidy), and to see humor in life—even if this humor, like wearing the scout hat to work or Ethel's comment about the file in the cake, can only be savored after the fact. From Ethel and Albert we learn that grace under pressure is not nearly so important to self realization as are civility and kindness under pressure.

Before we leave this *Ethel and Albert* analysis it is important to recognize that a depiction critique is as much a product of its own time as is the program being critiqued. Thus, lessons that from a late-1980s perspective may appear simplistic, sexist, or sociologically abrasive may not have seemed so to viewers actually living in the Eisenhower era. We must understand that a program's lessons are frozen in the context of its time and may be rendered quaint, frivolous, or irrelevant by the passage of years. In the case of "The Income Tax," the episode's protrayal of environment and society seem the most anachronistic aspects; but its teachings on our fundamental human responsibilities and especially on our standards for personal evaluation remain timeless.

Remember that as John Fiske and John Hartley point out, "Television [and radio, too] is a human construct, and the job that it does is the result of human choice, cultural decisions and social pressures. The medium responds to the conditions within which it exists."[18]

Notes

1. Ben Stein, *The View from Sunset Boulevard* (New York: Basic Books, 1979), xii.
2. Michael Leahy, "Our Cities Are Big Bad Places—If You Believe Prime-Time TV," *TV Guide* (May 3, 1986): 5–6.
3. Ibid., 7.
4. Stein, *View*, 70–71.
5. Ibid., xi.
6. William Cohen and Gary Hart, "TV's Treatment of Washington—It's Capital Punishment," *TV Guide* (August 24, 1985): 5.
7. Hugh Sidey, "Snowcroft's Concerns," *Time* (May 4, 1987): 17.
8. Jack Shaheen, "The Arab Stereotype on Television," *The Link* (April/May, 1980): 2–3.
9. Cathy Schwichtenberg, "*The Love Boat*: The Packaging and Selling of Love, Heterosexual Romance, and Family," in Horace Newcomb, ed., *Television: The Critical View*, 4th ed. (New York: Oxford University Press, 1987), 127-28.
10. Mike Oppenheim, "TV Isn't Violent *Enough*," *TV Guide* (February 11, 1984): 21.
11. Michael Pacanowsky and James Anderson, "Cop Talk and Media Use," *Journal of Broadcasting* (Fall 1982): 750.
12. David Schoenbrun, "In Defense of TV's Newscasters," *TV Guide* (April 25, 1987): 6.
13. Jason Robards, "Television So Often Promotes Drinking Instead of Combating It," *TV Guide* (May 4, 1985): 39.

14. J. L. McCary, *Human Sexuality* (New York: Van Norstrand, 1973), 106.
15. Michael Leahy, "Don't Mis-Judge Working-Class America," *TV Guide* (December 21, 1985): 12.
16. Carl Grabo, *The Creative Critic* (Chicago: University of Chicago Press, 1948), 108.
17. Robert Coles, "What Makes Some Kids More Vulnerable to the Worst of TV?," *TV Guide* (June 21, 1986): 7.
18. John Fiske and John Hartley, *Reading Television* (London: Methuen & Company, 1978), 17.

Symbols, Myths, and Structures

It has been said that radio and television do not really mirror reality but rather that they structure and mold reality into organized patterns for efficient conveyance. With this perspective in mind, we now examine some of the coding systems from which these organized or semi-organized patterns are derived. As mentioned at the start of Chapter 11, understanding such electronic pedagogies is vital for thorough critical experiencing of the broadcast/cable curriculum.

Symbols and Archetypes

The basic building blocks for any codes are the individual units that can be isolated or combined to carry and amalgamate meaning. For our purposes, these symbols are, in Hal Himmelstein's words, "nothing more or less than organizing ideas by which *people* develop perspectives about their relationship with their world."[1] Thus, as Theodore Meyer Greene adds, a symbol is "entirely the product of human contrivance. . . . It has no basis in nature or in logic; the meaning of a pure symbol is arbitrarily attached to it by individual *fiat* or social convention."[2]

Those symbols whose meaning accrues solely from individual fiat are of little use in the mass media, of course, where transference of commonly accepted meaning is crucial. Such *personal* symbols, then, are of utility only in inter- or intra-personal communication, in which we share a highly proprietary meaning with a small group of friends, lodge, sorority, or church members, or just with ourselves. Personal symbols are the province of the secret handshake, cryptic emblem, or the waxed and flattened tulip from an eighth-grade sweetheart. They have immense meaning for us as individuals but little utility in communicating with the world at large unless, like the broken-horned unicorn in Tennessee Williams's *Glass Menagerie,* the symbol's essence comes to be expressed in more universal terms.

Social symbols are understood by a much wider public, perhaps even by an entire society, and thus can be readily appropriated by radio and television. Sometimes, however, rather than borrowing a pre-existing social symbol, the media themselves will create and market one of their own as a means of more certainly controlling how the message will be decoded. Thus, what Horace Newcomb calls the "embedded significance" of the broadcast-used social symbol can be attributed to either of two conditions:

> Some of that significance rises from the field of reference within the formula or type of the work. Other significance is rooted in the symbol's relation to the world outside popular entertainment forms.[3]

The leather-jacketed, ducktailed hood, for instance, was a media-borrowed and media-amplified symbol of youthful defiance in the 1950s; but this symbol was turned inside out by the Fonz on *Happy Days,* who became the epitome of integrity and humane conscience. The Tootsie Pop sucker was a child's confection until *Kojak* made it a symbol of tough virility. And "Where's the Beef?" was an old lady's search for the perfect (Wendy's) hamburger until Walter Mondale used the slogan in the 1984 Democratic presidential primary to pop Gary Hart's image bubble.

The broadcast commercial's self-contained brevity both recruits and creates social symbols as a matter of virtual necessity in order to register concepts in a bare minimum of time. Thus the nerd symbol/character in the following Ogilvy & Mather spot presents a clear need that the product emblem can address.

Production Note: Gloria must have a husky, sexy voice.

DUANE: Once upon a time, believe it or not, I was a nerd. Like last week.

(SFX: PHONE RINGS)

GLORIA: (Filter Mic) Hello?

DUANE: Oh Gloria, this is Duane. I got your number from your brother.

GLORIA: Oh, hi Duane. What are you wearing?

DUANE: Me? Just cazhing about in my polyvinyl leisure suit and matching pencil case. (PHONE CLICK) Well, not exactly

matching, per se. I—(DIAL TONE) Oh. (Fading off)
Obviously I had to change style.

CLERK: Hi, can I help you? Whoa, what's that on your suit?

DUANE: Oh, sour ball. Must have stuck to me on the bus again.

CLERK: Okay. You need OP sportswear.

DUANE: OP?

CLERK: Yeah, right away. Over here.

DUANE: Yo, quite an array of back-to-school apparel.

CLERK: Yeah, and they're durable.

DUANE: I love durable.

CLERK: They're stylish.

DUANE: My middle name.

CLERK: And look how they fit you.

DUANE: Can I use your phone?

CLERK: Sure.

(SFX: PHONE RINGS)

DUANE: Gloria, it's me. I'm wearing OPs.

GLORIA: Why don't you come over, Duane?

DUANE: I can't, Glo. Got to stay home and wax my slide rule.
          (PHONE CLICK) Sometimes you gotta play hard to like.[4]

(Reprinted with permission of *Adweek*)

When symbols can cross cultures and times and still preserve their central meaning, they become archetypes. Most social symbols, in fact, have their genesis in underlying, enduring *archetypes* that have simply been given a more specific rendering by a given culture. Take the concept of the comic, for example. As Northrop Frye points out, an ancient Greek pamphlet, the *Tractatus Coislinianus*, "sets down all the essential facts about comedy in about a page and half."[5] Frye recounts that the *Tractatus* lists three kinds of comic characters:

1. The *alazons* or imposters who pretend to be more than they are "though it is more frequently a lack of self-knowledge than simply hypocrisy that characterizes them."[6]

2. The *eirons* or self-deprecators who thus make themselves invulnerable because they castigate themselves before others can grab the opportunity.

"Central to this group is a hero, who is an *eiron* figure because, as explained, the dramatist tends to play him down and make him rather neutral and un-formed in character."[7]

3. The *bomolochoi* or buffoons "whose function it is to increase the mood of festivity rather than contribute to the plot . . . with established comic habits like malapropism or foreign accents."[8]

To these three *Tractatus*-specified types, Aristotle would add a fourth:

4. The *agroikos* who can be surly, unsophisticated, or solemn depending on the comic context. We find the first "in the miserly, snobbish, or priggish characters whose role is that of the refuser of festivity, the killjoy who tries to stop the fun"[9] and the second in the simple, even "hayseed" figure who, in his or her innocence, often expresses the uncomplicated ideal. The solemn vari-ant is "what in vaudeville used to be called the straight man . . . who allows the humor to bounce off him, so to speak."[10]

Thus, in the OP radio commercial, Duane is the classic *eiron*, whose self-deprecation comes close to transforming itself into the *alazon*'s boasting through the sudden and comic self-importance that the product provides. Glo-ria is the "killjoy" *agroikos* figure who "refuses festivity" from Duane only to have the tables ironically turned when he hangs up on her. The clerk, on the other hand, functions as the "straight man" *agroikos* type who "allows the hu-mor to bounce off him" while he seriously sells the product to Duane and to us.

These comedic archetypal symbols are not, of course, limited to advertis-ing; they can also help propel sitcoms. This is perhaps most strikingly present in ensemble comedies, such as *Cheers*, which seem virtually to mirror Frye's descriptions of Greek dramatic theory. Consider, for example, the many vi-gnettes between Cliff, the knowledge-bluffing mailman, and Norm, the tubby accountant who so blatantly embraces his own flaws and failures. As Frye points out, "The multitude of comic scenes in which one character compla-cently soliloquizes [Cliff] while another makes sarcastic asides to the audience [Norm] show the contest of *eiron* and *alazon* in its purest form, and show too that the audience is sympathetic to the *eiron* side."[11] In other words, viewers side with *eiron* Norm over *alazon* Cliff. Even though Frye wrote the descrip-tion of their interaction more than thirty years before *Cheers* was conceived, his observation remains eminently pertinent because both it and the sitcom are based on the same enduring set of archetypal symbols.

Cheers proprietor and hero-figure Sam represents another dimension of the *eiron* role who deprecates himself for his lack of intelligence while his largely "unformed" character makes him ripe for waitress Diane's (later, and owner Rebecca's) irritatingly over-bearing proddings. Diane, and her replace-ment, Rebecca, play *alazons* to Sam's *eiron* in the same manner that Norm balances Cliff so that we do not tire of either context. (Recall our earlier discussion of balance in Chapter 10.) The other *Cheers* regulars tend largely to fulfill *agroikos* functions: the "killjoy refuser of festivity," Dr. Frazier Crane; the simple, innocent bartender, Coach, who was replaced, on the death of his role-player, by the equally simple and innocent Woody (a "hayseed" besides); and the surly, feisty Carla, who constantly strives to stand in the way of Diane's or Rebecca's manic enthusiasms. Carla, in fact, may be the program's most complicated character because her "fun-stopping" *agroikos* rampages are balanced by wistful revelations of *eiron*-like self-censure.

Notice that there are no *bomolochoi* among *Cheers* regulars because, by definition, these buffoon figures only function "to increase the mood of festivity rather than contribute to the plot." Instead, *bomolochoi* enter and leave the bar as minor or random episode characters who exist, like Carla's hairy ex-husband Nick Tortelli, only to incite the regular ensemble's interplay. In fact, when the *Cheers* creators attempted to fashion a spinoff sitcom built around Nick, his inherent buffoon limitations, as *Chicago Tribune* critic Clifford Terry pointed out, proved a dead weight:

LEADEN 'CHEERS' SPINOFF BARELY RATES A WHIMPER
By Clifford Terry

The premiere episode of "The Tortellis," an NBC sitcom that makes it debut at 8:30 P.M. Thursday on Channel 5, starts off with Nick Tortelli (played by Dan Hedaya) dreaming that he is in heaven and has been condemned to eternal damnation. "You cheated on both your wives," says a ghostly voice. "You were dishonest in business. You were a terrible father." To which the accused replies, "Don't I get any points for consistency?"

Granting that he might, the same can't be said for the show, a spinoff of "Cheers" that is nothing to shout about.

"The Tortellis," whose main characters will be introduced in Thursday's "Cheers" episode, centers on Nick, the ex-husband of Carla, the barmaid in Sam Malone's Boston saloon played by Rhea Perlman.

In the opener, directed by James Burrows and written by Ken Estin, he has followed his present wife, Loretta (Jean Kasem)—a blond "My Friend Irma"-style airhead with a Marilyn Monroe voice—to Las Vegas. It seems she had fled from New Jersey to the home of her sister, Charlotte (Carlene Watkins), to get away from Nick, an unregenerate "slug," after finding him in the shower with the Avon lady. (His explanation was he was trying out a new brush.)

Before long, Charlotte—the comely, cynical mother of a young boy (Aaron Moffatt)—has agreed to let the Tortellis stay on if they share the rent, and not long after that, they are all joined by Nick and Loretta's son (Timothy Williams) and his new bride (Mandy Ingber). Complications then arise when Nick, who hopes to make it big as a TV repairman, finds that he is strongly attracted to his sister-in-law.

Lacking the sophisticated, off-center humor of "Cheers," "The Tortellis" is filled with leaden lines. When Loretta asks, "Are we the biggest boobs in town or what?", Charlotte answers, "Not in this town." When Charlotte tells Nick she is a substitute schoolteacher, he answers, "What a coincidence. I went to school." When Nick asks Charlotte, "Can't you take a joke?" she answers, "Not when it's married to my sister."

Neither are the characters themselves appealing, unless you enjoy watching a neanderthal type swatting his son on the head with a newspaper and pulling his ears.

Executive producers of "The Tortellis," which will move to its regular Wednesday night time slot Jan. 28, are Glen Charles, Les Charles and James Burrows, creators of "Cheers," as well as Patricia Nardo.

(Courtesy of F. Richard Ciccone, *Chicago Tribune*)

Archetypal symbols function regardless of whether audiences, creators, or critics are aware of these symbols' presence. This occurs because archetypes are inherently enduring and transcend the limitations of any given place or time. Even though the social symbols based on these archetypes are quite apparent, the reason some social symbols seem more effective than others often is due to the degree to which they conform to our implicit if deep-seated archetypal expectations of them. The more the critic, at least, can come to recognize archetypal patterns, the easier it is for that critic to understand and perhaps even anticipate programmatic success or failure. It is not necessary to explain to a mass readership why the *bomolochoi*-dependent *Tortellis* is archetypally flawed as a comedic vehicle. In apprehending this flaw, however, the critic becomes more adept in ferreting out the manifestations of such a defect as a means of providing public advisement.

When an archetype is abused, either intentionally or unintentionally, the communicative fallout can be devastating. This is particularly true when the message tries to cross cultures without adequate attention to archetype-encasing social symbols. Thus, Pepsi-Cola's existence-glorifying slogan "Come Alive—You're in the Pepsi Generation" was translated in Taiwan as "Pepsi-Cola Will Bring Your Ancestors Back from the Dead." Competitor Coca-Cola did no better with social-symbol decoding on the Chinese mainland, where its identity line converted to "Bite the Waxy Tadpole." More tragically, Adolph Hitler's Nazi *swastika* was a social-symbol distortion of an archetypal emblem that represents the mystic lifeforce in the cultures of India and Japan as well as among Native Americans and that, when called a *gammadion* (four Greek gamma symbols radiating from a common center), was also used by the early Christian church to represent Christ as its core. Hence, though the archetype recurs, the social constructs for it can change and even reverse its meaning.

Radio/television critics, of course, seldom need wrestle with anything of such profundity. Nevertheless, the presence of archetypes as repetitive meaning patterns must at least be acknowledged because, as Frye maintains, "we could almost define popular literature, admittedly in a rather circular way, as literature which affords an unobstructed view of archetypes."[12]

Whether this literature is conveyed directly in print or via the electronic media is unimportant except that television is coming to possess the more pervasive influence. Rose Goldsen, in fact, would argue:

Television now holds a virtual monopoly on whatever artistic and symbolic forms have a chance to be widely shared throughout the society. All the images, all the tales and ballads and chants and songs and stories that come through that screen, show-and-tell aspects of social reality that then become familiar to all.[13]

Ritual, Mystique, and Myth

In making her case, Goldsen has led us beyond a discussion of symbols into the larger arena of ritual. Even though a social or archetypal symbol carries meaning to the mass audience, it only acquires an involving storyline or narrative when immersed in a ritual—what Robert Smith calls "an act, or series of acts, which brings about a satisfactory resolution of the problem with which the program deals."[14] Thus, as John Fiske and John Hartley observed about popular crime shows:

> A programme like *Ironside* converts abstract ideas about individual relationships between man and man, men and women, individuals and institutions, whites and blacks into concrete dramatic form. It is a ritual condensation of the dominant criteria for survival in modern complex society. Clearly in this condensed form individual relationships can be scrutinized by the society concerned, and any inappropriateness can be dealt with in the form of criticisms of the programme. Hence, *Ironside*'s ritual condensation of relationships is supplanted by *Kojak*'s, which is supplanted in turn by *Starsky and Hutch*. Each of these fictive police series presents a slightly different view of the appropriate way of behaving towards other people.[15]

Whichever series ritualistically solves its problems in the most gratifying, most appealing way becomes the most esteemed. This is as true of game shows, sitcoms, and newscasts as it is of crime dramas. Any series develops its own ritual or formula, and even though the specific units within it will vary from episode to episode, the basic problem-solving progression will remain constant.

The same observation applies to radio formats. The aural service's hot clock is, in the final analysis, a ritualistic apportioning of an hour that accustoms us to when our need for news, weather, musical entertainment, traffic reports, or simulated conversation will be fulfilled. The format that successfully harmonizes with the life cycles of its target listeners is the format whose ritual thus possesses what Frye calls "magic":

> If we turn to ritual, we see there an imitation of nature which has a strong element of what we call magic in it. Magic seems to begin as something of a voluntary effort to recapture a lost rapport with the natural cycle. This sense of deliberate recapturing of something no longer possessed is a distinctive mark of human ritual. Ritual constructs a calendar. . . . But the impetus of the magical element in ritual is clearly toward a universe in which a stupid and indifferent nature is no longer the container of human society, but is contained by that society, and must rain or shine at the pleasure of man.[16]

A well-programmed radio station, in other words, gives us the sense that we are in control of our day, not only through the conveyance of coping information, but also via tension release that comes from well-selected and scheduled music and features. "Rituals," perceptual psychologist Rudolf Arnheim points out, "not only express what people feel but also help them to feel the way the situation requires."[17]

On television, we encounter the ritual of the anchor who bids us hello, then unveils all manner of tragedies but still reassures us at the end with a cheery good-bye. This pattern is matched by the ritual of the game show or sports event, which starts with the 'natural' challenge of human and situational obstacles to conquer and ends when someone or some team succeeds in this quest and is primed for new contests to be subsequently aired. Similarly, the ritual of the soap opera that transports us through the week and then, through a major Friday event, magically suspends time until Monday, is akin to the sitcom that enables us to string together humorously packaged problem revelations and solutions over time and in convenient and familiar half-hour patterns. The difference, on the other hand, between soap opera and sitcom rituals, is, as Horace Newcomb puts it:

> While the situation comedy is doomed to repeat itself in every episode of every series, changing only in the actual "situation" that precipitates the action, the soap opera will grow and change. . . . We see the same characters on typical evening dramas. But the soap opera characters change. They grow older; they marry; they have children; their problems are always appropriate to their situation.[18]

Since Newcomb made this observation, it should be noted that sitcoms like *Cheers* and *The Cosby Show* have adopted problem-solving rituals that are fueled by character change. Sam and Diane/Rebecca do mature through the cross-pollinating ebb-and-flow of their *Cheers* relationship. *Cosby*'s Theo does become more responsible and watches his sisters meet new challenges as their lives take them more and more beyond the nurturing boundaries of the Huxtable home. Unlike *Happy Days*' Richie Cunningham, who was the same boy in progressively larger-size slacks, characters in some of our newer sitcoms are engendered by a ritual that allows for psychological as well as physical growth.

Because it is usually easier to believe in characters who grow and change as we do, it can be argued that these newer sitcoms have a stronger *mystique*. Simply put, mystique is belief in the ritual's change device. We really want to accept that we know our world better now than before the newscast began; that the game show or sportscast has honestly established the better players; that our illegitimate heroine will really find the identity and support of her natural father; that our sitcom 'family' will continue to triumph so appealingly; that the radio station really did make our day brighter than it otherwise would have been. These and other electronic media mystiques are continuously generated and tend to be mutually supportive.

Hence, when we lose faith in one of them it can have a negative impact on our total belief perception of radio/television. This is why radio's payola scandals of the late 1950s and television's counterpart quiz-show riggings were so damaging, at least in the short term, to the industry. For when the public found that the songs they heard were determined by bribes, and their quiz show champions had cheated to win, all the rituals on the air were suddenly in danger of the loss of mystique. Through public hearings and public firings, broadcasting's damage control efforts did seem to succeed, but there are critics who would argue that, at least for the people who remember the 1950s, radio/television mystique has never fully recovered.

Commercials, like programs, try to cultivate their own sense of mystique. It is not enough that the audience understands the portrayed problem-solving ritual; they must also believe that the depicted solution is attainable and attainable best through application of the specific product or service being advocated. In the Figure 12–1 ninety-second spot for Multi-Action Tide, for instance, the familiar ritual of detergent use/endorsement is lightly satirized as a means of building up product mystique. After all, a product that is not afraid to kid itself must be legitimate since we tend to believe in people who are honest about themselves. This is effective advertising because it breaks old stereotypes of housewives who swoon over clean laundry and substitutes a more believable ritual in which viewers are invited to answer some mystique-enhancing questions for themselves.

Commercial mystique does not always require television or ninety seconds to be realized. The following one-minute radio spot builds belief in pleasurable sailing on a boat from Southwest Marine Sales because the copy demonstrates that the sponsor knows the precise feeling that the ritual of sailing is supposed to engender.

ANNCR: For your pleasure—a daydream from Southwest Marine Sales. The sails are full. The vessel glides quietly and gracefully through the water. White, foaming waves, cascade over the deck. The refreshing spray a coolant from the mid-day sun's warming rays. Seagulls soar overhead---specs of white against a backdrop of blue. Gentle gusts of a salt-scented breeze and you. The strain of muscles conquering wind and wave. The thrill of motion. <u>This</u> is sailing. Man and the elements. Willful. Strong. Exciting. This passage a thought from Southwest Marine Sales---Texas' largest sailboat dealer. See Texas' finest sailing vessels at Southwest Marine Sales, today, on Highway 146 at the Seabrook Shipyard. Once sailing's in your blood, you may never be a land-lubber again.

SAATCHI & SAATCHI COMPTON INC.
625 Madison Avenue, New York, N.Y. 10022
Telephone: (212) 754-1100

CLIENT: PROCTER & GAMBLE CO.
PRODUCT: TIDE (MULTI-ACTION)
TITLE: "SOCKS"
COMML. # PGTX 0029   TIMING: 90 SECONDS
DATE: 4/7/86   PAGE 1

1. WOMAN 1: It's like something from Mars. I can't believe it.

2. You won't believe it. It's incredible. Unbelievable. I'm repeating myself.

3. ANNCR: (VO) Which statement is true?

4. (SFX: TYPING) One, this woman would be enthusiastic about anything.

5. Two, this woman is crazy.

6. Three, this woman tried new Multi-Action Tide. The answer is three!

7. Introducing new Multi-Action Tide!

8. It'll knock your socks off,

9. and it'll get 'em cleaner!

10. WOMAN 2: It gets things cleaner than any detergent. I mean the way it works is just so amazing!

11. I mean it works! It really works!!!

12. (SFX: TYPING) ANNCR: (VO) One, this woman was a high school cheerleader and never got over it.

13. Two, this woman sees what she wants to see.

14. Three, this woman tried new Multi-Action Tide.

15. (MUSIC UNDER) This woman tried new Multi-Action Tide!

Figure 12–1 Tide "Socks" Photoboard (Copywriter, Jeffrey Frey; Art Director, Robert Meyerson, Saatchi & Saatchi Compton Group, Inc.)

1. With ingredients so special, so superior, we had to bring them to you in a whole new form.

2. Just one sheet in the washer...

3. (SFX: SPLASH) ...and the most effective detergent ingredients ever created

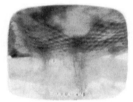

4. are released.

5. Then come whiteners more effective than any bleach.

6. Then you keep that same sheet of Multi-Action Tide for your dryer...

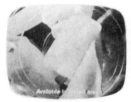

7. where the fabric softener is activated for unbeatable static control.

8. WOMAN 3: I could believe cleaner and harder. But cleaner and easier just blows my mind!

9. (SFX: TYPING) ANNCR: (VO) One, this woman's mind was blown a long time ago.

10. Two, this woman leads a very dull life.

11. Three, this woman tried...you know the answer.

12. For the cleanest, brightest, most static free wash you've ever had from one product,

13. new Multi-Action Tide.

14. (SFX: EXPLOSION) It'll knock your socks off,

15. and it'll get 'em cleaner!

231

> Southwest Marine. Number One at making daydreams
> reality.

(Courtesy of Wally Wawro, WFAA–TV)

When a ritual is so meaningful and so believable (mystique-rich) that it can be endlessly retold over time to carry the values of our society, it becomes a *myth*. We can change the symbols attached to the myth at will and still not vary the fundamental point this mythic story makes because its underlying value structure (recall our discussion of values in Chapter 8) is more or less eternal. As Rollo May has put it:

> We find our myths all about us in the unconscious assumptions of our culture; we mould the myths and we use them as images in which we can recognize ourselves, our friends, and our fellows; we use them as guidelines to our ways of life.[19]

Popular use of the term notwithstanding, a myth is not a falsehood; it is simply a value or faith statement that cannot be scientifically verified. Hence, as in our discussion of the four ways of knowing in Chapter 4, myth is much more the province of the mystic than that of the scientist.

More than two decades ago, Sprague Vonier, then station manager of WTMJ–TV in Milwaukee, randomly compiled a list of myths he detected in the prime-time television of his time. Vonier pointed out that this list was by no means exhaustive but did include many of the mythic attitudes most often conveyed to electronic audiences. Among the items on Vonier's inventory were:

> A man's home is his castle.
> Fair play is important.
> Everyone has a right to speak his mind.
> Everyone is entitled to the best education of which he is capable.
> People should be kind to animals and children.
> Everyone is created equal.
> No man is beyond redemption.
> We expect justice at the hands of the law and usually get it. When we don't, we try to correct the situation.
> We must strive to be well liked, to please others, to win the acceptance of the community.[20]

We can, without much difficulty, find these same myths undergirding today's programs because as Vonier wrote in 1965:

> They find their footings in a heritage of Anglo-Saxon law, of protestant ethical concepts, of democratic principles of government and a heritage of English literature. They are the same popular philosophical and ethical concepts which have under-

lain other media of mass entertainment, the movies, popular magazines, radio drama and even the comic strips.[21]

For the critic, the apprehension of myths not only fosters an understanding of our culture but also helps make sense of the symbolic patchwork that is electronic media content. Creators as well as consumers need to become more sensitive to this symbolic richness if for no other reason than to understand the cumulative meaning and impact of radio/television messages. With this realization in mind, Robert Smith advises:

> Programs are unyielding to analysis only if we insist on dealing with them atomically, one by one. If we look for the underlying rhythms that tie them to one another and to the stories of past cultures, both literate and illiterate, we may find that they lead us into the rich tapestry of the Western tradition. If we can see through the idiosyncracies of each program to its underlying structure, we may find that it takes on new meaning, or rather, the meaning it has for us becomes clear.[22]

Thus, as novelist Joyce Carol Oates observed, the cops of *Hill Street Blues* were compelling not because they were crimefighters like so many others on the air, but because "the Hill Street police are figures of Sisyphus rolling their rocks up the hill and the next day rolling them up again, and again. . . . It is always the next morning, it is always roll call."[23] Though many watchers of the program were not familiar with Sisyphus, the deceitful Corinthian king, they became very familiar with his myth of futile, Hades-bound endurance by watching as the hellish rock of anarchy kept threatening to roll back over 'The Hill' and crush its protectors.

It is inevitable that the electronic media function, albeit semiconsciously, as the perpetuators of myths because, asserts Professor John Cawelti, these media

> communicate to nearly everyone in the culture by depending on an established repertory of basic stories and other artistic patterns in a fashion analogous to the traditional bard's use of epic formulas and a well-known mythology. These conventional patterns guarantee a high degree of accessibility. Of course mere accessibility is no guarantee of artistic interest. However, there is a sense in which the best popular art is not only fairly easy to interpret, but compels audiences to want to understand it, because it deals in an interesting way with stories and themes that seem important.[24]

Thesis, Antithesis, and Synthesis

Another way of analyzing how symbols are manipulated into ritual and mythic structures is to examine how a creator interposes two opposites to generate a new amalgamation. The idea of these two opposites (the thesis and antithesis) and their resulting combination (the synthesis) is generally attributed to the works of Plato, Kant, and Hegel. This idea received its most explicit development, however, in Johann Gottlieb Fichte's *Science of Knowledge*. To Fichte, these three entities were interdependent in the science and arrangement of thought: "Just as there can be no antithesis without synthesis, no synthesis without antithesis," he wrote, "so there can be neither without a thesis—an absolute positing."[25]

Even though Fichte's statement of his premise becomes increasingly complex as his writing proceeds, its basic thrust was clearly captured by Karl Popper, who explained in his *The Open Society and Its Enemies*:

> First a thesis is proffered; but it will produce criticism, it will be contradicted by opponents who assert its opposite, an antithesis; and in the conflict of these views, a synthesis is attained, that is to say, a kind of unity of the opposites, a compromise or reconciliation on a higher level. The synthesis absorbs, as it were, the two original opposite positions, by superseding them; it reduces them to components of itself, thereby negating, elevating, and preserving them.

The impact of this structure's adoption is perhaps most noticeable in music, where, beginning in the nineteenth century, composers abandoned the sonata-allegro practice of a simple restatement (recapitulation) of contrasting themes in favor of a coda, or similar terminal device. The purpose, explains Aaron Copland, "is to create a sense of apotheosis—the material is seen for the last time and in a new light. . . . What sense does it make to go through all the turmoil and struggle of the development section if only to lead back to the same conclusions from which we started?"[26]

If all this does not seem very relevant to radio/television criticism, let us add that this same structural phenomenon can be found not only in programming but even more concisely in commercials as well. Consider the following spot, for example:

COUNSELOR: Bob, Helen, as a trained counselor, I believe every marriage can be saved.

BOB & HELEN: Yeah, sure, we'll see about that.

COUN: Now Bob, what's the problem?

HELEN: Cheap jerk here won't buy me a new TV.

COUN: Now Helen, I asked Bob.

BOB: There's nothing wrong with the old set.

HELEN: Yeah? The vertical hold is so bad that I can't tell Laverne from Curly.

BOB: It's Shirley.

HELEN: Yeah, see he's always ---

COUN:	Now Bob, how about a new set?
HELEN:	This cheap jerk?
COUN:	You know, cheap jerk, uh, Bob, what you two need is---
BOB & HELEN:	A divorce!
COUN:	No, Granada TV Rental.
BOB:	Granada TV Rental?
COUN:	Why put up with a lousy picture? Rent a big brand name color TV for just $11.95 to $29.95 a month.
BOB:	No more ghosties?
HELEN:	Or fuzzies?
COUN:	Any problems, Granada provides free repairs.
HELEN:	Wow!
COUN:	Or Granada gives you a free loaner.
BOB:	Wow!
COUN:	Problem solved?
BOB & HELEN:	Yeah.
COUN:	Next problem: drinking beer and smoking stogies in bed ---
HELEN:	I need a brewsky and a stogie to relax me after a hard day.

(Courtesy of Dick Orkin)

Here, the thesis is that TV sets with prime-grade picture quality can be costly, and its antithesis is that poorly functioning receivers are a major family irritant. The resolving synthesis is Granada—the company that can provide a prime picture quality economically. Therefore, there is no longer any reason to put up with inferior video.

In Figure 12–2, we see how this same schema can underlie a television advertisement. You need data generation systems that keep your office contemporary, posits the thesis; but the noise of these systems can prove a counterproductive office irritant, argues the antithesis. Fortunately, (synthesis) with Exxon systems, you acquire modernity but without the aural shock.

For program examples of this dynamic, we need only to turn to the two scripts in the Appendices. In the case of *Ethel and Albert*'s "The Income Tax," the thesis states that it is important to be honest while the antithesis counters

EXXON OFFICE SYSTEMS

INK JET

LENGTH: 30 SECONDS

JOHN HUSTON V.O.: The shocking thing

about the office of the future . . .

is the sound of it.

So at Exxon Office Systems, we've created the EXXON 965 Ink Jet Printer.

It can print just about anything . . . as fast as 90 characters per second.

And it's incredibly quiet.

Now the automated office will never sound the same again.

For more information call 800-327-6666.

Exxon Office Systems. It's the future . . . without the shock.

The Future . . . without the shock

Figure 12–2 Exxon "Ink Jet" Photoboard (Courtesy of Kathryn Spiess, Marsteller Inc.)

that compulsive honesty invites suspicion or financial harm. These two contrasting views are synthesized in the show's conclusion, which demonstrates that reasonable candor will preserve both self-respect and well-being. In *The Cosby Show*'s "Theo's Holiday," the thesis tells us that asserting one's self-sufficiency is a hallmark of maturity. The ironic antithesis, however, maintains that the working world expects but does not nurture this self-sufficiency. Fortunately, a supportive family can promote maturing independence through selective guidance in the ways of the world (the synthesis outcome).

The following review by *New York Times* critic John O'Connor demonstrates what occurs (or more precisely, fails to occur) when thesis and antithesis are never synthesized. As O'Connor states at the beginning of his piece, in this cable special, "we have the entertainer as singer (thesis) doing battle with the entertainer as concerned advocate" (antithesis) but with no apparent resolution or amalgamation (synthesis) of these two polarities.

TV: STREISAND'S 'ONE VOICE' ON HBO
By John J. O'Connor

In "Barbra Streisand: One Voice," on the Home Box Office cable channel tonight at 10, we have the entertainer as singer doing battle with the entertainer as concerned advocate. Fortunately, the singer wins, though just barely.

I must confess to a chronic allergy to show business personalities who become soapbox orators. Whether it's Charlton Heston on the right or Jane Fonda on the left, just for starters, the sincerity-laden performances inevitably tend to leave me cringing in embarrassment before such profound superficiality. For the most part, I am entirely in Ms. Streisand's corner so far as her causes are concerned, but I keep wishing she would just sing. That's what she does best.

This pay-cable special was taped Sept. 6 in the exquisite garden of Miss Streisand's imposing California home. Warming up the audience, Robin Williams says, "Welcome to the Malibu Shakespeare Festival." An exclusive audience of 500 Hollywood celebrities paid $5,000 a couple, with the proceeds going to politicians, including the then-campaigning Senator Alan Cranston, Democrat of California, and to the Barbra Streisand Foundation. A note at the end of the program explains that the foundation "supports qualified charitable organizations committed to antinuclear activities, the preservation of our environment, our civil liberties and human rights."

That would have been enough to make the star's point. But Ms. Streisand believes that more is more. We first hear her voice on the tape-recorded invitations sent out for the event. Mentioning the "billions of dollars that are being spent on weapons," she urges her friends to "please join me at my home, under the stars. We'll have dinner." Then, emerging from some artificially created mists, she strolls onto the small stage dressed all in white, her blonde hair having that casual just-washed look, and sings "Somewhere" from "West Side Story." That much done nicely, she looks around at her impeccably manicured property and comments, solemnly, on how "this place is really special to me, the awesome balance of nature."

Backed up by a fine eight-member ensemble playing electronic instruments under the musical direction of Randy Kerber, Ms. Streisand maneuvers her way smoothly through a generally familiar repertory: "People," "Send in the Clowns," "The Way We Were," "Happy Days Are Here Again." A tribute to Judy Garland with "Somewhere Over the Rainbow" is lovely. She is still trying, unsuccessfully, to push the score from "Yentl," with music by Michel Legrand and lyrics by Marilyn and Alan Bergman, but "Papa, Can You Hear Me" remains forgettably gooey. And her closing rendition of "America the Beautiful" owes an enormous debt to the definitive soul version associated with Ray Charles. Barry Gibb of the Bee Gees appears for a couple of duets, and that is a mistake, breaking the momentum of what should be a Streisand juggernaut. Sitting on a stool at center stage, the star is most effective when most simple and unaffected.

That still leaves, of course, the polemics to get through. Confronted with Chernobyl, Ms. Streisand worries about cheese from France and apples from Oregon. "We're all downwind," she says, "and it terrifies me." She adds: "I mean, aren't we all the same really? Lovers are lovers, no matter under what government they make love." Entertainers seem to have an instinct for trivialization.

But perhaps, for all that, the spectacle can be effective; Senator Cranston was re-elected.

(Copyright © 1986 by The New York Times Company. Reprinted by permission.)

Semiotics

A much more recent development in the analysis of message structure in general—and one that was almost immediately applied to electronic media content in particular—has occurred via the rise of semiotics. Coined by philosopher Charles Sanders Peirce, the term *semiotics* refers to the study of sign systems. Peirce, as well as Swiss linguist Ferdinand de Saussure, provided much of the basic theory that has fueled increased scholarly attention to this subject during the last two decades. At the outset, however, it must be said that this interest has not been shared by practicing radio/television critics and currently remains largely the tool of university researchers and their graduate students.

Because semiotics is the study of sign systems, it is important here to delineate signs from the symbols with which we were concerned at the beginning of this chapter. Even though much metaphysical hairsplitting can be indulged in, Frye put the distinction in its most comprehensible terms when he wrote that signs are simply those symbolic units "which, conventionally and arbitrarily, stand for and point to things outside the place where they occur."[27] Thus, for our purposes, all signs are symbols; they are the symbols that possess the greatest utility since they free us from the bonds of our immediate and concrete perceptual environment.

When we deal with semiotics, we face two basic concerns. These concerns are, in the words of Fiske and Hartley, "the relationship between a sign and its meaning; and the way signs are combined into codes."[28] These signs can be verbal, auditory, or visual, of course, and this is what makes a semiotic analysis of the electronic media much more complex than that of the verbal-only world of print. In any event, according to Saussure, the fundamental process for semiotic scrutiny can be reduced to this equation:

$$signifier + signified = sign$$

The signifier is the vehicle, the physical entity, that carries the meaning. Thus, in the Navy public service announcement in Figure 12–3, the signifier is the aircraft carrier. The signified is a mental concept that comprises the meaning's core. In this PSA, the signifier is the concept of adventure. The sign, or resulting associative sum, is that working with the Navy's equipment and activities can make your life adventuresome.

Applying this semiotic decoding to the following radio spot, we find the signifier to be the 500-pound parrot, the signified the idea of selling unwanted and unusual items, and the amalgamating sign the message that Cincinnati Surburban Press classifieds can market anything.

(SFX: PHONE RINGING)

WOMAN: Cincinnati Surburban Press Classified, can I help you?

MAN: (Whispering) I would like to sell a very unusual parrot.

WOMAN: A very unusual--?

MAN: Parrot. Yes, he weighs 500 pounds and he eats raw meat.

WOMAN: Could you speak up, sir?

MAN: I'm afraid he'll hear me.

PARROT: Brawk! Bruno wanna steak. (in background)

MAN: (To Parrot) Coming, Bruno!

WOMAN: Well, sir, your ad will appear in our family of 19 Cincinnati Suburban Press newspapers, reaching over 240,000 homes.

MAN: Oh good, good.

WOMAN: And at a very low cost.

PARROT: Bruno wanna steak, now!

MAN: Yes, Bruno. Uh, nice birdie!

WOMAN: And how would you like the ad to read, sir?

MAN: One very large parrot, well-mannered, must sell.

PARROT: Hey, who're you talking to?

MAN: Nobody.

PARROT: Give me that phone.

(SFX: PHONE NOISES)

PARROT: (To Woman) Who's this?

WOMAN: Cincinnati Suburban Press Classified.

U.S. Navy Public Service TV

"FLIGHT OPERATIONS": 30 Seconds (also available in :20 and :10 versions) QUAQ 0837

ANNCR: Flight Operations - Hawaiian Islands

155 is the

go bird. 10° right rudder.

Bring up 155 on No. 2 elevator.

Cloud tops at 28,000 feet. Alpha Hotel your wind is down the deck

at 28 knots.

Launch aircraft.

Stand clear. Stand clear. Most jobs promise you the world.

The Navy delivers. See your recruiter.

Navy. It's not just a job, it's an adventure.

NAVY. IT'S NOT JUST A JOB, IT'S AN ADVENTURE.

Figure 12–3 U.S. Navy "Flight Operations" Photoboard (Courtesy of Navy Recruiting Command, Department of the Navy)

PARROT: I'm the parrot. I wanna place an ad.

WOMAN: Parrot?

PARROT: Used human for sale.

WOMAN: Used human?

PARROT: House broken.

WOMAN: House broken?

PARROT: Does tricks, too. Listen to this. Bawk! Hey, Howard go
            mow the lawn, take out the trash, bawk. Bring my
            slippers, roll over. Bawk! Play dead, ya little wimp---

WOMAN: (Under Parrot's list) Now wait a minute. Who is this?
            Hello? Sir? Are you still there?

ANNCR: Everything sells faster in Suburban Classified. Cincinnati
            Suburban Press.

(Courtesy of Christine Love, Sarley/Cashman Creative Services)

To understand the interrelationship of the three parts of our equation better, it is sometimes interesting to switch signifiers between two pieces of content. For a moment, therefore, let us imagine that the aircraft carrier was
placed in the previous radio commercial and that the 500-pound parrot became the signifier in the Navy PSA. In the case of the radio spot, the change
would not cause a meaning shift since an aircraft carrier could be construed
as an unwanted, unusual item, as was the parrot. That the Cincinnati Suburban Press classified can sell anything is a message that could still arise as the
cumulative sign. Likewise, if transferred to the TV spot, the 500-pound parrot
could still logically relate to the 'signified' of adventure and, if the fowl was
owned by the Navy, might even comprise a workable if bizarre manifestation
of the sign (working with the Navy's equipment and activities can make *your*
life adventuresome). More likely, however, the sign would become something
to the effect that Navy service exposes you to exotic things.

Much of what we call creativity involves just such unconventional signifier
manipulation because it establishes wholly new constructs by which we can
apprehend established truth. Thus, critic comprehension of semiotic mechanisms might make it easier to detect and explain truly creative expression in
radio/television.

However derived, signs can be classified as to whether they possess first-,
second-, or third-order signification. First-order signs are those for which the
specific content is vital. In the above radio commercial, for instance, it is important to the sponsor that listeners understand it is the *Cincinnati Suburban
Press* classifieds (not just any classifieds) that can sell anything. By definition,
most advertising promotes first-order signs since it is the specific brand, rather
than the brand category, that clients are paying to market.

Second-order signs, in contrast, derive their significance, say Fiske and Hartley, "not from the sign itself, but from the way the society uses and values both the signifier and the signified. In our society a car (or a sign for a car) frequently signifies virility or freedom."[29] The car manufacturer and its advertising agency then try to parlay this second-order signification into first-order specificity by convincing you to attribute this virility or freedom only to their model, as is the thrust of the classic Cadillac commercial in Figure 12–4.

An industry-wide (generic) promotion to buy American cars, drink coffee, or use gas appliances, on the other hand, would be a second-order signification effort because it stresses the value of U.S. cars, of coffee drinking, or of gas appliances themselves without referencing a specific (first-order) brand.

Particularly when teamed up with other signifiers, second-order signs can acquire third-order signification, or what Fiske and Hartley call "a comprehensive, cultural picture of the world, a coherent and organized view of reality with which we are faced. It is in this third order that a car can form part of the imagery of an industrial, materialist and rootless society."[30] Third-order signs thus are beyond the scope or control of individual programs or creators and flow instead from the aggregate impact of the media's first- and second-order sign use.

Radio/television critics can explore these third-order signs not in their previews and reviews, but only in their most incisive and comprehensive think pieces (commentaries), in which that rare attempt is made to put an entire programmatic landscape into cultural perspective. A rereading of Janet Maslin's critique on "Prime Time Cereal" in Chapter 3 and of Steve Daley's "'Roots' Entrenched in Television's Soul" as well as of Scott Bennett's "Static in TV's Preacherland Tells of Flaws in Our Society" (both in Chapter 8) reveal glimmers of third-order sign analysis. These three pieces also indicate just how difficult it is for a broadcast/cable critic to ascend to a third-order vantage point within the limitations of a single, brief article.

Whether they are dealing with first-, second-, or third-order significations, most semioticians who concern themselves with the electronic media tend to treat pictorial and linguistic signs as equals, not only in these signs' import but in how they function as meaning conveyances. As a critical tool, there is nothing wrong with this operational presumption as long as we respect Robert Smith's caution not to

assume that the analogy works more exactly than seems to be the case. For instance, if television pictures sometimes function like words, we may be led to assume that pictures are words, groups of pictures function like sentences, and that they are held together by a "grammar." Such pitfalls are characteristic of analogical thinking. We can avoid them by remembering that, although television may yield to structuralist inquiry based on the linguistic model, we have not yet found a visual "language." What we have found is associative groups that sometimes bear structural similarities to languages.[31]

The Dream Realized

GMEE0935   30 Seconds

MUSIC: CADILLAC THEME IN AND UNDER.

(Anncr VO): Ever since that summer job way back then...

you've dreamed of having...

your own Eldorado.

Now you've realized your dream.

Your 1985 Eldorado is a very special Cadillac...

with a very special way...

of moving you like no other car.

You were right all along.

Eldorado is a car that...

dreams are made of.

SINGERS: BEST OF ALL, IT'S A CADILLAC.

Figure 12–4   Cadillac "The Dream Realized" Photoboard (Courtesy of Lori Wacker-man, D'Arcy Masius Benton & Bowles, Inc.)

The more broadcasting and cable content piles sign on sign to generate ever greater complexities of meaning, the greater is the critical temptation to use some standard system through which this conglomerated meaning can be screened. The danger in such a practice is that the critic forgets that radio/television content creation is more art than science and therefore ignores De-Witt Parker's reminder that "in allowing more than one meaning, artistic signs differ from the scientific, where the ideal is always that one sign should have only one meaning."[32] Linguistically no less than pictorially, "the notion that it is possible to reduce language to sign language, to make one word invariably mean one thing," asserts Frye, "is an illusion."[33]

Perhaps the greatest contribution semiotics and any other symbolic or structuralist approach make to critical thought is to remind broadcast/cable critics that, as concerns meaning construction and transmission, no program or spot content can be automatically dismissed as either obvious or trivial until a judicious dissection is first performed. Through such a dissection, the critic may come to know more than fruitfully can be relayed to the public; but this is much better than apprehending less than that of which one's audience is aware.

Notes

1. Hal Himmelstein, *On the Small Screen* (New York: Praeger Publishers, 1981), 97.
2. Theodore Meyer Greene, *The Arts and the Art of Criticism* (Princeton: Princeton University Press, 1940), 102.
3. Horace Newcomb, "Television and Cultural Theory." Presentation at the Conference on Postindustrial Culture, February 1977, at the University of Wisconsin, Milwaukee.
4. Larry Dobrow, "The Best Ads," *Adweek Radio 1985 Issue* (July 1985), 28.
5. Northrop Frye, *Anatomy of Criticism* (Princeton: Princeton University Press, 1957), 166.
6. Ibid., 172.
7. Ibid., 173.
8. Ibid., 175.
9. Ibid., 176.
10. Ibid., 175–76.
11. Ibid., 172.
12. Ibid., 116.
13. Rose Goldsen, *The Show and Tell Machine* (New York: The Dial Press, 1977), 285.
14. Robert Smith, *Beyond the Wasteland: The Criticism of Broadcasting,* rev. ed. (Annandale, Va.: Speech Communication Association, 1980), 20.
15. John Fiske and John Hartley, *Reading Television* (London: Methuen & Company, 1978), 90.
16. Frye, *Anatomy,* 119–20.
17. Rudolf Arnheim, *Toward a Psychology of Art* (Berkeley, University of California Press, 1967), 68.

18. Horace Newcomb, *TV: The Most Popular Art* (Garden City, N.Y.: Anchor Books, 1974), 174.
19. Rollo May, *Existential Psychotherapy* (Toronto: CBC Learning Systems, 1967), 22.
20. Sprague Vonier, "Television: Purveyor of Parables," *Journal of Broadcasting* (Winter 1965–66): 5.
21. Ibid., 6.
22. Smith, *Wasteland*, 24.
23. Joyce Carol Oates, "For Its Audacity, It's Defiantly Bad Taste and Its Superb Character Studies," *TV Guide* (June 1, 1985): 7.
24. John Cawelti, "With the Benefit of Hindsight: Popular Culture Criticism," *Critical Studies in Mass Communication* (December 1985): 369.
25. Johann Gottlieb Fichte, *Science of Knowledge*, trans. by Peter Heath and John Lochs (New York: Appleton-Century-Crofts, 1970), 113.
26. Aaron Copland, *What to Listen for in Music* (New York: Mentor, 1957), 118–19.
27. Frye, *Anatomy*, 73.
28. Fiske and Hartley, *Reading*, 37.
29. Ibid., 41.
30. Ibid.
31. Smith, *Wasteland*, 32–33.
32. DeWitt Parker, *The Principles of Aesthetics*, 2nd ed. (Westport, Conn.: Greenwood Press, 1976), 57.
33. Frye, *Anatomy*, 335.

Composite Criticism

In this final chapter, it seems appropriate to explore an aggregate methodology that encompasses, at least in part, virtually every critical perspective we have previously examined. This four-part schema, which we are labeling *composite criticism,* has its roots in the writings of George Santayana and Jerome Stolnitz. In his teaching, Thomas Olson then refined the methodology and specifically applied it to the task of critiquing radio/television. In brief, composite criticism provides a tool by which one can, within a single critique, examine a work from four different perspectives; these perspectives also have a distinct relationship to the four communication process components set forth in Chapter 2. This process thereby places the broadcast/cable work within the real-world context that gives it life and determines its success or failure.

Composite criticism's quartet of perspectives is divided into intrinsic and extrinsic pairings and cross-divided into appreciation and evaluation activities. Therefore, to begin to understand how each perspective is orientated, we must first define the terms that collectively identify them:

Intrinsic pertains to the work itself and the properties internal to it. The focus here is on the work in isolation rather than within any particular social or historical context.

Extrinsic, in contrast, places the work within the environment in which it is created and displayed and examines it as an interactive agent with sender and/or receiver.

Appreciation is the process of favorably and sympathetically inventorying the work's merits and the difficulties that had to be surmounted in its production. Of special concern is the cataloguing of the work's pleasure potential.

Evaluation determines whether the work's capabilities were realized. It systematically compares beauties and faults in the form, content, and scope of the work.

By cross-pollinating these operations, we arrive at the four procedures from which composite criticism germinates:

> Intrinsic Appreciation
> Extrinsic Appreciation
> Intrinsic Evaluation
> Extrinsic Evaluation

In examining each procedure in detail, we want to become aware of how they all share the tasks of criticism, as *criticism* was defined in Chapter 1:

> knowledgeable comprehension, positive/negative ascertainment, and resulting carefully considered judgment as a means of reasonably estimating the value of the particular work under scrutiny.

Intrinsic Appreciation

To understand the focus of intrinsic appreciation, it may be necessary to review what was said in Chapter 9 about art as a vehicle for igniting pleasurable experiences. Our concern here is to compile a register of all the enjoyments the work generates. We wish to become aware of its materials, how they are organized, and the resulting expressive capabilities. One but by no means the only way to accomplish this is to apply Chapter 10's logic of aesthetic form as a detector of realized beauty. Our thrust here is exclusively toward the successful apprehension of pleasure—for failures, remember, are the province not of appreciation, but of evaluation.

There is no morality, no right and wrong, in the case of intrinsic appreciation—only the attempt to identify aesthetic (as we have defined the term) happiness. As DeWitt Parker reminds us:

> The spirit of art is fundamentally non-moral, for the aesthetic attitude is one of sympathy—an attempt at once to express life and to feel at one with it; it demands of us that we take the point of view of the life expressed and, for the moment at any rate, refrain from a merely external judgment. Through art we are compelled to sympathize with the aspiration towards growth, towards happiness, even when it leads to rebellion against our own standards and towards what we call sin. The sympathy, realism, and imagination of art are antagonistic to conformist morality.[1]

In other words, intrinsic appreciation leads us to relish the work for itself rather than for any moral or practical purpose to which the work might be put. Even though this concept may be especially difficult for pragmatic Americans to accept, it is absolutely essential to the attainment of thoroughgoing criticism.

Like the shower murder scene in Alfred Hitchcock's movie *Psycho,* we may hate the event but love its treatment; from just such paradoxes can intrinsic appreciation most fully be comprehended. Yet, some moralistic high brows have a great deal of trouble accepting the validity of intrinsic appreciation—not only because they see it as unprincipled hedonism, but, more to the point, because they also view its application to radio/television as an endorsement of the masses' unrefined tastes. It is to these people that former CBS commentator Eric Sevareid was referring when he wrote:

> There is, and always has been, a broad swatch of professional intellectuals who fear and detest anything new, particularly if it is adaptable to the pleasure of the great mass of ordinary people. This particular type of intellectual neither knows nor likes ordinary people. This is why they write about "humanity" and not about persons. They are like the English Puritans who hated bearbaiting, not because it gave pain to the bears but because it gave pleasure to the spectators.[2]

Instead of starting from a plateau of disdainful intellectualism, former *Washington Post* television-radio critic Lawrence Laurent long ago argued that, "The complete television critic begins with a respect and a love for the excitement and the impact of the combination of sight and sound—pictures which can be viewed, and words which can be heard, by millions of people at one time."[3] This respect and love is but another facet of intrinsic appreciation and allows the critic to approach his or her subject with initial optimism instead of terminal cynicism.

The following Ed Bark review illustrates that the inclusion of intrinsic appreciation does not require fawning acceptance of the work being critiqued. Even though *Popcorn Kid* is appreciated as a "good comedy snack," with a "freshness to the cast," "nice writing, a few chuckles," and "Norris' infectious enthusiasm" as "an appealing dream merchant," Bark still exercises his evaluative prerogative to find fault with, and project dangers for, this series.

'POPCORN KID' HAS SOME COMEDIC KERNELS
By Ed Bark

Fresh popped from MTM Productions—the premium Orville Redenbacher of series television—comes CBS' *The Popcorn Kid,* a finger-lickin' good comedy snack.

Sneak-previewed Monday, *Popcorn* moves to its regular time slot tonight (Friday, 7:30 P.M., Channel 4), where the chances for long-term success seem promising opposite NBC's soon-to-be-canceled *Amazing Stories* and ABC's fading *Webster.* Whoa, though, *Popcorn Kid* had only a 12.9 rating and 19 percent share of the viewing audience Monday, not nearly good enough to beat equally soft competition from NBC's suddenly potent *Valerie* (18.7/28) or the second half-hour of ABC's *MacGyver* (16.2/24).

The premiere episode set up shop at the Majestic Theater, a grand old Kansas City movie palace that opened during the Depression era. Sixteen-year-old romantic Scott

Creasman (Bruce Norris), dreaming of breaking into show biz someday, is marking time by star-gazing behind the Majestic candy counter. He is joined by prim Gwen Stottlemeyer (Penelope Ann Miller); empty-headed Lynn Holly Brickhouse (Faith Ford); black, athletic Willie Dawson (Jeffrey Joseph); goofy projectionist Marlin Bond (John Christopher Jones) and Majestic manager Leonard Brown (Raye Birk), whose crusty exterior coats the usual melted butter of a heart. (In future episodes, why not introduce a wacked-out character named Skip "Kernal" Sanders?)

Popcorn's ensemble is typically mixed and on the surface nothing to stay home about. Still, there is a freshness to the cast, even though they look like ads for Johnny Miller Menswear in their powder blue, synthetic Majestic uniforms. Norris in particular is an appealing dream merchant whose love and knowledge of the cinema make him mature beyond his years at a time when most teens might think Hedy Lamarr is a new hair mousse.

Not surprisingly, Monday's episode added jeopardy in the form of the proposed desecration of the Majestic into a multiplex.

"Places like the Majestic shouldn't be ripped apart just so people can make a few more bucks," Norris protested. He later won the day by persuading the unseen owner of the Majestic, a Mr. Tuttle, to declare the theater a landmark and thereby get a tax break.

On tonight's show, unavailable for preview, the vacant Lynn Holly enters the Kansas City Dream Queen Pageant, but Norris is hardpressed to find a talent for her. Two Fridays from tonight, Ed Asner will play himself as guest of honor at the Majestic's Ed Asner Film Festival.

Popcorn Kid is a welcome little visitor. Nice writing, a few chuckles (including those behind the candy counter) and Norris' infectious enthusiasm for life on a grand stage. It's playing in home theaters everywhere, but Monday night's disappointing "box office" portends only a brief run.

(Reprinted with permission of *The Dallas Morning News)*

Extrinsic Appreciation

Extrinsic appreciation extends sympathy for the work by attempting to ascertain the situational problems with which it was forced to cope. It acknowledges the show's attainments in meeting the industry's own standards of profitability and popularity. In other words, through extrinsic appreciation, we examine the content as a creature of the broadcast/cable business, keeping in mind the constraints endemic to that business, such as those identified in Chapters 5 and 6 on Productional Ingredients and Business Gratifications. Bark engaged in just such a procedure in his *Popcorn Kid* review when he commented on the show's disappointing "numbers" and on the specific competitive arena within which it must do battle.

Despite the sophisticated hardware and software involved, John Fiske and John Hartley remind us that "television [like radio] is a human construct, and the job that it does is the result of human choice, cultural decisions and social pressures. The medium responds to the conditions within which it exists."[4] Extrinsic appreciation takes such pressures into account before the more judicial aspects of composite criticism are allowed to come into play.

In this way critic and consumer alike can come to enhance their delight in a radio/television creation because, as George Boas asserts, "When one is acquainted with the technique involved and knows its problems, one enjoys the artist's victory over its difficulties, his peculiar manner of overcoming them."[5] If we know, for instance, the intricacies faced by writers and producers of made-for-TV movies in sculpting their scripts around the mandate for a certain length and certain schedule of commercial breaks, we acquire a more benevolent understanding of the artistic hurdles these creators face. We better comprehend the formulaic straitjacket they must still attempt to tailor to their dramatic needs. Similarly, by understanding what happens to a theatrical film that must be edited to the length and subject matter restrictions of commercial television, we learn to draw distinctions between the original and its necessarily abbreviated network edition. Film director Milos Forman, in fact, would argue that unless the original director is contracted to do the television editing, the over-the-air version of the movie is:

> just a dishonest *Reader's Digest*. . . . Would you call a gallery owner an exhibitor of art if to accommodate better the space of his gallery, (he) cut six inches of Picasso here, eight inches of Modigliani here, or chopped the feet off of Michelangelo's David because the ceiling was too low?[6]

Editing challenges are, of course, just one of many considerations with which electronic communicators must deal on a continuous basis. In helping his production students take several others of these into account, Professor George Wilson compiled the following checklist of concerns. Though these are expressed as television items, they can contribute with little or no adaptation to an extrinsic appreciation of radio as well:

> The novice television producer-director has a tendency to forget, or overlook, the fact that a television program's success or failure with respect to drawing a large mass audience may often be due to factors beyond the immediate control of those who plan, organize, produce and direct the program. Quite often factors which conspire for a program's success, or failure, are under the control of management rather than those who function in a creative capacity. As you view current offerings of broadcasting stations or networks, attempt to speculate (since complete information will frequently not be available to you) on the following:
>
> A. Do the program adjacencies (the program before it and the one following) conspire for the success of the program?
> B. Is the competition from programs on other stations or networks of such a nature as not to threaten the success of the program?
> C. Do the track records of the producer and director from previous productions auger well for the excellence of this program?
> D. Is the program blessed with one or more superstars?
> E. Was this program a success last season (if so, it will probably be a success this season)?
> F. Does the exposure factor conspire for the program's success? (Overexposure of programs in a series over a period of years

tends to make the programs tired and shopworn with respect to viewer attraction.)

G. Have the program compilers carefully considered the demographics of the segments of the audience that you think they are trying to reach? (Research tends to show that audiences react quite differently according to various attitudes they acquire as a result of numerous factors. Consider the following:)

1. Appeals to younger people
2. Appeals to older people
3. Appeals to those with education
4. Appeals to those without much education
5. Appeals to those of a conservative bent
6. Appeals to those with a liberal bent
7. Appeals to blue collar workers
8. Appeals to white collar workers
9. Appeals to males
10. Appeals to females
11. Appeals to rural dwellers
12. Appeals to urban dwellers
13. Appeals to buyers of low-cost mass-produced items
14. Appeals to buyers of high-cost items

(Courtesy of George P. Wilson)

These and other elements all are appropriate to the practice of extrinsic appreciation insofar as they help the critic learn and sympathetically convey the electronic media's structural, situational, and expressive limitations. In referring to such an analysis of a painting, Boas avows that the question "becomes not whether the painter has painted a picture, or even such and such a picture, but whether he has painted within the given restrictions."[7]

Radio/television program properties, as we have observed, have multiple "painters" and multiple sets of "restrictions," so Boas's observation takes on manifold importance for the broadcast/cable critic. In essence, extrinsic appreciation is an exercise that emphasizes what theorists label *contextual* criticism. As Jerome Stolnitz explains it, "Contextualism has placed art in its natural setting. Fine art is not a 'spiritual mystery.' It arises in the circumstances of human living and it answers to human needs. . . . We now see that different kinds of art can all be valuable 'in their own way.'"[8] It is just such valuation that conscientious radio/television critics should seek to bring to the coverage and eventual enhancement of the field they survey.

Intrinsic Evaluation

As stated at the beginning of this chapter, evaluation takes the appreciation-derived list of the work's pleasures and sympathetically modified capabilities and compares this list with that work's faults and missed opportunities. Negative as well as positive ascertainments now enter the critical process through application of whatever sets of standards are deemed relevant. With intrinsic evaluation, we examine the program in isolation and attempt to estimate its value without regard to the way it was scheduled or initial audience reaction to it. In this way, the audience is led to see beyond realized pleasure to latent possibilities that although perhaps not attained in the first apprehension, should be sought after in future listening or viewing experiences. Thus, as Parker points out, "the analysis and constant attention to the subtler details demanded by theory may bring to notice aspects of a work of art which do not exist for an unthinking appreciation. As a rule, the appreciations of the average man are very inadequate to the total possibilities offered, extending only to the more obvious features."[9]

Though we must consider the work within its genre (sitcom, soap opera, etc.) intrinsic evaluation does not stop there; it is also willing to judge the work as a completely unique property. To Stolnitz, all intrinsic evaluation:

> respects the uniqueness of the particular work. Like aesthetic perception itself, it sees what is distinctive about the work, what sets it off from "similar" works. Criticism by rules, however, presupposes that works can be classified into "kinds" and are therefore subject to the criteria which measure goodness in each "kind."[10]

For our purposes, and those of many radio/television critics, both genre and individualistic approaches to intrinsic evaluation are viable and mutually supportive. If they were not, we would have great difficulty discussing the contribution of such break-through programs as *All in the Family* or *Hill Street Blues,* which enriched their genres by innovatively restructuring long-established conventions.

In the following *Variety* review by Frank Beermann, for instance, *Crime Story* is evaluated on its own merits via a cross-referencing with two other like-genre series (*Kojak* and *Miami Vice),* which the critic believes to have influenced its development. Thus, of *Crime Story* itself, Beermann tells us that "the preem [premiere episode] was well constructed. It had action galore and solid acting in the major roles" but that "none of the actors, except for old cop Farina, bring any new nuances to their roles." The critic thereby balances appreciation with evaluation and moves on to place the program in its generic frame by comparing the similarities of *Kojak* and *Crime Story.* Evaluatively, we are told that, in the case of Torello's cops, "None of those took on any sign that they might become individuals as did some of the Kojak squad"; but, the critic sympathetically adds, "that may happen later." The reader of Beermann's piece also learns that, as equated with the same producer's *Miami Vice, Crime Story* "may be on more solid ground" because its writer and star are both ex-cops. On the other hand, because of the greater sense of realism that flows from its cop creators, *Crime Story's* "heavy use of music" ironically may be "even more disruptive" than in *Miami Vice,* where authenticity is less of a factor:

CRIME STORY
By Frank Beermann

Like Kojak, "Crime Story's" Torello is a police lieutenant. Although Torello works in Chicago and Kojak in New York, there are many similarities between them. Both cling to their ethnic backgrounds—Kojak as a Greek-American and Torello as an Italian-American. And both Telly Savalas and Dennis Farino come from the same backgrounds.

Further, both came from the cities in which the action of their series takes place. As a consequence, both are able to bring authentic native-land accents to their work. In fact, Farino may be the only actor on TV outside of Robert Conrad who used a Chicago working class accent in his work.

Beyond those similarities, both characters are dedicated police officers who sometimes override the civil rights of the malefactors they are in contact with, and with plenty of script approval.

All of which is by way of saying that there is nothing particularly original about "Crime Story," the latest Michael Mann entry in the NBC–TV schedule.

Mann is the producer of "Miami Vice" and, as such, can do no wrong over at NBC—yet. In this venture, he may have another hit.

The preem was well constructed. It had action galore and solid acting in the major roles. Farina is himself an ex-Chicago cop. Writer Chuck Adamson, also, once walked a beat in that city, and much of the material for the series will be based, it is said, on his experiences.

Because of that background, this series may be on more solid ground than "Miami Vice," which seems little more than a cartoon strip with rock music. Still, some of the obscurity of the older series was present in the Chicago skein. And Mann continues his heavy use of music in this one. It seems, probably because the new one is more rooted in reality than the Miami series, even more disruptive.

It is also more eclectic than in "Miami Vice." Whereas that series uses almost all rock, the new one runs the gamut from rock to blues to jazz—depending on the characters being focused on. It also is questionable if all segments of society lived with as much musical imperative as the rock generation—this series is placed in the 1960's.

The preem indicated that there will be one major criminal on whom Torello will fix during the season. His name is Ray Luca, who made the jump from street punk to gang boss in the first episode and solidified that move in the second. (The series was preemed on Sept. 18, and the second episode played on the next night.) It is easy to guess that Torello will continue to pursue the increasingly powerful Luca while he solves other crimes along the way. Luca can be expected to become a fugitive who never has to leave town.

Torello is head of something called the major crime unit, and because Chicago is such a big town, there is no shortage of those to keep him from pursuing his arch enemy.

Luca is played in stet young gang punk style by Anthony Denison. Another stock figure is gang boss-fence Phil Bartole played by Jon Polito in the old recipe. In fact none of the actors, except for old cop Farina, bring any new nuances to their roles. Darlanne Fluegel plays his loving wife, and Stephen Lang played a young lawyer who is expected to become a major (if high-minded) defender of those accused along the series way.

There is also a group of cops—members of Torello's unit. None of those took on any sign that they might become individuals as did some of the Kojak squad, but that may happen later.

Much of the success or failure of the series may hang on its ability to attract audience away from its Tuesday-night rival "Moonlighting." Given the inexplicable popularity of that show these days, it may be hard to do. But the show may be strong enough to warrant NBC's moving it to another night and let another sacrificial goat take the moon rays.

(Courtesy of Syd Silverman, *Variety*)

In applying intrinsic evaluation to a program there are, of course, many more possible aspects to treat than those covered by Beermann. No single critique can touch on all elements of a work's structure and content but instead must focus on those components the critic believes put the program into the clearest perspective for the public. In previous chapters, we have addressed productional ingredients (Chapter 5), ethics and values (Chapter 8), aesthetics (Chapters 9 and 10), and symbols, myths, and structures (Chapter 12). Any and all of these vantage points can yield appropriate intrinsic judgments as long as the critic is able to translate the perspective used into consumer-discernible terminology.

Extrinsic Evaluation

This final component of composite criticism focuses on the effects of the work on the audience. It is this activity that preoccupies congressional hearings and pressure group crusades—unfortunately, to the total exclusion of composite criticism's other three aspects. By itself, extrinsic evaluation can be both simplistic and damaging because it fails to consider the work's benefits (intrinsic appreciation) and the complexity of the electronic media's creative/transmission process (extrinsic appreciation) as well as ignoring the work's specific content and structure (intrinsic evaluation).

If, on the other hand, we use extrinsic evaluation in consort with the other three procedures, the resulting critique acquires substantial relevance and importance for art because it reveals artistic power as well as artistic character. Depiction, as discussed in Chapter 11, is perhaps the most obvious mechanism for evaluating effects, but an assessment of business or audience gratifications (Chapters 6 and 7) is just as potent in this regard. So, too, are analyses of ethics and values (Chapter 8) and symbols, myths, and structures (Chapter 12) insofar as these approaches probe the enhancement or debasement of audience perceptions and beliefs.

As a counterpart to his previously presented extrinsic appreciation-related inventory, Wilson has also developed a three-part evaluation instrument that asks his students to estimate what he labels program "impact" (another way of conceptualizing audience effects). Here, again, as they relate to audio-compatible functions, the items on this list can be applied to radio assessment as well.

Principles for Evaluating the Impact of TV Programs

I.   INSTRUCTIONAL VALUES OF THE PROGRAM
    A. Is new information presented on places, processes, methods, techniques, events, or people?
        1. Give examples of this new information.
        2. What is the value of this information?
    B. Are new insights presented on social, psychological, or emotional problems or relationships?
        1. What are they? Be specific.
        2. How important or valuable are these new insights?
    C. Are new and fresh insights on character and personality presented?
        1. What are they?
        2. Why are these insights important?
    D. Are new ideas or concepts presented?
        1. What are they?
        2. Why are these concepts important?
    E. Are old ideas presented in a new, novel, or different interpretation?
        1. What are they?
        2. Why do you deem these important?

II. SOCIAL VALUES--Does the program further the democratic process [or, even more fundamentally, the human condition]?
    A. By reinforcing or stressing concepts, processes, or procedures?
        1. What are they?
        2. Why is it important to reinforce them?
    B. Are desirable mores, codes, or customs reinforced in the program?
        1. What are they? Be specific.
        2. Why do you feel it important for the mass audience to continue to accept these values?
    C. To what extent does the program point out, dramatize, or highlight social problems that need solving?
        1. What are these problems?
        2. Why do you feel they are important?
    D. To what extent does the program suggest specific ways to improve a social problem or situation?
        1. Recapitulate the solutions--briefly.
        2. Do you find these solutions practical?
           Realistic?
           Believable?

III: HOW DOES THE PROGRAM CONVEY ETHICAL VALUES?
    A. Is the information or interpretation presented accurate? (Or is it distorted, false, or one-sided?)
        1. In what way? Be specific.

    2. Defend your agreement or disagreement with the ethical
       values presented.
  B. Does this interpretation illuminate and inspire human des-
    tiny?
    1. In what way? Be specific.
    2. Why do you agree (or disagree) with the interpretation?
  C. Is the interpretation time-less? In what way? Timely? In
    what way?
    Universal? (Applicable to other cultures and peoples) In what
    way?

(Courtesy of George P. Wilson)

Wilson's last point about timeless and timely interpretations deserves special recognition. As we found in our analysis of *Ethel and Albert,* it is important to look at a work's impact as relates both to its time and to our time. In
this application of what we have labeled extrinsic evaluation, we may find that
some program elements are time-bound whereas others can strike a responsive chord regardless of how many years later the program matter is apprehended. Part of this has to do with the technology available to the artist at the
time because audience impact is determined to a degree by the tools used. In
speaking of the new electronic media potentials brought by satellite transmission, for example, video artist Nam June Paik asserts that "just as Mozart mastered the newly-invented clarinet, the satellite artist must compose his art from
the beginning suitable to physical conditions and grammar."[11] The greater
part of timely/timeless, however, has to do less with tools than with how the
audience perceives the work in relation to what else was/is available at the
time. Hence, to extend our same-composer example, "Mozart's music may appear serene and cheerful to a modern listener, who perceives it in the temporal context of twentieth-century music," writes psychologist Rudolf Arnheim,
"whereas it conveyed the expression of violent passion and desperate suffering
to his contemporaries in relation to the music they knew."[12]

In a world of *Milton Berle, The Adventures of Ozzie and Harriet,* and *Father Knows Best,* our *Ethel and Albert* referent holds up well as an effective
and audience-involving portrayor of values and issues. When placed next to
The Cosby Show, One Day At a Time, and *Night Court,* however, its comparative poverty of productional tools makes it much easier to overlook the
timeless human relationships Ethel and Albert depict for us. The astute critic
will recognize this dynamic in the programs he or she reviews and may even
call our attention to the most aged of reruns if they possess meaningful impact potential for the current audience. As David Handler recounts:

> Hair styles change. Values change. The way shows look and sound changes. Good
> acting and writing [intrinsic elements] don't. If we love the people—if they absorb
> us, make us laugh or cry [an extrinsic evaluation]—then a show isn't dated. It's a
> classic.[13]

Composing the Composite Critique

Despite the seeming immensity of the task, it is possible for a cogent critique to encapsulate all four composite criticism elements in building a comprehensive assessment of the program material under scrutiny. In fact, this is not only possible but comes close to being mandatory if we are fully to meet the terms of criticism's definition assembled in Chapter 1. By using composite criticism, the critic is doing no more than dutifully retracing the road the creator(s) traveled in constructing the work. As Melvin Rader reminds us:

> No artist can create without appreciating the values that he wishes to express; without contemplating the expressive medium, elements and forms; and without criticizing the work as it takes shape under his hand. The artist himself is a beholder and judge, and the fineness of his art depends largely upon the quality of his appreciation and judgment.[14]

Thus, by replicating this creative process through composite criticism, critics place the work in honest, realistic perspective for themselves and consumers alike.

 The following critique of *The Morning Program* by *Time's* Richard Zoglin is an appropriate illustration of composite construction. Read the review in its entirety before we isolate its intrinsic/extrinsic elements:

SOMETHING TO EMBARRASS EVERYONE
By Richard Zoglin

On the first day, Co-Hosts Mariette Hartley and Rolland Smith told their new TV audience, "We want to be your friendly wake-up call." On the second day, Hartley pasted a HIT SHOW ON BOARD sign on Smith's lapel. By day three, she was fairly doubled over with laughter at the good time being had: "It's such fun waking up with all of these people!" But the credo for *The Morning Program* came at the end of its fourth show. As part of a tribute to Martin Luther King Jr.'s birthday, the cast sang *We Shall Overcome.*

 CBS's new entry in the early-morning wars had an armada of foes to overcome, even before it went on the air. Fans of the old *CBS Morning News* were outraged by the network's cancellation of that long-running broadcast, whose low ratings had persisted for years despite a revolving door of hosts and formats. CBS News staffers resented the fact that the fluffy newcomer would be produced by the network's entertainment division. Rivals were publicly contemptuous. Bryant Gumbel, co-host of the front-running *Today,* scoffed before the new show even aired, "Desperate people do desperate things."

 After the program's debut last week, most viewers probably agreed. In an effort to look different from its morning competitors—*Today* and ABC's *Good Morning, America*—*The Morning Program* has come up with something to embarrass everyone. Smith, a straightlaced former anchorman for New York City's WCBS–TV, and Actress Hartley, who once filled in as a *Today* co-host, engage in strained banter on an elaborately homey set. The show's regular features include personal ads, in which singles promote themselves via 30-second video clips, comedy routines that, good or bad, do not go down easily at 7:55 A.M., and Hartley's dog Daisy, which gets petted a lot. All of this is witnessed by a studio audience that on opening day found even Mark McEwen's weathercasts worthy of applause.

The Morning Program has more conventional features as well: celebrity interviews, daily health tips, movie reviews and short news inserts. But Hartley, babbling constantly, is inexcusably cheerful, and the whole enterprise pushes too fast and too hard: *Hour Magazine* on speed.

Still, the show seems to have an appealing goal in sight: a friendly kaffee-klatsch in the tradition of radio's long-running *The Breakfast Club.* Some of the ideas work. Bob Saget, the show's announcer and "sidekick," narrated a funny home video of his own wedding. Writers Roy Blount Jr. and Calvin Trillin were on hand with wry commentaries. And a few of the segments (like an interview with a Wall Street executive at the gym where he goes boxing before work) struck just the right, what's-new-this-morning? tone.

Criticizing *The Morning Program* as fluff is unfair, almost like blaming *Late Night with David Letterman* for not running news inserts. The show's main problem seems to be a failure of nerve. It tries to break from the morning mold but retains enough *Today*-like elements to make the entertainment features jarring. Another sort of host—a folksy Arthur Godfrey type, perhaps—might have made the format more palatable. Even Smith and Hartley could eventually relax and turn into pleasant morning companions. Right now they are working too hard at chemistry to notice that the ingredients are not jelling.

From the standpoint of intrinsic appreciation, Zoglin tells us of the program's "appealing goal" to be "a friendly kaffee-klatsch in the tradition of radio's long-running *The Breakfast Club.*" The premiere show featured "a funny home video," "wry commentaries" by Blount and Trillin, and a few segments that "struck just the right, what's-new-this-morning? tone." There is a further possibility of enjoyment if the hosts can "eventually relax and turn into pleasant morning companions." Sympathizing with the program's gargantuan task, Zoglin practices extrinsic appreciation by pointing out that "CBS's new entry in the early-morning wars had an armada of foes to overcome, even before it went on the air." The critic details some of these factors (outraged fans of the predecessor program, divisional jealousies within CBS, contempt from other networks) and takes pains to recognize that, since the program is trying to be entertainment-centered rather than news-centered, attacking "*The Morning Program* as fluff is unfair."

Having benevolently taken these factors into consideration, Zoglin's intrinsic evaluation is fair without needing to be charitable. The show "has come up with something to embarrass everyone" in its effort to look different with a "straitlaced former anchorman" trying to engage in "strained banter on an elaborately homey set." Many of the comedy routines "do not go down easily at 7:55 A.M." and combine with the "babbling," "inexcusably cheerful" Hartley to push the whole enterprise "too fast and too hard."

The extrinsic evaluation result, of course, is that the program segments are just too "jarring" to be that self-proclaimed "friendly wake-up call." The format and co-hosts are simply not "palatable" in the early morning, with the ingredients "working too hard at chemistry to notice" that the audience does not want *"Hour Magazine* on speed" at this time of day.

Notice that, even though we discussed the four composite criticism items in the order in which they were first presented earlier in the chapter, Zoglin's arrangement and interspersing of them was much different. In fact, there is no right or wrong sequence to the process. As long as all four composite bases are covered, they can be introduced in any order the critic sees fit to convey best the essence of his or her perception. Similarly, there is no requirement that our four vantage points each receive equal space or time. Apportionment will vary widely from critique to critique based on the program in question. As long as one does not try to justify a ten-paragraph hatchet job with but a single sentence of sympathy, the fairness of the process does not hinge on an equal number of words being devoted to laudatory versus negative comments.

When critics and critiques are perceived as fair by people in the industry, the potential that their observations will be heeded (though not necessarily acceded to) increases. More than thirty years ago, Harold Fellows, then president of the National Association of Radio-Television Broadcasters (now the NAB) asserted to his membership:

> Those who weigh our deficiencies against our great contributions of fine showmanship and superb informational service, and emerge with a tempered and reasoned appraisal of our industry, are men and women whose voices should be heard.[15]

For another example of composite criticism in action, we turn to a TV-movie review by *The Toronto Star's* Jim Bawden. In this instance, a much greater proportion of the critique is devoted to a sympathetic portrait of the creator (extrinsic appreciation) than to the other composite elements, but all nonetheless are responsibly covered by the time Bawden's piece is concluded.

JUTRA'S FINAL FILM IS LIKE HIS LIFE—FULL OF QUESTIONS
By Jim Bawden

It's unfortunate Claude Jutra's last film, *My Father, My Rival,* could not have been one of his best. For the acclaimed Quebec director to have ended his career with something as spectacularly wonderful as *Mon Oncle Antoine* would have been just and fitting. Instead this hour-long drama, starring Wendy Crewson and Lance Guest, offers a bite of life rather than a whole slice.

My Father, My Rival (tomorrow at 9 on Global's Channel 22) was the last film made by Jutra before he mysteriously disappeared last November. The director suspected he was suffering from Alzheimer's disease and wandered away from his Montreal home on Nov. 5. He has not been seen since.

Jutra's final work looks at the problems of adjustment of a lonely boy who has just lost his mother. Scott (Lance Guest) focuses on his pert swimming teacher who is about to leave town to study music at university. Years pass and she returns, aged 25, ready for a career as a high school teacher. At 18, the boy experiences new pangs which are those of desire.

In terms of subject matter, this is familiar Jutra turf. It is kind-hearted, sympathetic to all characters, beguiling in spots, touching at other moments.

In truth, it has been some time since Jutra masterpieces *Mon Oncle Antoine* (1971) and *Kamouraska* (1973). The bursting of Quebec's film industry bubble in the mid-'70s left him a director without a country. He switched to TV films, even acted himself. But his glory days were behind him.

Jutra struck out, making the not-bad *Dreamspeaker* for CBC, then *Surfacing* and *By Design* in English. The immense popularity of *Mon Oncle Antoine* did not make him any money. It was made for $250,000 for the National Film Board and profits went back to the government.

Montreal-born Jutra trained as a doctor (as had his father and grandfather). Shortly after graduating in 1949 he won a Canadian Film Award for an experimental short called *Mouvement Perpetuelle*. By 1963 he had made his first feature, a remarkable little work called *A Tout Prendre*. Jutra shot it as a private 16mm venture, and starred in it too. The New York Times' film critic Bosley Crowther wrote, "He handles the camera and direction with such inventiveness and flexibility that it's a wonder we haven't heard from him with a picture made subsequent to this."

In person Jutra was desperately shy, hard to interview. He lived in a series of low-rent flats in Montreal, never married and once told me, "I never felt part of any of the fashionable movements of the '60s." His eye was always on the next project.

By 1972 The Manchester Guardian was hailing him as "Canada's Truffaut" but soon afterward his career was plainly in decline. His pictures continued to be interesting but never again approached greatness. Something had gone out of Claude Jutra. The waning of his talents had already begun and perhaps he spotted the first symptoms of the wasting disease.

My Father, My Rival was shown on American pay TV as *Dark but Full of Diamonds* (the title of the novel). The film suffers because it has no definite sense of place—it was deliberately obscured to make it more palatable to U.S. audiences. The conflict between son and father (Tom Hauff) is not well enough defined. The son thinks of his doctor father as stuffy and prematurely old. Why the young teacher (played by a pert Wendy Crewson) should be drawn to the father instead of the son isn't well explained either.

Jutra gets more out of the material than you have a right to expect. The story could have become manipulative but there are no heavies here. The father has been as desperately lonely as his son. Yet they can only communicate through the bright, young music teacher.

Despite the theme, the film, made for Insight Productions, is positively buoyant at times, especially when it is capturing Scott's earlier impulsive, juvenile love for his teacher. At such moments Jutra seems to be telling us anything is possible. As usual Jutra doesn't take sides, makes no moral judgments. He had never done so in his impressive if uneven director's career and it's this humanity that makes *My Father, My Rival,* worth sitting through.

(Reprinted with permission—The Toronto Star Syndicate)

My Father, My Rival is, according to Bawden, "kind-hearted, sympathetic to all characters, beguiling in spots, touching at other moments." "Despite the theme," the film is "positively buoyant at times," writes the critic and thereby gives us the essence of the pleasure (intrinsic appreciation) that can be derived from watching it. As we have said, the sympathetic extrinsic appreciation that pervades this review touches compassionately on Jutra's illness, his "desperately shy" nature, and his financial difficulties due to "the bursting of Quebec's film industry bubble" and the National Film Board's proprietary rights to his greatest masterpiece. All of this gives the master his due and allows evaluation of *My Father, My Rival* to proceed without seeming to be callous or cold-hearted.

Intrinsically, maintains Bawden, the film "suffers because it has no definite sense of place." Yet, even in this evaluation, the critic balances his statement with the extrinsic appreciation revelation that "it was deliberately obscured to make it more palatable to U.S. audiences." Unfortunately, however, there are other flaws: "conflict between son and father is not well enough defined"; "why the young teacher should be drawn to the father instead of the son isn't well explained either." Still, "Jutra gets more out of the material than you have a right to expect" (a statement that is both appreciative and evaluative). Ultimately, for the audience (extrinsic evaluation), "Jutra seems to be telling us anything is possible." He "doesn't take sides, makes no moral judgments" but his film radiates a "humanity that makes *My Father, My Rival,* worth sitting through."

Composite criticism, then, gives us a multiplicity of orientations that, in the hands of an observant and articulate critic, coalesce into a single unified and useful critique. By using all four of the composite-encompassing tools in the reviewing of programs, we avoid those prejudicial extremes that can torpedo creator-critic-audience communication. If we restrict ourselves to a single perspective, on the other hand, distortion and myopia can easily set in.

Imagine, for example, a hypothetical interchange between an extremist, self-indulgent videographer and a straitlaced, self-proclaimed protector of community morals. In analyzing his program called "Nude in a Seven-Course Cantonese Dinner," the videographer evidences an exclusionary concern with the pleasure and enjoyment that the work's imagery brings to him. The community protector, in contrast, is willing to discuss only how this taped depravity will corrupt the behavior of the town's youth.

These two viewpoints certainly will engender argument, but they will not promote dialogue. The videographer is engaging solely in intrinsic appreciation while the protector is restricting his purview to extrinsic evaluation. The failure of each party to consider the other's process (and their mutual ignoring of intrinsic evaluation and extrinsic appreciation) will, of course, result in an unproductive standoff. The only thing worse would be for a *critic* to adopt such a one-eyed approach because this would either mislead or antagonize not only one person but also the entire audience whom that critic is supposed to serve.

Even though it is important to look at both intrinsic and extrinsic factors, however, one need not always derive a uniformly positive or uniformly negative conclusion in regards to our internal and external perspectives. Hence, in the reviews of ABC's courageous *Something about Amelia,* which dealt directly with the subject of incest, some critics lauded the show's acting and storyline (positive intrinsic evaluation) while nonetheless reproaching it for a vagueness that might cause children to misconstrue normal parental shows of affection into acts of evil perversion (negative extrinsic evaluation).

The reverse also can legitimately occur. Several years ago, the students at a black inner-city high school staged a performance of *Fiddler on the Roof,* the musical portrayal of the triumphs and tragedies of a group of Russian Jews. The performance was simultaneously taped for cable access showing. Even though television reviewers found the result to be artistically rough and productionally primitive (negative intrinsic evaluation), they still praised the program's powerful community impact as a statement of one ghettoized people's sensitizing sympathy for a divergent group of ghetto dwellers (positive extrinsic evaluation). This illustrates Northrop Frye's contention that

> No discussion of beauty can confine itself to the formal relations of the isolated work of art; it must consider too, the participation of the work of art in the vision of the goal of social effort.[16]

In summary, when space and subject permit, composite criticism can comprehensively fulfill criticism's requirements because it intersects all four of the communications process components discussed at length in Chapter 2. We can, in fact, refine that chapter's diagram of criticism and the communications process (Figure 2–1) by substituting composite criticism's individual elements for what we therein referred to simply as *critic.* See Figure 13–1.

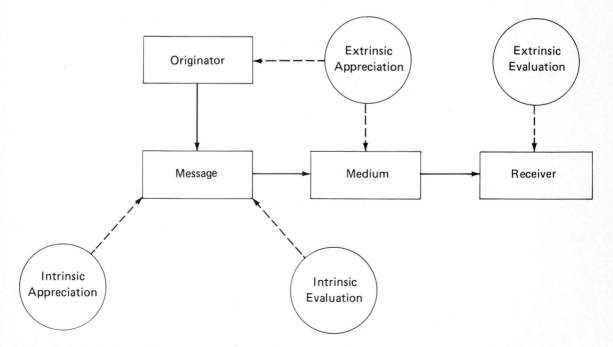

Figure 13–1   Composite Criticism and the Communications Process

Thus, in examining Figure 13–1, we are reminded that extrinsic appreciation focuses mainly on the originator and the medium by illuminating and sympathizing with the difficulties both entities face as well as with the problems one function might cause the other (the incompetent originator abusing the medium or the deadline-dominated medium providing insufficient time for originator preparation, for example).

Extrinsic evaluation, meanwhile, is mainly concerned with the effects of the transmission on the receiver. It thus emphasizes the communications process result or alleged result in terms of predicted audience impact.

Finally, because they *are* intrinsic, intrinsic appreciation and intrinsic evaluation concentrate on the beauty or pleasure potential of the work itself and thus scrutinize message form and content factors that help or inhibit the realization of this potential.

Using the unadorned term *criticism* to encompass the four-faceted procedure we have labeled *composite criticism,* Stolnitz aptly encapsulates its dimensions and benefits by concluding:

> Criticism calls our attention to the sparkle or charm of the sensory matter, the subtlety of form and the way in which its formal structure unifies the work, the meaning of symbols, and the expressive mood of the entire work. Criticism gives us a sense of the work's "aesthetic intention," so that we do not make illegitimate demands upon it. Criticism also develops aesthetic "sympathy" by breaking down the prejudices and confusions which get in the way of appreciation. It explains the artistic conventions and social beliefs of the artist's time. It relates the work of art to the great world and shows its relevance to our own experience.[17]

A Final Annotation

Composite criticism is the most eclectic of the many critique methodologies we have explored in these thirteen chapters. There are other procedures, particularly in the area of quantitative research, that we lacked the space to explore. Instead, we have attempted to construct a fundamental frame of reference that makes sense in terms of the mutual needs and evaluative interests of radio/television creators, consumers, and critics. Above all, the objective is to make the subject and practice of criticism approachable by all literate people with an interest in the electronic media and their improvement.

As indicated in the beginning of this book, criticism is a constructive tool rather than a destructive weapon. Its use as such requires that critiques and the persons who fashion them function as stimulators and not inhibitors of the field they survey. Particularly in the ever-changing environment of radio/television, critics certainly cannot claim always to possess the right answers. But it may not be too much to expect that, over time, they at least ask the right questions.

1. DeWitt Parker, *The Principles of Aesthetics,* 2nd ed. (Westport, Conn.: Greenwood Press, 1976), 272.
2. Eric Sevareid, "A Little Less Hypocrisy, Please," (New York: Television Information Office, 1968), 2.
3. Lawrence Laurent, "Wanted: The Complete Television Critic," in Robert Lewis Shayon *et al., The Eighth Art* (New York: Holt, Rinehart and Winston, 1962), 156.
4. John Fiske and John Hartley, *Reading Television* (London: Methuen and Company, 1978), 17.
5. George Boas, *A Primer for Critics* (New York: Greenwood Press, 1968), 81.
6. "Cutting Controversy," *Broadcasting* (January 27, 1986): 63.
7. Boas, *Primer,* 33.
8. Jerome Stolnitz, *Aesthetics and Philosophy of Art Criticism* (Boston: Houghton Mifflin, 1960), 474–75.
9. Parker, *Aesthetics,* 11.
10. Stolnitz, *Art Criticism,* 482.
11. Nam June Paik, "La Vie, Satellites, One Meeting—One Life," in John Hanhardt, ed., *Video Culture* (Rochester, N.Y.: Visual Studies Workshop Press, 1986), 219.
12. Rudolf Arnheim, *Toward a Psychology of Art* (Berkeley: University of California Press, 1967), 67.
13. David Handler, "Which Old Favorites Are Still Choice—and Which Aren't," *TV Guide* (April 4, 1987): 20.
14. Melvin Rader, *A Modern Book of Esthetics,* 5th ed. (New York: Holt, Rinehart and Winston, 1979), 16.
15. Harold Fellows, "Address, NARTB Convention," *Broadcasting–Telecasting* (April 23, 1956): 35.
16. Northrop Frye, *Anatomy of Criticism* (Princeton: Princeton University Press, 1957), 348.
17. Stolnitz, *Art Criticism,* 494.

The Cosby Show

"Theo's Holiday"

THE COSBY SHOW
"Theo's Holiday"
Show #0221-22

Written by
John Markus
Carmen Finestra
Matt Williams

DR. WILLIAM H. COSBY, JR.

CARSEY-WERNER CO.

(Script provided courtesy of Kim Tinsley, Director of Public Affairs, *The Cosby Show*)

THE COSBY SHOW
"Theo's Holiday"
SHOW #0221-22

CAST

Cliff Huxtable..Bill Cosby
Clair Huxtable..Phylicia Rashad
Denise Huxtable..Lisa Bonet
Theo Huxtable..Malcolm-Jamal Warner
Vanessa Huxtable..Tempestt Bledsoe
Rudy Huxtable ....Keshia Knight Pulliam
Cockroach..Carl Payne

SET

ACT ONE   PAGE

Scene 1:   INT. KITCHEN—EVENING (DAY 1)   (1)
Scene 2:   EXT. HUXTABLE'S FRONT STOOP—THE NEXT   (4)
                 MORNING (DAY 2)
Scene 3:   INT. LIVING ROOM—CONTINUOUS ACTION   (6)
                 (DAY 2)
Scene 4:   INT. THEO'S ROOM—CONTINUOUS ACTION   (8)
                 (DAY 2)
Scene 5:   INT. LIVING ROOM—A MOMENT LATER (DAY 2)   (10)

ACT TWO

Scene 1:   INT. THEO'S ROOM—LATER THAT AFTERNOON   (13)
                 (DAY 2)
Scene 2:   INT. DINING ROOM—MOMENTS LATER (DAY 2)   (16)
Scene 3:   INT. KITCHEN—CONTINUOUS ACTION (DAY 2)   (19)
Scene 4:   INT. LIVING ROOM—CONTINUOUS ACTION   (21)
                 (DAY 2)
Scene 5:   INT. THEO'S ROOM—THAT EVENING (DAY 2)   (25)

ACT ONE

Scene 1

FADE IN:

INT. KITCHEN—EVENING (DAY 1)
(Cliff, Clair, Denise, Theo, Vanessa, Rudy)

(THERE IS A SUMPTUOUS MEAL ON THE TABLE. THE HUXTABLE
FAMILY IS EATING DINNER. ALL THE CHILDREN EXCEPT THEO
ARE LAUGHING)

THEO: No, really. I could do it.

VANESSA: Could you see Theo up on a billboard?

(THE KIDS LAUGH)

THEO: Hey, it won't be just billboards. It'll be catalogues, magazines, TV . . .

DENISE: Hah!

CLAIR: If your brother is serious about a career, I think we should encourage him.

DENISE: But, Mom, a model.

THEO: Why not?

RUDY: Because you're Theo.

(THE GIRLS LAUGH)

CLIFF: Wait a minute. I can't just sit back and watch my man take all this abuse.

THEO: Thanks, Dad.

CLIFF: I happen to think you're a very handsome fellow, and could make a go at modeling.

THEO: I know I could. You see, most of these guys in the magazines, when they pose, look like this . . .

(THEO STRIKES A MODEL-LIKE POSE)

THEO
(CONT'D):   That's not natural. If I were doing it, I'd stand like this . . .

(THEO SHOWS HIS VERSION OF A NATURAL POSE. IT LOOKS PRETTY GOOD)

GIRLS: Oooooo.

CLIFF: Son, you're a natural.

THEO: Dad, I read that a model, even one who's starting out, can make five hundred dollars a day. And the great thing is, I could start when I'm eighteen.

CLIFF: What about college?

THEO:	I could go, but that's four years out of my modeling career.
CLAIR:	Theo, your father and I have never said you had to go to college. But we do feel that it can help you lay a foundation for the rest of your life.
THEO:	Mom, at five hundred dollars a day, I don't need a foundation.
CLIFF:	You think you'd be ready to go out on your own at eighteen?
THEO:	I could do it. I know it's going to be hard, but I could do it.
DENISE:	Uh-huh, sure.
THEO:	I could.
CLIFF:	I don't think you really know how hard it is.
THEO:	I know I'd have to find my own place, pay bills, and all that stuff. But I could do it.
CLIFF:	You say you can do it, but you don't really know because you haven't tried it.
THEO:	I manage my life pretty well right now.
CLIFF:	Theo, right now you are going through life on the Doctor and Mrs. Huxtable Scholarship Fund.

(THE CHILDREN AD LIB 'YEAH,' 'RIGHT')

THEO: (TO HIS SISTERS)	Hey, you're on it, too.
(TO CLIFF)	I don't need that much. If I get one day's work as a model, I'll have enough to live on for a month. And I figure if I get in a bind, you and Mom. . .
CLIFF/CLAIR:	No.
THEO:	But you could. . .
CLIFF/CLAIR:	No.

THEO:	You wouldn't help me at all?
CLIFF:	Once you're out in the real world, you can't rely on your mother and me. You have to make it on your own.
CLAIR:	But, of course, we'd be happy to help you get started.
CLIFF:	No.
CLAIR:	C'mon, Cliff. Theo, how much do you think you'd need?
THEO:	Oh, five hundred dollars.
DENISE:	Theo, get real.
CLIFF:	You'll need more than that.
THEO:	All right. A thousand.
CLIFF:	Tell you what. We'll give you two thousand dollars to get you started.
THEO:	Hey, with two "G's" in my pocket, there'd be no looking back.
CLIFF:	You sound confident.
THEO:	I am.

(GETTING UP AND PICKING UP HIS OVERNIGHT BAG)

	Can I be excused?
VANESSA:	Where are you going?
THEO:	I'm spending the night at Cockroach's.
CLAIR:	You're coming back, aren't you? You're not going out into the real world so soon?
THEO:	No, Mom. I'll be back tomorrow.
CLIFF:	What time?
THEO:	Around ten.
CLIFF:	Ten. Got it. See you then.

(THEO STARTS TO EXIT)

RUDY:	Bye Mr. Model.

(THEY ALL LAUGH AND <u>AD LIB</u> 'GOODBYES' TO THEO. THEO EXITS)

CLIFF: Is everyone going to be here around ten tomorrow?

(THE KIDS <u>AD LIB</u> 'YES')

DENISE: Why?

CLIFF: I need all of you for a project.

CLAIR: What project?

CLIFF:

(SMILING AS HE GETS UP)

           Let's just say we're going to be helping Theo get ready
           for the real world.

DENISE/
VANESSA/
RUDY: Oooooo.

(CLIFF STRIDES OUT AS WE:)

<u>DISSOLVE TO:</u>

<u>ACT ONE</u>

<u>Scene 2</u>

<u>EXT. HUXTABLE'S FRONT STOOP — THE NEXT MORNING (DAY 2)</u>
(Cliff, Theo, Vanessa)

(VANESSA SITS ON THE STOOP. THEO ENTERS, CARRYING HIS OVERNIGHT BAG)

THEO: Hey, Vanessa.

(VANESSA LOOKS AT HIM, PUZZLED)

THEO:
(CONT'D):   What's wrong?

VANESSA: You must be mistaking me for someone else. My name's
           not Vanessa.

THEO: Huh?

VANESSA: My name is Margo Farnsworth.

THEO: What are you talking about?

VANESSA: I'm Margo Farnsworth. I have an apartment in this
           building.

THEO: Whatever you say, Margo.

(THEO STARTS UP THE STAIRS)

VANESSA: Wait. I know who you are. The landlord told me that a
           young man who's eighteen and on his own is coming
           here to rent an apartment.

(A BEAT)

THEO: Oh, I get it. Very funny.

VANESSA: What's so funny?

THEO: I'm eighteen and I'm on my own.

VANESSA: That's right. and you're here to rent an apartment.

THEO: Fine. Okay. I'll rent an apartment. Who do I talk to?

VANESSA: The landlord. Just ring the doorbell. I hope you get into
           the building. Some very nice people live here.

THEO: Right. Okay, Vanessa.

VANESSA: Who?

THEO: Never mind.

(THEO WALKS UP TO THE DOOR AND RINGS THE BELL)

SFX: DOORBELL

(A BEAT. CLIFF ANSWERS THE DOOR)

CLIFF: Hello.

THEO: Hi, Dad.

CLIFF: Who?

THEO: Oh. I mean, Mr. Landlord.

CLIFF: You must be here for the apartment. I'm Harley.

(EXTENDING HIS HAND)

Harley Weemax.

THEO: Theodore Huxtable.

CLIFF: Oh, yes. Huxtable. Your parents were here a little earlier. They left an envelope for you.

(HE HANDS THE ENVELOPE TO THEO)

CLIFF
(CONT'D):   You got nice folks.

(THEO OPENS THE ENVELOPE AND PULLS OUT A STACK OF FAKE MONEY)

THEO: This is play money.

CLIFF: It's good here.

THEO:
(FINDING A NOTE AND READING IT)

"Dear Theo, here's your two thousand dollars to get started. Good luck. We love you very much. Mom and Dad."

CLIFF: Beautiful people. C'mon, I'll show you the apartment.

CUT TO:

ACT ONE

Scene 3

INT. LIVING ROOM — CONTINUOUS ACTION (DAY 2)
(Cliff, Clair, Theo, Rudy)

(CLIFF ESCORTS THEO IN)

CLIFF: Welcome to the Real World Apartments. As you can see, we have a beautiful lobby. All the woodwork is original.

(CLAIR ENTERS FROM THE KITCHEN)

CLAIR:
(TO CLIFF)   Hi, Harley.

CLIFF: Hi, Millie.

THEO: Millie?

CLIFF: Yeah, this is Millie Farquar. She owns the Wagon
                    Wheel Restaurant here.

CLAIR: Howdy, You'll have to stop by for some grub.
                    We're right off the lobby. Open twenty-four hours.

THEO: Good one, Mom.

CLAIR: Who?

THEO: I mean, 'Mrs. Farquar.'

CLAIR: It's 'Miss'. Hope to see you real soon.

(CLAIR EXITS BACK INTO KITCHEN)

CLIFF: You'll like eating at the Wagon Wheel. I
                    recommend the Bacon Burger Dog.

(CLIFF AND THEO HEAD TOWARD THE STAIRS)

CLIFF (CONT'D):   We have a few rules here at Real World
                    Apartments. Rent is due on the first of every
                    month, no exceptions. No loud music after ten
                    o'clock. No pets and no children.

(RUDY ENTERS DOWN THE STAIRS IN A VERY NICE BUT
CONSERVATIVE OUTFIT. SHE'S CARRYING A BRIEFCASE)

RUDY: Hi, Harley.

CLIFF: Hi, Mrs. Griswald.

THEO: Oh, no.

(RUDY CROSSES TO THE KITCHEN AS CLIFF AND THEO HEAD UP
THE STAIRS)

CLIFF: Let's go see the apartment.

CUT TO:

ACT ONE

Scene 4

INT. THEO'S ROOM — CONTINUOUS ACTION (DAY 2)
(Cliff, Theo)

(THEO'S ROOM IS TOTALLY STRIPPED AND EMPTY. CLIFF AND
THEO ENTER. THEO IS STUNNED)

THEO: Dad!

CLIFF: Who?

THEO: Where's my stuff? My stereo? My posters? My bed?

CLIFF: It's an unfurnished apartment.

THEO: I don't believe this.

CLIFF: Believe what? I'm just showing you an unfurnished
         apartment. And this is not a dream.

THEO:
(CALMING DOWN) Okay. Unfurnished. I got it.

CLIFF: Good.

THEO: So how much is it?

CLIFF: Six hundred dollars a month.

THEO: For one room?

CLIFF: Hey, that's what they go for nowadays.

THEO: I guess I'll have to take it.

CLIFF: Not so fast. How old are you?

THEO: Eighteen.

CLIFF: Sorry.

THEO: What?

CLIFF: I don't rent to people that age. All they want to do is party.

THEO: Did I say I was eighteen? I'm sorry. I meant I've been on
         my own since I was eighteen. I'm actually twenty-three.

CLIFF:　Good.

(THEO STARTS TO TAKE MONEY OUT OF THE ENVELOPE)

THEO:　I've got the six hundred dollars for the rent.

CLIFF:　Wait. I'll need the first month's rent and the last month's rent.

THEO:　Why?

CLIFF:　I need the last month's rent in case you try to move out early without paying.

THEO:　That's twelve hundred dollars.

CLIFF:　And I need another month's rent as security to cover damages.

THEO:　That's eighteen hundred dollars!

CLIFF:　You add like a twenty-three year old.

THEO:　All right. It's a lot of money, but I need a place to live. Here you go.

(THEO STARTS TO HAND CLIFF THE MONEY)

CLIFF:
(MOVING HIS HAND AWAY)

　　　I can't take it.

THEO:　Why not?

CLIFF:　I'll need references.

THEO:　References?

CLIFF:　Yes. Someone to vouch for your character, like your employer. You do have a job, don't you?

THEO:　Uh . . . not now. But I'm going to get one. I'm a model.

CLIFF:　A model, huh? I'm going to need proof that you'll be able to pay your rent.

THEO:　I'll pay it. I promise.

CLIFF: I can't feed my family on a promise. I need a letter stating that you have a steady income.

THEO: Where am I going to get that?

CLIFF: From your modeling agency.

THEO: I don't have one.

CLIFF: If you want to work as a model, you have to have an agent. But you're in luck. There happens to be a modeling agency right here in the lobby. Ask for Kitty La Rue.

THEO: Kitty La Rue. Thanks.

(THEO EXITS)

CUT TO:

ACT ONE

Scene 5

INT. LIVING ROOM — A MOMENT LATER (DAY 2)
(Cliff, Denise, Theo, Vanessa, Rudy)

(DENISE AND VANESSA ARE QUICKLY REARRANGING THE ROOM. THEY'RE PLACING THE COFFEE TABLE IN FRONT OF ONE OF THE CHAIRS TO LOOK LIKE A DESK)

CLIFF (O.S.):
(LOUDLY)

You can't miss it. The modeling agency is right at the bottom of the stairs.

DENISE: Hurry.

(VANESSA CROSSES TO THE CORRESPONDENCE DESK AND TURNS THE CHAIR AROUND AND SITS IN IT. THEO ENTERS DOWN THE STAIRS)

VANESSA: Welcome to the Firestone Modeling Agency.

THEO: This is the modeling agency?

VANESSA: Yes it is. I'm the receptionist, Kitty La Rue.

THEO: I thought you were Margo Farnsworth.

VANESSA: You must have me mistaken for someone else. Do you
            have an appointment?

THEO: No. The landlord sent me. I'm a model and I need an
            agent.

VANESSA: Well, we're always looking for new faces. I'll ask Ms.
            Firestone if she'll see you.

(VANESSA CROSSES AROUND THE COUCH TO DENISE)

VANESSA
(CONT'D):   Excuse me, Ms. Firestone.

DENISE: Yes, Kitty?

VANESSA: There's a gentleman here who needs an agent.

DENISE: How does he look?

VANESSA: Not bad.

DENISE: Send him in.

(VANESSA CROSSES TO THEO)

VANESSA: Ms. Firestone will see you.

(THEO CROSSES AROUND THE COUCH TO DENISE. VANESSA
EXITS)

THEO: Hi.

(WITHOUT RESPONDING, DENISE GETS UP AND STUDIES THEO'S
FACE. SHE THEN CIRCLES HIM, CHECKING HIM OUT)

DENISE: Do you always stand like that?

(THEO STRAIGHTENS UP)

DENISE
(CONT'D):   Would you mind walking across the room for me?

THEO: Huh?

DENISE: Just walk over and back.

(THEO, VERY SELF-CONSCIOUSLY, WALKS ACROSS THE ROOM AND
BACK)

DENISE
(CONT'D):
(WATCHING) Uh-huh . . . hmm . . . Uhhh . . . Um-hmm . . . Do you
have any experience?

THEO: No. But I look good.

DENISE:
(CHUCKLES TO HERSELF, THEN)

          Darling, come with me.

(DENISE ESCORTS THEO TO THE FRONT DOOR, AND OPENS IT)

DENISE
(CONT'D):   Take a look. That's New York City. I could throw a
stick out there and hit twenty guys who look just like
you. What makes you think you're special enough to
be a Firestone model?

THEO: I'm a natural. I'm sure if I get that first job, I'll never
stop working.

DENISE: I like your attitude. Let me see your pictures.

THEO: I don't have any.

DENISE: You're not going to get work without pictures. You
need to go to a good photographer and get a full set of
prints done. It will cost you eight to twelve hundred
dollars.

THEO: Look. Could you do me a favor? I'm trying to get an
apartment. Could you just write me a letter saying
I'm working as a model?

DENISE: You don't have an apartment?

THEO: No.

DENISE: How am I going to get in touch with you if I ever
want to hire you?

THEO: Write the letter, then I'll have the apartment and
you'll know where to find me.

DENISE: That would be dishonest. Now if you'll excuse me, I
             have to call Paris.

(DENISE EXITS. THEO THINKS A BEAT, THEN CROSSES TO THE
FRONT DOOR AS CLIFF ENTERS)

CLIFF
(CONT'D):   Where are you going?

THEO: To get a reference. Don't let anyone take that
             apartment.

CLIFF: I can't promise anything, but I'll try.

(THEO EXITS OUT THE FRONT DOOR. RUDY ENTERS FROM THE
KITCHEN, NIBBLING ON A COOKIE)

CLIFF
(CONT'D):   Mrs. Griswald, where did you get that?

RUDY: Millie made it.

(RUDY EXITS UP THE STAIRS AS WE:)

FADE OUT:

END OF ACT ONE

ACT TWO

Scene 1

FADE IN:

INT. THEO'S ROOM — LATER THAT AFTERNOON (DAY 2)
(Cliff, Theo, Cockroach)

(THEO ENTERS WITH COCKROACH WHO'S WEARING A SUIT
AND TIE)

COCKROACH: Man, you weren't kidding. There's nothing in here.

THEO: I know, Cockroach. They're going all out for this.
             That's why you've got to be good.

COCKROACH: You have nothing to worry about.

CLIFF (O.S.): Hello.

THEO: In here.

(CLIFF ENTERS)

CLIFF: Mrs. Griswald told me you were back.

COCKROACH:
(EXTENDING HIS HAND)

               Hi, Mr. Weemax. I'm Horton W. Dansberry.

THEO: Instead of a letter, I decided to bring my employer.

CLIFF:
(TO COCKROACH)

               You're his employer?

COCKROACH: Yes.

CLIFF: What line of business are you in?

COCKROACH: I'm in oil.

CLIFF: Oil?

COCKROACH: Yes. Let me give you one of my cards.

(COCKROACH HANDS CLIFF A CARD)

CLIFF:
(READING)   'Cockroach Oil.' Very nice card. Isn't it expensive to
               have them hand-drawn like this?

COCKROACH: Only the best for my company.

CLIFF:
(TO THEO)   You work for this man?

THEO: Yes I do.

CLIFF: I thought you said you were a model.

THEO: I am. I'm the spokesman for Cockroach Oil.

COCKROACH: Let me tell you something about this man, Mr.
               Weemax. He's a fine spokesman. Responsible,
               dependable, and hard-working. He's the reason
               Cockroach Oil is what it is today.

CLIFF: That's all I have to hear. Mr. Huxtable, welcome to
                your new apartment.

THEO: Awright. Here you go.

(THEO PULLS OUT HIS MONEY AND GIVES CLIFF A STACK OF IT)

THEO
(CONT'D):   I did it, Dad.

CLIFF: Who?

THEO: Come on, Dad, isn't this what it was all about?
                Getting an apartment on my own? I showed you I
                could do it. Now, let's get my furniture back in here.

CLIFF: I don't know what you're talking about.

THEO: Hold it, time out, time out. I have to talk to my Dad.
                Could you find him for me?

CLIFF: I'll see if he's here.

(CLIFF EXITS)

COCKROACH: Who's playing your Dad?

(CLIFF ENTERS)

THEO: My Dad.

CLIFF: Hey, Son. Mr. Weemax said you were looking for me.

THEO: Dad, how much longer will this go on?

CLIFF: Son, the real world stops for no man. But in your
                case, twenty-four hours.

THEO: Twenty-four hours? What am I supposed to do?

CLIFF: In the real world, you'd have to get furniture for
                your apartment, towels, sheets, pillowcases, food.
                You'd have to get a phone, contact the electric
                company . . . I told you it wasn't going to be easy.

THEO: That's okay. I can do it.

CLIFF: My boy.

| THEO: | How do I get my furniture? |
| CLIFF: | I'll ask Mr. Weemax. |

(CLIFF EXITS)

| COCKROACH: | This is fun. |
| THEO: | That's because it's not happening to you. |

(CLIFF ENTERS)

CLIFF:	Bye, Doctor Huxtable. Love that guy. Your Dad told me you're looking for furniture.
THEO:	Yeah. Would you happen to know where I could find some?
CLIFF:	Yes I would. There's a very nice furniture store right next to Millie's restaurant. Come on, I'll show you.

(CLIFF EXITS)

COCKROACH:	Who's Millie?
THEO:	Mom.
COCKROACH:	Amazing. I wish we did stuff like this at my house.

(THEO AND COCKROACH EXIT)

CUT TO:

ACT TWO

Scene 2

INT. DINING ROOM — MOMENTS LATER (DAY 2)
(Cliff, Clair, Theo, Cockroach)

(THE DINING ROOM HAS BEEN TURNED INTO A USED FURNITURE SHOWROOM, WITH ALL OF THEO'S THINGS — BED, DESK, STEREO, BOOKSHELVES, ETC. — ARRANGED WITH PRICE TAGS HANGING FROM THEM. THE STORE OWNER, CLAIR, TAKES INVENTORY AS CLIFF LEADS THEO AND COCKROACH INTO THE ROOM)

| THEO: | My stuff. |
| COCKROACH: | They really cleaned you out. |

THEO:
(TO CLIFF)   Millie runs the furniture store?

CLIFF: That's not Millie. That's Amanda.

CLAIR: Hey, Harley, who you got there?

CLIFF: Couple of customers, Amanda.

CLAIR: Send them over.

(CLIFF NUDGES THEO AND COCKROACH TOWARD CLAIR, THEN
EXITS)

CLAIR
(CONT'D):   Gentlemen, welcome to Amanda's Furniture City,
                where money talks and nobody walks. If you like it,
                touch it. If you break it, you buy it. If you don't see it,
                we don't have it. But we'll get it. Now, what can I do
                for you?

THEO:
(LOOKING AT A PRICE ON THE STEREO)

                A hundred and fifty dollars for my stereo?

CLAIR: It's not yours yet. But tell you what. Because I like
                your face, for a hundred and thirty-five you can walk
                out with it.

THEO: That's a lot of money. I only have two hundred
                dollars to furnish my whole apartment.

CLAIR: Does your friend have any money?

COCKROACH: No.

CLAIR:
(TO THEO)   Who's he?

THEO: My boss.

CLAIR: Better get yourself a new boss.

THEO:
(LOOKING AT THE PRICE TAG ON THE BED)

                Two hundred dollars?

CLAIR: That's for both beds.

THEO: Can I buy just one?

CLAIR: No. I can't break the set.

THEO: Why not?

CLAIR: They'll get lonely, okay?

(COCKROACH LAUGHS. THEO GIVES HIM A DIRTY LOOK)

THEO: Everything's so expensive. What am I going to do?

CLAIR: You come here for advice or furniture? Look, time is money. You've got to figure out what you need.

THEO: I need it all.

CLAIR: Well, you're not going to get it with two hundred dollars. But, you're in luck. Here at Furniture City, we accept all major credit cards.

THEO: I don't have any credit cards.

CLAIR: You're in luck. Here at Furniture City we accept personal checks.

THEO: I don't have a checking account.

CLAIR: Then you're about to leave Furniture City.

THEO: Mom . . .

CLAIR: Who? Look, my friend, I really want to help you out. What you need to do is go to the bank and get a loan.

THEO: All right. Where's the bank?

CLAIR: It's very easy to find. Just go through Millie's restaurant and make a left.

THEO: C'mon, Cockroach.

COCKROACH: I can't wait to meet the banker.

CLAIR: When you get everything straightened out, come on back. We never close.

(AS THEO AND COCKROACH START TO EXIT)

COCKROACH: I might be back to buy that stereo.

(THEO PULLS COCKROACH OUT OF THE ROOM)

CUT TO:

ACT TWO

Scene 3

INT. KITCHEN — CONTINUOUS ACTION (DAY 2)
(Cockroach, Theo, Denise)

(DENISE IS RINSING SOME DISHES. THEO AND COCKROACH HAVE
ENTERED AND THEO IS CLOSING THE DINING ROOM DOORS
BEHIND THEM)

COCKROACH: Hi, Denise.

THEO: Wait a minute. She's not Denise.

DENISE: Yes, I am.

THEO: You are?

DENISE: Yes.

THEO: Good.

COCKROACH: Theo, I'm starving. Before we go to the bank, can we
             take a break?

THEO: Sure.

(THEO AND COCKROACH START UNLOADING THE
REFRIGERATOR)

DENISE: I'll get you some plates.

THEO: Thanks.

(THEO AND COCKROACH CARRY THE FOOD TO THE TABLE.
DENISE BRINGS PLATES AND SILVERWARE OVER. THEY START TO
DIG IN. DENISE STANDS BEHIND THEM AT THE TABLE)

DENISE: So, what have you got there?

THEO: Chicken . . .

(UNSEEN BY THEO AND COCKROACH, DENISE PULLS OUT A
SMALL NOTE PAD AND STARTS WRITING)

THEO
(CONT'D):   . . .some tuna, carrot salad.

DENISE: Would you like sodas?

THEO/
COCKROACH: Yeah.

(DENISE FINISHES WRITING, RIPS OFF THE SHEET OF PAPER AND
LAYS IT ON THE TABLE)

DENISE: That comes to twenty-four dollars and fifty cents.
                 That's without the tip of course.

THEO: Hey, what is this?

DENISE: You're eating in Millie's Restaurant.

THEO: I thought you were Denise.

DENISE: I am. Denise Farquar, Millie's daughter. Now pay up.

COCKROACH: Good one. Unbelievable.

(COCKROACH STARTS TO TAKE A BITE OF CHICKEN)

THEO: Put that chicken down.

COCKROACH: I'm hungry.

THEO: You got the money for it?

COCKROACH: No, but you have enough.

THEO: Cockroach, I can't spend this much on one meal. I
                 still have furniture to buy. I have to get my phone,
                 my utilities. I am on a budget.

COCKROACH: Okay. Denise, how much is an apple?

DENISE: A dollar. But that doesn't include tip.

COCKROACH: We'll take two.

THEO: We'll take one and split it.

DENISE: All right.

(AS COCKROACH CUTS THE APPLE IN HALF:)

DENISE
(CONT'D):   There's a fifty cent charge for splitting. That comes
to a dollar and a half.

THEO: Fine. Here you go.

COCKROACH: Keep the change.

THEO: Cockroach!

COCKROACH: Hey, she's nice.

DENISE: Thank you. Hope to see you again real soon.

THEO: Not at these prices you won't.

(DENISE EXITS)

ACT TWO

Scene 4

INT. LIVING ROOM—CONTINUOUS ACTION (DAY 2)
(Rudy, Vanessa, Clair, Cliff, Theo, Cockroach)

(RUDY SITS AT THE DESK. CLIFF LISTENS AT THE KITCHEN DOOR.
VANESSA SITS IN A CHAIR WITH THE COFFEE TABLE IN FRONT
OF HER. CLAIR STANDS NEXT TO VANESSA, GOING OVER A PIECE
OF PAPER)

CLAIR: Just go right down the checklist.

CLIFF: They're coming.

(CLIFF RUSHES TO THE COUCH. HE AND CLAIR QUICKLY SIT
DOWN. THEO AND COCKROACH ENTER)

VANESSA: Would you two please have a seat? I'll be with you as
soon as I finish here.

THEO:
(QUIETLY TO COCKROACH)

    Vanessa.

COCKROACH: Just be cool.

VANESSA:
(TO CLIFF AND CLAIR)

> Your application for the loan is in perfect order. It looks good. I'm going to recommend approval.

CLIFF: Oh, golly. That is so marvelous.

(TO CLAIR)   Honey, we can buy our dream house.

CLAIR: And raise a family.

(THEY KISS)

VANESSA: Now, what we have to do is have the loan approved by the president of the bank, Mrs. Griswald.

(VANESSA CROSSES TO RUDY)

VANESSA
(CONT'D):   Mrs. Griswald?

RUDY: Yes.

VANESSA: Would you look at this application and tell me what you think?

(RUDY LOOKS AT THE PAPER A BEAT AND SAYS:)

RUDY: Approved.

VANESSA: Thank you, Mrs. Griswald.

RUDY: . You're welcome.

(VANESSA CROSSES BACK TO CLIFF AND CLAIR)

VANESSA: Congratulations.

CLIFF: Oh, golly. I'm so glad we came to this bank.

CLAIR: Me too. Now we can start planning for our future.

(TO VANESSA)

> Thank you for all your help.

(CLIFF AND CLAIR EXIT UP THE STAIRS)

VANESSA: Next.

(THEO AND COCKROACH CROSS TO VANESSA)

THEO: Who are you now?

VANESSA: I'm Ms. Covington. And would you please not eat
               those apples in my office?

(THEO HANDS HIS APPLE TO COCKROACH. HE SETS THEM DOWN)

VANESSA
(CONT'D):   What can I do for you?

COCKROACH: Theo, let me handle this.

(TO VANESSA)

               This gentleman works for me. My name is Horton W.
               Dansberry. I'm the president and owner of
               Cockroach Oil. I'd give you my card, but I ran out.

VANESSA: I see.

(WRITING ON THE PAD)

               Where's Cockroach Oil located?

COCKROACH: Our headquarters are on the top floor of the
               Cockroach Oil Building. It's a forty-nine story
               building.

VANESSA: And the address?

COCKROACH: Nine-eighty-one East Fifty-fourth Street.

VANESSA: Got it.

(REACHING FOR THE PHONE)

               Could you give me the phone number? I need to
               confirm this information.

COCKROACH: Uh . . . we don't have a phone.

VANESSA: You own a forty-nine story building and you don't
               have a phone?

COCKROACH: Uh . . . the telephone pole out front blew over.

THEO: Forget him. Look, I really need a loan. I have to buy furniture, food, a portfolio . . .

VANESSA: How much money do you need?

THEO: I'd say, uh, twenty-five hundred dollars.

VANESSA: I see.

(WRITING ON THE PAD)

            Have you ever taken out a loan before?

THEO: No.

VANESSA: That's too bad. Mr. Huxtable, you have no credit history, and your boss doesn't own a telephone. It doesn't look good.

THEO: But I really need the money. I'll pay it back. I promise.

VANESSA: Well . . . I do like to give young people who are starting out a break. I'm going to recommend that you get the loan.

THEO: Awright.

VANESSA: Mrs. Griswald, could you come here?

RUDY:

(CROSSING TO VANESSA)

            What do you want? I'm busy.

VANESSA: This young man wants a loan. I recommend we give it to him.

(RUDY STUDIES THE NOTEPAD FOR A BEAT, THEN:)

RUDY: No.

VANESSA: But . . .

RUDY: No.

THEO: Why not?

RUDY: You have nothing.

(RUDY CROSSES BACK AND SITS AT HER DESK)

VANESSA: Sorry. I tried. Tell you what. Once you start working and have some money, come back and we'll be glad to give you a loan.

THEO: But I need it now. Are there any other banks in this building?

VANESSA: Yes, but they're all owned by Mrs. Griswald.

RUDY: That's right.

DISSOLVE TO:

ACT TWO

Scene 5

INT. THEO'S ROOM — THAT EVENING (DAY 2)
(Theo, Cliff, Clair, Rudy)

(THEO'S ROOM IS BARE EXCEPT FOR HIS STEREO, A PILLOW AND A COUPLE OF BLANKETS. A SINGLE LIT CANDLE, SET IN A DISH ON THE FLOOR, IS THE ONLY LIGHT IN THE ROOM. THEO SITS ON HIS BLANKETS MUNCHING CONTENTEDLY ON SOME CRACKERS)

SFX: KNOCK

THEO: Come in.

(CLAIR AND CLIFF ENTER. CLAIR CARRIES A COVERED PLATE)

THEO
(CONT'D): Hi, Mr. Weemax, Amanda.

CLAIR/CLIFF: Who?

CLIFF
(CONT'D): Son, it's Mom and Dad. Don't you recognize us?

CLAIR: We thought we'd drop by and see how you're getting along in your new apartment.

THEO: Pretty good. I did all right. I got everything I need and I still have twenty-three dollars left over.

CLIFF: Good for you. So, how do you like the real world?

THEO: Well . . . it's a lot tougher than I thought. But you know what? So am I.

CLAIR:

(INDICATING THE CANDLE)

Don't you have any electricity?

THEO: Not yet. I bought my stereo before I knew I had to pay a fifty dollar deposit to get my utilities turned on.

CLIFF: That's pretty steep.

THEO: Yeah. I found out the electric company is owned by Mrs. Griswald.

CLAIR: Well, Theo, we can't stay long.

(HANDING THEO THE PLATE)

Here, your father and I fixed you a home-cooked meal.

(THEO UNWRAPS THE PLATE)

THEO: Awright! A Bacon Burger Dog.

(THEO DIGS IN)

CLIFF: Son, we're very proud of you. If there's anything you need just call us.

THEO: Thanks. I could use a chair, but other than that, I've got everything I need.

CLAIR: This is everything you need?

THEO: Sure. In fact, even when I'm a model and making lots of money, I'm going to live like this.

CLIFF: I see. You're willing to live like this on your money, but on our money you want to live like the rich and famous.

THEO: I never thought of it that way.

CLAIR: Then I guess you learned a pretty important lesson today.

THEO: Yes, I did. I learned that when I go out in the real world, I never want to do business with anyone in my family.

<u>FADE OUT</u>:

<u>END OF SHOW</u>

APPENDIX B

Ethel and Albert

"The Income Tax"

ETHEL AND ALBERT

Friday, March 23, 1956

SPONSOR: The Ralston Purina   TIME: 10:00—10:30 P.M.
         Company

<u>CAST</u>

ETHEL.................................Peg Lynch
ALBERT..............................Alan Bunce
GILBERT ....Walter Abel
GRACE ....Cele MacLaughlin
RALPH BUNDERSON ....John Gibson

"The Income Tax"

WRITER: Peg Lynch   PRODUCER-DIRECTOR: Walter Hart

(Script provided courtesy of Peg Lynch)

<u>SCENE: (LIVING ROOM)</u>

ALBERT: (HAT AND COAT ON) Ethel! ETHEL! Oh—

ETHEL: (COMING IN) For Heaven's sake—

ALBERT: Come here—

ETHEL: I thought you'd gone to work.

ALBERT: Gone to work! I was looking for my sales report and I found this.

ETHEL: What?

ALBERT: (RISES) A letter. From the Income Tax Department. It isn't even OPENED!

ETHEL: What?

ALBERT: When did this come?

ETHEL: I don't know—don't even know what it is—

ALBERT: You with your passion for swooping things off the desk—you probably just jammed it in a drawer—and—

(READING LETTER)

ETHEL: Well—don't get so excited. It isn't April 15th yet. You've got time. Here's that book with the minutes of the Woman's Club. Maybelle wanted it.

ALBERT: OH MY GOSH!

ETHEL: What?

ALBERT: The tax inspector wants to look over my 1954 tax returns!

ETHEL: You mean—you're—you're being checked?

ALBERT: Yeah!

ETHEL: You paid your tax and mailed it in, didn't you?

ALBERT: YES!

ETHEL: I wonder why they're checking you?

ALBERT: Yeah—Well—I suppose—it's—you know—just routine.

ETHEL: (WORRIED) Uh-huh. (BRIEF PAUSE) You think maybe we put down a little too much for charity?

ALBERT: NO!—No—I give to charity. You're allowed to give so much.

ETHEL: Think maybe we stretched it a little?

ALBERT: No . . . I was perfectly honest about everything—

ETHEL: Think maybe you took too much off for business expense?

ALBERT: (SITS) N-no . . . no . . . I . . . It's just a routine check . . .

ETHEL: There must be SOMETHING THEY'RE QUESTIONING!

ALBERT: Well—I—He's probably going to question why I got the letter two weeks ago and didn't call him—you with this phobia for cleaning off the desk—I—(RISES) (LOOKS AT WATCH) It's after nine. Maybe I'd better phone right now.

ETHEL: The phone's here. Put the blame on me. Say—you know—your wife put the letter in the desk and—you know—you just happened to find it now—Maybe you could be—you know—kind of—amusing telling about it.

ALBERT: (QUICK LOOK AT HER) Yeah. Tax office. (PICKS UP PHONE)

ETHEL: Maybe you could be kind of funny about how I'm always swooping things in desk drawers—and you know—putting your things—

ALBERT: Yeah—Main 4090.

ETHEL: (CROSSES AWAY) You put down exactly what you were making, didn't you?

ALBERT: (CLEARS THROAT. LITTLE LAUGH) Hello . . . This is Albert Arbuckle,—and—I got a letter two weeks ago from your department—seems to have gotten misplaced and I just found it—

ETHEL: Tell them it was my fault.

ALBERT: Yes—(LAUGHING) (SOBERS) All right.

ETHEL: What did they say?

ALBERT: Girl on the switchboard. She's connecting me with someone else.

ETHEL: Tell them it was my fault.

ALBERT: Hello. Hello, Sir. (FRIENDLY LAUGH) I seem to have misplaced a letter from you people two weeks ago apparently—about a tax inspection and—

ETHEL: Tell him it was my fault.

ALBERT: Albert Arbuckle, 444 Edgecombe Road. Yes. That's right, sir. Thank you. (TO ETHEL) Going to look up the letter. I suppose he's going to send somebody out to the house here. Wednesday night would be all right, wouldn't it?

ETHEL: You'd better have him come tonight!

ALBERT: Tonight?

ETHEL: Not having called them for two weeks—then if you put the man off—maybe he'll think—you know—that you're—well, "fixing" your books.

ALBERT: Oh!—Look—Hello. . . . Yes?—

ETHEL: Tell him any time is all right so he doesn't think anything's crooked.

ALBERT: Yes—well—any time—(LOOKS AT ETHEL) Tonight would be fine!

ETHEL: Want to ask him for dinner?

(ALBERT SHAKES HEAD "NO")

I could make a cake.

ALBERT: 8:30 . . . Yes . . . yes—all right, sir. Thank you. 'Bye. I've got to have my cancelled checks—my check stubs and my sales slips—

(TAKING OFF COAT AND HAT)

I have to have everything that will show ANYTHING WE SPENT for 1954. Let's head for the attic.

SCENE DISSOLVES TO ATTIC

ETHEL: Now here is the account book for 1954 but I can't find the cancelled checks for 1954! You know—it makes me kind of mad the government wanting to know about 1954—

ALBERT: Well—it's the law.

ETHEL: If they want to know about 1954 why don't they come around in 1954 instead of making us prowl around looking for cancelled checks and stubs and sales slips—when I'm right in the middle of a devil's food cake . . .

ALBERT: The government doesn't care that you're in the middle of a devil's food cake.

ETHEL: I guess they will be when I stop buying butter!

ALBERT: (LOOKS AT HER. GIVES UP. GOES BACK TO LOOKING)

—OH LOOK—my old boy scout hat—

ETHEL: Why do we have to have sales slips?

ALBERT: It is what the man said!

(PUTTING HAT ON WHILE HE LOOKS FURTHER THROUGH BOX)

ETHEL: Do you mean to tell me that President Eisenhower is interested in my buying a nylon blouse for $6.95 in 1954?

ALBERT: President Eisenhower isn't interested in your nylon blouse—It's the tax department we're dealing with! Oh—look at the time—Going to be so late getting to the office—and I've got an appointment—

ETHEL: Run along—I'll spend the whole day in the attic if necessary—looking for things—

SOUND: (DOORBELL)

(THEY LOOK AT EACH OTHER. ALBERT GRABS HER ARM)

GRACE: (OFF) Yoo-hoo—Ethel!

ETHEL: It's just Grace.

ETHEL: (LOOKING AT HIM) BE RIGHT DOWN, GRACE . . . .

GRACE: Brought over some samples for my new draperies—want to see what you think!

(STARTS SPREADING THEM OUT OVER BACK OF LOVE SEAT. ALBERT COMES RUSHING DOWNSTAIRS)

ALBERT: —Hello, Grace—(RUSHING TO DESK)

GRACE: Good morning, Albert. My, you're late today.

ALBERT: Mmm.

GRACE: By the way, have you got the Woman's Club book with the minutes of the meetings?

ETHEL: Oh yes—saw it this morning—somewhere—better get to work, dear.

ALBERT: Uh-huh!

GRACE: I can't go to the meeting tonight—Maybelle Bunderson wants the book. Are you going to be home tonight?

ETHEL: I should say we are—somebody's coming.

GRACE: Why don't you call Maybelle up and have her husband pick up the Woman's Club book on the way home from work—?

ETHEL: No. No—

GRACE: What do you think?

ETHEL: That's nice. We're going to be busy tonight. (SLIDES OVER TO GRACE) The income tax man is coming out.

(GRACE LOOKS AT HER)

          Albert's being checked. For 1954.

(GRACE LOOKS AT HER. TURNS AND LOOKS AT ALBERT)

ALBERT: (HEARS THIS. LOOKS UP AND AROUND AT GRACE)

          Well—it's—it's just a routine check.

GRACE: Uh-huh.

ALBERT: I mean—it could happen to anybody.

GRACE: Uh-huh.

ALBERT: Nothing to worry about—(TURNS TO GO) (LITTLE LAUGH)

GRACE: Where did Al Capone go?

ETHEL: Alcatraz. That was for tax evasion, Grace!

GRACE: I know—I just always think of Al Capone when anything funny comes up about taxes.

(ALBERT GOES OUT)

ETHEL: Oh—Uh-huh! I do, too. But Albert hasn't—

GRACE: No—no—OF COURSE NOT.

(LOOKS AT HER. PUTS ARM AROUND HER)

          I know Albert is as honest as the day is long—and I don't blame him for wanting to impress the tax man that he

is—but if you want my honest opinion I just don't think
that thing is going to do the trick.

ETHEL: What thing?

GRACE: Wearing a boy scout hat!

ETHEL: OHHHH! He wasn't doing it to—Oh—

(GRABS HIS HAT. RUSHES TO DOOR)

ALBERT! DEAR!

SOUND: (CAR DRIVES OFF)

—Oh—well, this is one day that Albert won't forget for a
long time!

SCENE DISSOLVES

MIDDLE COMMERCIAL

SCENE: (LIVING ROOM)

ETHEL: Did you find the cancelled checks for Community Chest?

ALBERT: No . . . I can't find that anywhere!—I've got my record
book for '54 pretty much in order—I hope but I—

SOUND: (DOORBELL)

(THEY LOOK AT EACH OTHER)

(ALBERT GOES TO DOOR)

ALBERT: Good evening.

MR. B.:   Good evening. Mr. Arbuckle?

ALBERT: Yes—won't you come in?

MR. B.:   Thank you. Had a little trouble finding the house.

ALBERT: Oh—we should have turned the porch light on for you.
This is my wife.

ETHEL: How do you do?

MR. B.:   How do you do?

ALBERT: Well—let me take your coat—

MR. B.:   Oh—I—

ETHEL: I'll take your hat—

ALBERT: Maybe he'd like some coffee, dear. Pretty cold out.

MR. B.:   (ALBERT GETTING HIM OUT OF COAT)

            No—no—no—thanks anyhow—

ETHEL: Won't you sit down?

MR. B.:   Thank you.

ETHEL: Certainly been warm for February, hasn't it?

MR. B.:   Hasn't it?

ETHEL: Hardly know what to expect.

MR. B.:   Well—way it goes. You can't tell much about the
            weather—you expect it to snow and it's real warm, then
            you expect it to be nice and it snows. (LAUGHS)

ETHEL: (LAUGHS) Yes—it certainly—is—well—soon be spring, I
            guess.

MR. B.:   Oh yes . . . (LITTLE POLITE LAUGHING)

ALBERT: Well, there's still a chance we could have a blizzard
            before spring.

MR. B.:   (AGREEING) Oh yes. Oh yes. I've seen blizzards in June.

ALBERT: Is that so?

MR. B.:   Yep. Of course you can't tell much. Been having funny
            weather all over the last few years. I personally think
            it's on account of the atom bomb experiments.

ETHEL: Uh-huh.

MR. B.:   All those blizzards last year. Colorado. Nebraska.

ALBERT: Yep.

MR. B.:   I was born in Nebraska.

ETHEL: No! Well, isn't that interesting!

MR. B.:   Yes—well—

(LOOKS FROM ONE TO THE OTHER)

            Really—it's certainly very pleasant talking to you, but
            I—(GETS UP)—really can't stay—

ALBERT: Oh? (RISES)

MR. B.:   No, I just thought I'd pick up the book and be on my way—I'm a little late tonight. Haven't even had dinner.

ALBERT: Oh—you want to take the records with you?

MR. B.:   Oh yes—sure—that's the idea, I guess.

ALBERT: (CROSSES TO DESK) Oh. I see. Well, that's all right. Better explain a few things then, I guess. Here's the complete record for 1954 . . . This is my total income for '54.

MR. B.:   What?

ALBERT: My total income for 1954. Listed right here. Here!

MR. B.:   (LOOKS) Oh—well—that's pretty nice!

ALBERT: A—yes—that's my GROSS income of course—

MR. B.:   Yeah! Well, that's all right. You're doing fine.

ALBERT: (LOOKS AT HIM) A—yes—well, here I've listed my deductions—right here—business expenses and all that and I think you'll find everything in order—

ETHEL: (CROSSES TO THEM) We're awfully sorry about the letter. It's really my fault—it came two weeks ago and I must have put it in a drawer by mistake—

ALBERT: Dear—

ETHEL: I just want him to know it's my fault . . . . it's why he didn't call—

ALBERT: (JOVIALLY) It doesn't matter dear—we're getting it all settled now. Well, here's the account book. I probably don't have it quite as well organized as a regular accountant would—but I think you'll find everything is in order. It's always quite a job making out an income tax!

MR. B.:   Oh—you're telling me! Now we got another coming up.

ETHEL: Yes—well—I guess it makes a lot of work for you.

MR. B.:   Well—guess it's kind of a headache to everybody.

ALBERT: Now here are my cancelled checks—kind of hate to let them go—they're the only receipts I have—you want those, too?

MR. B.:   I don't know anything about cancelled checks. My wife just said to pick up a book.

ETHEL: Your wife?

MR. B.:   Aren't you the Arbuckles?

ETHEL: Yes—who are you?

MR. B.:   Ralph Bunderson. Maybelle called me and said I should stop here on my way home tonight and pick up some books for the Woman's Club or something—

ETHEL: OH—oh—Maybelle—You're Maybelle Bunderson's husband—Yes—yes—the minutes of the meetings—

MR. B.:   Didn't Maybelle call you?

ETHEL: Yes—yes—she did—I just forgot—Now where's the book? Get his coat, dear—Oh—here it is—We're in kind of a dither today—we're expecting the tax man.

MR. B.:   Tax man?

ETHEL: Yes. Albert's being checked. For 1954.

MR. B.:   Oh. (LOOKS AT HIM)

ETHEL: Just routine.

MR. B.:   Uh-huh. (LAUGHS) Maybe you took off a little too much for entertainment, huh? (NUDGES ALBERT)

ETHEL: (PUSHING HIM OUT) Well—thanks for picking it up—Tell Maybelle I'm sorry—Awfully nice meeting you—'Night—

MR. B.:   Goodnight—

(ALBERT NODS)

ETHEL: (CLOSES DOOR) Well—don't look at me—I forgot he was coming!

ALBERT: HE MUST HAVE THOUGHT I WAS CRAZY—standing there telling him how much money I made in 1954!

ETHEL: Well—I'm sorry—never mind that now . . . Did you find the Community Chest Check?

ALBERT: NO . . . I can't find it!

ETHEL: Well, it makes me nervous not having that. They're always suspicious when you put down too much for charity—What if he questions you?

ALBERT: I'll tell him I lost the check . . . which apparently I have. I've got some checks for other charities. Here's the list.

ETHEL: I just wish Reverend Sheridan would see what you put down for contributions to the collection plate—

ALBERT: Look—

ETHEL: I'll go upstairs and look in that box in our closet—there's some things in that—possibly some cancelled checks—(GOES)

ALBERT: Ahh—

ETHEL: (CALLING) You look in that check file once more—

ALBERT: (LOOKING) Yeah—O.K.

SOUND: (DOORBELL)

(ALBERT LOOKS UP. GETS UP. GOES TO DOOR. OPENS IT)

GILBERT: Good evening. Mr. Arbuckle?

ALBERT: Yes.

GILBERT: Gilbert. Henry Gilbert from the tax office.

ALBERT: Won't you come in?

GILBERT: (CROSSES IN) Thank you. (BRIEFCASE. GLASSES)

ETHEL: (OFF) ALBERT! DID YOU FIND THE COMMUNITY CHEST CHECK!

ALBERT: Oh—well—NO DEAR . . . NEVER MIND.

ETHEL: (OFF) Well—just don't mention it at all—maybe he won't even notice it—

ALBERT: (LITTLE LAUGH) DEAR—

ETHEL: (OFF) You can always tell the tax man that it was an OUT OF POCKET contribution—I think that's what they say—

ALBERT: ETHEL!

(GILBERT CROSSES INTO L.R.)

ETHEL: (COMING DOWN)

(ALBERT CROSSES INTO L.R.)

    I'm coming right down—You can tell the tax man that you just handed over some cash for charity—and there isn't any way he can check on you—that's what a lot of people do—and—

(ALBERT IS TIGHT-LIPPED)

    What's the matter with you?

(SHE TURNS SLOWLY)

GILBERT: Shall we get started, Mr. Arbuckle?

SCENE DISSOLVES

(ETHEL AND ALBERT LAUGHING. ALBERT HAS ARM AROUND HER)

ALBERT: Well—now what did I tell you, dear—everything's all right, huh?

GILBERT: Oh yes—sure—(PUTTING ON COAT) This was just a routine check—everything seems to be in fine order—

ALBERT: Thank you . . . I'm afraid my wife was expecting to visit me in prison!

(ETHEL LAUGHS)

    Sneak a file into a cake!

GILBERT: (LAUGHS) I wish they were all like your husband. Makes our work easier when taxpayers keep nice neat accounts. Well—goodnight.

ETHEL: Do you find many people trying to—evade their tax?

GILBERT: Oh no—no indeed—you'd be surprised. Most people seem to be fundamentally honest. Many times in checking, of course, we find honest mistakes—income they FORGOT to declare—OR with a joint return such as you have—sometimes the wife might have some kind of income—perhaps it's so small she forgets about it—or she doesn't want to tell her husband just so she can have some pin money of her own—

(BOTH HE AND ALBERT LAUGH)

(ETHEL SMILES AND THEN SUDDEN THOUGHT)

> SO—as I'm leaving I always ask one last question—"Are you sure you have declared everything and that you have NO OTHER INCOME?"

ALBERT: Oh—Positive! (LAUGHS) Aren't we, dear? Wish we did—we—

(ALBERT LOOKS AT ETHEL)

ETHEL: A—

(LOOKS AT ALBERT. THEN TO GILBERT)

> Could I talk to you for just a minute?

GILBERT: (LOOKS AT ALBERT) Why—yes—surely!

(ETHEL BECKONS HIM TO ONE SIDE)

ETHEL: I don't want Mr. Arbuckle to know about this—But I do get some money from the upstairs rent of a house—and I also cook and bake things and sell them—I just wanted to ask you this one little question—would you call that income?

GILBERT: You—cook and bake things and sell them?

ETHEL: Uh-huh.

GILBERT: You—collect rent money?

ETHEL: Yes. But I wasn't sure that would be called income.

GILBERT: Yes. That's called income.

ETHEL: I haven't said anything to Albert—it's sort of a little nest egg that I've hidden away—I've been accumulating for some time—in case he loses his job or something—you know—

GILBERT: Yes. Very nice of you.

ETHEL: Thank you.

GILBERT: Uh-huh. May I ask—a—how much you have accumulated?

ETHEL: Well, I think I've done very well. It's about eleven hundred and twenty-five dollars and thirty three cents. I'm building it right up!

(GILBERT LOOKS AT HER. STARTS TO TAKE OFF COAT)

ALBERT: What's the matter?

GILBERT: It seems—

ETHEL: Don't tell him—I've wanted this to be a surprise!

GILBERT: It will be! It seems that your wife has an income.

ALBERT: Income—from WHAT?

GILBERT: From sort of a home bakery and real estate business.

ALBERT: WHAT?

ETHEL: Oh—Honestly—I didn't want you to know about it—it's what I use to buy your birthday and Christmas presents from—so I don't spend YOUR money—

ALBERT: What money do YOU have?

ETHEL: You know Mother rents out the upstairs of her house to the Wilkersons and since I own the house jointly with her—she sends me half the rent. Then I sometimes sell my devil's food cake—you know how crazy everyone always is about it—

(TO TAX MAN)

It's the dark red kind—and I have a special 22 minute frosting—

(HE NODS)

ALBERT: Never mind the frosting! Go on—Go on—

ETHEL: Then in the fall I make quite a bit of mince meat—sell that—just to my friends—kind of a secret recipe—and you know my wonderful grape jam—Well I've sold some of that.

ALBERT: Is that all?

ETHEL: Well, I've really done quite well on Argyle socks and braided rugs. And two needlepoint chair covers. Maybe a few other things.

ALBERT: (CHOKED)

(LOOKS AT TAX MAN)

How much have you made?

GILBERT: Eleven hundred and twenty-five dollars and thirty-three cents.

ALBERT: Well! Where is it,—for Pete's sakes—it isn't in our savings account!

ETHEL: Of course not! It's right here where we could get it in case you lost your job!

ALBERT: It's HERE? In the HOUSE? (BRIEF PAUSE) WHERE? WHERE IS THE MONEY?

ETHEL: In a mason jar.

ALBERT: In a mason jar! WHERE? Ethel?

ETHEL: Oh. Downstairs in the vegetable pantry on the bottom shelf in back of the watermelon pickles and the stewed tomatoes—just pull out the board.

ALBERT: Excuse me. (TO TAX MAN)

SCENE DISSOLVES TO ALBERT POURING MONEY OUT OF MASON JAR TO TABLE. MUSIC IN B.G. ALBERT POURS ANOTHER OUT AS GILBERT TALKS . . . .

GILBERT: Naturally you'll have to file amended returns for the years since you started this—and there is also the possibility, Mr. Arbuckle, that you will be in a higher tax bracket—ALSO there is accumulated interest dating from the day on which you should have reported this income—6% a year—not to mention other penalties that might be imposed. You realize, of course, Mrs. Arbuckle, what we have to do is determine how much of this was income in 1954, which is the year we are investigating. For the moment—let us discuss 1954.

SCENE DISSOLVES

(TO CARD TABLE FILLED WITH PAPERS. GILBERT AND ETHEL ARE WORKING. ALBERT IS COUNTING MONEY.)

ETHEL: Now the cake cost about 55 cents to make—the frosting about 56—so that's $1.11 . . . and I sell it for $2.50 . . . and I sold—

(LOOKING AT LITTLE BOOK)

about a cake a week . . .

GILBERT: (HARRASSED IN SHIRT SLEEVES) 52 cakes . . . $1.50 each . . .

ETHEL: Now the mince meat . . . well, about four dollars for meat—I make about two gallons of mince meat at a time—the last batch didn't turn out too well because my apples were a little too sweet—

GILBERT: Ummmmmm————

ETHEL: You need really tart apples for mince meat—but if you can't get them—put in a cup of vinegar—

ALBERT: Darling—the man doesn't care how to make mince meat!

ETHEL: He wants the expenses—and if I use vinegar which I did last time—that would be about $.10.

GILBERT: Thank you. How much mince meat did you make in 1954?

ETHEL: Roughly?

GILBERT: ANY way.

ETHEL: About 32 quarts. And I sold it for a $1.02.

GILBERT: A—why the two cents?

ETHEL: Stamps.

GILBERT: Stamps. (TO ALBERT) Been wondering for years why I didn't like mince meat—it's got stamps in it.

ETHEL: No—I mail out post cards to my friends telling them I've made it and to come and get it—

GILBERT: Ummm. Now. You say you collect $15 a month rent from your Mother's house—do you have any expenses in connection with jointly owning this home?

ETHEL: No.

ALBERT: NO EXPENSES! For Pete's sakes—it was in 1954 I paid for the new roof on your Mother's house—$350.—What do you mean—no expenses?

ETHEL: That's right—I didn't think of that as an expense—I mean—I just—well, Mother didn't ASK you to, you OFFERED to—and I'm sure if she knew you felt this way about it—she wouldn't have taken a red cent—

ALBERT: I DON'T BEGRUDGE YOUR MOTHER THE MONEY I JUST SAID IT WAS AN EXPENSE. That was the year I paid for new brass pipes for the plumbing too—and wallpaper for the downstairs. Every year it's something!

ETHEL: Mother has never ASKED you for a penny!

ALBERT: I didn't say she had!

GILBERT:

(GETTING INTO SUIT COAT)

I think I'll run along. I just remembered that my mother-in-law's visiting US and I was supposed to take them to a movie. Now don't worry. Bring all this stuff and come to my office in the morning. I didn't realize you had so many expenses in connection with that house. In fact, the way I see it—from the looks of these figures, the government may wind up owing you a refund.

ALBERT: Oh, well, that would be wonderful.

GILBERT: We'll figure it out tomorrow. Don't worry!

ALBERT: Well, I'm just terribly sorry about the whole thing.

ETHEL: I don't know why you two are making such a fuss. I simply saved money you didn't know you had. And I'll tell you this much there isn't a woman in the world that hasn't got a nest egg somewhere—even if it's a small one.

GILBERT: Not my wife! I keep track of every penny in my house!

(ETHEL LAUGHS AND HUMS AS SHE GOES TO COFFEE TABLE AND OPENS MASON JAR. THEY WATCH HER, THOUGHTFULLY. HE TURNS TO ALBERT. SLOWLY)

You know, I think I'll get on home and have a little talk with MY wife! Goodnight—Goodnight—

ALBERT: Thanks very much, sir, and I'll be at your office in the morning. Goodnight.

GILBERT: Goodnight. (GOES OUT)

ETHEL: Well, he was rather nice when he loosened up a bit, wasn't he?

ALBERT: Well!

ETHEL: Aren't you pleased? Because I saved all that money
           you're getting a refund.

ALBERT: Yes, that's wonderful . . . except, dear, . . . you haven't
           really SAVED. You just counted the money coming IN,
           not the money going OUT.

ETHEL: Well, I've GOT the money—that's all I know!

ALBERT: And it's going in the bank! Hiding it in a mason jar! For
           Pete's sakes, honey . . . that's like people who hide it in
           mattresses and old shoes. Now. Dear. (SITTING AT
           DESK) I want to have a little talk with you about money.

ETHEL:
(PICKS UP JAR. CLUTCHES IT)

           A woman likes to have a secret nest egg.

ALBERT: But a bank will give you interest on it, dear . . . . (PAPER
           AND PENCIL) Now at 2½ or three percent interest . . . .
           on $1125. . . .

ETHEL: Where's the flashlight?

ALBERT: In the back entry. Or if you invest it in some stock you
           could get as high as six percent . . . and in ten years . . .
           (FIGURING)

ETHEL: Where's the spade, dear?

ALBERT: In the garage. Let's see, ten times twenty-seven fifty—
(ETHEL TIPTOES OUT)

           —with compound interest—

(LOOKS UP)

           Spade!

(LOOKS AFTER HER. THROWS PENCIL IN AIR AND LEANS BACK IN
DESPAIR)

SCENE FADES OUT

MUSIC: UP

Suggested Exercises

1. For the next several days, keep a running tally of how many times you hear people use the term *criticism* or its derivatives. In what percentage of these cases was the term used in a negative sense? What are the implications of this finding for the practice of criticism as defined in this chapter?

2. Watch a thirty-minute television program of your choice and compile a balance sheet of its strengths and weaknesses. How do these two columns compare?

3. Repeat exercise 2, but this time, listen to a selected radio station for a one-hour period.

4. Read the following Clifford Terry review of *Harry*. Then dissect this piece as to its coverage, or lack of coverage, of each of the five steps in S. Stephenson Smith's critical process.

ARKIN HITS BOTTOM IN 'HARRY'
By Clifford Terry

Last March, Alan Arkin turned up in a based-on-fact made-for-TV movie called "A Deadly Business," bringing home one of his finest performances as a convicted forger and bank robber who turned FBI informant to blow the whistle on New Jersey's corrupt, mob-controlled toxic waste-dumping industry.

At 7:30 P.M. Wednesday night on ABC-Ch. 7, Arkin returns to prime time in a new sitcom, "Harry," and what a difference a year makes. Playing a wheeling-dealing scrounger/manipulator who works as the head of purchasing for a metropolitan hospital, he has found himself in a vehicle that could very well mark the nadir of his incredibly erratic career.

Just what kind of hustler is Harry Porschak? Well, in the opening episode alone, he collects bets for a "kidney stone pool," cleans up on "maternity bingo" and plays gin with a 78-year-old stroke victim, taking him for $650. Just what kind of hospital does Harry work in? Well, it is so poor, says one staff member, that the CAT-scan equipment "is actually powered by a cat," and the X-ray machine is so often broken that "they're reduced to asking people to *describe* their insides."

Created by Susan Kramer, the show's premise quickly wears thin, while the characters are more annoying than endearing. They include Harry's arch-enemy, the despotic, imperious Nurse Duckett (Holland Taylor of "Bosom Buddies"), who squints like Ben Turpin when she becomes exasperated; the blustery, bumbling hospital administrator (Kurt Knudson); the prudish, fastidious expediter (Thom Bray), who spies on his colleagues by hiding in lockers and garbage cans with a tape recorder; the house psychiatrist (Barbara Dana); the idiot savant math whiz (Matt Craven) and the supposedly lovable neurotic (stand-up comic Richard Lewis), who passes himself off as a doctor to his ladyfriends even though he flunked out of medical school at the University of Guatemala.

In the opener, the nurse and the expediter try to nail Porschak for allegedly peddling over $100,000 in hospital supplies for his personal gain, and the laugh-track-fortified dialogue isn't any better than the storyline.

Shrink to Harry: "I have to see a manic-depressive in two minutes. If I'm late, she gets very upset. Of course, then she gets very giddy."

Administrator to Harry: "If you've got anything to say to me—anything to get off your chest—now's the time."

Harry to administrator: "OK—I think Meryl Streep does too many accents."

ABC has stuck "Harry" into the time slot that has been occupied by one of the network's few hits, although we have been promised that Howard Hesseman and his gifted students will return to the air sometime this spring. As for now, let the record show that "Head of the Class" has been replaced by the bottom of the barrel.

(Courtesy of F. Richard Ciccone, *Chicago Tribune*)

5. Estimate the number of book reports/reviews you have completed to this point in your life. Compare this number to the approximate number of radio/television program reports you have prepared. What do you conclude from this comparison?

6. List five specific examples of how a critic can serve as audience protector.

7. Which of the dozen characteristics that constitute the critic's overall role are represented in the Don Merrill review of *L.A. Law?* Which are found in the Clifford Terry *Harry* piece printed above? In comparing the number of critic role characteristics covered by each review, which deals with more points? Does this make the piece the more effective review? Why or why not?

Chapter 2
The Critic and the Communications Process

1. Dissect Don Merrill's Chapter 1 review of *L.A. Law* by isolating which, if any, of Merrill's comments relate to (a) originator criticism, (b) message criticism, (c) medium criticism, and (d) receiver criticism.

2. Repeat exercise 1 using a review by one of your local newspaper critics as the focal point.

3. Write a one-page message-evaluating description of the worst television series you can find. Then repeat the exercise using the *best* (in your opinion) series as your referent. Which paper was easier to construct? Why?

4. Evaluate the accuracy or inaccuracy of Gunter Anders's observation about radio by citing examples from your own experience as to how you use that medium.

5. For the next six television commercials you see, speculate on the identity of their intended receivers. Were these types of receivers successfully appealed to in your estimation? Why or why not?

6. Repeat exercise 5 using the next six radio commercials you hear.

7. Repeat exercise 5 again, using a television program or a particular radio station's primary format as your subject. Is it more difficult to guess a commercial's target audience or the target for a program or format? Why?

Chapter 3
The Species of Criticism

1. Into which species of criticism would you place Alan Bunce's *Performance Today* piece in Chapter 2? Don Merrill's Chapter 1 writing on *L.A. Law?* Are there elements of more than one critical species in either of these columns?

2. Read the following Ed Bark critique. Does it relate to one or more than one critical species? Which? What statements within the Bark article most lead you to your conclusion?

'NIGHTLINE' IS ARENA IN MAYOR'S RACE
By Ed Bark

Don't ignore those candidate forums, but know that ABC's *Nightline* is the main arena for Dallas' major mayoral candidates.

It's where the elite meet to show their 30-second spots. Tune in any *Nightline* next week, and you'll be swayed or dismayed by words, images and music from the video campaigns of Jim Buerger, Jim Collins, Fred Meyer or Annette Strauss. Collins hasn't bought nearly as many 30-second commercials as his opponents, but he'll be making an unprecedented video appeal on election eve. His *Insight: A Dallas Mayor's Campaign,* a half-hour commercial for Collins' candidacy, is scheduled to be telecast at 7:30 P.M. Friday on Channel 27. Channel 8 is charging Collins $30,000 for the privilege of pre-empting ABC's *The Charmings.* Each *Nightline* ad has a price tag of $1,150. The station limits candidates to two *Nightline* appearances per week, to keep their messages from colliding during the same commercial break.

IDEAL AUDIENCE

Nightline is a strong vehicle for any candidate running for anything. Seen in an average of 100,000 homes nightly in the Dallas–Fort Worth viewing area, the program attracts an upscale audience with an appetite for public affairs and a probable interest in voting.

Thursday's *Nightline* accommodated commercials for Buerger, Strauss and Meyer. Make no mistake, this is where the real candidate debates are taking place. Some impressions:

Buerger, who was first out of the box with a blitz of TV spots last month, used his visually arresting law-'n'-order spot. Resembling one of the "Crimestoppers" segments on Channel 5's newscasts, it exploits the base fears of the electorate. We see stand-ins for a police officer, a citizen and a thug. We hear a narrator warn, "Today, police officers are forced to spend thousands of man-hours writing traffic tickets." (The voice drips with disdain for "traffic tickets.")

"Meanwhile," the narrator continues, "the Dallas police are so understaffed, it takes nearly 10 minutes to respond to crimes."

The words are reinforced by pictures of a hammer smashing through a window, the flash of a switchblade knife, a woman screaming as she is grabbed from behind and finally a gun going off, with the barrel pointed directly at viewers. All the while, an officer is seen dutifully writing out a traffic ticket to an attractive woman.

TAILORING THE IMAGE

Then comes Buerger, looking relaxed in his living-room easy chair. His wife and two daughters are at his side, innocently playing a board game on a coffee table. We wouldn't want them hurt, would we?

"Let's be careful on the roads," Buerger says. "Traffic safety is important, but so is fighting crime. As mayor, we'll take up to half the officers now writing tickets and transfer 'em to neighborhood patrol. Makes sense, doesn't it?"

The Strauss spot is 30 seconds of plain talk, with the candidate shown, studio-portrait style, against an unadorned, light gray backdrop. Strauss tells voters she is woman enough for the job of mayor.

"Some say that Dallas is not ready for a woman mayor," she says in part. "I disagree. I'm Annette Strauss, and I think the voters will look at qualifications and record of experience. Protecting our neighborhoods, strengthening business and fighting crime and drugs are not jobs for a beginner. I'm running on a record of performance, not on promises."

The delivery is good, and the candidate is photographed flatteringly. But the spot is not particularly memorable, save for its starkness.

Meyer is portrayed as a flesh-pumping man of action. A narrator extols the candidate's business sense and leadership qualities, while Meyer joyously shakes hands with a black man, a fireman and a good ol' boy in a western-cut shirt and gimme cap. The musically accompanied spot opens in the manner of the TV series *Dallas,* with three framed scenes of the city giving way to "Dallas" spelled in bold block letters. The final image is a freeze frame of Meyer reaching out to shake someone else's hand while surrounded by buoyant supporters hoisting his campaign placards.

Meyer himself speaks only briefly. "Our No. 1 job is to build economic opportunities in every area of our city," he says from a lectern.

It is a slick, traditional and ordinary spot.

Calculating, but effective use of television gave Buerger the edge in Thursday's *Nightline* "debate."

(Reprinted with permission of *The Dallas Morning News)*

3. To ascertain this column's function beyond mere personality portraiture, list the things learned about the broadcast media's workings from reading Jim McFarlin's profile of Bob Allison.

4. Fashion five current topics that, in your market, would make for an effective audience reaction column. Have any of these topics been discussed recently by local or national critics? Why, or why not, do you suppose?

5. Assume that a given program being aired this evening has come to you via preview cassette. Write a 300-word preview of it that covers what you believe to be the most important consumer advisory elements.

6. For the next two to three weeks, keep a record of the television programs reviewed or previewed by critics appearing in your local newspaper. What percentage of the shows selected for critical treatment are *audience* successes? On the other hand, what percentage are clear failures from a rating/share standpoint? Do(es) the critic(s) more often agree with or contradict consumer preferences as revealed by the numbers? What does this suggest about the critic orientation toward the public?

7. What, as presented in her "Prime Time Cereal" piece, are Janet Maslin's contentions about broadcast/cable advertising? If you were to compose a similar piece using cat and dog food advertising as your focus, what contentions would flow from your opinion essay?

Chapter 4
Knowledge Processing

1. Is Jim McFarlin's Chapter 3 piece on Bob Allison empirical, normative, or both? Cite specific evidence from this article to support your conclusion.

2. Repeat exercise 1 with Marc Gunther's "A Man and a Woman" preview (also in Chapter 3) as your focus.

3. Figure the share, rating, and CPM in the case of a population of 1.5 million with a sample size of 220, of which 134 are viewing TV, 56 are tuned to our program, and a 30-second commercial costs $1,750.

4. The following Ed Bark critique would seem primarily to deal with the scientific way of knowing. Does it also contain vestiges of (a) the mystic and/or (b) the rhetorician? If so, what portions of Bark's piece evidence these approaches?

CHANNEL 8 UPSET WITH ARBITRON
By Ed Bark

Most viewers have a healthy distrust of the ratings.

When a favorite show is canceled, the standard response is, "They never asked me what I watch." It's a helpless feeling. Ratings seem to be mysterious marauders, arriving black-caped in the dark to steal away a loved one.

Sometimes television stations get the same impression. In the Dallas–Fort Worth viewing area, Channel 8 executives say they are tired of being taken for a roller-coaster ride by the Arbitron ratings service, which is in competition with the A.C. Nielsen Co. for the big money stations pay in return for audience information. For the first time in this market, Arbitron, in a recent letter to Channel 8, has acknowledged several problems and promised to correct them in time for the four-week May ratings sweeps, an audience measurement period used by stations to set advertising rates.

"There's too much at stake for them (Arbitron) not to do a better job," Channel 8 sales manager Buff Parham said Monday. "Hopefully, they realize how crucial the problem is."

If not, "the rhetorical question is how long can we afford bad data?" Parham said. For Arbitron, that's a chilling question. Channel 8, the area's ABC affiliate station, is Arbitron's most valuable client in the D/FW market. Channel 4 (CBS) and Channel 5 (NBC) subscribe only to Nielsen. Channel 8 takes both services, but anything can happen in a soft economy.

Channel 8 and Arbitron have been at odds since October about how Arbitron selects the 400 D/FW households it has equipped with computerized ratings meters. Overnight ratings from these meters supply stations with the audience numbers they use to sell advertising time locally. In the view of Parham and Channel 8 research director Christi Keane, Arbitron's ratings have bounced up and down too much in comparison to Nielsen's.

"If they were consistently low or high, that would be all right," Keane said.

In a four-page letter sent to Keane March 20, Arbitron acknowledged that from late 1986 to January 1987, its sample of metered households became "progressively weaker" in these areas:

* Adults ages 18 to 34 who are heads of households.
* One-to-two person households vs. three-to-four person households.
* Single TV set households vs. multiset households.
* Hispanic households.

The weaknesses in these viewer groups are "a repeat of something experienced earlier in 1986 in Houston," Arbitron says. "Younger households seem to be more affected by the economy. They are turning over at a more rapid rate than anticipated. Replacements are not coming as quickly as planned."

Younger households, under-represented in Arbitron's sampling, are affecting the three other subgroups, too. "They are all tied together," Arbitron says.

It all sounds rather Byzantine until Arbitron concludes that Channel 8 is strong among "the types of households that switch channels most often. . . . These are the subgroups that deteriorated in Arbitron's meter sample in late 1986."

For instance, if Arbitron has an inadequate sampling of Hispanic households, then are Channel 8's 10 P.M. newscasts, simulcast in Spanish on KESS–AM radio, being shortchanged?

Efforts are being made to correct these imbalances, Arbitron says. So what do we have here? Is it an instance of a powerful station leaning on a vulnerable ratings service and threatening to cancel it unless the ratings improve?

No, says Parham, because Channel 8 was satisfied with its performance in Arbitron's four-week February ratings sweeps book.

"But we're not happy with how we got there," he said. "We had a good book, and the sample was still screwed up."

Channel 8's 10 P.M. newscasts in fact had slightly higher ratings in Arbitron than in Nielsen during the February sweeps. But Arbitron gave lower marks than Nielsen to the station's 5, 6 and 6:30 P.M. newscasts and important syndicated programs such as *The Oprah Winfrey Show, Hour Magazine, Entertainment Tonight* and *Donahue.*

If Channel 8's Arbitron numbers perk up significantly in the May Sweeps, do Channels 4 and 5 have the right to be skeptical?

Parham laughed and let the question pass.

(Reprinted with permission of *The Dallas Morning News*)

5. Is the Don Merrill Chapter 1 review of *L.A. Law* a good example of the way of the critic? To answer this question, analyze it in the same manner that we analyzed David Remnick's *Playground Pros* piece.

6. Listen to one hour of programming on a tightly formatted music radio station. Now, write three brief descriptions of this experience—one from each of the perceptual triad perspectives.

7. Repeat exercise 6 using an hour-long television program as your referent. Was exercise 6 or 7 easier to accomplish? Why?

8. Dissect the Clifford Terry preview of *Harry* presented in the Chapter 1 exercises in this Appendix as to how it reflects, or does not reflect, each plane of the perceptual triad. Does your finding dovetail with how informative or uninformative you perceived this particular preview to be?

Chapter 5
Productional Ingredients

1. Using a one-hour action/adventure program as your subject, analyze the contribution made by, and appropriateness of, its musical soundtrack. Is the music a programmatic enhancement or is it a crutch for shoddy plot or dialogue? Would the music be missed if omitted? Are its instrumentation, tempo, type, and volume well suited to the program's character?

2. Compose a critique that compares an hour's programming on two competing radio stations as to clarity, execution, continuity, and aptness of task. Which of these four elements was easiest to discuss? Which most difficult? Why?

3. Cite your own experience to explain Parker's comment that, "In music we get so close to ourselves that at times it is almost frightening."

4. Dissect Alan Bunce's Chapter 2 review of *Performance Today* to ascertain if or how he commented on the program's musical clarity, execution, continuity, and aptness of task.

5. Examine the late news shows of two local television stations. How do the on-camera talent try to behave as trustworthy friends? Which station's performers are most successful in this regard? Does this also make that station's newscast the better of the two? By what criteria is better to be judged?

6. Watch a game show host other than Pat Sajak and analyze his performance in terms of the following: (a) communication with the viewer; (b) communication with the studio audience; (c) communication with the contestants; (d) techniques of and success at controlling the pace of the show.

7. Analyze the nonverbal communication of the actors in a selected sitcom. How much of this nonverbal portrayal would be discernible to the audience if the show was performed on a stage instead of on television?

8. Repeat exercise 7 using a different sitcom. Then compare the two shows as to the amount and clarity of their casts' nonverbal communication.

9. In the case of exercise 7 (and, if completed, exercise 8), how many of the detected nonverbal behaviors were set up by a directorial shot change? In what percentage of cases was the shot change necessary to audience perception of the behavior?

10. List and compare the number of separate shots in two different sitcoms. Is there a relationship between number of shots and show pacing? Between number of shots and amount of dialogue? Between number of shots and sense of viewer involvement?

11. Repeat exercise 10 using two action/adventure shows as your subjects.

12. Repeat exercise 10 using episodes from two soap operas as your subjects.

13. Applying our explanation of the horizontal camera plane's shot types, write a technical description of each shot in the Michelob Classic Dark commercial in Chapter 4.

14. Select a one-hour drama or action/adventure show for viewing. Analyze that production's exploitation of the vertical camera plane. Is the exploitation a help or a hinderance to character development? To the sense of character interaction?

15. View any sitcom episode. While watching, note the occasions when you do not feel yourself placed at Pepper's "point of optimum receptivity." Were these occasions a help or hinderance to your sense of involvement in the storyline?

16. Repeat exercise 15 using a one-hour drama or action/adventure show as the object of analysis.

17. Dissect Tom Shale's Chapter 4 review of *A Year in the Life* to discover if and how he discussed each of television's six visual stage-molding ingredients.

18. Repeat exercise 17 with David Remnick's Chapter 4 *Playground Pros* preview as your referent.

19. Listen to sixty minutes of a music-formatted radio station in order to analyze how aural volume and transitions are used or abused in the hour's various program elements. What, if anything, would you have done differently to further format cohesion?

Chapter 6
Business Gratifications

1. Define what, in your estimation, constitutes "the public interest." In light of your definition, which broadcast or cable offerings seem the *most* effective public interest servants? Which seem the *least* effective in this role? How do your *most* and *least* selections compare in terms of their apparent business/financial success?

2. Analyze the radio stations in your locality in terms of the specific audience that you believe each is trying to attract. Which stations seem the most successful in this regard? To what factors would you attribute their success?

3. List the specific business gratifications alluded to in the *Broadcasting* article on *Amerika*. Which of these apparently were achieved by the show and which were not?

4. Repeat exercise 3 using Ed Bark's "Channel 8 Upset with Arbitron" piece printed in this Appendix's Chapter 4 exercises as your point of reference. In this case, what business gratifications has the station achieved or failed to achieve?

5. Repeat exercise 3 using Jim McFarlin's Chapter 3 profile of Bob Allison as your referent. In this instance, how did Allison's business gratification goals (a) parallel and (b) clash with the goals of the stations employing him?

6. Isolate at least six specific examples of counterprogramming by television stations in your market. What universe is each station apparently trying to reach in this endeavor? Is this counterprogramming maintained or abandoned in preceding and following shows?

7. As an ABC programming executive, what would you recommend to mitigate John Sias's problems in scheduling the start of *ABC Monday Night Football?* As a critic, would your recommendation be any different? Why or why not?

8. Listen to an hour of a radio station's programming and try graphically to construct the hot clock it seems to be using. Listen also to the preceding hour to see if, or how, the hot clock changes.

9. Repeat exercise 8 with a closely competing station. Do the two stations' hot clocks seem to mirror each other or do they evidence counterprogramming strategies?

10. Answer the chapter's five schedule and flow analysis questions in terms of the 9 P.M. programs aired by two competing television stations in your market.

Chapter 7
Audience Gratifications

1. What, according to Tom Shales's Chapter 4 preview of *A Year in the Life,* are the gratifications the audience might derive from this show? Which of these gratifications apparently would not be shared by Shales himself?

2. According to Lon Tuck's Chapter 5 piece on WGMS, which of the seven use/gratification factors does that station seem to be providing to its listeners?

3. Repeat exercise 2 in terms of WKBD's movies as described in Marc Gunther's Chapter 6 "Looking at the Big Picture" column.

4. Select a one-hour television series and write your own analysis of the use/gratification factors it is most likely to service. Include in your assessment which of these factors would not be appealing to you personally and why.

5. Watch a vintage sitcom and compare its gratifications with those provided by a first-run sitcom. In what ways, if any, do the gratification patterns vary between the two shows? What, in your opinion, are the reasons for this variation or the lack of it?

6. Repeat exercise 5 using two different programs.

7. Repeat exercise 5 by cross-comparing the programs studied in exercises 5 and 6. Do your findings remain fundamentally the same regardless of which old show is compared to which new show? What is/are the reason(s) for this consistency or inconsistency?

8. Read *The Cosby Show* script in Appendix A. To which audience gratifications does it seem to cater? Would these gratifications vary from one demographic group to another?

9. Repeat exercise 8 using the *Ethel and Albert* script in Appendix B. In addition to the questions posed above, ask yourself whether this show's gratification patterns would be different for a viewer in the 1950s than for a viewer of today.

10. List your own four best media friends as found in either radio or television programming. What is it about them (and about the programs on which they appear) that makes them so appealing to you?

11. State the precise problem-solving claims made by each of the next six radio commercials you hear and the next six television commercials you see. What devices were used to convey these solutions? Were any other gratifications involved in these commercials?

12. Compare how problems are developed in a soap opera installment and in an episode of a sitcom. How many problems are present and how many are solved within each show's boundaries?

13. Into which of Gans's "taste publics" do you fall? Into which do/did your parents and grandparents fall? How do your program choices reflect or contradict your taste-public membership? How do/did your parents' choices reflect or contradict theirs?

14. Select what in your opinion is the most violent program series currently on the air. Write a position paper on it that addresses the question of whether the series' violence, in whole or part, would seem to have a socially beneficial catharsis effect. What type of viewer would be most incited (positively or negatively) by this violence?

Chapter 8:
Probing Ethics and Values

1. Watch three continuous hours of television programming on a single channel. Make a list of all the values that are expressed or implied during these three hours (in the aired commercials as well as the programs).

2. Repeat exercise 1 during the same time of day, but watching a different channel. Do the values displayed vary between the two channels in number or type? What is the reason for this similarity or discrepancy?

3. Reread Marc Gunther's Chapter 3 piece on "A Man and a Woman." As evidenced in this writing, what personal values does Gunther himself seem to hold?

4. Repeat exercise 3 using Janet Maslin's Chapter 3 essay on "Prime Time Cereal" as your subject.

5. Select a one-hour dramatic series and analyze how it serves or fails to serve each of the six elements that Ralph Smith found critics to value.

6. Repeat exercise 5 using a news-magazine, talk show, or sitcom as your subject.

7. Scrutinize the Ed Bark 'Nightline' column printed in this Appendix's Chapter 3 exercises. Which element or elements that Ralph Smith found critics to value was evidenced in the commercials for each of the Bark-mentioned candidates? Which of these values does Bark seem most to favor—or can't this be inferred from his writing?

8. Cite at least four electronic media portrayals that would support Parker's contention that "the good must know its alternative or it is not good."

9. Should J. B. Stoner's commercial have been guaranteed broadcast access? Is there any other type of message that should be accorded such guarantee? Write a brief opinion essay that sets forth and illustrates your position.

10. As a critic, can you evolve a defense of a Family Viewing plan? Could you devise a way by which such a plan could function effectively while still being constitutional?

11. Reread Jim McFarlin's Chapter 3 profile of Bob Allison. Are elements of the Protestant ethic and/or social Darwinism alluded to? If so, does each element seem to reflect the views of Allison, of McFarlin, or of the Detroit electronic media establishment?

12. Select any sitcom, drama, or action/adventure episode and dissect how it mirrors or contradicts Protestant ethic and social Darwinism tenets.

13. Repeat exercise 12 using a newscast as your point of reference. Watch the newscast for three succeeding days before drawing your conclusions.

14. Repeat exercise 13 by choosing a newscast from a different station or network. Are the Protestant ethic and social Darwinism present to the same degree on both channels? Why or why not?

15. Read the *Ethel and Albert* script in Appendix B and analyze how it embraces or avoids the Protestant ethic and social Darwinism.

16. What specific values does Scott Bennett espouse in his "Static in TV Preacherland" piece? Are these values related to the Protestant ethic and/or social Darwinism?

Chapter 9
Aesthetics and Art

1. Listen to an hour of a given radio station's music programming. Then write five brief aesthetic analyses of it as seen from the respective orientations of Absolutism, Individualism, Objectivism, Cultural Relativism, and Biopsychological Relativism.

2. Repeat exercise 1 using a one-hour television series as your referent.

3. Inventory all the possible pleasures of *A Year in the Life* that Tom Shales isolates in his Chapter 4 preview. Which of these pleasures seem to be enjoyed by Shales himself?

4. Repeat exercise 3 using Tony Scott's Chapter 8 preview of *LBJ: The Early Years* as your reference point.

5. According to his Chapter 1 review, which of art's six tasks does Don Merrill believe to be served by *L.A. Law?* Cite specific quotes from Merrill's piece to document your findings.

6. Repeat exercise 5 using Lon Tuck's Chapter 5 review of WGMS as your subject.

7. View a game show and identify which of art's six tasks it seems to fulfill. Then view another game show and conduct the same analysis. Are the two programs similar or divergent in the artistic tasks they meet?

8. Repeat exercise 7 using two soap operas. What (if any) artistic task-serving is common to both game show and soap opera genres? Which tasks apparently are not served by either program type?

9. Examine the Philips Lighting (Chapter 8), Michelob and Celentano (both Chapter 4) television commercials and ascertain which of the six artistic tasks each seeks to serve.

10. Repeat exercise 9 in terms of the following radio spots: First Federal Savings (Chapter 2) Lotus Esprit Turbo (Chapter 4) and Newscastle Brown (Chapter 5). Does there seem to be any significant difference between the artistic tasks served by radio as contrasted with television spots?

11. List your three favorite role models as chosen from characters in currently running television series. Contrast these with what, in your opinion, are the three least desirable role models. What particular qualities motivated your assessment?

12. Repeat exercise 11 using newspersons as your referents.

13. Reread Lon Tuck's Chapter 5 piece on WGMS in order to isolate the tension-release factors he believes this station provides. Compare these tension-relieving elements with those of *Training Camp* as revealed in John O'Connor's Chapter 7 review. How do these two critics indicate their approval or disapproval of the tension-release mechanisms they detected in their sub-jects?

14. Find a television program (nonnews) that you believe "inspires fear, distrust and indignation." Describe how this inspiration is realized and whether you believe this to perform a positive service for the audience.

15. Repeat exercise 14 using a current radio-featured song lyric as your referent.

16. Analyze the *Ethel and Albert* script in Appendix B as to how many of the six artistic tasks this episode accomplished and how this accomplishment was handled.

17. Keep a log for several days of your own radio/television program choices. Then label each choice as to whether it primarily represents a fine, folk, or popular art orientation.

18. Select one complete day's programming out of *TV Guide* and at-tempt to categorize each program as a fine, folk, or popular art. Where were the fine and folk arts most likely to be found (at what times and on what pro-gram services)?

Chapter 10
The Logic of Aesthetic Form

1. Reread Lon Tuck's WGMS piece in Chapter 5 to ascertain whether he believes that station's programming possesses organic unity.

2. Write your own critique of a local radio station's three-hour program block with the concept of organic unity as your focal point.

3. Repeat exercise 2 using a different radio station. In comparing the two outlets, does the one possessing the greater sense of organic unity also seem to be the "better" station? By what criteria did you arrive at this determination?

4. Scrutinize the 6 P.M.-to-midnight programming of a local network affiliate television station. Does its schedule suggest the presence of organic unity? Why or why not?

5. Repeat exercise 4 using an independent (nonnetwork) station. Which of the two stations' schedules seems to be the more organically unified? Can you speculate on the reason(s)?

6. Isolate the theme of the next six television commercials you see. Does the theme's articulation rest more on visual or aural parts of the communica-tion?

7. Watch a made-for-TV movie. List how many and what type(s) of the-matic variation are contained therein. Did each of these variations assist or in-hibit your enjoyment of the feature?

8. Analyze how the newscast on two local television stations are/are not balanced as to (a) point of view within controversial stories, (b) heavy and soft news features, (c) feature length, (d) on-camera talent type and use.

9. Reread Mike Harris's Chapter 9 review of *The Australian Film Institute Awards* in order to uncover the specific balance lacks that harmed the telecast.

10. Plot the evolution of a daytime soap opera during the course of a week. What factors seem to determine the evolutionary pace? Does evolution ever break down? If so, where and why?

11. Repeat exercise 10 with a single episode of an action/adventure show as your subject. What are the differences in evolution's handling within a self-contained action/adventure episode as compared to the continuing episodes of a five-day-a-week soap?

12. Critique and compare the evolution of two competing radio stations' morning drive-time programming.

13. Graph the hierarchical patterns of an episode from each of two different action/adventure shows. Is the show with the more skillful hierarchy also the better show overall? Why or why not?

14. Repeat exercise 13 using two sitcoms as your referents.

15. Prepare your own logic of aesthetic form critique of *The Cosby Show* script in Appendix A.

16. Conduct a logic of aesthetic form analysis of a current dramatic series episode.

17. Repeat exercise 16, focusing on a different dramatic series. Is the show that better conforms to Parker's logic also the more enjoyable one for you? Is it also the most appealing one for the public as evidenced by the comparative ratings and shares? If not, why not in your estimation?

18. Repeat exercise 16 and 17 using two sitcoms (other than *The Cosby Show*) as your subjects.

19. Analyze Tom Shales's Chapter 4 preview of *A Year in the Life* as to how many logic of aesthetic form components it covers.

Chapter 11
Depiction Analysis

1. Describe, in as detailed a manner as possible, the physical environment in which a selected, locale-specified sitcom or dramatic series is placed. Based on your own knowledge, what elements of this depiction clash most with the reality of that locale?

2. Reread Ed Bark's *Nightline* political commercial column printed in this Appendix's Chapter 3 exercises. What is society like (at least, in Dallas) according to the political spots Bark described? Do the social depictions in these messages clash with one another? Do we have any clues as to Bark's own conceptualization of Dallas society?

3. How is the ethnic or occupational group to which you belong depicted in the electronic media? Write a brief critique that cites specific examples of your findings and takes a position on the legitimacy or fraudulence of these depictions.

4. Analyze five radio commercials and five television commercials from the standpoint of the consequences predictions they make. Which consequences are reasonable based on normal product category expectations? Which are outlandish or incredible?

5. Watch a daytime soap opera for a three-day period. What does it show to be the consequences of sex and love? Does it define or distinguish between these two concepts in any way?

6. Listen to three hours of radio music programming. In terms of the lyrics aired, answer the same questions posed in exercise 5.

7. Select an episode of an action/adventure show and list each act of physical violence. In how many acts are the consequences of that violence sanitized?

8. Repeat exercise 7 focusing on another action/adventure program. Which program is more violent? Which program is more unrealistic because of the percentage of its violence that is sanitized?

9. What are the consequences of actions as depicted in the cereal commercials discussed by Janet Maslin in her Chapter 3 "Prime Time Cereal" commentary? Does Maslin find these consequences credible?

10. Select two television series in which parenting is a prominent depiction. How are the responsibilities of parenting shown in each program? Are there major differences between the two about what these responsibilities are? Are there differences as to the advocated methods for carrying out these responsibilities?

11. Study the visual (on-location) stories in a network newscast. In which cases did the picture seem more important than the subject of the story itself?

12. Repeat exercise 11 by focusing on a local station newscast. Did it appear more or less susceptible than the network to the emphasis of pictorial values over substantive content?

13. Identify the self-evaluative standards taught by the following spots: the Red Cross "rescue" (Chapter 7), the J. B. Stoner candidacy pitch (Chapter 9), and the John Smith's Yorkshire Bitter "anniversary" (Chapter 10).

14. Watch three different sitcoms. How is happiness defined in each? How much importance does the program attach to the pursuit of happiness?

15. Repeat exercise 14 using three game shows as your point of attention. As a group, do the sitcoms or the game shows make happiness attainment more important as a self-evaluative standard? Why is this the case?

16. Conduct your own five-part depiction analysis of an hour-long drama or action/adventure program.

17. Repeat exercise 16 using a newscast as your referent.

18. Use *The Cosby Show* script in Appendix A as the subject for a complete depiction critique.

Chapter 12
Symbols, Myths, and Structures

1. Analyze two current sitcoms as to the possible presence and interaction of *alazons, eirons, bomolochoi,* and *agroikos* within them. Is the show that more clearly and extensively mirrors these types the more enjoyable program? Why or why not?

2. Identify and explain the symbols used in the "I Am Michigan" television spot presented in Chapter 11. Which of these symbols could as easily be used in the promotion of *any* state? Which seem exclusive to Michigan? Which could be used by some states but not by others?

3. Listen to a selected disc jockey's entire on-air shift. What symbols/ archetypes does the disc jockey exploit in developing communication with the audience?

4. Describe the problem-solving progression (rituals) used in the episodes of two currently aired sitcoms. Was the ritual of one show more believable (more mystique-rich) than that of the other? If so, did this believability make it the more enjoyable sitcom? Why or why not?

5. Repeat exercise 4 using two action/adventure programs as your subjects.

6. Analyze the ritual put in place by your favorite radio station's morning drive-time programming. Does this ritual mirror your own morning lifecycle? If so, via what devices?

7. Scott Bennett's Chapter 8 commentary on "TV's Preacherland" to a large extent deals with mystique. As Bennett defines it, what is this specific mystique? What created it? Can it and should it be sustained by the electronic media?

8. During a period of a week's viewing, compile a list of myths that were conveyed by the programs you observed. Are any of Vonier's items also on your list?

9. Dissect five television news-magazine stories to see whether they mirror a thesis/antithesis/synthesis progression. Do the stories that conform to this progression seem more or less complete than other stories? More or less balanced? More or less accurate?

10. Describe how the thesis/antithesis/synthesis structure is exploited in Chapter 4's Michelob Dark "Soy Sauce" television commercial.

11. Find two other sitcoms that, like *The Cosby Show* and *Ethel and Albert*, regularly follow the thesis/antithesis/synthesis pattern.

12. Ascertain the signifier/signified/sign components of the next six television commercials to which you are exposed.

13. Repeat exercise 12 for the next six radio commercials you hear. Is this structure more difficult or easier to detect in radio than in television? Why?

14. Discuss the semiotic structure of the Barbra Streisand *One Voice* special as described in the chapter's John O'Connor preview. In the critic's view, did the selected signifier/signified/sign elements make the program more or less effective than it might otherwise have been? What first, second, and third order signs were relied on? Was this reliance justifiable? Why or why not?

15. What are the first, second, and third order signs in the two Marcy Fitness commercials described by Barbara Lippert in her Chapter 9 review? What is the critic's attitude toward the appropriation of these signs and the interrelationship the spots seem to establish between them?

Chapter 13
Composite Criticism

1. Isolate all the intrinsic appreciation elements mentioned by Don Merrill in his Chapter 1 *L.A. Law* critique and by Marc Gunther in his Chapter 3 "A Man and a Woman" piece.

2. Watch the television program you dislike the most and write an intrinsic appreciation inventory for it. Make this inventory as extensive as possible.

3. Apply George Wilson's extrinsic appreciation checklist to a prime-time television program of your choice.

4. Repeat exercise 3 by adapting the checklist to preparation of an extrinsic appreciation of a local radio station's early evening program block.

5. Isolate the extrinsic appreciation elements in Lon Tuck's Chapter 5 piece on WGMS and Marc Gunther's Chapter 6 column, "Looking at the Big Picture."

6. Reread the Clifford Terry preview of *Harry* printed in this Appendix's Chapter 1 exercises. List all of Terry's intrinsic evaluation comments and, across from them, all of his intrinsic appreciation statements. Are these two lists balanced? If not, what does the imbalance imply about the show and/or about the critic?

7. Find the intrinsic evaluation elements in Tony Scott's Chapter 8 preview of *LBJ: The Early Years* and in Jim Bawden's preview of *The War Reporters* in Chapter 11.

8. Use George Wilson's "Impact" instrument to conduct an extrinsic evaluation of an action/adventure or dramatic series episode.

9. Repeat exercise 8 with a sitcom as your subject. Does Wilson's instrument seem to work more or less effectively in an extrinsic evaluation of this program genre? Why?

10. Cull out the extrinsic evaluation aspects of Jim McFarlin's Chapter 3 profile on Bob Allison and of David Remnick's *Playground Pros* preview in Chapter 4.

11. Conduct a composite critique of *The Cosby Show* script in Appendix A.

12. Repeat exercise 11 with the *Ethel and Albert* script in Appendix B as the referent. (Keep in mind the chapter-presented information about the program's history and production.)

Index

A

ABC, 40–41, 42–43, 71, 103–105, 108–109,
    111, 116, 121, 128, 134, 137, 139,
    140, 190, 249, 258, 262, 316,
    317–318
ABC Monday Night Football, 108–109, 128
Absolutism, 156
Access, 142–145
Action/adventure programs, 31, 64, 92, 128,
    169, 180, 183, 203, 227, 253–255
Actors, television, 85–87
Adam–12, 211
Advertising:
    business of, 9, 10, 45–47, 102, 103, 105,
        107, 108, 110, 126, 134
    examples of, 30–31, 80–81, 122–124, 143,
        165–166, 169–170, 181, 182,
        186–187, 204, 207–208, 214,
        222–223, 229–232, 234–235, 236,
        239–241, 243
    structure of, 15, 137, 180, 186, 191–192,
        234–235, 239–241, 242, 251

techniques of, 13, 14, 139, 167–168,
    184–185, 196, 203, 207, 213, 222,
    224, 226, 229, 242
Adweek, 167–168, 184–185
Aesthetics, defined, 155–156, 163
Afterschool Specials, 139
Agroikos, 224–225
Alazons, 223–224
Allen, Leslie, 8, 9
Alley, Robert, 138
All in the Family, 14, 210, 211, 253
Alternation, 184
Altheide, David, 75, 79
American Academy of Pediatrics, 208
Amerika, 40–41, 103–105, 111
Amos and Andy, 206
AM radio, 50, 74–75, 76–77, 106, 119, 121
Anders, Gunther, 28
Anderson, James, 211
Antin, David, 94
Antithesis, 233–237
Appreciation, defined, 247
Aptness of task (musical), 79–82
Archetypes, 223–227

Aristotle, 127–128, 178, 224
Arizona Daily Star, 36
Arlen, Michael, 94
Arnheim, Rudolf, 79, 86, 165, 192, 228, 257
Art:
　defined, 163
　sources of, 171–174
Artistic tasks, 163–171
Ask Your Neighbor, 36–39, 83
Audience reaction column, 35, 39–41, 47
Australian Film Institute Awards, 161–162
Awards, 13, 161–162

B

Bach, Johann Sebastian, 161
Balance, 185–189, 190, 193, 195, 196–197
Balanchine, George, 64
Banks, Allen, 138–139
Baran, Stanley, 84
Barbra Streisand: One Voice, 237–238
Bardic mediator, 146
Bark, Ed, 249–250, 317–318, 320–321
Bawden, Jim, 211–212, 260–262
BBC (British Broadcasting Corporation), 10,
　53, 125
Beacon Hill, 158
Beardsley, Monroe, 2, 3, 12, 164, 165–167,
　199
Becker, Alton, 59
Becker, Samuel, 72, 101
Bednarski, P. J., 16
Beerman, Frank, 253–255
Beethoven, Ludwig van, 158, 161, 172–173
Bell, Clive, 13, 156
Bennett, Scott, 151–153
Bernikow, Louise, 121, 126
Beverly Hillbillies, 53
Bierbaum, Tom, 140
Biopsychological relativism, 160–162, 189
Blackmur, Richard, 13
"Blue Book," 10–11, 53
Blue Knight, 211
Boas, George, 99, 151, 179, 251, 252

Bomolochoi, 224–226
Book reports, 6
Breakfast Club, 259
Broadcast Education Association (BEA), 103
Broadcasting, 103–105
Brown, Les, 11, 20, 29, 35, 101, 103, 111, 112
Browning, Robert, 164
Bullard, George, 21
Bunce, Alan, 24–27, 29–30, 32, 43, 83, 179,
　196
Bunzel, Peter, 23–24
Businessmen, portrayal of, 138, 211

C

Cagney & Lacey, 203
Camera/character arrangement, 92, 96,
　178–179
Camera in motion, 93, 96
Camera planes, 90–92, 93, 96
Camera shot types, 90, 91, 93, 94–95, 96
Canada, 158–160, 212–213, 260–262
Cannon, 31
Caplan, Gerald, 159–160
Car & Driver, 44
Carson, Johnny, 121, 141
Casualness, 141
Catharsis, 127–128
Cavell, Stanley, 191
Cawelti, John, 44, 86, 233
CBN (Christian Broadcasting Network), 139
CBS, 7, 8, 31, 102, 103, 104, 105, 108, 111,
　119, 144, 158, 249, 258–259
Channels of Communication, 20, 101, 103
Cheers, 224–225, 228
Chiaroscuro lighting, 88
Chicago Sun-Times, 16
Chicago Tribune, 15, 133–135, 187–189,
　225–226, 315–316
Chilberg, Joseph, 91–92
Children's programming, 136, 138–139, 143,
　144–145, 167, 191, 206–207, 215
Christian Science Monitor, 8, 9, 24–27,
　29–30

Clarity (musical), 74–75, 82
Clios, 13
CNN (Cable Network News), 106, 183
Cohen, Hilary, 23
Cohen, William, 205–206
Colbys, 86
Coles, Robert, 215
Collison, Perce, 8
Commercials. *See* Advertising
Communications Act of 1934, 142–143
Communicator, defined, 22
Companion-seeking, 120–122
Comstock, George, 116, 128
Consequences, depicted, 207–210, 216, 218
Continuity (musical), 78–79, 82
Cooney, Joan Ganz, 139
Copeland, Gary, 127
Copland, Aaron, 64–65, 68, 71–72, 73, 234
Cosby Show, 40, 108, 111, 119, 150–151,
    170–171, 206, 209, 228, 237, 257,
    267–295
Cost-per-thousand (CPM), 55, 102, 107
Counterprogramming, 107
Crime Story, 253–255
Critic:
    background of, 19–21
    burden of, 13
    as entertainer, 15–16
    as guide, 11–12
    role of, 11–17
    way of the, 60–64
Critical process, 3
Criticism:
    contextual, 252
    defined, 5, 20, 248, 264
    eclectic, 59
    genre, 253
    historical, 26
    literary, 12
    medium, 22, 27–30, 33, 219, 263–264
    originator, 21–27, 33, 263–264
    re-creative, 26–27
    scientific, 8–9, 15, 54–56, 60, 62–63, 232,
        244
Critique, defined, 3

Crosby, John, 10–11, 27
Crown, Peter, 90
Cultural relativism, 158–160

D

Daley, Steve, 133–135, 187–189, 242
Dallas, 215
Dallas Morning News, 151–153, 249–250,
    317–318, 320–321
Dann, Michael, 108, 119
Davis, Dennis, 84
da Vinci, Leonardo, 92
Day After, The, 40–41, 105
Defenders, 4–5
Dennis, Everette, 6
Dependency, 117
De-regulation, 148
Detroit News, 21, 36–37, 40–41, 42–43,
    109–111
Dewey, John, 178
Diamond, Edwin, 144
Dignity, human, 139–140
Director, television, 86, 91, 94, 179
Disc jockeys, 36–39, 76–79, 82–84
Disney, Walt, 132
Dobyns, Lloyd, 108
Docudrama, 136–138
Documentaries, 60, 62–63, 108, 126, 140, 212
Dominance, 192
Dominick, Joseph, 87, 90–91
Drama programs, 3–5, 13–14, 42–43, 86, 92,
    93, 96, 107, 124–125, 136–138,
    149–150, 164, 180, 193, 233
Ducasse, C. J., 157
Dynasty, 86, 215

E

Eirons, 223–225
Eisenstein, Sergei, 94
Eleanor & Franklin, 137
Eliot, T. S., 12

Ellington, Duke, 179
Emmys, 13
Empathy, 128, 165–167
Empiricism, 49–52, 56, 58, 59, 60, 62, 72
Entertainment-seeking, 116–117
Entertainment Tonight, 32
Equilibrium, 160–161. *See also* Balance
Escapism, 64, 82, 118–120, 126, 167, 215
Ethel and Albert, 195–199, 217–219,
        235–237, 257, 297–314
Ethics, 131–153, 187, 191, 232–233,
        256–257
Ethnic depictions, 206–207
Evaluation, defined, 248
Evolution, 190–192, 195, 197, 198
Execution (musical), 75–78, 82
Expressive plane, 65–68, 71, 78
Extrinsic, defined, 247
Extrinsic appreciation, 250–252, 255, 259,
        261–262, 263–264
Extrinsic evaluation, 255–257, 259–260, 262,
        263–264

F

Fallen Idol, 91
Fame, 216–217
Family, 71
Family Feud, 65
Family Ties, 40, 209, 211
Family viewing, 145
Fantasy Island, 107
Father Knows Best, 211, 257
Fear, 88, 168–171, 197, 203, 205, 249
Federal Communications Commission (FCC),
        6, 10, 32, 52, 53, 76, 106, 141, 145,
        148
Feldman, Edmund, 180, 185–186
Fellows, Harold, 260
Fichte, Johann Gottlieb, 234
Fiddler on the Roof, 263
Fine art, defined, 171, 252
First Amendment, 7, 144, 145
Fiske, John, 116, 146, 219, 227, 238, 242, 250

Flow analysis, 107–111
FM radio, 74–75, 76–77, 106, 121
Folk art, defined, 171–172
Forman, Milos, 251
Formats, radio:
    critiques of, 24–27, 29–30, 36–38, 51,
        76–79
    execution of, 49–51, 75, 81–83, 84, 106,
        109, 141, 168, 179, 183, 184, 190,
        227–228
    types of, compared, 64, 75, 96, 118–119,
        121–122, 126, 173
Fowler, Mark, 148
Freedom of expression, 142–145
Frye, Northrop, 7, 132, 163–164, 173,
        223–224, 226, 227, 238, 244,
        263

G

Game shows, 65, 85, 106, 139, 180, 183, 227,
        228
Gans, Herbert, 125
Geist, Christopher, 120
Gestalt psychology, 86–87
Gillette, Frank, 90
Gitlin, Todd, 107
Golden Girls, 209
Goldsen, Rose, 79, 128, 226–227
Good Morning, America, 258
Gossip column, 9, 11, 26, 35, 36–39, 47,
        260–262, 320–321
Gotshalk, D. W., 171
Gould, Jack, 7, 11, 15
Grabo, Carl, 7, 13, 99, 119–120, 147–148,
        179, 215
Grant, Bud, 104–105
Grapes of Wrath, 202
Greeks, ancient, 2, 50, 79–80, 127–128, 138,
        155, 177, 223–224
Greene, Theodore Meyer, 12, 23, 26–27, 50,
        65, 74, 80, 84–85, 141–142, 151, 163,
        164, 178, 221
Gunther, Marc, 40–41, 42–43, 109–111

H

Hadas, Moses, 174
Ham, Al, 119
Handler, David, 257
Happiness ethic, 213
Happy Days, 222, 228
Harris, Mike, 161–162
Harrison, Bernie, 11
Harry, 315–316
Hart, Gary, 205–206, 222
Hartley, John, 116, 146, 219, 227, 238, 242, 250
Hauser, Arnold, 8, 167
HBO (Home Box Office), 114–115, 237–238
Head of the Class, 316
Hegel, Georg Wilhelm Friedrich, 234
Henry, William, 20–21
Herbener, Gerald, 178
Hertzog, Albert, 27–28
Hickey, Neil, 17
Hierarchy, 191–194, 195, 197–198
Highway to Heaven, 80
Hill Street Blues, 4–5, 14, 93, 96, 107, 202, 211, 233, 253
Himmelstein, Hal, 221
Hoberman, Ben, 121
Hollywood Squares, 65
Holocaust, 126
Honesty, 136–138
Honeymooners, 173
Hot clock, 109, 190
Houseman, John, 86, 87
Howard, Ken, 86
Howdy Doody, 136
How the West Was Won, 126
Humphrey, Hal, 11
Huntley (Chet) and Brinkley (David), 187
Hurd, Volney, 9–10
HUTs (homes using television), 54, 103

I

I'll Take Manhattan, 104
Individualism, 157

Intellectuals, 32, 53, 171, 249
Intrinsic, defined, 247
Intrinsic appreciation, 248–250, 255, 259, 261, 262, 263–264
Intrinsic evaluation, 252–255, 259, 262, 263–264
Inversion, 184–185
Ironside, 227
I Spy, 135

J

Jankowski, Gene, 7, 29, 102
Jencks, Richard, 144, 145
Jessup, Bertram, 125
Jones, Will, 16
Julia, 135
Jutra, Claude, 260–262

K

Kant, Immanuel, 234
Kate Smith Hour, 195–196
Kinescope recording, 196
Kipper, Philip, 93
Kitsch, 172, 194
Klein, Paul, 103
Knowing, ways of, 54–64
Kojak, 211, 222, 223, 253–255
Kreiling, Ernie, 32
Krinein, 2

L

L.A. Law, 3–5, 13–14, 43
Landry, Robert, 10, 29
Langfeld, Herbert, 190
Last Fling, 42–43
Late Night with David Letterman, 259
Laurent, Lawrence, 11, 15, 107, 249
Lawrence Welk Show, 31
Lazarsfeld, Paul, 11, 28–29

LBJ: The Early Years, 136–138, 206
Leahy, Michael, 203, 215
Lear, Norman, 101, 210
Leave It to Beaver, 120, 173, 211
Legal issues, 23–24, 141, 142–145
Leonardo da Vinci, 92
Levy, Mark, 120
Life Styles of the Rich and Famous, 115
Lighting and shadow, 88–90, 96
Lippert, Barbara, 167–168, 184–185
Livingston, Donald, 91
Locale, 202–204, 217
Lock-boxes, 145
Loevinger, Lee, 6, 32, 52
LOP (least objectionable program) Theory, 103
Los Angeles Herald Examiner, 23–24
Lou Grant, 149–150
Love Boat, 209
Lynch, Peg, 196, 297–314

M

McCain, Thomas, 91–92
McCary, J. L., 213
McCoy, Joe, 119
Macdonald, Dwight, 172
McFarlin, Jim, 36–39, 83
McGuire, Bernadette, 112
Mack, John, 105
MacKenzie, Robert, 80, 93
McLuhan, Marshall, 132, 164, 202
McNeeley, Jerry, 2
McQuail, Denis, 116
Magazine industry, 102, 106
Manipulation, 28, 32–33, 68, 70–71, 151–153, 171, 195, 202
Maslin, Janet, 45–47, 242
Maude, 210
May, Rollo, 232
Media literacy, 6
Medium criticism, 22, 27–30, 33, 219, 263–264
Menaker, Dan, 84
Meredith, Don, 120

Merrill, Don, 3–5, 13–14, 43, 85, 87, 139, 209–210
Merton, Robert, 28–29
Message criticism, 26–27, 33, 263–264
Miami Vice, 203, 253–254
Michelangelo, 23, 99, 100, 251
Milton Berle Show, 257
Mini-series, 40–41, 69–72, 103–105, 126
Minneapolis Tribune, 16
Miss USA Pageant, 104
Modigliani, Amedeo, 251
Moonlighting, 255
Moore, Tim, 83
Morality, 132–133, 149, 155–156, 157, 194, 215, 248–249
Morning Program, 258–259
Movies, broadcast, 109–111, 191, 192, 205, 206, 251, 260–262
Mozart, Wolfgang Amadeus, 9, 99, 100, 101, 257
Mr. Rogers' Neighborhood, 139
MTV, 78, 95, 106
Murder, She Wrote, 119
Music:
    as art, 64–68, 73–82, 125, 141, 161, 172–173, 179, 234
    radio, 8–9, 24–27, 32, 49–51, 74–78, 79, 80–82, 95–96, 109, 119, 122, 167, 169, 172–173, 183, 184, 194
    television, 31, 64, 70–71, 78, 80, 95, 106, 194, 237–238, 253–254
Music of Your Life, 119
Music videos, 64, 78, 79, 95
Mussolini: The Untold Story, 126
My Father, My Rival, 260–262
Mystic, 56–58, 63
Mystique, 228–232
Myth, 232–233

N

Napoleon and Josephine: A Love Story, 126
National Association of Broadcasters (NAB), 118, 260

National Association of Television Program Executives (NATPE), 16
National Commission on Working Women, 206–207
National Educational Television (NET), 125
NBC, 4–5, 69–71, 80, 104, 108, 111, 119, 120, 121, 135, 139, 188, 225, 249, 254–255
Neuman, Russell, 56
New Newlywed Game, 139
New Republic, 45–47
New York Herald Tribune, 10
New York Times, 7, 15, 20, 105, 114, 237–238
Newcomb, Horace, 86, 124–125, 222, 228
News programming:
  radio, 10, 84–85, 117, 124, 126, 136, 139, 164, 180, 187, 205, 211–212, 227
  television, 23–24, 36, 84, 92, 94, 96, 106, 108, 118, 124, 126, 136, 139, 140, 164, 180, 183, 187–189, 191, 205, 211–213, 228, 317–319
Newsweek, 10
Nickelodeon, 139
Night Court, 257
Nightline, 317–319
Normative perspective, 52–54, 56, 57, 58, 59, 60, 63, 72
North and South, 126
Nostalgia, 118–120
Notan lighting, 88
NPR (National Public Radio), 24–27, 29–30, 32
Nye, Russel, 173

O

Oates, Joyce Carol, 233
Objectivism, 157–158
O'Connor, John, 105, 114–115, 237–238
Olson, Thomas, 178, 186, 190, 247
One Day at a Time, 257
On-stage skill ingredient, 82–87
Opinion essay, 35, 44–47, 151–153, 159–160, 188–189, 317–318
Oppenheim, Mike, 209
Organic unity, 178–179, 191, 194, 196

Originator criticism, 21–27, 33, 263–264
Our World, 108
Ozzie and Harriet, Adventures of, 257

P

Pacanowsky, Michael, 211
Paik, Nam June, 257
Painter, F. V. N., 12, 155
Paley, William, 8
Parker, DeWitt, 73, 76, 82, 83–84, 88, 122, 127, 142, 149, 163, 165, 168–169, 177, 180, 183, 185, 186, 189, 190, 193–195, 198, 244, 248, 253
Payola scandals, 229
PBS (Public Broadcasting System), 42–43, 64
Peirce, Charles Sanders, 238
People meters, 54, 113
People's Court, 115
Pepper, Stephen, 11–12, 91, 92
Perceptual triad, 64–72
Performance Today, 24–27, 29–30, 32, 43, 83, 179
Personality/gossip feature, 35, 36–39, 260–262, 320–321
Personal symbols, 221–222
Peter the Great, 126
Petticoat Junction, 53
Picasso, Pablo, 158, 168, 251
Pike, Kenneth, 59
Pilot (episode), 43–44
Pittman, Robert, 95
Plato, 79–80, 234
Point of optimum receptivity, 92
Pollack, Jeff, 119
Poltrack, David, 103
Pop art, defined, 172–174
Popcorn Kid, 249–250
Popper, Karl, 234
POV (point-of-view) shot, 93–94
Powers, Ron, 128
Prairie Home Companion, 141
Previews:
  examples of, 42–43, 60–61, 69–72, 114–115, 212–213, 225–226,

Previews (*con't.*)
    237–238, 260–261, 315–316
  functions of, 11, 41–42, 44, 114, 242
Prime Time Access Rule, 106
Prior restraint, 143
Problem-solving, 122–125, 165, 227–229
Productional/technical plane, 68, 71–72, 73
Promotional announcements (promos), 35,123
Protestant ethic, 146–151, 232
PSAs (public service announcements), 57–58,
    122–124, 239–241
Psycho, 249
Psychographics, 107, 113
Psychology,86–87,116,119,128,135,160–162,
    167–168, 193, 208, 215, 228, 257
Public broadcasting, 24–27, 29–30, 32,
    42–43, 64, 139
Pudovkin, V. I., 85

R

Rader, Melvin, 125, 258
Radio formats. *See* Formats, radio
Ratings, 51, 54–56, 102–107, 108, 113, 121,
    134, 139, 249–250, 320–321
Reaction shots, 93, 162
Reader's Digest, 251
Reasonableness, 2, 3, 8
Receiver criticism, 30–33, 116, 263–264
Recurrence, 183
Religion, 70–71, 138, 143, 146–147,
    151–153, 226, 242
Rembrandt, 198
Remnick, David, 60, 62–63
Renaissance person, 20
*Report on Public Service Responsibility of
    Broadcast Licensees*, 10–11, 53
Responsibilities, depicted, 210–213, 216, 218
Retro TV, 120
Reverse angles, 93–94
Reviews:
  examples of, 4–5, 24–26, 51, 140,
      161–162, 167–168, 185, 249–250,
      254–255, 258–259
  functions of, 24, 43–44, 65, 242, 253

Reymer & Gersin Assoc., 118, 121–122
Rhetoric, defined, 58–59
Rhetorician, 58–60, 63
Rhythm, 190, 233
Ritual, 227–229, 232, 233
Robards, Jason, 213
Roots, 40, 103, 126, 134–135, 242
Roper Organization, 117–118
Rossman, Jules, 43, 44–45
Rubin, Alan, 118
Russin, Joseph, 101

S

St. Elsewhere, 71, 93
Santayana, George, 117, 132, 155, 247
Sarnoff, David, 164
Saussure, Ferdinand de, 238
Schaefer, George, 86
Scheduling, 107–111, 126, 139, 184, 191,
    209, 228, 251, 253
Schoenbrun, David, 213
Schramm, Wilbur, 11
Schwichtenberg, Cathy, 209
Scientific criticism, 8–9, 15, 54–56, 60,
    62–63, 232, 244
Scott, Tony, 136–138, 206
Seldes, Gilbert, 11, 14, 15, 32, 91, 92, 122,
    173–174, 198–199
Self-evaluation, 213–215, 217, 219
Semiotics, 238–244
Sensuous plane, 64–65, 71, 78
Sesame Street, 134, 139
Sessions, Roger, 79
Sevareid, Eric, 249
"Seven Dirty Words" (Pacifica) Case, 145
77 Sunset Strip, 39
Sexual content, 87, 167–168, 184–185,
    208–209, 213–215
Shaheen, Jack, 206
Shales, Tom, 69–72, 80, 104–105
Shares (audience), 51, 54–56, 102, 103, 104,
    106, 107, 108, 113, 249–250
Shayon, Robert Lewis, 11, 20, 47, 50, 111,
    128, 147
Shot duration, 94–95, 96, 178–179

Shot transitions, 94–95, 96
Sias, John, 108–109
Siepmann, Charles, 10, 11, 53
Signified, 238–241
Signifier, 238–242
Signs, 238–244
Simon, John, 14–15
Singer, Samuel, 21, 75
Situation comedies:
   contemporary, 87, 108, 170–171, 206,
      224–225, 228, 267–295
   creation techniques of, 86, 92, 106,
      139–140, 169, 180, 184, 193, 226,
      227, 228
   critiques of, 3, 64, 65, 114–115, 194–195,
      209–210, 225–226, 249–250
   historic, 53, 70, 173, 191, 195–199, 206,
      228, 297–314
60 Minutes, 119
Skornia, Harry, 11
Slater, Dan, 127
Smith, Ralph, 9, 10, 33, 53, 135, 138, 140,
   141
Smith, Robert, 54, 56, 58, 60, 72, 135, 227,
   233, 242
Smith, S. Stephenson, 3
Smooth Talk, 42–43
Snow, Robert, 75, 79
Snowcroft, Brent, 206
Soap operas, 106, 158, 164, 168, 180, 184,
   202, 228
Social Darwinism, 147–151
Social symbols, 222–223, 226, 227
Society, depicted, 205–207, 216, 218, 227
Something about Amelia, 116, 262–263
Sound transitions, 95–96
Sound volume, 95–96
Special Treat, 139
Sports programming, 108–109, 114–115,
   120, 128, 168, 180, 228
Square Pegs, 70
Stage-molding ingredients, 87–97
Starsky and Hutch, 227
Stein, Ben, 23, 100–101, 138, 202–203, 205
Stengel, Robert, 11
Stereotypes, 138

Stolnitz, Jerome, 2, 3, 13, 14, 142, 155–156,
   157, 171, 186, 247, 252, 253, 264
Stoner, J. B., 143
"Sweeps," 110
Symbols, 221–227, 232–233, 238, 244
Symons, Howard, 144
Syndication, program, 31, 109, 190
Synthesis, 233–237

T

Talk shows, 36–39, 75, 83, 106, 121,
   258–259
Tartikoff, Brandon, 121
Taste publics, 125–126
Television Age, 16
Television Information Office (TIO), 117–118
Tension-release, 167–168, 170, 197–198, 207,
   228. *See also* Catharsis
Terry, Clifford, 225–226, 315–316
Thematic variation, 180–185, 190, 194–195,
   196
Theme, 179–180, 184, 194–195, 196, 233,
   261
Thesis, 233–237
"Think piece," 44–47, 151–153, 159–160,
   242, 317–318
Thorn Birds, 40, 104, 126
3–2–1 Contact, 139
Time, 258–259
Tinker, Grant, 101
Today, 258–259
Tonnage, 102–103, 105–108, 126
Toronto Star, 159–160, 211–212, 260–262
Tortellis, 225–226
Tractatus Coislinianus, 223–224
Training Camp, 114–115
Transposition, 183
Transvaluation, 132
Truth, 56, 60, 101, 232
Tuck, Lon, 76–79, 81–82, 190
Tunstall, Jeremy, 22
Turner, Charles, 78
TV Guide, 3–5, 80, 85, 93, 139, 205–206,
   209–210

Twilight Zone, 133
227, 87, 209–210

U

UHF television, 106
USA Cable Network, 139
USA Today, 102
U.S. Congress, 27, 28, 121, 142, 143, 144,
    145, 255
U.S. Supreme Court, 23–24
U.S. Surgeon General, 27

V

Valuation, 2, 3, 5, 8, 13, 51, 52, 56, 63, 101,
    107, 135–142, 180, 189, 194, 252
Values, 131–153, 179–180, 194, 232, 257,
    258
Variety, 9, 10, 136–138, 140, 161–162,
    253–255
Variety, program, 138–139
VCRs, 41, 110–111, 126, 153
VHF television, 106
Vietnam, 128, 137, 205
Violence, 127, 128, 142, 157, 169, 203,
    208–209, 211–212
Vivas, Eliseo, 22–23, 33, 133, 164, 180–183
Vonier, Sprague, 133, 232–233
Voyage of the Mimi, 139

W

Wagner, Richard, 73
Wakshlag, Jacob, 91–92

Wald, Richard, 100
War and Remembrance, 104
Warner, Charles, 106
War reporters, 211–213
Washington Mistress, 205
Washington Post, 15, 60, 62–63, 69–72,
    76–79, 104–105, 107, 249
Weber, Max, 146
Welch, Roy Dickinson, 73
Wheel of Fortune, 85
White, Llewellyn, 9, 11
White, Steve, 120
Williams, David, 36
Williams, Robert, 91, 95
Williams, Tennessee, 222
Willson, Meredith, 28
Wilson, George, 251–252, 255–257
Winds of War, 40, 104, 126
WKRP in Cincinnati, 194–195
Wolters, Larry, 15
Women, depiction of, 138, 167–168
World War II, 10, 40, 104, 126, 137
Wright, Charles, 22, 117
Wright, Robert, 105
Wurtzel, Alan, 87, 90–91

Y

Year in the Life, 69–72, 80
Young, Richard, 59
Youngblood, Gene, 148

Z

Zettl, Herbert, 88
Zoglin, Richard, 258–260